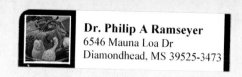

THE COLD WAR

THE
COLD
WAR

A MILITARY HISTORY

EDITED BY

ROBERT COWLEY

Random House Trade Paperbacks
New York

LIBRARY OF CONGRESS CATALOGING-IN-PUBLICATION DATA
The Cold War: a military history/edited by Robert Cowley
p.   cm.
Includes index.
ISBN 0-8129-6716-X
1. Cold War.   2. Military history—20th century.   I. Cowley, Robert.
D843.C577245 2005   909.82'5—dc22   2005042138

Printed in the United States of America

www.atrandom.com

246897531

Book design by Simon M. Sullivan

Contents

LIST OF MAPS

Introduction

Some years ago, while cleaning out their garage, my wife's aunt and uncle came on a scrapbook that she had kept in prep school. It was from 1963, and we pored over the photographs of ski weekends, class play programs, and dance invitations. Among copies of her school newspaper, I spotted a story she had written. It was set in the near future, in a classroom, and it was about the day the Bomb fell: "There was a large quake and the room seemed to turn upside down. We were thrown from our seats. A large crash shattered the window and threw the pieces into the four corners of the room. Sirens screeched. I had difficulty trying to breathe in the fog that now filled the room. We got to our feet and made our way through the crowded halls to the air raid shelter."

Life, for the narrator, would never be the same. A year after the Cuban Missile Crisis, apocalypse was still on our minds. We were not quite halfway through the Cold War, and the Bomb—Bombs, rather—seemed to be our undeserved future. As I read my wife's story, written in her properly neat schoolgirl script, the memory of the nuclear clock resurfaced, its hands perpetually stuck at one minute to midnight.

The Cold War lasted almost half a century—from 1946 until 1991, when the Soviet Union ceased to exist—and occupied the greater part of our lifetime. (If one accepts the position of historians such as Michael Howard, you can extend its chilling sway back to the October Revolution of 1917.) The expression was apparently coined by the preeminent journalist of the middle years of the century just ended, Walter Lippmann. According to his biographer, Ronald Steele, Lippmann borrowed the phrase from the French *La Guerre Froide*, "The Cold War," which people used to describe the "Phony War" of 1939. *The Cold War* was the title of a collection of Lippmann columns that appeared at the end of 1947, by which time it was clear that the West was on a collision course with the

Soviet Union. The man who handled PR for the self-important financier and presidential confidant Bernard Baruch later claimed that his client was the originator, but there is no evidence to back him up—no speech such as Winston Churchill's "Iron Curtain" pronouncement at Fulton, Missouri, on March 5, 1946.

Whatever the origin of the conflict or the expressions that defined it, one thing is clear: The Cold War was a war, and at times a very hot one, even if the two superpowers almost never clashed openly or directly. This anthology details some of the exceptions: the aerial duels between Soviet and Allied pilots over "MiG Alley" in the Korean War (Dennis E. Showalter's "The First Jet War") and the near shoot-downs of military reconnaissance planes over the Soviet Union (R. Cargill Hall, "The Truth About Overflights"). "Ferrets," planes that flew along the margins of the Soviet empire, photographing army and navy bases and radar installations, were not always so lucky: At least fifteen were shot down; almost two hundred air crewmen died or disappeared into Soviet prisons. But the destruction of a single aircraft, Major Rudolf Anderson's U-2, over Cuba on October 27, 1962, nearly propelled the world into war. That date must take a dubious pride of place as the most dangerous in the entire Cold War (Dino A. Brugioni, "The Invasion of Cuba"). One is tempted to add those hours, almost exactly a year earlier, when U.S. and Soviet tanks stood muzzle-to-muzzle at Checkpoint Charlie in Berlin, the only time that ground forces confronted each other, ready to trade shots in anger.

As one perceptive interpreter of the struggle, Martin Walker, has pointed out, "The Cold War was truly a global conflict, more so than either of the century's two world wars." One can approach it from many angles—economic, social, political. All are valid, all are interrelated. But the Cold War was primarily a military phenomenon, and its military implications are the subject of this anthology.

In the sense that it was global, involved so many millions, and mobilized such a substantial part of national economies, the Cold War was a total war. It was a struggle that manifested revolutionary and patriotic fervor on both sides: Democracy is as much an ideology as Communism. (The Red Scare was the chief manifestation of that fervor in the U.S.; the various postwar Stalinist purges in the Soviet Union or the cultural revolution in China were its counterparts.) Because there could be no genuine coexistence between the two worldviews—though the sides intermittently paid lip service to the notion—both East and West aimed for total victory. A middle ground was out of the question. For most of those years, the West held a decided edge in wealth and technological sophistication. It managed the feat of producing guns and butter at the same time. The Communist empire couldn't, and didn't, and that may have been its signal weakness and eventual undoing.

Is there a person over the age of thirty whom the Cold War didn't somehow affect? For those of us who are as old as I am (seventy), it occupied most of our adult lives. Serving in the military was a given, especially in the 1950s and 1960s, the years of maximum chill. People I knew did time in Korea and Vietnam; a number are contributors to this book. As children, many of us learned to crouch underneath our school desks, in premature rehearsal for the inevitable. In cities, black circles with yellow triangles, radiation symbols, indicated the presence of fallout shelters stocked with food and water. There, the fortunate survivors of a nuclear blast might hole up days, weeks even, until battery-powered radios notified them that radiation had decreased and it was safe to venture outside—to what? But that was a question one skirted. Talk-show guests argued whether it was ethical to bar interlopers with a gun, even if it was tantamount to a death sentence. Civil defense was clearly something of a boondoggle, but it kept a great many people employed and busy. A war mentality was part of our lives. I remember once, in the early 1970s, I was having problems with the water supply in the Connecticut house I rented. My landlord took me to inspect the pumps. He led me to a concrete structure sunk into a hillside, unlocked a door, and switched on the light. I saw bunks with mouse-eaten mattresses, shelves stocked with rusting food cans, and dusty olive-green containers that held water. The water pump was also located here, and as my landlord checked and adjusted it, I asked him what this artificial grotto was. Oh, he explained, it was once a bomb shelter. "You know—the Great Fear."

The Great Fear. Although there now seems something faintly ludicrous, even pathetic, about the examples just cited, we also did experience moments of genuine terror. The Cuban Missile Crisis was one of them, perhaps the worst. I can't forget October 27, 1962, a warm and sunny morning when I walked down Broadway on Manhattan's West Side, doing the sort of errands I always did on Saturdays. Suddenly, a thought overwhelmed me: This might be my last weekend on earth. Should I send my then-wife and two small daughters, one of them just five months old, to stay with my parents in the country? It didn't seem such a wild thought. I returned to my apartment to find that Major Anderson had been shot down. But Armageddon would have to wait. My older daughter wanted to go to the park.

George Feifer (who wrote "The Berlin Tunnel," anthologized here) was a graduate exchange student in Moscow that fall. Few people there, he once told me, were aware of the Cuban Missile Crisis; the Soviet media had blacked out all mention of it. "But they knew something big was up," he added, "even if we didn't know precisely what until Khrushchev made a talk at the end, hiding lots of things and twisting others into a Soviet victory. I knew much more than most people, because while the crisis was on, I happened to bump into a friend from the American embassy staff on a busy street. He told me. Still, I knew too little to be scared that I might be killed by an American nuclear bomb at any moment."

The precarious two weeks of the Cuban Missile Crisis came close to overshadowing the emergency in Europe of a year earlier, the erection of the Berlin Wall. But the Wall never caused the same amount of trepidation, certainly not among ordinary people, nor in Washington or Moscow. The confrontation at Checkpoint Charlie was one of those dicey moments when overly aggressive subordinate commanders got out of control, as they did, with potentially more dangerous consequences, in Cuba. Although the U.S. publicly fumed and blustered and made calming promises of support to West Germany and the beleaguered citizens of West Berlin, Washington was privately relieved. "It's not a very nice solution," John F. Kennedy remarked at the time, "but a wall is a hell of a lot better than a war." Khrushchev agreed. "We didn't want a military conflict," he said in the tapes that became his memoirs. "There was no necessity for one. We only wanted to conduct a surgical operation."

"Surgical" was the right word. By staunching the refugee hemorrhage, the East Germans and their Soviet bosses had saved their nation from dissolving, as it would three decades later when the Wall did come down. A stasis then existed that people on both sides learned to live with. But the Communists paid a high price for their military gamble in Berlin. They had handed the West its most enduring propaganda triumph, one it never lost an opportunity to play up for the rest of the Cold War.

I can testify to the effect that the Wall had on me in the mid-1970s, when it was enjoying its dour heyday. The idea that it might come down in my lifetime seemed inconceivable. The memory of a late-night walk near the Brandenburg Gate, as close as the Wall would allow me to get to East Berlin, is still vaguely unsettling. I became aware of uniformed shadows in a darkened guard tower and of the reflection of West Berlin streetlamps bouncing off binocular glass. But it was more than that. Those binoculars were following me.

"Before I built a wall," Robert Frost wrote, "I'd ask to know / What I was walling in or walling out." Exactly. Staring from a high floor of a building set against the Wall—I was lunching in the headquarters of a prominent West German newsmagazine—I could see nothing but the shabby buildings and empty streets of East Berlin (propaganda, propaganda). An occasional scurrying figure seemed all but swallowed by the voracious chill of Socialist space. Below, against a backdrop of blocked windows, Dobermans strutted with fierce nervous intensity, ready to maul anyone rash enough to cross the intervening space—if, indeed, a fleeing human could get that far. I might as well have been regarding the yard of a huge open-air prison.

The Berlin Wall and the Cuban Missile Crisis occupy central places in the history of the Cold War. Thereafter, with one notable exception, the war scare of 1983 (recalled here by John Prados), the long face-off between the U.S.S.R. and the West "took on," in the words of the historian John Lewis Gaddis,

> a certain stability, even predictability, after 1962. Neither side would ever again initiate direct challenges to the other's sphere of influence. Anomalies like a divided Germany and Korea—even absurdities like a walled capitalist West Berlin in the middle of a communist East Germany, or an American naval base on the territory of a Soviet ally just off the coast of Florida—came to seem quite normal. . . . Not the least of the Cold War's oddities is that its outcome was largely determined before two-thirds of it had even been fought.

The military focus of the Cold War now shifted back to Asia, Vietnam in particular. I'm surprised how many knowledgeable people disassociate the struggles in Southeast Asia from the Cold War. One can argue that the French came out on the losing end of a colonial war, and the Americans of the civil war that followed it. But both the French and the Americans, along with their allies, were fighting Communists: Not just the conquest of territory but the dominance of an ideology was at stake. The part that the Chinese Communists played in displacing the French is incontestable, as both Douglas Porch and Williamson Murray make abundantly clear in these pages. Later, in the war between the two Vietnams, the Chinese and the Soviets fought a war by proxy, pouring the resources of war into the Communist North. It's worth quoting at length the military historian John F. Guilmartin, Jr.:

Vietnam was clearly a major chapter in the Cold War. Viewed from a narrowly military and geographic perspective, it was an unequivocal American defeat. Viewed within the broader context of the Cold War, it was an operational defeat and a strategic victory. The Soviets and the Chinese spent heavily supporting North Vietnam, and in the case of the Soviets, they expended resources that they couldn't spare. When, over the long haul, their bills came due, they couldn't be paid. Vietnam wasn't the only cause of the Soviet decline, or even the biggest one—expenditures on strategic weapons systems were more important, with conventional military hardware close behind. But Vietnam could have been the straw that broke the camel's back.

It would be impossible to list the ways in which the Cold War changed our lives. Wars do that. Let me suggest a few random examples, each of them with a military antecedent.

Jet planes are obvious. The swept-wing B-47 bomber of 1950 is still the model for airliners. Or take Japan's hold on world markets. It is rooted in the early 1950s, when we pumped money into the country, our recent enemy, and made it our main staging base for the Korean War. Take the interstate highway system. It was originally conceived and funded as a way of moving troops and speeding evacuation from cities threatened by nuclear attack. Or Len Deighton and John le Carré: The Cold War turned the spy thriller into a literary genre. Or American popular culture, whether it was Levi's or Elvis Presley—who, after all, served as a private in West Germany. It was first spread by the GI's who garrisoned our Roman Wall. They left behind an enduring legacy of desire for material things. In the end, the Cold War may have been won as much on the sound stages of L.A. as in the missile silos of North Dakota. Not even Stalin's greatest creations, the Iron Curtain and the Red Army, could turn back *Dallas* and *Dynasty*, those television epics of Western (both upper- and lower-case) wealth. I think of Dennis E. Showalter's remark: "It may not have been the Stars and Stripes that rose over Moscow—but the Golden Arches are good enough." The people on the other side wanted what we had, even if it was our greedy worst.

I

FIRST SKIRMISHES

The Day the Cold War Started

JAMES CHACE

On May 7, 1945, at General Dwight D. Eisenhower's headquarters at Rheims in France, Germany surrendered unconditionally to the Allies, formally ending almost six years of war in Europe. It took less than a year, three seasons only, for the Grand Alliance of the United States, Great Britain, and the Soviet Union to fall apart, and with it, lasting hopes of a peaceful international order. In that time the Soviets had swallowed much of Eastern Europe, and the West was beginning to accept, however reluctantly, the inevitability of a divided continent. The Soviets were also occupying northern Iran and were threatening to extend their influence, if not their outright domination, to the Persian Gulf. But as the year 1946 began, no country felt the menace of Soviet expansionist pressure more than Turkey. The Russians were asking— demanding, rather—to be allowed to establish naval and army bases in the Bosporus and Dardanelles. Would control of the eastern end of the Mediterranean be next? Soviet troops began to mass on the borders with Turkey.

As early as January 5, 1946, the new American president, Harry S. Truman, worried out loud to his secretary of state, James Byrnes, that the Soviets intended to invade Turkey. "Unless Russia is faced with an iron fist and strong language," Truman said, "another war is in the making." Then he added (and remember, this was a time when the American armed forces were demobilizing thousands of men each day), "Only one language do they understand—'How many divisions have you?'" A month later, the Soviet ruler, Joseph Stalin, gave a speech announcing a new five-year plan. He went on to attack capitalism and to remark threateningly that his nation should be prepared for "all kinds of eventualities." Back in Washington, Justice William O. Douglas remarked to the secretary of the navy, James Forrestal, that Stalin's speech sounded like "the declaration of World War III."

The gloves were off. The former British prime minister, Winston Churchill, spoke at Westminster College in Fulton, Missouri, on March 5; Truman introduced him. "From Stettin in the Baltic to Trieste in the Adriatic," Churchill said, "an Iron Curtain has descended across the Continent." His words were not a call for war—not yet—but a counsel of preparedness. The time had come to check Soviet expansionism. "From what I have seen of our Russian friends and allies during the war, I am convinced that there is nothing they admire so much as strength, and there is nothing for which they have less respect than for weakness, especially military weakness." Stalin could not let the Fulton speech go without a public comment: "Mr. Churchill is now in the position of a firebrand of war."

Truman's January 5 outburst, Stalin's February broadside, or Churchill's Missouri warning: One might pick any number of symbolic days when the ideological and military struggle that was to consume the world for the next forty-five years began. James Chace, the biographer of Dean Acheson, argues that the pride of date belongs to August 19, 1946. That was the day when the Truman administration publicly rejected Stalin's call for joint Soviet-Turkish defense of the Straits—and backed up its words by dispatching a naval task force to Istanbul. For the first time (and not for the last), the United States had proclaimed to the Soviets that, to protect its interests, it was not afraid to resort to arms.

─────────

JAMES CHACE, who died in the fall of 2004, was a distinguished historian, foreign policy analyst, editor, and teacher. He is best known for his biography, *Dean Acheson: The Secretary of State Who Created the American World,* as well as several books on international affairs, including *Solvency, America Invulnerable* (with Caleb Carr), *The Consequences of the Peace,* and a memoir, *What We Had.* His final book was *1912: Wilson, Roosevelt, Taft & Debs—the Election That Changed the Country.* The former managing editor of *Foreign Affairs* and editor in chief of *World Policy Journal,* Chace was the Henry Luce Professor in Freedom of Inquiry and Expression at Bard College.

I N LATE AUGUST 1946 the world's largest aircraft carrier, the *Franklin D. Roosevelt*, accompanied by two destroyers, weighed anchor for Gibraltar and the eastern Mediterranean. The ships were to rendezvous off Lisbon with three more American destroyers and two cruisers dispatched from British waters. Their final destination: Istanbul. There they would join the U.S.S. *Missouri*, the battleship on which the Japanese surrender had taken place a year earlier. The *Missouri* had already arrived in the Straits of the Dardanelles on April 5.

And for what purpose was this formidable array of sea power intended? None other than to confront the Russian navy at the mouth of the Black Sea if required. At the very least, this flexing of military muscle was aimed at making the Soviets think twice about putting any more pressure on Turkey.

Twelve months after the end of World War II, the tensions between Moscow and Washington had reached a breaking point. In Iran, the Soviets, who had occupied the northern part of the country during World War II, had refused to withdraw their forces six months after the end of the war (the length of time they had agreed to in 1943). They bowed to U.S. pressure only in the spring of 1946. In Greece, Stalin was supporting the Greek Communist bands who were fast bringing the country to the brink of civil war. With Soviet-controlled governments in Poland, Bulgaria, and Romania, and Communist parties active throughout Europe, it seemed to Western leaders that Soviet expansion had to be countered.

As early as December 1945, Soviet troops were massing on the Russo-Turkish border. Meanwhile, at least two hundred Soviet tanks crossed the Iranian border, and about a third of these mobilized along the frontier between Iran and Turkey. By the summer of 1946, the United States decided to risk the end of the wartime alliance in a naval show of force—one that signaled a virtual end to American efforts to accommodate the demands of the Soviet Union. Relations between the two powers would never be the same again.

Even during the halcyon days of the wartime alliance, Stalin was insisting on a Russian military presence in the Dardanelles and Bosporus (together known as the Straits), the vital gateway in and out of the Black Sea for the Russian fleet headquartered at Sebastopol. At the Yalta summit in February 1945, Stalin declared that the Montreux Convention—which the great powers had signed in the 1930s, giving Turkey the right to defend the Straits—must be revised. Churchill and Roosevelt had agreed. But then Stalin spoke in more threatening tones, asserting that he found it "impossible to accept a situation in which Turkey had a hand on Russia's throat."

Stalin's demands escalated after the war in Europe, and in June 1945 he insisted that the Kars and Ardahan districts of eastern Turkey, ceded by Moscow to Turkey in 1921, would have to be returned to the Soviet Union. In addition, he demanded that the Turks consent to Soviet bases in the Straits.

A month later, meeting with Truman and Churchill at Potsdam outside the ruined city of Berlin, Stalin and his foreign minister, Vyacheslav Molotov, declared that the bases were not enough: Turkey and Russia should become joint custodians of the Straits. Neither Truman nor Churchill thought much of that idea.

Stalin's desire to acquire the lost territories in eastern Turkey may well have been inspired by Lavrenti Beria, head of the secret police and, like Stalin, a Georgian. According to Khrushchev's memoirs, at one of those "interminable" suppers with Stalin, Beria "started harping on how certain territories, now part of Turkey, used to belong to Georgia." He then convinced Stalin that "now was the time to get those territories back. He argued that Turkey was weakened by World War II and wouldn't be able to resist."

As Soviet demands intensified, Washington took a hard line. By the time Secretary of State James F. Byrnes returned from the Moscow Conference in December 1945, Truman was complaining to him: "There isn't a doubt in my mind that Russia intends an invasion of Turkey and seizure of the Black Sea Straits to the Mediterranean. Unless Russia is faced with an iron fist and strong language another war is in the making. Only one language do they understand—'How many divisions have you?'"

The Turks also had no intention of satisfying Soviet demands. In the weeks after Potsdam, the Turkish foreign office believed a Soviet invasion was likely, but, they said, "We would rather die on Turkish soil than be deported to

Siberia." The American ambassador in Ankara was convinced that Moscow wanted to convert Turkey into a Soviet satellite, and, from Moscow, George F. Kennan warned that no concessions would satisfy the Soviet Union, whose aim may have been to establish, as he put it, a "friendly" regime in Turkey.

Kennan, who had been trained in Russian from the 1920s, was serving in the Soviet capital as deputy to Ambassador W. Averell Harriman. He had long chafed at being on the sidelines as Washington made decisions affecting America's relations with the Soviet Union. At one point he was so despondent about being marginalized that he seriously considered resigning from the foreign service altogether.

But in February 1946, Washington asked for his views of Soviet behavior, and he seized the occasion to send an eight-thousand-word message to the State Department—the so-called Long Telegram—describing the "Kremlin's neurotic view of world affairs" that would make it impossible for the Soviet Union to coexist with the West. "Here was a case where nothing but the whole truth would do," he wrote later. "They had asked for it. Now, by God, they would have it."

The Soviet leaders, he believed, could compensate for the "traditional and instinctive Russian sense of insecurity" only by going permanently on the attack "in [a] patient but deadly struggle for total destruction of [a] rival power, never in compacts and compromises with it."

As he had hoped, his warnings were heeded back home, and now American policy makers closely scrutinized his analyses of Soviet intentions.

By late March 1946, Kennan was convinced that Stalin was insatiable: "Nothing short of complete disarmament, delivery of our air and naval forces to Russia and resigning of powers of government to American communists" would alleviate Stalin's distrust, and even then he would probably "smell a trap and would continue to harbor the most baleful misgivings."

As the crisis deepened, former Soviet foreign minister Maxim Litvinov, who had been associated with a more friendly policy toward the United States in the 1930s, gave a revealing interview on June 18, 1946, to the CBS correspondent in Moscow, Richard C. Hottelet. The old Bolshevik explained that there "has now been [a] return in [the] U.S.S.R. to [the] outmoded concept of geographical security." When Hottelet asked if Soviet policy would be mitigated if the West were to give in to Soviet territorial demands, Litvinov said that "it would lead to [the] West being faced after [a] period of time with new series of demands."

On August 7, 1946, Moscow sent a detailed memo to the Turkish government and copied Washington. Moscow now demanded a joint Turkish-Soviet defense system in the Straits, which would necessarily require Soviet bases.

In the absence of Secretary Byrnes, who was in Paris, Undersecretary of State Dean Acheson took charge. For Acheson, the Soviet message marked a turning point. It meant that Moscow was bent on expansion whenever and wherever the opportunity presented itself. Acheson's policy up till now had been to press the administration to seek common ground with the Soviets. This approach was no longer acceptable. While the Soviets may not have been planning a direct military assault on Turkey, their demand for bases in the Dardanelles implied eventual projection of Soviet power into the eastern Mediterranean. Even if it meant war, Acheson was prepared to recommend a hard line to Truman, and the president was ready to follow it.

At fifty-three, Acheson was nearing the peak of his power and performance. Before the war he was an acerbic and brilliant young lawyer, once described by a partner as "the shiniest fish in the sea," and service in Franklin Roosevelt's State Department had smoothed some of his sharper edges. Now with Truman as president, he was second in command under Secretary of State Byrnes. But for much of Byrnes's tenure, Acheson was acting secretary of state in Washington, as Byrnes was out of the country 350 of the 562 days he was in office, negotiating with the British, the French, and the Russians.

Tall and imposing, with his guardsman's mustache and his seemingly imperious manner, Acheson was also without guile or self-importance. Although he appeared to some the personification of a British diplomat, his close friend and colleague Sir Oliver Franks, the British ambassador to Washington, described him more accurately as "not at all an English or British type. He is a pure American type of a rather rare species. He is imbued with a love of cabinet making and gardening, never forgetting and ever going back to the roots from which it all springs." Acheson was, said Franks, "profoundly American in this regard" and, above all, "a blade of steel."

Acheson was a realist, not an ideologue. Despite his distaste for the Soviet regime, he believed that the United States had to deal with the Soviet Union as a great power whose interests might well conflict with those of the United States, but whose cooperation should be sought whenever possible.

During the tough negotiations with Moscow over Soviet withdrawal from Iran earlier that year, and in his efforts to persuade Stalin to internationalize atomic energy, Acheson had persisted in trying to find ways to satisfy the Soviet Union's security concerns. But he was also becoming convinced that the United States would have to assume a more prominent moral, military, and economic role in confronting any Soviet probe.

The problems bedeviling American foreign policy were not like headaches, he said that June—when you "take a powder and they are gone." Instead, "They are like the pain of earning a living. They will stay with us until death."

Most of the books that lined the front room of his redbrick house in George-town were biographies and treatises on nineteenth-century British statesmen—Melbourne, Palmerston, Disraeli, Salisbury—and Acheson was steeped in their thinking and history. At the end of World War II, he had been prepared to concede Great Britain its traditional sphere of influence in Iran and to let Britain contest Russia there, as it had a century before in the so-called Great Game of Asia. But now he perceived how weak Britain actually was, and he rec-ognized its consequent reliance on America to back it up in the Middle East.

Even while the United States had been following a policy of trying to coop-erate with the Soviet Union on a whole range of issues, Acheson was deter-mined to demonstrate America's commitment to Turkey. Unlike northern Iran and Eastern Europe, which Soviet troops occupied as a result of World War II, the Straits were a strategic point that had been free of Russian control. If Moscow intended to seize them, the truly expansionist nature of Soviet foreign policy would be revealed.

The opportunity to take a stand presented itself a bit ghoulishly, in the per-son—more precisely, the body—of Mehmet Munir Ertegun, the Turkish ambassador to the United States, who had died in Washington during World War II. Traditionally, chiefs of mission who died in service were returned by warship. Acheson decided that he would return Ertegun's body to Istanbul on the battleship *Missouri*. Although the direct Soviet threat to Turkey was on the ground, the majesty of the *Missouri*, with its 16-inch guns, its enormous bulk, and its especially strong armor, made it a perfect symbol of U.S. resolve.

Despite the arrival of the battleship at Istanbul in early April, the Soviets kept their pressure on the Turks; nonetheless, the presence of the *Missouri* as an emblem of American protection allowed the Turks more freedom to reject Soviet demands. The Dardanelles was, as Acheson saw it, the "stopper in the neck of the bottle," and if Great Britain was too weak to take action, America must be prepared to step in.

Two days after the Soviet memo of August 7 demanding that the Turks allow the Russians to share in the defense of the Straits, the Yugoslavs, under Stalin's then ally Marshal Tito, forced down an unarmed U.S. Army transport plane. Acheson, impatient to take action, began meeting with high-level officials from the State, War, and Navy departments, along with the Joint Chiefs of Staff, to decide what to do. In Acheson's mind, the worst policy would be one of bluff. The Russians must be certain that America would support Ankara if Turkey were attacked.

The risks of bluffing were also uppermost in the thinking of Secretary of the Navy James Forrestal. Forrestal, a workaholic former Wall Street banker, was obsessed with the Communist threat to the point of paranoia. His obsession with the Red menace eventually forced him to resign as secretary of defense in 1949. Not long after that, he committed suicide by jumping out of a window at the Bethesda Naval Medical Center.

When Forrestal dispatched the *Missouri* to the Straits in March, he wanted the Eighth Fleet, the striking arm of the Atlantic Fleet, to accompany it and then to remain in the Mediterranean for maneuvers as a first step toward establishing a permanent naval presence there. At the time, he told Winston Churchill that Truman had refused to send such a task force to accompany the *Missouri*, and Churchill responded that "a gesture of power not fully implemented was almost less effective than no gesture at all." Now Forrestal was determined to send all the ships needed to confront the Russians at the mouth of the Black Sea. Throughout the sweltering Washington summer, high-level discussions between the departments of State, War, and Navy would produce one of the toughest policy recommendations yet offered to Harry Truman.

Flanked by Forrestal and top Pentagon brass, Acheson presented the report on August 15 to the president and awaited his reaction. "In our opinion," the report read, "the primary objective of the Soviet Union is to obtain control of Turkey. . . . If the Soviet Union succeeds in obtaining control of Turkey, it will be extremely difficult, if not impossible, to prevent the Soviet Union from obtaining control over Greece and over the whole Near and Middle East."

Should this happen, the report went on, Moscow would be in a much stronger position to threaten India and China. "The only thing which will deter the Russians will be the conviction that the United States is prepared, if necessary, to meet aggression with force of arms."

The report concluded, "In our opinion therefore the time has come when we must decide that we shall resist with all means at our disposal any Soviet aggression and in particular, because the case of Turkey would be so clear, any Soviet aggression against Turkey."

The president did not hesitate. "We might as well find out," Truman responded, "whether the Russians are bent on world conquest now as in five or ten years." He was prepared to pursue the policy to the end.

At this point, according to Acheson, General Eisenhower, then army chief of staff, leaned over and asked him in a whisper if it was clear to the president that the course they were recommending could lead to war. Before Acheson could reply, the president asked whether the general had something to say. Acheson repeated Eisenhower's question.

As Acheson tells it, Truman took from his desk drawer a large map of the Middle East and the eastern Mediterranean and asked those present to gather around him. Unfolding the map, Truman gave a short lecture on the historical background and current strategic importance of the region. It was vital to protect the Straits from any Soviet incursion; otherwise, he said, echoing the report's conclusion, Soviet troops would soon be used to control all of Turkey, and in the natural course of events, Greece and the Near East would fall under Soviet domination.

When he finished, he turned to Eisenhower in good humor and asked if he was satisfied now that the situation was understood. Eisenhower joined the others in general laughter and said that he was.

Four days later, Acheson reacted to the Soviet proposal. He rejected any notion that the U.S.S.R. should share responsibility with Turkey for the defense of the Straits. The Montreux Convention could be revised, but the United States considered the Turkish Straits a matter of concern to its own strategic interests. Turkish sovereignty remained inviolate. Acheson did not have to spell out the administration's willingness to risk war.

The Cold War started on August 19, 1946.

Confronted by American resolve—symbolized by the naval task force in the eastern Mediterranean, headed by the *Roosevelt* and the *Missouri*—the Russians backed down. A month later, their tone on the Dardanelles was much softer. And after Stalin's death in 1953, the question of even revising the Montreux Convention was abandoned.

A week after Acheson had sent his reply to Moscow, *New York Times* reporter James Reston noted a shift in Acheson's thinking. While the undersecretary had previously held out for a "liberal policy" toward the Soviet Union, "when the facts seemed to merit a change—as he seems to think they now do in the case of the Soviet Union—he switched with the facts."

Three years later, as secretary of state, Acheson was dining with President Truman in his private railway car on the way back to Washington from the dedication of the new United Nations Building in New York. Acheson's wife mentioned Central Asia, and that got Truman started. The waiters cleared away the dishes, and the president began to lecture on the history of Central Asia, the various emperors, the military campaigns, the migrations of populations. Toward the end of his exposition, Mrs. Acheson said, "This is amazing. I wouldn't have been surprised that you would know all about the Civil War, but this part of the world, I've never known anyone who knew anything about it."

The president laughed and then told her why: "Well, my eyesight isn't any good. I was never any good playing games where you have to see what you're doing at a distance. I couldn't hit a ball if it hit me in the nose, so I spent my time reading. I guess I read nearly every book in the library. I got interested in this part of the world, and ever since I've read everything about it I could find."

But, as Acheson commented, what Truman discussed that late afternoon was not simply a collection of unconnected events but the reasons why these migrations took place, and the pressures that were pushing them. His depth of understanding about the region was worthy of a scholar.

For Truman, as for Acheson, the Turkish crisis meant that the Soviets would not be content with a sphere of influence in Eastern Europe. Instead, they were engaged in a policy of renewed expansion. Especially in the Mediterranean and the Near East, where the Russians had traditionally sought territory and access to the sea, and where the British had stood fast against them, the Americans must now be prepared to draw the line. With the Truman administration's willingness to risk a hot war over the control of the Dardanelles, the Cold War had actually begun.

Four years later, the American Mediterranean task force that had been established at the end of 1946 was designated the Sixth Fleet. With this action, the navy's emphasis on the Pacific, which had been the central priority in naval thinking since the 1930s, came to an end. Henceforth, American naval strategy, built around the revived nineteenth-century practice of stationing American warships in friendly ports, was focused on the containment of the Soviet Union—the ultimately successful foreign policy objective of the United States for the next forty-five years.

Cloak-and-Dagger in Salzburg

HARRIS GREENE

On a local level, as opposed to a geopolitical one, the Cold War had an even earlier start. In Austria, for example, tensions between the former allies flared almost from the moment World War II ended. With help from the local populace in early April 1945, the Soviets had overrun Vienna: The city would subsequently be divided into four occupation zones—American, British, French, and Russian—as was the entire country. Vienna, like Berlin, was deep in the Soviet zone. Austria would remain occupied for the next ten years; it was not until 1955, when the treaty making the entire country neutral went into effect, that the last foreign troops left.

Austria hardly resounded with the sound of music in those first years of peace. Much of the country, especially those areas that the Russians had shouldered through, had been savaged by war. People lived squalid lives on the edge. Former concentration-camp inmates and refugees from Eastern Europe—displaced persons, or simply DPs—roamed the landscape; as late as the mid-1950s, thousands still lived in camps. Former POWs searched for wives and families who had themselves become displaced in the final convulsions of 1945. Desperately poor people, hungry and jobless, were willing to do anything to survive. Only black marketers and spies seemed to thrive: Intrigue became a profession in a world unnaturally filled with unexplained kidnappings, disappearances, and murders. A movie such as *The Third Man*, set in Vienna in 1947, seemed less fiction than documentary.

Once the occupation armies arrived, they immediately put their intelligence organizations to work. Local Nazis had to be corralled. But another concern came to dominate: What was the other side up to? Already the Iron Curtain was descending. In Salzburg, Mozart's birthplace, the operations chief of the U.S. Army's 430th Counter Intelligence Corps (CIC) was a man named Harris Greene. For him, the Cold War would begin on January 20, 1946. The story he related fifty years later may have had the flavor of a Keystone Kops misadventure, but it was a gambit in a game that was becoming increasingly hazardous and at times deadly.

———

The late **HARRIS GREENE** served with the CIC in postwar Italy and Austria and worked for the CIA from 1949 until his retirement in 1980. In the years that followed, he turned to—what else?—spy novels, publishing six.

THERE ARE DIFFERING OPINIONS on when the Cold War began. But I contend that it began, at least on a small scale, in occupied Austria. I can even cite the exact date: January 20, 1946, barely six months after the end of World War II. I was there, serving as operations chief for the U.S. Army's 430th Counter Intelligence Corps (CIC) Detachment in Salzburg.

The key player in the historic drama that unfolded that Sunday was Richard Kauder, alias "Klatt," a pudgy, forty-year-old Viennese with a weakness for women. Kauder was born Jewish but converted to Roman Catholicism to avoid the arrows and slings of Austrian anti-Semitism. A journalist, he had been recruited late in 1937 by the Abwehr, the military intelligence arm of the German armed forces, to run a small but important network of Russian spies.

When war between Russia and Germany came in June 1941, Kauder's agents at first supplied valuable information from Moscow. Kauder's network dissolved, however, after it passed on "bad" intelligence that helped set up a military disaster for the Germans in the great tank battle of Kursk in July 1943. After Kursk, the Germans never again seized the initiative against the Soviets, and they retreated until Berlin and the end of the war.

Kauder's military intelligence unit retreated with the rest of the German army, and when the hostilities were over, he ended up in the American zone of Austria. He fell into the hands of the Strategic Services Unit (SSU), the temporary American counterintelligence organization in Salzburg, which tried without success to debrief him.

One day in January 1946, the otherwise uncooperative Kauder came to his SSU contact officer and asked for protection. He said he believed he was being closely followed. SSU came to us at the 430th CIC Detachment and asked us to watch over Kauder.

Because of the heavy demands on our arrest and internment of German Nazis, SS, and Gestapo, we could spare only Special Agent George Milovanovich, from Ohio. George, who died in the 1950s, was a real linguist, speaking English, Russian, Hungarian, Serbian, Croatian, Czech, and Slovak. He was well over six feet tall but knew nothing about war or violence. He was hopeless at rounding up Nazis and was thus selected for "minding" Kauder. We gave him a submachine gun without an ammunition clip and told him to arrest anyone who wanted to seize Kauder.

The evening of January 20, 1946, was clear and cold in Salzburg. Freshly fallen snow crunched beneath the tread of the few passersby in that defeated and occupied city. CIC got a phone call from Milovanovich asking for "backup." He was in Kauder's apartment, and he didn't like what he saw from the window. Kauder's house, located in a blind alley, was filled with American MPs, he said. This was news to CIC. We rounded up people and sent two jeeps, carrying four CIC agents and four SSU personnel, to investigate. The vehicles arrived at Kauder's place at ten-thirty P.M.

Meanwhile, Milovanovich noted an MP, with pistol and 505 MP on his helmet liner, climbing the stairs to Kauder's flat. Despite the lack of bullets in his weapon, Milovanovich decided to brazen it out.

"Stop!" he shouted from the top of the stairs. The MP did not stop.

"*Halt!*" cried Milovanovich. The MP did not halt.

Finally, Milovanovich decided to use Russian. "*Stoi!*" he shouted. This time the "MP" *stoi*-ed, but he also pulled out his .45-caliber pistol, the one the Viennese called "pocket flak" because of its ammo size. Clearly unused to the weapon, he fired it wildly. At that moment, the two jeeps bearing the CIC and SSU men arrived. Firing, mostly into the air, became general. An "MP" tried to slug a CIC man with his pistol but was disarmed. In a matter of moments, four of the "MPs" were surrounded by armed CIC and SSU men, who marched them off to imprisonment. In front of Kauder's house sat a huge automobile, a Nazi Horch, with double rear tires four feet in diameter. Inside the Horch lay a preferred instrument of Soviet kidnapping: a Persian rug in which a captive could be wrapped so tightly that he could barely breathe, much less cry out.

At CIC headquarters, the prisoners were brought before me. Their "MP" uniforms revealed, under the U.S. jackets, the complete uniform of the Soviet army. In Salzburg, a Soviet repatriation mission with quasi-diplomatic status had been operating since the war's end. Although the Americans knew the mission was mostly NKVD (Soviet secret police), the Soviets spent most of their free time at the American PX buying food and giving no cause for worry. The four prisoners were from this mission.

How did the Soviets get ahold of American MP uniforms? An alcoholic American warrant officer had been virtually living at the Soviet mission, where he was fed vodka nonstop. Since he was the logistics officer for the MP battalion in Salzburg, getting uniforms from him was not difficult.

The Soviet group stood impassively in a circle around me. I informed the leader of the prisoners, Major Passichnik, that he and his little team would spend the night at the Landesgericht jail, a stopping point for hundreds of German SS and Gestapo officials en route to the U.S. internment camp. The major could not believe his ears.

"You are going to put us in a *German* cell?" he thundered. "Why don't you put us in an American CIC prison?"

Because, I told him, the Americans don't have their own prison or cells. This inability to match the NKVD cell for cell or prison for prison so shocked this gentleman that he and his fellow prisoners went meekly across the square to incarceration.

We still had not informed CIC's Vienna headquarters of the situation and the arrests; nor could we do so without also informing the Soviet high command: The CIC's communications landlines ran through the Soviet zone of Lower Austria to Vienna. The report on the prisoners would have to go to Vienna by air.

Salzburg had an airport. But it was a tiny one, commanded by a U.S. Air Force first lieutenant named Frost. We approached the lieutenant, who initially and promptly turned down the request to fly to Vienna as too dangerous. He said he would fly to the American airfield at Tülln, twelve miles outside Vienna. This was quite unsatisfactory, because it meant that any messenger could be intercepted by the Soviets outside Vienna. (The remaining officers at the Soviet mission in Salzburg had already advised NKVD headquarters near Vienna to intercept any reports on the prisoners.) We virtually promised Lieutenant Frost a medal for delivering top-secret info and convinced him to fly to Vienna and land at dawn on a street in an American ward. Frost had but one airworthy plane, a Piper Cub, which had been used as an artillery-spotting craft.

Fortunately, Frost hadn't arrived until after the war and was desperate to win any sort of a decoration. Once he agreed, we wrote up the report on the Soviet repatriation mission, placed it inside double envelopes (top-secret style), and delivered it to the lieutenant, who immediately took off in his Piper Cub.

Frost, recognizing the nonfighting character of his aircraft, headed north until he reached the Danube River and then flew "on the deck," skimming the Danube's murky waters, often scarcely fifty feet above the river. In Soviet-controlled Lower Austria, two MiGs rose to demand why he was flying over Soviet-controlled territory, but they did not dare dive down on the Piper Cub lest they find themselves in the Danube. So Frost flew on, landing the Cub at daybreak in an American-controlled ward on a street that had been cleared of traffic. He came to a stop a few feet from a wall. Frost hopped out, jumped into a waiting CIC jeep, and was conveyed to General Mark W. Clark, former military chief on the Italian front and now American high commissioner for Austria. Clark read the CIC report intently.

For three days, the Soviets in Vienna demanded the release of the prisoners in Salzburg, and for three days, Clark stalled, blasting his Soviet opposite number, Field Marshal Konyev, every time the latter called or came to a four-power meeting.

Back in Salzburg, Major Passichnik and the other three prisoners were raising hell, promising their Austrian jailer all sorts of dire consequences. The jailer was both happy to have the Soviets in his grasp and appalled by the threats he was hearing, and daily he sent a list of them to the Americans.

Finally, having toyed with the Soviet field marshal enough, Clark told me by telephone to let the prisoners go. I had the Soviets showered and shaved and brought before me in freshly pressed uniforms. In English and German, I dressed them down for breaking their diplomatic status and said I was returning them to the Soviet high command.

It was a quiet three-car convoy that set out for the "border" between the Soviet and the American zones with the Russians on board. The country road led north from Salzburg to Linz and thence east to the railroad bridge that crossed the Enns River into Lower Austria. Upon reaching the Enns, I explained to the Soviets that they must walk across the railroad bridge until they saw fellow Russians. We watched intently with binoculars what transpired. We noted that the NKVD had arrived with a Black Maria—a truck with a canvas top. As each of the Soviets, led by Passichnik, clambered into the truck, he was "aided" by a rifle butt to his posterior; 1946 was still the era of Stalin, and the penalty for failure was not a pleasant one.

After a brief stay in an interrogation center in Germany, Kauder was back in Vienna. The Americans never established which side he had been working for, but we felt he was a Soviet double agent who had purposely fed the Germans bad information about Kursk. Kauder was given his freedom by SSU and remained in Austria. American intelligence lost track of him in 1950.

As for Lieutenant Frost, he got a Bronze Star for his low-level flight in the Piper Cub. He had taken part in a war, after all—the Cold War.

The Great Rescue

DAVID CLAY LARGE

Vienna and Berlin were the only cities on the historical fault line of the Iron Curtain where the two sides directly confronted each other. While Vienna's potential for trouble diminished with time, Berlin's only seemed to grow. The divided city was 110 miles within the Soviet zone of occupation—and later, East Germany (or the German Democratic Republic, as it was formally called). Berlin became the most dangerous flash point of the Cold War. Its importance, early on, was strategic. If the Soviets could force their former allies to evacuate Berlin, demoralization and a sense of abandonment by the U.S. might spread over Western Europe. They might have achieved a principal goal: a unified, demilitarized, and politically nonaligned Germany—which, no doubt, would eventually drop into the Communist camp. Who could tell which countries might follow? It was the domino argument—or the "bandwagon effect," as it was called then—but it made sense, perhaps more than it would in Asia in the 1960s. Later, as the two sides hardened their positions and allowed them to petrify, the importance of Berlin became largely symbolic, especially with the building of the Wall in 1961. But that is getting ahead of our story.

Another event played just as decisive a part in turning Berlin into a symbol. That was the Soviet blockade of the Western-held sectors of the city, severing all road, rail, and river access. The Soviets made the introduction of the Western deutsche mark in June 1948 as their excuse, but the underlying purpose was to prevent the establishment of a separate West German state. In this chess game, the response of Great Britain and the United States was to institute an airlift, utilizing the three twenty-mile-wide air corridors the Soviets had allowed them in 1945. So began

"The Great Rescue," as David Clay Large aptly calls it. The airlift has to be counted one of the genuine triumphs in the history of military logistics: By the time the Soviets backed down in May 1949, Western Allies had achieved a practically bloodless strategic victory. In just four years, they had transformed Berlin from Hitler's capital to the "outpost of freedom," the symbolic bastion of the so-called free world.

———

DAVID CLAY LARGE is a professor of history at Montana State University and an authority on modern German history. Among his books are *Where Ghosts Walked: Munich's Road to the Third Reich; Berlin;* and, most recently, *And the World Closed Its Doors: The Story of One Family Abandoned to the Holocaust.* Large is working on a book about the 1936 Olympic games. He divides his time between Bozeman, Montana, and San Francisco.

I N 1958, SOVIET PREMIER Nikita Khrushchev observed that Berlin was the "testicles of the West," which he had only to "squeeze" to make his adversaries scream. Moscow's most painful pressure on this tender part occurred a decade earlier, in 1948–49, when the Soviets closed off all road, rail, and river traffic between the Western sectors of Berlin and the Allied zones of occupation in western Germany. This most audacious of modern blockades produced an even more ambitious response from the Western Allies: the fabled Berlin Airlift, which managed to break the Russian stranglehold after eleven months. Ever since, the Big Lift has been justifiably celebrated as a magnificent example of fortitude, technical skill, and organizational prowess. Yet the enterprise was, from the outset, a highly risky expedient that provided some of the most dangerous moments in the early Cold War.

Berlin had been a bone of contention between Soviet Russia and the Western Powers even before the Cold War began. The Americans and British had allowed the Red Army to overrun the Nazi capital in May 1945 on the understanding that they would gain immediate access to the city, which was to be governed jointly by the Four Powers (Britain having agreed to give France part of its sector of occupation in exchange for some of the American sector). But once ensconced in Berlin, the Soviets obstructed Western entry for about eight weeks. During their time of exclusive control, they began stripping the region of industrial machinery and shipping it back to Russia. By the time their Western "partners" arrived, in early July, the Soviet forces had taken away almost 70 percent of Berlin's heavy industry.

At the same time, the Russians sought to establish the basis for political control over the entire city by employing handpicked German Communists to staff municipal offices. Walter Ulbricht, who had been living in exile in Moscow (and avoiding Stalin's purges by prodigies of toadying), was put in charge of a "Communist Action Group" that placed reliable functionaries in key administrative posts. Paul Markgraf, a Stalinist thug, became chief of police, while Arthur Pieck, son of German Communist Party chairman Wilhelm Pieck, took over the department of personnel. Lenin once said that whoever controls Berlin controls Germany, and whoever controls Germany controls Europe. Lenin's successors had obviously taken this wisdom to heart.

Despite early friction with the Soviets, the Western Powers hoped for harmonious Four-Power administration of Berlin and Germany in the immediate postwar era. To avoid provoking the Russians, they did not press for a written agreement defining land access across the Soviet zone to their sectors in Berlin. Perhaps they took it for granted that the surface routes would not be impeded. At any rate, only access by aircraft was guaranteed through a specific arrangement in 1945, which established three air corridors into the city, each twenty miles wide. "The Soviets were very legalistic in that respect when it suited them, and they caught us," observed an American diplomat with unimpeachable hindsight.

Legalism, however, was not very evident in the administration of Berlin and Germany in the first years after the war. The Potsdam Agreement of August 1945 called for treating Germany as a single economic unit, but each military government evolved policies unique to its occupation zone, and each applied its own interpretation of the "Four-D" principles: de-Nazification, demilitarization, decartelization, and democratization. Not surprisingly, the greatest discrepancies were between the three Western zones and the Soviet zone. The sharply diverging approaches meant that meetings of the Allied Control Council (responsible for all of Germany) and the Allied Kommandatura (responsible for Berlin) often degenerated into verbal mud fights, with the Soviets accusing the Western Powers of coddling former Nazis and fomenting remilitarization, while the Western Allies charged Moscow with looting Germany in order to keep it permanently unstable and ripe for Communist domination.

The divisions among the occupation powers were especially intense in the former Nazi capital, which was rapidly becoming known as the "Capital of the Cold War." In preparation for municipal elections to be held in October 1946, German Communists, backed by the Soviets, forced a merger of the Social Democratic Party (SPD) and the Communist Party into the Socialist Unity Party (SED). The fusion was supposed to apply citywide, but Social Democrats in the Western zones decisively rejected this shotgun marriage, preferring to remain single and free of control from Moscow. In the October elections, the SPD won 48.7 percent of the municipal vote; the conservative Christian Democrats (CDU) 22.2 percent; and the SED 19.8 percent. Given their first chance at free elections in over thirteen years, the Berliners had overwhelmingly rejected the version of "democracy" sponsored by the SED.

The Soviets and their SED clients were not amused. Unable to alter the results of the election, they acted as if the new city government were illegitimate, overriding its policies unless approved by the Kommandatura, and harassing and sometimes even kidnapping non-Communist functionaries. A standoff arose when the city assembly appointed Ernst Reuter as lord mayor. He was a former Communist who had split with the party in 1921 because he could not tolerate its subordination of German working-class interests to the demands of Moscow. Upon joining the SPD, he had become a vocal opponent of the Nazis and had spent the war years in exile in Turkey. Upon his return to Berlin in 1946, he worked to rally local Socialists against the Soviets. Unwilling to accept such an independent spirit as lord mayor, the Russians vetoed Reuter's appointment. Yet the intrepid Reuter continued to speak for the city, and most Berliners saw him as their leader (he duly became mayor of West Berlin once the city was formally divided).

As it grew increasingly evident that Germany and Berlin were becoming prime battlegrounds in the emerging Cold War, the Western Powers started taking measures to protect and rehabilitate "their" Germany. In early 1947 the Americans and British fused their zones economically into "Bizonia." (France, intent upon keeping Germany divided and weak, kept its zone separate for a time.) The Russians, who had been extracting war reparations in the form of coal and manufactured goods from the Western zones, were officially prevented from continuing this practice. A few months later, George Marshall, the new American secretary of state, announced his famous plan for European economic recovery, the Marshall Plan, in which he pointedly included Germany. The program was also open to the Soviet Union and the regions in Eastern Europe that it controlled, but Marshall expected Moscow to spurn the aid, which it promptly did. If the Soviets in 1946–47 were bringing down an Iron Curtain across Europe, the Western Powers were drawing some lines of demarcation of their own.

The Soviets bitterly protested the Western initiatives as violations of the Potsdam Agreement and as steps toward the formal division of Germany. They retaliated in the most effective way they could: by interfering with traffic into Berlin. Claiming "technical difficulties" on the rail lines, they restricted the number of freight trains allowed to pass through their zone, thereby creating a serious food shortage. In early 1948, with their Berlin garrisons feeling the pinch, the Americans and British launched a baby airlift with a few planeloads of supplies, a preview of the much larger lift to come. Although the Allied Kommandatura continued to meet during this crisis, Robert Murphy, political adviser to the American military government, reported that the agreement had become impossible "even on the most routine questions." General Lucius Clay, the U.S. military governor, sensed "a feeling of new tenseness in every Soviet individual with whom we have official relationships." He feared war might come with "dramatic suddenness."

The situation was so menacing because, following extensive postwar troop withdrawals from continental Europe, Western strength on the ground was very thin relative to the massive Soviet presence. According to American intelligence estimates in early 1948, the Russians had eighty-four divisions stationed in eastern Germany and in other satellite countries, while the West could muster only sixteen divisions stationed in Germany, Austria, the Benelux countries, and France. American officials worried that the Russians might be inclined to exploit their conventional superiority through a rapid push westward. "All the Russians need to reach the Rhine is shoes," said Undersecretary of State Robert Lovett.

Yet heightened tensions with the Soviets did not prevent the Western Powers from taking further steps to ensure the political and economic viability of western Germany. In early June 1948 they instructed German officials in the Western zones to draft a constitution for a new federal state "best adapted to the eventual re-establishment of German unity at present disrupted." They also announced that they would begin formulating an "Occupation Statute" to define relations between themselves and the new German government. Finally, on June 18 the Western military governments announced that a new currency, the deutsche mark, would replace the inflated reichsmark (the old Nazi currency) in their zones. The new currency was not designated for use in Berlin, but when the Soviets tried to impose an Eastern-zone currency on the entire city, the Americans, having secretly flown in loads of deutsche marks in case they might be needed, started issuing the new bills on June 24. Now Berlin had competing currencies to match its competing ideologies: Western deutsche marks stamped with a large B for Berlin, and Soviet-issued reichsmarks bearing thumb-sized coupons stuck on with potato glue. No sooner had the Russians introduced their "wallpaper marks" (so named by the Berliners) than their representative on the Kommandatura, Major General Alexander Kotikov, stalked out of the Allied body, allegedly in response to the equally abrupt departure of his American counterpart, Colonel Frank Howley. Now even the pretense of cooperation was gone.

The battle of the bills turned into a full-scale battle for Berlin, because the Soviets, citing additional technical difficulties, stopped all road traffic coming into Berlin on June 18, the day the deutsche mark was launched in western Germany. On June 24 they halted rail and barge traffic as well, and they cut deliveries of electrical power and coal from the Eastern sectors to the west. In the following weeks they also established checkpoints along their sector border in Berlin to monitor (but not yet prevent) the passage of goods and people.

While the currency imbroglio provided the immediate backdrop for these dramatic measures, it was not the central issue behind the blockade. The Soviets hoped to use their stranglehold over Berlin to force the Allies to rescind their plans for a West German government, which Moscow resolutely opposed. The Soviets also wanted to regain the right to extract reparations from the Western zones, especially from the coal-rich Ruhr. These were the immediate goals; down the line they hoped to show the Western Powers that it made no sense for them to stay in Berlin, deep within the lair of the Bear.

Colonel Howley, commandant of the American sector in Berlin, labeled Russia's decision to impose a full blockade "the most barbarous in history since Genghis Khan reduced conquered cities to pyramids of skulls." His comment was a bit hyperbolic, ignoring as it did some rather more barbarous decisions of recent vintage. Yet the Soviet move was indeed a bitter blow to the 2.1 million people living in the Western sectors of Berlin. It promised more hardships on top of the miseries endemic to the entire city in the late 1940s. The capital of the Cold War was still a living monument to the horrors of World War II. Enormous piles of rubble blocked central streets; bands of displaced persons, German and foreign, roamed the town, looting, robbing, raping, and murdering. The most prosperous business was the black market, where everything was traded, from pieces of coal to Lucky Strike cigarettes, long the city's currency of choice. But while all Berliners had to contend with high crime and chronic shortages, those in the Western sectors now faced a life-or-death crisis, since most of the food and energy they required came either from western Germany or from the Soviet-controlled zone of occupation. No wonder they cheered when Ernst Reuter called upon the world to help Berlin "in the decisive phase of the fight for freedom."

The primary targets of this appeal, the Western Allies, were in something of a quandary about how to respond. Official Washington was caught off guard and full of trepidation. George Kennan, head of the State Department's Policy Planning Staff, recalled: "No one was sure how the Russian move could be countered, or whether it could be countered at all. The situation was dark and full of danger." France waited to see what action its partners might take. Only Britain adopted an immediate unequivocal stance. Foreign Secretary Ernest Bevin announced that Britain would neither abandon Berlin nor back away from plans for a separate West German state.

On the scene in Germany, General Clay also appeared steadfast, at least outwardly. Interpreting the Russian move as a bluff designed to frighten the West out of Berlin, he publicly promised that the Americans would not leave. "If Berlin falls," he said, "Germany will be next. If we intend to defend Europe against Communism, we should not budge." In private, however, he worried that if Berlin could not be fed, a starving populace would force the Western Powers out in order to get the blockade lifted.

None of the Allied officials contemplated a fight by the tiny Western garrison in Berlin, which in total comprised about fifteen thousand troops. A possibly more viable option involved breaking the blockade by dispatching an armed convoy from western Germany. General Clay was an avid proponent of this gambit, going so far as to lay plans for a six-thousand-man task force to storm 110 miles down the autobahn from Helmstedt to Berlin. Clay asked General Curtis LeMay, commander of the U.S. Air Force in Europe, to provide air support in case the Russians started shooting—an eventuality LeMay did not expect but which he welcomed as a fine opportunity for a preemptive strike on all Russian airfields in Germany. "Naturally we knew where they were," LeMay said. "We had observed the Russian fighters lined up in a nice smooth line on the aprons at every place. If it had happened, I think we could have cleaned them up pretty well, in no time at all."

But of course "it" didn't happen. The State Department thought the convoy option was far too risky, while the Pentagon dismissed it as militarily unworkable. As General Omar Bradley, chairman of the Joint Chiefs of Staff, wrote later, "The Russians could stop an armed convoy without opening fire on it. Roads could be closed for repair or a bridge could go up just ahead of you and then another bridge behind and you'd be in a hell of a fix."

If the Western Powers were unwilling to confront the Russians with ground forces, and were equally determined to stay in Berlin, they had to find a way to keep the city supplied, pending a still-hoped-for diplomatic solution. In the given circumstances, an airlift of some kind seemed the obvious answer, but at first only Foreign Secretary Bevin pressed it with any vigor. He argued forcefully that an airlift would at once reinforce the morale of the West Berliners and show Moscow that "we are not powerless but on the contrary possess a wealth of technical ability and spectacular air strength." Clay, having reluctantly given up his convoy idea, soon came around to Bevin's view. But the State Department and Pentagon still dithered, worried that this gambit, too, posed the risk of war, and that the Soviets might take advantage of Western preoccupation with Berlin to strike elsewhere. Finally, on June 26, President Truman put an end to all the equivocation by ordering that an airlift to Berlin be made operational as soon as possible. To Secretary of the Army Kenneth Royall's objection that this might mean war, he replied that America would "have to deal with the situation as it developed."

Even if, as Clay and Bevin were convinced, an airlift did not lead to war, there were legitimate reasons to doubt that it could save Berlin. No one had ever attempted to air-supply such a huge population with almost everything it needed for survival over a prolonged period. The Americans had been successful in airlifting supplies "over the Hump" of the Himalayas from India to China in 1942–43, and the British had supplied their troops similarly in Burma, but these missions had been limited largely to military materials and had operated in uncontested (and uncongested) airspace. Moreover, at the beginning of the airlift, the West did not possess spectacular air strength, at least not in the form of cargo planes readily available in the region. The U.S. Air Force in Europe had only two C-54 Douglas Skymasters, which could ferry almost ten tons, and 102 battered C-47s, known as Gooney Birds, with a three-ton capacity. The British air command in Germany could deploy a total of fourteen Dakotas, their version of the C-47. The French had six Junkers and one Dakota, all derelict.

Existing loading and landing facilities were also inadequate. America's primary air base in western Germany, Rhein-Main, had a runway of good length, but its surface was not designed for heavy transport use. The RAF's Wunstorf base in the British zone had little hardstand for parking and loading. At the Berlin end, Tempelhof, in the American sector—built largely by the Nazis in the 1930s—had a massive administrative complex, but its single runway (another was soon added) was surfaced with tire-busting steel planks, and the approach to it from the west required coming in between high apartment buildings and a four-hundred-foot-tall brewery chimney. A cemetery near the field reminded pilots where they would end up if they miscalculated the approach. Gatow, in the British sector, was much easier to fly into but lacked a good off-loading area. There were no airfields at all in the French sector, though Paris allowed the Americans to start building a new one (with German labor) at Tegel in July 1948. Because access to Tegel was impeded by transmitting towers belonging to the Soviet-controlled Radio Berlin, France's Berlin commandant politely asked the Russians to dismantle them. When the Russians refused, he ordered the things blown up. This was France's major contribution to the airlift.

As soon as the lift got under way, a call went out for cargo planes from all over the world. In the American case, aircraft arrived from bases as far away as Guam, Alaska, Hawaii, and Panama to make up what was at first labeled the "LeMay Coal and Feed Delivery Service" and later rechristened "Operation Vittles." Although the build-up was impressive, the enterprise at this point was definitely seat-of-the-pants. "It was a cowboy operation when I got there in July," recalled an American pilot. "It was a joke if you could take off after your buddy and get back to Rhein-Main before he did. It did not matter how you beat him, just so long as you beat him." Loading operations were also chaotic, with trucks smashing into planes and even driving into spinning propellers. In the early days, pilots experimented with low-level drops over Berlin's Olympic Stadium to avoid time-consuming landings, but all the food ended up as puree, while coal became coal dust. Worse, although the deliveries increased each week, they were not nearly enough to meet Berlin's needs, even in summer. Observing this painful reality, Robert Murphy, Clay's aide, speculated on July 9 that "within a week or so we may find ourselves faced with a desperate population demanding our withdrawal to relieve the distress."

Clearly, a great leap forward in terms of organizational sophistication was required if Western Berlin was to avoid going Red—or dead. Fortunately, even as Murphy was issuing his grim prognostication, measures were being taken to make the operation more viable. Dozens of American C-54s, along with newly arrived British Yorks and Sunderland flying boats (which landed on the Havel

River and Berlin's many lakes), were integrated into the system. The larger aircraft were able to carry bulky items like generators and power plant machinery, necessary to replace energy transmitters from the East. As for food, it was now delivered almost exclusively in dehydrated form, which made for less weight and more efficient packaging, if not for better eating. So many items arrived as powder that a cartoon showed a stork flying into Berlin carrying a diapered bundle labeled POWDERED BABY.

The most crucial advances were key logistical and technical innovations introduced by General William H. Tunner, a veteran of the "Hump" who arrived in July to become commander of the Combined Airlift Task Force. Tunner's notion of an airlift sounded like something out of a primer by Henry Ford: "There is no frenzy, no flap, just the inexorable process of getting the job done. In a successful airlift, you don't see planes parked all over the place. They're either in the air, on loading or unloading ramps, or being worked on." Tunner quickly imposed a rigid routine whereby planes were dispatched according to type, airspeed, and cargo loads, which avoided bunching up en route or on the ground. Pre-established flight plans put an end to races through the corridors. Improvements in air traffic control around Berlin made it possible to bring in planes at very short intervals. A special training facility in Great Falls, Montana, prepared air and ground crews to work together efficiently in this exacting environment.

Among inhabitants of the Western sectors, improvements in the airlift did not immediately dispel widespread fears that their "outpost of freedom" would be slowly strangled to death. The first months of the blockade brought significant reductions in daily food rations, which had been meager enough to begin with. Because the Eastern sector was better supplied, West Berliners now began crossing regularly into the East to buy goods (at hugely inflated prices) or to beg handouts from Eastern friends and relatives. The Soviets tolerated such exchanges, believing they would further a material dependency on the East without substantially undercutting the blockade. They remained confident that all of Berlin would soon fall into their hands without their having to fire a shot.

By late fall 1948, however, Tunner's innovations were bearing fruit (albeit dehydrated): Berliners were not starving to death, and the local economy had not ground to a halt. The children of Berlin could take delight in occasional drops of candy attached to tiny parachutes; the kids called the planes "chocolate bombers." Yet everyone in Berlin understandably worried that the coming months might be a very different story, for harsh weather conditions would both increase demand for supplies and render their delivery much more difficult. It was estimated that Berlin required a minimum of 5,650 tons of food and coal per day to survive during the winter months; in October the lift had managed 4,760, and in November 3,800—not encouraging statistics. There was another danger as well. Alarmed by the airlift's successes, the Russians were now sending signals that they might not continue to tolerate this Allied expedient. Soviet planes began staging mock air battles over Berlin, while ground batteries practiced antiaircraft drills in the northern corridor. Red fighters even buzzed Allied cargo and passenger planes. If these sorties escalated from harassment to actual shooting, the airlift might lead to war after all.

As it turned out, the Soviet interference, while dangerous and provocative, did not become more extensive; indeed, it abated somewhat with the onset of winter. As so often in the past, the Russians seemed to be counting on nasty weather to come to their aid.

The Western Allies confronted the approach of winter with a new display of commitment to Berlin. On October 22, President Truman authorized the dispatch of sixty-six more C-54s to Germany, raising the total to 225. In November the new airport at Tegel became operational, greatly increasing the city's receiving capacity. Meanwhile, advanced radar installations and improved cockpit instrumentation were making it possible for planes to fly "when birds walked," as the pilots put it. After returning from a trip to Washington, Clay announced, "The airlift will be continued until the blockade is lifted."

While the strength of the Western commitment, both material and moral, should not be doubted, the subsequent months turned out to be not quite the white-knuckle experience that everyone had feared. The primary reason is that old General Winter sided this time with Russia's antagonists. January 1949 was a meteorological miracle, with clear skies and no hard frost. During that month, the airlift managed an amazing 5,546 tons a day. With relatively mild conditions continuing through March, and daily deliveries sometimes exceeding 6,000 tons, many Berliners in the Western sector found themselves actually *gaining* weight; a few more months of this and they would begin to look like Bavarians.

At the peak of the Berlin Airlift, in spring 1949, planes were landing every ninety seconds and turning around within six minutes. Many of the planes did not return empty, but "backlifted" export goods or ferried out passengers, mainly sick children and politicians.

Many Berliners were not content simply to grab for this lifeline from the sky;

they contributed their part to make the airlift a success. Residents of the Western zones helped unload planes, worked as ground mechanics, and drove the trucks that distributed food and coal. To supplement the powdered largesse from the West, they grew vegetables on every available scrap of soil. Perhaps most important, they maintained morale by regularly displaying their famous *schnauze* (irreverent wit). "Aren't we lucky," they joked, "just think what it would be like if the Americans were running the blockade and the Russians the airlift." A radio program called *Die Insulaner* ("The Islanders"), beamed from the American sector, featured easily identifiable Berlin types offering a running commentary on life in the beleaguered city. Older Berliners still remember the *Insulaner* theme song, which described the sound of four-motored aircraft as "music to the ear" and expressed longing for the day "when the lights are on and the trains are moving."

All of which is not to say that there was no self-pity or resentment, even toward the Western Allies. Some claimed that Berlin would not be in such a fix if the West had not "given" a third of Germany to the Soviets. Others complained about having to pay high prices for dehydrated foods that they didn't like anyway. Yet on the whole, the Berliners were deeply appreciative of the effort being made on their behalf, and they relished the chance to work hand in glove with the Western Powers against the hated Russians. In the end, they were certainly more thankful and cooperative than their countrymen in the Western zones, who howled in protest over a "Berlin tax" imposed by the new German Economic Council in Frankfurt to help relieve the distress of the city.

By spring 1949 the airlift was so successful that it seemed capable of going on forever. The preparations for a West German state had also proceeded apace, with the drafting and passage of a Basic Law, or constitution, for the new entity. Another epochal creation, the North Atlantic Treaty Organization (NATO), was formalized in April. Short of going to war, there was little that the Soviets could do to impede these developments. They had blockaded Berlin partly to strengthen their hand in dealing with their former allies on the German question; instead, they were being dealt out of the game.

The Western Powers, moreover, were putting pressure on the Russians through a small but painful counterblockade consisting of trade sanctions that prohibited shipments of crucial raw materials and manufactured goods from the Western zones to the East. The Soviet zone stopped receiving key items such as hard coal from the Ruhr, electrical motors, ball bearings, transmission systems, diamond drills, and optical equipment. The losses were all the more grievous because the economy in the Russian zone was in terrible shape due to earlier industrial pillaging and ongoing mismanagement by *Sowjetische Aktiengesellschaften*—Soviet-controlled companies known by their apt acronym, SAGS.

Obviously, this was not what the Soviets had intended when they launched their blockade, so they decided to bargain. In March 1949 their delegate to the United Nations Security Council, Yakov Malik, began meeting secretly with his American counterpart, Philip Jessup. After lengthy negotiations, the Soviets agreed to lift their blockade if the West consented to hold a Council of Foreign Ministers meeting on Germany in May. When this deal was announced in early May, many Berliners remained skeptical, fearing a Russian trick. But at one minute after midnight on May 12, 1949, all the lights finally came on in Berlin for the first time in eleven months, and the trains started rolling again between Berlin and western Germany.

There were no lavish celebrations in Berlin when the blockade was lifted. After all, the Cold War that had occasioned it was still very much alive, and everyone knew that the Soviets could cut off the city again if they chose to. In fact, they continued to interfere periodically with surface traffic, causing the Allies to keep flying in supplies through September 1949. Also, Berlin was now split sharply into two sections, with each part increasingly taking on its own character. Berliners had to wonder whether their city would ever become one again.

The Western Allies remained concerned about their own status in the divided city, but for the moment they could take quiet pride in the tremendous accomplishment that the Berlin Airlift represented. Some 238,616 flights had transported over two million tons of supplies into the blockaded city. Seventy-seven British and American airmen had lost their lives in the operation. These were painful losses, but remarkably few given the scope and duration of the undertaking.

Like many successful military operations—and the Berlin Airlift was essentially military, despite the participation of some civilian crews from commercial airlines—this enterprise had further payoffs down the line in terms of technical innovations and logistical lessons. "A lot of the procedures that were developed [for the airlift] were used to upgrade the air traffic control system in the United States," wrote a veteran of the campaign. One of these innovations is taken for granted today by all air travelers: those wandlike torches used to guide airplanes on the ground. In the military realm, with operations on distant battlefields demanding massive transport of men and material, the lessons of the lift were especially useful.

As for the Berlin Airlift's place in postwar politics, we can see that this initiative, along with the crisis that provoked it, helped to establish the parameters within which the victors and vanquished of World War II would operate for the next half century. By remaining steadfast in Berlin, the Western Allies placed an outer limit on Soviet expansionism in Europe. The Russian threat to Berlin, and the cooperative response it occasioned, helped spur the creation of NATO. The experience was also instrumental in forging the most important new bilateral partnership in the second half of the twentieth century—the bond between the United States and West Germany, founded in May 1949. As Robert Murphy correctly noted, it was through this cooperative effort that "the American people, for the first time in their history, formed a virtual alliance with the German people."

Alas, Murphy should have said "part of the German people." East Germany was left out of this embrace, and out of the "economic miracle" that emerged from it. As many feared in 1949, there would be more Berlin crises down the line to test the ties between West Berlin and its Allied protectors. In 1958, Moscow threatened once again to drive the Western Powers out of Berlin and to integrate the entire city into the Soviet-dominated East German state. The fact of the matter, of course, was that the tender testicles of the West had become the loose sphincter of the East—an opening through which thousands of East Germans were fleeing every year. The Berlin Wall that went up in 1961 to stanch the flow was in many ways as cruel as the Berlin Blockade, but it also turned out to be just as double-edged, since it purchased "security" at the price of continued economic stagnation and political oppression.

In 1951, Mayor Reuter of West Berlin, which was now a separate political entity and part of the West German state, dedicated a monument in front of Tempelhof Airport to commemorate the airlift of 1948–49. The structure consisted of a twenty-meter-high concrete slab with three prongs arching toward the West, symbolic of the air corridors into the city. Its base was inscribed with the names of the airmen who died in the lift. Looking at the monument now, in the wake of German reunification, one might propose that it stands not only for the enduring ties between Berlin and the West, but also for an act of faith in a perilous time that helped to make German unity possible fifty years later.

Incident at Lang Fang

EUGENE B. SLEDGE

When World War II came to its abrupt atomic end in the summer of 1945, few paid much attention to Mao Tse-tung and his Chinese Communists. They seemed, as John Lewis Gaddis has written, "little more than an obscure group of revolutionaries who engaged in long marches, lived in caves, and lectured one another on their own peculiar understanding of Marxist-Leninism." Even Stalin was inclined to put them down then, calling the Chinese Communists "Margarine Marxists," substitutes for the real thing. Though Mao's enclaves occupied considerable territory, mainly in North China, they were disconnected and concentrated mostly in rural areas, lacking significant urban bases. Mao's armed forces were small, numbering no more than three hundred thousand, many of whom belonged to scattered guerrilla bands. With the surrender of the Japanese, the Communists saw a chance to consolidate many of these enclaves. They also began to push into Manchuria, where, after their August 1945 blitzkrieg, the Soviets were busy stripping factories of heavy machinery and herding off thousands of Japanese prisoners to work in Siberia as slave laborers. At this point, curiously, the Soviets had friendlier dealings with Chiang Kai-shek's Chinese Nationalist government than with Mao's Communists. No one yet contemplated a Far Eastern Iron Curtain.

But even as the Communists were racing to establish themselves in Manchuria, with its rich deposits of coal and iron, so were the Nationalists. They were at the same time bent on taking over as much of North China as possible, and established themselves in major cities such as Beijing and Tientsin. The Communists resisted their drive north, which (in the words of the French military historian Lionel Max Chassin) "produced clashes . . . and, as the situation became more confused, each side accused the other of provoking civil war." Meanwhile, that fall Chiang asked for American help, ostensibly to aid in the disarming and repatriation of Japanese troops, who numbered upward of two million men. By the middle of October 1945, in an operation largely forgotten today, fifty-three thousand U.S. Marines had landed in China. Though the Americans were eager to accommodate their wartime ally, the poor fighting qualities of Nationalist troops and the entrenched corruption of the government dismayed them. The U.S. was determined to persuade Chiang to include the Communists in a ruling coalition. But strict neutrality was out of the question. The presence of American troops blocked the Communist advance and furthered Chiang's grand Manchurian design. With the help of the U.S. Tenth Air Force, he was able to airlift three entire armies north. The Communists responded angrily, attacking American troops, who were notably reluctant to become involved in combat. "Too many Marines who had fought in World War II, and wanted to go home now that it was over, died protecting a bridge or a railroad track in the wasteland of northern China."

The man who wrote this was a Private 1st Class in the 1st Marine Division named Eugene B. Sledge. He was one of two thousand marines who had arrived in Beijing on October 9 to take over from the Japanese. Sledge was a veteran of Peleliu and Okinawa, and he and his fellow marines were still outfitted in the tropical cotton they had worn in the Pacific. With forty members of a reinforced rifle platoon, he would be sent to protect the division's radio relay station at a godforsaken rail town called Lang Fang. Finding themselves in the unwilling midst of a new war, the marines looked around for someone else to fight the Communists for them. The solution they chanced on could not have been more ideal.

EUGENE B. SLEDGE, who died in 2001, was the author of *With the Old Breed,* an account of his ordeals as a young marine at Peleliu and Okinawa that is widely regarded as one of the most vivid memoirs of World War II. Sledge went on to become a professor of zoology and ornithology at the University of Montevallo in Alabama.

N THE AUTUMN OF 1945, soon after the end of World War II, the 1st Marine Division was sent to northern China. Our mission was to disarm the Japanese, prevent a Communist takeover, and maintain order. Those of us who were stationed in Peking had the "good duty," and we knew it. But late in October, a sergeant came into the British Legation, where most of the 5th Marine Regiment was billeted, and announced that a detachment from K Company was scheduled to pull a tour of guard duty. A reinforced rifle platoon with two light-machine-gun sections, as well as my 60mm mortar squad, would be sent to protect the division's radio relay station at Lang Fang, which was located along a railroad line midway between Peking and Tientsin. We received these orders with a noticeable lack of enthusiasm, but we knew we had not been sent to northern China for rest and rehabilitation.

The next morning dawned crisp and clear. Having been issued ammunition and C rations, our detachment of roughly forty marines and a corpsman, under the command of a lieutenant, boarded five trucks and a jeep and set out for Lang Fang. After we passed through one of the big tower gates in the huge wall surrounding Peking, we looked back and saw Chinese soldiers pulling the gate shut behind us. Our convoy went out into the windswept countryside, while we kept a sharp lookout for possible Communist ambush. Some miles down the road, we moved through an ancient walled village, virtually unchanged since the time of Kublai Khan and Marco Polo. It was crowded with Chinese peasants. Not a single person could be seen outside the walls—grim evidence of the terrible unrest and chaos infecting the countryside.

We soon arrived at Lang Fang, an unwalled village of about five hundred people. Our convoy entered a modern walled compound; atop one small building was a radio antenna. Behind the radio station were our quarters, in some one-story wooden barracks-type buildings. Several of us were detailed for guard duty along the compound wall. My post was on the fire step overlooking a narrow intersection lined with rows of single-story houses of mud and brick. Looking through a fire port and over the parapet, which had barbed wire stretched on top, I realized that we would be easy prey for any snipers in nearby houses.

Several curious Chinese children gathered in the street, and I began talking with them as well as I could, considering my limited knowledge of their language. I tossed a couple of pieces of C-ration candy to them, and they shouted their appreciation. Immediately, a crowd of about fifty people gathered, shouting and holding out their hands. Those of us who were on the wall soon ran out of candy and started tossing hardtack biscuits to them. They begged for more. Then a sergeant double-timed up and told us to save our rations in case we were cut off. (A chilling thought, to be sure!) In the late afternoon, my buddy and I were relieved by the next watch, and we set out beyond the compound gate in search of fresh eggs.

About a block to our right, we noticed the Japanese camp, which had several imposing brick buildings. Curious about our recent enemy, we went up to its gate, where a sentry snapped to and saluted us. We returned his salute. (All Japanese troops of all ranks saluted all marines regardless of rank. I was told they respected us because we had defeated the best troops they had.) We entered the camp, knowing from what we had seen in Peking that the Japanese were now on their best behavior around Americans. An officer invited us to two tables neatly spread with white tablecloths. On one were servings of tea and cookies; on the other were several fine samurai sabers. The officer saluted, bowed, and, pointing to the tables, said in perfect English, "You are welcome to anything you wish." Just then, another marine ran up and told us we were not allowed in the Japanese camp yet. The Japanese officer seemed confused by our sudden departure.

Grumbling mightily, we headed back into the village, still in search of eggs. Some Chinese peasants walked past us in the narrow streets; others sat on benches in front of their houses. A few had winter lettuce or other items for sale, but no eggs. The faces of Lang Fang's inhabitants were tanned and weather-beaten, revealing lives of hard labor and exposure to harsh conditions. The image of these terribly poor people, dressed in drab, dark blue winter clothing, and of the barren, windswept brown landscape was depressing.

Across the track, beyond the sooty, tile-roofed brick railroad station, we saw a group of several hundred Chinese troops bivouacked. They had stacked arms and were lounging around eating rations. Clad in mustard-colored uniforms, wrap leggings, and sneakers, they also wore the type of fatigue cap that made their ears stick straight out. We noted that their rifles were Japanese Arisakas. There were also numerous Nambu light machine guns, the kind that had given us so much misery during the war. In my limited Chinese, I asked each group of soldiers if there were any eggs for sale. Finally, a tall fellow produced a basket of fresh eggs, and we bought a dozen. Suddenly, I noticed that none of these soldiers was the least bit friendly, unlike most of the other Chinese we had encountered; in fact, they were taciturn and sullen. It was unnerving that such battle-hardened veterans as my buddy and me could have been so oblivious to the mood of these troops.

Carrying our paper bag of eggs, we hurried back across the track, only to be met by a frantic runner who told us that those were Communist troops we had been wandering among! As this was the second runner who had been sent after us, we expected to be disciplined. But our lieutenant did not notice us when we eased past him back into the compound. Soon we heard the word going around that there was a strong indication of Communist activity around the village after dark. We realized that we had already had a close call across the track.

In northern China at this time were many different armed groups: Japanese, Japanese-trained and -equipped Chinese puppet-government soldiers, Chinese Communists, Chinese Nationalists, Chinese bandits, and U.S. Marines—all armed to the teeth and vying to fill the power vacuum resulting from Japan's surrender. To the south, Chiang Kai-shek's Nationalist troops were locked in a bloody civil war with Mao Tse-tung's Communists. U.S. planes were flying Nationalist troops up to Peking to oppose the Communists in the north. In Lang Fang and many other areas, even the surrendered Japanese were allowed to retain their arms, under U.S. supervision, in order to help fight the Communists; they were tough, highly trained, and well-disciplined troops who were best able to oppose Mao's followers until the arrival of sufficient Nationalist forces. The Chinese puppet troops were considered of doubtful reliability, while the bandits had no motivation to fight other than a love of plunder from the helpless farmers. The bandits sometimes called themselves Communists, but only when it seemed convenient; we came to believe that they would side in any fight with whoever they thought would win.

The 1st Marine Division's original assignment, to disarm and repatriate Japanese troops, went ahead on schedule, but as the situation became more chaotic, many of us increasingly found ourselves fighting the Communists in lonely outposts and along the railroad lines. The Communists bitterly objected to the U.S. presence and fired propaganda blasts at our high command—as well as bullets at marines out in the boondocks. Too many marines who had fought in World War II, and wanted to go home now that it was over, died protecting a bridge or railroad track in the wasteland of northern China.

One of the many incidents involving some of these various forces occurred at Lang Fang on October 26, shortly after the egg quest. Breaking out our C rations for dinner, we heated stew and coffee and boiled eggs. As the orange sun began to sink through the dust and haze, we started to shiver in the chilly evening air. We wore tropical cotton dungarees, and although we had sweatshirts, we had been in the Pacific so long that we were not acclimated to even the slightest cool weather. Some of us walked around inside the compound, trying to warm ourselves.

Just before sunset, a Chinese messenger arrived at the gate with a note from a puppet general seeking permission from our commanding officer to test-fire a light machine gun in a sandbagged position on top of a two-story building near the railroad station. With permission apparently given, we watched several puppet soldiers working with the Nambu. To our amazement, they aimed the machine gun directly at the area where my buddy and I had been among the unfriendly troops; then they fired several long bursts. We all knew that meant trouble.

Initially, however, silence returned as darkness fell. We drifted into our quarters, wrapped ourselves in blankets, and tried to stay warm. The sentries on duty around the wall simply shivered.

Then, in under half an hour, we heard rifle fire in the distance. The order came: "Break 'em out on the double!" Someone yelled, "Everybody outside on the double with weapons and ammo—let's move!" I pulled on my field shoes, grabbed the .45-caliber Thompson submachine gun I had carried through both Peleliu and Okinawa, rammed a twenty-round magazine in place, and tumbled outside. I headed for the fire step with everyone else. We were told to remain neutral in this fight, but if we saw anyone stick his head over the wall, we were to blow it off. The volume of rifle fire increased, and we began to hear the crash of 81mm mortar shells in the village. A Chinese ran through the dark, narrow streets tooting on a bugle. He sounded more like some drunk on New Year's Eve than any bugler I had ever heard. We were all apprehensive. Though the firing was almost unnoticeable compared to Peleliu and Okinawa, we had reason to be concerned. Here we were, about forty U.S. Marines in the middle of what could explode into a vicious battle between two opposing Chinese forces numbering in the thousands. We had survived fierce combat in the Pacific, and none of us wanted to stretch his luck any further and get killed in a Chinese civil war. We felt abandoned and expendable.

Then the word was passed along that Japanese troops were going out to guard the railroad station with two tanks. Most of us were not assigned to specific guard stations, so we ran the short distance to the wall bordering the road, to watch this incredible scene. With our weapons slung or buttstocks resting on the fire step, we silently watched as the tanks and about thirty infantry passed no more than a few feet from us. Nervously, I fingered the web sling on my Thompson—the impulse to bring up the weapon to aim at our very recent enemies and squeeze the trigger was almost more than I could suppress. The marine next to me expressed my feelings, and probably those of many of the other men, when he said, "It sure is hard not to line 'em up and squeeze 'em off."

As the lead tank slowly clanked past us, its headlights shining, we saw a Japanese officer in dress uniform and cap, Sam Browne belt, campaign ribbons, and white gloves standing erect in the turret with his samurai saber slung over his shoulder. I wondered if I would ever understand the Japanese military. The infantrymen wore helmets and cartridge boxes but no packs. They carried Arisaka rifles, with bayonets fastened to their belts. The tank treads and hobnailed shoes churned up dust as they went past us and disappeared behind village buildings.

Returning to our previous positions along the wall, we learned that our CO had sent word to the Japanese major that we were neutral, but the U.S. government would hold him responsible if any marine was injured.

The sound of firing lasted until about midnight. Just before dawn, the Japanese came past us and returned to their barracks. At daylight, several puppet soldiers came to our gate and begged for treatment of their wounds. Our corpsman bandaged them, but he was ordered to conserve his supplies for our use. Other wounded soldiers were sent to the Japanese barracks.

The sun rose in a cloudless sky of brilliant blue. We soon heard the familiar sound of approaching Corsair engines. We watched with great satisfaction as several of the beautiful gull-winged marine fighters flew back and forth and circled over us. The pilots waved and gave us the thumbs-up sign. The Corsairs provided a great boost to our morale, as well as an impressive show of force for any watching Communists. We no longer felt isolated.

I do not remember how many days we remained in Lang Fang before another patrol relieved us, but it was not long. During this time, we were ordered to remain in or near the compound—not that any of us had the least desire to go exploring. We played baseball in a field just outside the compound gate and stayed vigilant. Fortunately, everything was quiet, and we soon returned uneventfully to Peking.

The final G-2 report of the incident mentioned that four to five thousand Communists had attacked the village but that the marine patrol had not been molested. There was only a brief reference to the Japanese tanks, and none to the infantry with them. I have no idea whether the U.S. government really would have held the Japanese major responsible if any Americans had been injured in the skirmish. And I never learned who ordered the Japanese to send out a patrol with tanks to guard the railroad station.

The incident at Lang Fang became a bland paragraph in a routine report. But to the marine combat veterans involved, this close call was an unforgettable experience, not so much for what happened but for what could have happened to a small group of fugitives from the law of averages. The wheel of fortune had spun once more—and again we had survived.

The Escape of the *Amethyst*

SIMON WINCHESTER

How drastically military momentum can change in just three and a half years. In the fall of 1945, when Eugene Sledge had his encounter with the sullen detachment of Communist troops, the Nationalists held a distinct advantage. Against the advice of American military advisers, Chiang sent his best armies north into Manchuria. They took the most important cities, but the Communists held the countryside and threatened rail connections. For Chiang, it was a strategic trap from which he would never escape.

The Communists, close to defeat in the early months of 1946, would regroup; as time went on and their armies grew, the initiative in the civil war would pass to them. They began to sever the supply links to the armies holding the Manchurian cities: Trapped, the Nationalists had no choice but to surrender. The Communists then pushed southward, taking advantage of Nationalist demoralization and inept generalship. Still, the Nationalists began 1948 with a three-to-one superiority; by the end of the year, the Communist forces outnumbered them. Many of their troops were former Nationalists; even generals went over to their side. They captured vast stockpiles of American arms, left behind by the fleeing Nationalists. Now they had material superiority, too. But Mao was convinced that the Americans were preparing to mount an invasion, leading him to announce a "lean to one side" doctrine. That side was, of course, the U.S.S.R. The Iron Curtain now extended to Asia.

In the spring of 1949, as the blockade of Berlin was fizzling to an end, Chiang's Nationalist armies were close to collapse. If the Soviets in the West had suffered a reverse that checked their expansionist hopes in Europe, in the East the armies of Mao's People's Republic were on the verge of achieving Communism's most resounding (and most enduring) victory. They occupied the greater part of China north of the Yangtze, and on April 20 would begin to cross the divided nation's greatest river. That was the same day that the British frigate *Amethyst* came under fire from Communist guns as it made its way up the Yangtze. Its mission was to bring supplies to the British embassy in Nanking, the Nationalist capital that Chiang's government was already abandoning. The Communists would occupy it, unopposed, on April 24, by which time a badly damaged *Amethyst* had crawled to the relative safety of a protective island. The frigate would spend the next 101 days there, trapped and a virtual captive of the Communists. During that interval, which lasted into midsummer, Chiang would flee to Taiwan and the Reds would take China's largest city, Shanghai.

What followed all depends on your point of view. For the West, and Great Britain especially, the *Amethyst*'s dash for freedom was the stuff of legend—and, inevitably, a movie. Was it indeed one of the rare epics of the burgeoning Cold War? But as Simon Winchester learned when he visited the site, the Chinese regard the escape of "The Imperial Make-Trouble Vessel" as a tale of bloodied bullies slinking away, a humiliation for the British Empire in particular and white prestige in general. For over a century, the Royal Navy had roamed the major rivers of China unchallenged. Suddenly, it seemed a little less invincible. The psychological impact of the *Amethyst* incident (as Chassin writes) "did more for a Communist victory than any strategic maneuver could possibly have done."

SIMON WINCHESTER has published eighteen books, including *Their Noble Lordships, Prison Diary: Argentina, The Professor and the Madman, The Map That Changed the World, Krakatoa,* and *The Meaning of Everything.* His next book is *A Crack in the Edge of the World: America and the Great California Earthquake of 1906.* This article is adapted from Winchester's account of a journey up the Yangtze, *The River at the Heart of the World.* When not traveling, he can be found in New York City, on a farm in the Berkshires, or on the Scottish island of Luing.

Z HENJIANG, A MODERATELY SIZED and moderately ugly city that lies on the still-tidal waters of the Yangtze, a hundred miles inland from the river's mouth, has long been famous in China for the making of vinegar. Westerners with a taste for literature may also know it as the childhood home of a formidable lady named Pearl Sydenstricker, who, after her marriage, became Pearl S. Buck, Nobel laureate. But I had long known of the place for a quite different reason. There was supposed to be a relic in Zhenjiang—from 1949, back when it was known as Chinkiang—that would stir the heart of any English schoolboy of my generation: the anchor of the famous and heroic Royal Navy vessel H.M.S. *Amethyst*. I had come to Zhenjiang because I wanted to see it.

So I told my translator what I wanted and suggested she might ask where the anchor was to be found. She translated the vessel's name to herself—"*Amethyst*, how to say?"—and then suddenly snorted (for weeks she had been ribbing me about the British empire) with mock annoyance.

"I know the ship. Of course!" she said. "We call it the 'Imperial Make-Trouble Vessel.' What is the name? *Purple Stone Hero*, yes, that's it! We defeated it. All Chinese know the story. You came as pirates, and we made you run! You were forced to leave a part of your precious ship behind, here in Zhenjiang. You destroyed a junk with passengers on your way out. Killed many people. We will find the piece you left behind. The anchor. It was a great humiliation for your *precious* British empire."

I reeled slightly from this unexpected onslaught. The facts—or at least the facts as presented to us as schoolchildren—had cast the whole affair for me in a very different light.

His Majesty's Ship *Amethyst* was a sloop-cum-frigate, built in 1943, the eighth to bear her name in the Royal Navy's history. She was of 1,495 tons displacement, three hundred feet long, thirty-eight feet across, and had been built on the Clyde by Alexander Stephen & Sons. She had the typical arms for a ship of the *Black Swan* class: six 4-inch guns, two Bofors guns, and twin Oerlikons. She normally carried 170 officers and men.

She had had a perfectly respectable career in her two World War II years, sinking a submarine off Ireland, helping take the Japanese surrender in New Guinea. Come the peace and she was sent to the Pacific, and in 1949 she found herself attached to the 3rd Frigate Flotilla, an instrument of British imperial power that patrolled the seas in the rough triangle bounded by the western tip of Sumatra, Cape York in northern Australia, and the most northerly point of the Japanese island of Hokkaido. This was half a century ago, when Britain still kept a presence in the Far East: London felt there was much to do in the way of showing the flag and intelligence-gathering, and that gunboat diplomacy—with a fleet of cruisers, destroyers, frigates like the *Amethyst*, and gunboats themselves—was still the best way to accomplish this. (The phrase "gunboat diplomacy" was in fact specially coined about a century ago for patrols on the Yangtze.) In the case of China, a British naval presence on the Yangtze also enhanced the security of the British embassy in the country's capital, Nanking, three hundred miles upriver from the East China Sea.

At the time of this celebrated incident, the unfolding of which gripped half the world and all of my school, a number of Western nations—notably Britain, the United States, France, even Italy—had been allowed to patrol the Yangtze as if it were their own for nearly a hundred years. A slew of treaties had been imposed on China after the so-called Opium Wars of the mid-nineteenth century, giving these foreign countries certain rights on the river. They were allowed to patrol it with guns locked and loaded, for the purposes of protecting their own trade, their own interests, and their own citizens.

By today's standards, it was a bizarre arrangement—as outlandish and unimaginable as, say, letting Japanese warships patrol today's Mississippi to protect a Honda plant in Hannibal, Missouri, or allowing Chinese gunboats to sidle among the punts on the Isis to look out for the interests of Beijing students up at Oxford University. But in the nineteenth century, the Chinese were powerless to prevent such arrogance by foreign traders. It was an arrangement that had gone hand in hand with the similarly bizarre concept of extraterritoriality—by which foreign citizens in the "concession areas" of certain Chinese ports could be judged only by their own courts and not be subject to Chinese law.

The two concepts—foreign naval rights on Chinese rivers and the jurisdiction of foreign courts on Chinese land—came together in Nanking in the late 1940s. Here were a British embassy and a British community in the capital of a China that was rapidly falling apart. The Yangtze, in the spring of that year (and as so often before in Chinese history), was the fault line: To the north of it was the People's Liberation Army of the Communists; on the south bank, the broken armies of the Nationalists. Caught in the middle were the neutrals—the embassies and foreign traders in Nanking, and the gunboats on the Yangtze itself. The former needed protection, if not evacuation, and these were tasks that could be accomplished only by the latter.

In March 1949 the Foreign Office in London sensed that Nanking was in dire trouble. The British ambassador there, Sir Ralph Stevenson, was nervous. As early as November 1948, he had asked Admiral Sir Patrick Brind, the commander in chief of the Far East station in Hong Kong, if he could spare a guard ship, a small fighting vessel that could bring the essential supplies that had been delayed by the civil war. It would help raise the morale of the local foreign community, and it could assist in a possible evacuation. Brind had agreed, and in March 1949 he sent a destroyer, H.M.S. *Consort*. Now, in April, the embassy needed another.

At first the plan called for an Australian vessel to be sent, but at the last moment, the admirals decided to bring the *Amethyst* up from her antibandit patrols off the coast of Malaya and dispatch her instead. She was to relieve her larger and more powerful colleague, the *Consort*, which had been stationed at Nanking for the previous several weeks and needed revictualing.

The *Amethyst* was in many ways the ideal choice. Her captain, Lieutenant Commander B. M. Skinner, had made the trip before. He had some knowledge of the ever shifting sandbars, and of the places where the so-called chow-chow water could twist a small ship in half. On April 12 the small vessel set off from Hong Kong and entered the Yangtze by the Woosung Bar light on April 15. Four days later, on April 19, she began working up the river proper and passed the end of the estuary at Chiangyin. She stayed there overnight, her lights doused. She had steam up again at dawn, and at five A.M. on Wednesday, April 20, she was under way once more, into the mouth of the dragon. Everyone knew of the risks: General Zhu De's People's Liberation Army was on the left bank (as seen looking downstream), and Mao Tse-tung was warning publicly that his military leaders planned to lead their men across the great river at any moment. The *Amethyst*, entering so dangerous a scene, was about to make for herself a secure place in naval history, an immutable myth in the minds of a generation of British children, and a heroic role in motion pictures.

As the ship approached the section of the river where the Communists were known to be massing, Commander Skinner ordered precautions: Large Union Jacks were to be draped over the ship's sides. The guns were to be armed and readied. The speed was increased from the customary Yangtze cruising speed of nine knots to the "danger" speed of sixteen. The ship was officially a neutral and should not have attracted any hostile fire. But this was China, a country in a dangerously unpredictable mood.

As the *Amethyst* passed Low Island, near the end of a long north-south reach in the river, there was a sudden crackle of rifle fire from the shore. Skinner ordered his gunners to train and aim. Then the rifle fire was followed, more ominously, by the zoom and whine of shells, as a shore battery opened up. Huge splashes of water erupted off the starboard beam. More than a dozen rounds were fired. None hit the British ship. On the bridge, the officers made caustic remarks about Communist marksmanship. As the *Amethyst* rounded the bend and began to head due west along the river's muddy, duck-filled Kou-An Reach, the final leg on the way to Chinkiang, the order was piped: "Hands relax action stations." The danger, it was thought, was over.

The sun was rising into a cloudless midmorning sky as the ship drew abreast of Rose Island. She was at reduced speed, and her guns were trained fore and aft. No one aboard suspected a thing—when suddenly, without warning, without any cries or flags or bugle blasts, a shell flashed across the ship's topmast. Skinner ordered his crew to action stations once more and demanded speed. The telegraphs clanged urgently, and the motors began to roar. And then, in an instant, the Communists found their aim. At least three shells slammed into the ship and exploded: One hit the wheelhouse, turning it into a maelstrom of splintered steel and wood and severely injuring the coxswain. As he fell, he pulled the wheel—and the ship—hard over to port.

The wounded vessel was now racing directly toward the thick mud of Rose Island. Skinner ordered *hard a-starboard*, trying desperately to correct the course and prevent his ship from running aground. At the same time, he ordered his guns to open fire. But almost at that instant, two more shells hit the ship. The bridge detonated in a ball of fire, and everyone in or near it was killed or terribly wounded. Skinner was mortally injured and would live on for two agonizing days. The ship's executive officer, Lieutenant Geoffrey L. Weston, was hit by a piece of shrapnel the size of a matchbox. It tore through his lungs and lodged in his liver. It was this man, though bleeding heavily and barely able to speak, who took command.

Weston had to watch in impotent horror as the ship slid steadily into the mudflats and then stopped dead, stuck fast, right in the gun sights of the Communist batteries. He managed to croak one urgent flash signal to the commander in chief of the Far East station in Hong Kong: "Under heavy fire. Am aground in approx. position about 31 degrees 10 minutes North 119 degrees 60 minutes East. Large number of casualties."

Zhu De's gunners showed no mercy. Shell after shell tore into the ship, and within minutes the deck was an inferno, littered with dead and wounded men. The ship's power was cut, the radio was out, the sick bay suffered a direct hit, and the aft gun turret was ruined. The injured lay untended among the flames, and if not burned by the fires, they were hit by splinters from new shell bursts. For over an hour, the ship shuddered and shook under the barrage. Weston gave the order to evacuate—though not abandon—the vessel.

A small steaming party was left on board to keep the boilers ready, as well as medics and volunteers stayed to help tend the wounded. The rest swam or took life rafts to Rose Island or to shore—under a withering hail of machine-gun fire, which killed more of the terrified men as they swam. Those who made it set themselves up in the underbrush, watched, and waited. (By the end of the action, twenty-two of the 183 men aboard the *Amethyst* were dead, thirty-one were wounded, and one was never found.) The plan was to reboard the ship at nightfall, repair her, refloat her, and get away. The Communists stopped shelling about eleven A.M., and the river fell quiet. Everyone thought that a boarding party might come; one never did.

Why the Communists never captured the *Amethyst* or its sailors remains an abiding mystery of the saga. Prevailing wisdom has it that Zhu De saw the ship as a potent and valuable symbol. (Men were just pawns; ships were instruments of imperial aggression.) And perhaps in his eyes, a crippled British ship, its crew at his mercy, was a far more powerful symbol than that same ship firmly in Communist hands. The Communists appeared to regard the ship rather as a cat might a captured mouse: something to torment and torture but not to kill, not for now.

The valor of the British sailors—or whatever I imagined about them, in the jingoistic reveries of my world as a five-year-old—was seemingly without precedent or parallel. The ship's crew was briefly reinvigorated at the prospect of rescue, or as Shakespeare might have said, rebuckled and respurred. For, as anticipated, the H.M.S. *Consort* came in an attempt to help, speeding downriver from Nanking at an almost unimaginable speed of twenty-nine knots, flying seven ensigns and three Union Jacks. But the rescue was never to be: The *Consort* was caught in brutal shellfire, too. Ten of her men were killed, and she found it impossible to stop and help, her captain knowing full well that if she did so, she would be trapped as well.

The destroyer had no choice, savage though the leaving had to be, other than to blink a farewell to her crippled colleague and limp on toward the sea to lick her own wounds. The *London* and the *Black Swan* ventured upriver from Shanghai, but they also lost men in unacceptable numbers and turned back. A Sunderland flying boat made two attempts to land beside the stricken ship but was chased away by gunfire—to which a seaplane was naturally even more vulnerable, being thin-skinned and designed both to fly and to float. The *Amethyst*, as the whole world knew, was trapped and very much on her own.

And so she remained, a tiny gray warship held hostage to a mighty revolution's fortune, a symbol of the unfamiliar new realities of what was being called and understood as the Cold War. She was refloated, and for the first few days, she steamed about wildly, trying to find sanctuary beyond the reach of the guns, which, thankfully, for the moment, were silent. She landed all her wounded onto the relative safety of the Nationalist-held right bank, into the care of local doctors, and she would later send her dead to the bottom of the river, weighted with 4-inch shells. She dropped anchor off Ta Sha Island ("Big Sand Island") a few miles downstream from Chinkiang and just opposite the point where the Grand Canal, the world's most venerable artificial waterway, joins the Yangtze.

There, in five fathoms of water on a good holding ground of mud and sand, the *Amethyst* stayed put. The hostage drama that captivated half the world was to go on, miserably, for an extraordinary 101 days. There was to be no more firing, but there was no freedom, either.

The politicians in London fulminated impotently, and everywhere diplomats tried in vain to engage Washington and other influential capitals in an effort to do something, to use such muscle as they had to win the ship's release. All came to naught, and it was swiftly realized that only those on the spot had any chance of ameliorating the situation. The assistant naval attaché from the British embassy in Nanking, Lieutenant Commander John Kerans, eventually reached the *Amethyst* by land and took command of the vessel. He was later to

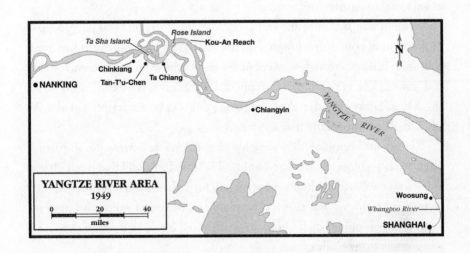

YANGTZE RIVER AREA
1949

0   20   40
miles

Rose Island
Ta Sha Island
Kou-An Reach
Chinkiang
Ta Chiang
Tan-T'u-Chen
● NANKING
● Chiangyin
YANGTZE RIVER
Woosung ●
Whangpoo River
SHANGHAI ●

N

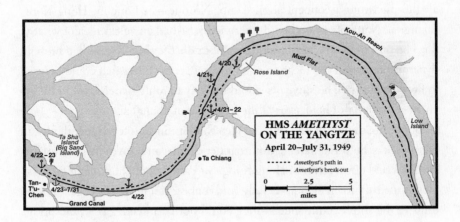

Kou-An Reach
Mud Flat
4/20
4/21a
Rose Island
4/21–22
Low Island
Ta Sha Island (Big Sand Island)
4/22–23
● Ta Chiang
Tan-T'u-Chen
4/23–7/31
4/22
Grand Canal

HMS *AMETHYST*
ON THE YANGTZE
April 20–July 31, 1949

- - - *Amethyst*'s path in
——— *Amethyst*'s break-out

0   2.5   5
miles

become the principal hero of the saga. A young third secretary at the embassy named Edward Youde, who spoke Chinese impeccably (though with a Welsh accent, it was later joked), walked and bicycled to the Communist lines and tried to reason with the senior cadres of the local leadership, to no avail. (Youde went on to become governor of Hong Kong and, sadly, the only holder of that office to die in harness, in 1986.)

Locals in sampans were allowed to come to the ship's side and sell food, paltry amounts of poor stuff for high prices. The ship's oil supplies dwindled away, both from leakage through buckled plates and because of the demand for light and power. The crew's morale dropped. Rats infested the vessel; some were larger than Simon, the ship's cat. The ship's dog, Peggy, was frightened of them and hid. The temperature rose and rose.

"Things are beginning to get mighty uncomfortable," wrote the ship's only surviving radio officer in his diary on July 22. "And I'm afraid that if our oil gets much lower we shall be shutting down again for 48 hours at a time; then it won't be uncomfortable anymore, it will be plain Hell. Even to write this I have got four sheets of blotting paper under my wrist, and it is soaked through now. . . . It is beginning to get really grim."

There was terrible tedium aboard, and above all a persistent and nagging concern that the firing might begin again or that the Communists might order all the men into a concentration camp. No one—in London, Hong Kong, Shanghai, Nanking, or on board the *Amethyst*—had any clear idea of what to do. The only plan officially bruited was to scuttle the ship; Kerans had brought dynamite and knew the location of all the sea cocks (valves that could be used to flood the hull). The survivors would then try to route-march back to the security of Nationalist-held areas or the free areas of Shanghai.

But by the middle of July, another idea was forming, quite independently, in the minds of both Lieutenant Commander Kerans and, unknown to him, Sir Patrick Brind down south in Hong Kong. Sir Patrick thought it might be possible for the ship to break out, secretly, and make a run for it. He began to send hints to the ship's commander—they could not be in code, as all the bridge codebooks had been destroyed—suggesting that plans for escape might be considered. London was officially eager for a diplomatic end to the situation and wanted no derring-do or risky maritime drama, but Admiral Brind, like Nelson at the battle of Copenhagen, had a penchant for turning a blind eye to official policy.

His hints, however, passed unnoticed, not just by the ever listening Chinese but by everyone aboard the *Amethyst*. They were, it has to be said, decidedly opaque. "The golden rule of *making an offing* and taking *plenty of sea-room* applies particularly" was one sentence, supposedly pregnant with meaning, transmitted by Brind. He sent it in the course of telling the ship's crew how best to weather an oncoming typhoon. It took two full weeks for Kerans to kick himself, realizing the old sailor had been offering much more than mere advice on seamanship. He was telling the commander, without letting the Chinese know, that he ought to *make an offing*—leave the shore—and give himself *plenty of sea-room*—get far out to sea. In other words: Break out, Mr. Kerans, and in short order.

Even before Kerans had deciphered the obscure hints from Brind, he had realized that escape was the only choice. Such negotiations as were occasionally going on between local British diplomats and the Communists were getting nowhere. Fuel oil was approaching the point at which he could not make the downstream journey even if he wanted to. Water, fresh food, morale—all were low. The men would soon have to go on quarter rations (they had been on half rations since July 11). And at the end of July, there would be a new moon. If there was any moment when it might be possible to slip past the watchful eyes of the Communist sentries, that would be it.

There were plenty of disadvantages. The ship, scarred and holed—the more serious holes plugged with blankets—was in poor shape. Only one of the big guns could be fired. The charts had been covered with blood or shredded, and no one aboard had much idea about how to navigate down one of the world's most complicated and always changing rivers. The engine room had lost seventeen of its men, almost half the complement. Even if the engines themselves held up during the high-speed run for cover, would the crew?

However, a decision had to be made. Kerans wrote a cable, using a code devised over the previous three months and having to do with the spelling of names of the nearest relatives of various crew members. He gave it to the signalman and marked it with the highest of all priorities—*Flash*:

Top Secret. C-in-C, repeated Concord, from Kerans. I am going to try to break out at 10 p.m. tonight, 30th July. Concord set watch 8290 [kilocycles].

This last essentially instructed the H.M.S. *Concord*, a destroyer stationed near the mouth of the Yangtze, to act as *Amethyst's* floating guardian angel and to listen in on a preassigned radio frequency as the captive ship's progress unfolded.

The plans were made meticulously. If the *Amethyst* were to pass out undetected, silence was imperative. The anchor could not be raised in the normal way; rattling the chain through the hawsepipe would make a din certain to awaken every Communist battery from Chinkiang to the outskirts of Shanghai. Instead, it was decided to knock the pin from one of the half-shackles that held together the lengths of anchor chain, and to let the chain fall into the water vertically, with thick grease on all the ship's surfaces that it might touch. The ship's perceived shape was important, too: A silhouette could be recognized. So mattresses and awnings and hammocks were arranged along the ship's sides to make her look as different as possible from usual. She reconfigured her lights, showing green over red, masquerading as a civilian vessel, a merchantman. Talking above a whisper was forbidden; smoking was banned; no one could use the intercom, certainly not the radio.

Two hours before the deadline, and with impeccably poor timing, one of the supply sampans arrived alongside. The crew members were Chinese, of course, probably part-time spies for the Communists. So the hammocks and the awnings had to be struck, and the sailors had to show their mood of customary weariness. No clue was to be offered the next day. The visitors said they had beer. They were told to come back with it the next day. Everything was made to sound normal.

At ten P.M. or a bit before on the hot and moonless night, better fortune intervened. A merchant ship, the *Kiang Ling Liberation*, suddenly appeared, heading down the half-mile-wide stream. Kerans whispered his orders. The sloop's engines were started—a huge blast of orange sparks from the funnel went unnoticed, to general pleased astonishment—and the little warship spun quickly into the river alongside the passing freighter. At the moment when the anchor chain appeared to be vertical, a quick blow from a hammer snapped a pin; a shackle opened and the anchor was slipped, with the silent, splashless plummet of an Olympic diver. Kerans accelerated and sailed in tandem with the *Liberation*, keeping to the merchantman's starboard side and thus hiding behind her bulk from the watchful gunners ashore.

The ruse worked, for a while. But near the town of Ta Chiang, both ships were challenged by a series of magnesium flares fired from a battery on the left bank, which hung high in the sky, illuminating the scene for hundreds of yards.

Heavy machine-gun fire broke out, and then the shore batteries began to pound, and shells and tracer bullets flew in all directions. The *Amethyst* was hit, forward of the bridge. There were no casualties; a few plates were buckled, and there was a small amount of flooding. She gunned her engines to the highest speed possible, determined to fly past the *Liberation* and get away from the battery at all costs. Observers on board say she scraped by the larger vessel with just eighteen inches to spare. Roaring downriver with a huge bow wave before her, she managed to get away almost unscathed. She sent a signal to Brind, noting laconically that she had been hit. It reached the admiral at a dinner party in Hong Kong, where a toast had been drunk at precisely ten P.M., as Kerans began his breakout: "To H.M.S. *Amethyst* and all who sail in her."

More signals came in to headquarters during the night. "Halfway," said one, as the *Amethyst* passed the midway point to the sea. "Hundred up," said another (a cricketing term meaning "a hundred runs scored," to which the admiral replied with the same sporting metaphor: "A magnificent century!"). A small passenger junk unexpectedly crossed the path of the fleeing and unlit ship. The bridge officers waited, sickened, for the awful crunch of smashed wood and the cries of the drowning. There was nothing they could do. Many may have died. But the *Amethyst* could not afford to stop.

The ship raced on, now straining at twenty-two knots, like a dog with a bone in its teeth. Mercifully, Kerans knew the river well enough, even at night, and managed with uncanny accuracy to avoid the sand spits and bars that might have brought the vessel to further grief.

At dawn they passed under the searchlights of Woosung Fort, where another Communist battery stood on the right bank, just where the Whangpoo entered the Yangtze. The searchlights briefly glanced off the hull — everyone on board holding their breath — and then the lights moved on. The *Amethyst* kept roaring onward. "Everything you've got!" Kerans instructed the engine room. "Damage to engines accepted."

And then, finally, there in the dim light of morning, under a plume of smoke on the wide gray waters of the outer estuary, was the familiar outline of the H.M.S. *Concord*. She saw the smaller *Amethyst* roaring down on her and made what has since become one of the Royal Navy's most famous signals: *Fancy Meeting You Again.* It was now beyond doubt that the H.M.S. *Amethyst*'s saga was over. After 101 days in captivity, she had broken free — though at a terrible cost. All told, 46 men had died on the ship and on those that had attempted to rescue her, and 93 more had been wounded. Even so, it was a moment of triumph for Britain, and one of the greatest, face-losing humiliations ever for the Chinese Communists.

But the Communists were determined not to see it in this light. "Do not make haste in celebrating the success," they cautioned in an official statement released to the press. "The whole case will not be closed so long as the culprits are not punished." Another statement warned: "As long as the British government still exists, the Chinese people must continue to go into the responsibility for the crime and insist on meting out severe punishment."

In the West, such tocsins were widely dismissed as sour grapes. The H.M.S. *Amethyst* limped back to Hong Kong, then to Britain, doing a lap of honor through the eastern lands of the empire on her way home. Everywhere, church bells rang, celebration dinners were served, ladies swooned over the sailors, officers were handed medals, most were promoted—it was one of the very last of fading Britain's finest hours. The king congratulated everyone concerned, some personally at a reception in Buckingham Palace. The movie studio British Lion made a film—which everyone at my school was required to see—starring all of the gang (Richard Todd, William Hartnell, Donald Houston, Akim Tamiroff) who had recently brought the cinema-going public so breezily through World War II.

The film (black and white, of course, and with stirring music) was called *The Yangtse Incident*. In a story rendered simple and gripping were seeds rich in the pride of England, and of our sour contempt for the people of China. As a twelve-year-old—the film was released in 1956, seven years after the events on the river—I believed in it implicitly. It must have colored the thoughts of many who saw it and made them think of China, particularly Chinese Communists, with the utmost loathing and hostility.

There is something droll in considering what the Chinese did after the *Amethyst* made good its exit. It is said they sent down divers and located the anchor—still attached to its several tons of chain—and pulled it from the river. They paraded it around town as a spoil of battle, a trophy that their men had wrested bravely from a fleeing imperial coward. How many of the locals accepted the story is anyone's guess, but it was not to be too much longer before the city of Chinkiang (Zhenjiang) had been swept clear of all its foreign residents, and the old British consulate had been turned into a revolutionary museum. It is said they dumped the relic there, in the gardens. The anchor, like the consulate itself, was part of the dastardly enginework of foreign oppression that the revolution had so brilliantly driven away.

But to find the anchor today? A baffling habit I have encountered in many Chinese is their mute insistence that *they do not know where anything is*. You ask an ancient who has lived all of his long life in Zhenjiang, "Where is the old British consulate?" and he will shake his head and wave you away with his hand, professing no clue, having no interest. My questions about the anchor itself produced still more puzzled refusal: "No, never heard of it. *Purple Stone Hero*? Not anywhere here. Doesn't ring a bell with me."

In the end, my interpreter and I found a man with a car who knew where the local museum was, and this turned out to be, unmistakably, the old consulate itself. No one knew it was; but its architecture—redbrick and of a complexity you find in an Escher painting, with seven linked buildings, lots of outside stairs and archways, and wings and extra windows—was classic Foreign Office Grade One issue. The building looked as though it might have been sent out from London in crates and set up on a spare weekend by the local staff. Consulates like this one existed all over the East, from Kashgar to Korea. They were built during that wave of British expansion and self-confidence that marked the latter half of the last century. Here the walls were still intact, ten feet tall; and I could make out bas-relief crests, with intertwined letters for "Victoria" and "Regina."

It was just as well the walls were high: Britain had attacked the Manchus here as far back as 1842, and a keen, long-standing bitterness had suffused the local population. It was a bitterness that may well have contributed to the locals' professed ignorance of any British memorial even a century and a half later.

The invaders' triumph back then had been a signal one. Seven thousand British soldiers had stormed over the city's double walls from their flotilla of men-of-war—the *Amethyst*'s predecessors, one might say. They had sacked the city within hours. The local governor had locked himself and his family into their house and set it ablaze, all dying on the pyre. From the British point of view, the rout of the city's defenders had been the culminating victory of the first Opium War. Within just one more month, the Chinese had been forced to hand over Hong Kong in perpetuity and pay $21 million in Mexican silver dollars, the currency of the day, in compensation. The Chinese, inevitably, saw it otherwise.

However, it took them many years to become strong enough to say so. Two decades later, China was still being pummeled and humiliated by foreigners and was forced to allow Chinkiang to be declared a treaty port in 1861, effectively relinquishing sovereignty over parts of the city to foreign administrations. The foreigners had high hopes for the place. A British concession was built, with its own waterworks and generating station—and, as in Shanghai and Nanking and forty-five other places in China, its own British laws and courts.

Britain, Germany, France, and Austro-Hungary set up consulates in the city; great British trading firms like Jardines and Swires kept hulks in midriver for mooring their steamers; and Standard Oil of New York (which was later to become Mobil Oil, a company with formidably strong connections in old China) had a farm of oil storage tanks. Japan toppled most of this comfort and prosperity when it captured the city in 1937; Zhu De's troops—who stormed across the Yangtze in 1949 even while the *Amethyst* was enduring her miseries in midstream—managed to finish it off. Few outsiders have lived in Zhenjiang since. The only foreigners I heard about while I was there were a couple of Algerians said to be working in a talc factory.

It was one thing to find the consulate, quite another to find the anchor. No one outside the building would say anything about the delights inside until I paid to get in. So I handed over one yuan to a crone behind the guichet and inquired. No, she said, there is no such thing as an anchor anywhere here. The cadre standing inside the gate said much the same: There were plenty of Sung dynasty pots and pans, but no anchor from a barbarian war vessel. "You have wasted your time," he said, and laughed bitterly.

Just then a young Chinese woman who worked at the museum came down the stairs. She had been reading a novel—the museum had few visitors—and was chewing on a sweet called sugared cow skin. She offered me one. She smiled warmly. "I heard there was an anchor here," she said in halting English. "But it is buried in grass, I think. Besides, they are doing some demolish work. Come with me."

My interpreter and I followed her up a hillock, through an archway, past a flight of stone steps that must have once seen processions of clerks and second secretaries and consuls. We came out onto a newly flattened area of wrecked brickwork, where one of the seven buildings had recently been flattened. Behind it was a small slope covered with jungle. The girl pointed to it. "There, I think. Use a knife, if you have one," she cried, and went off, back to her novel and her bag of sugared cow skins.

Thick laurel bushes had infested the hillside, and the branches slashed at my legs as I waded through to the edge of the cliff. And then, burdened by growth but unmistakably nautical, there was the anchor—four feet tall, its shank covered in some kind of cracked poultice, its ring solid, a half-shackle with a pin hanging loosely from it. The anchor's crown was firmly cemented to the ground, and the flukes rose sharp and spadelike into the surrounding bushes. It looked half a century old, but it had been built well, and it was neither rusty nor broken. The Admiralty commissioned its iron to last.

A small notice, half-illegible from dirt and growth, was mounted in front. I rubbed away the grime and read: "This was the anchor from the foreign Imperial War Vessel *Purple Stone Hero*, captured in the fourth month of 1949 by Heroic Members of the People's Liberation Army after the ship had made a cowardly run away down the Long River to the Sea."

I cut away some of the plants and took pictures. I had known Sir Edward Youde when he was governor of Hong Kong. I had liked him and gone to his funeral. His widow was living in Britain; I thought she might like to have a reminder. The little ship herself had long since been retired and scrapped. This, thousands of miles away in China, under a canopy of laurel leaves, was all that was left.

Or was it? Since coming back and poring over the pictures, I have begun to wonder.

The anchor in Zhenjiang is a much smaller device than that normally used to hold a warship. Its design is that of a fisherman's anchor, made specifically to hold a little craft. It is most certainly not the standard Admiralty "pattern stockless anchor," with which pictures show the *Amethyst*'s bows to have been equipped. My guess is that the Chinese have actually duped us, and themselves—not, one might say, for the first time. What stands among the undergrowth in Zhenjiang may well be another anchor, possibly from one of the *Amethyst*'s lifeboats—thus perhaps indeed a British anchor, and so a symbol of the treachery. But my guess is that the real half-ton of iron, together with all its chains—that which was so silently slipped on the night of the getaway—remains buried in the Yangtze mud. It might have been a good idea to raise it, but it was in all likelihood far too heavy and far too sunk for even the bitterest Chinese to recover it and put it on show. A lesser substitute had to do.

II

POLICE ACTION

The United States, the U.N., and Korea

JAMES CHACE AND CALEB CARR

It was four in the morning on June 25, 1950 (Korean time), when ten North Korean divisions led by tanks and supported by 1,643 guns crossed the 38th Parallel into an unsuspecting South Korea. In a rainy half-light, the Korean War began, "the first overt military assault," the historian John Lewis Gaddis has pointed out, "across an internationally recognized boundary since the end of World War II." The North Koreans envisaged a blitzkrieg operation of a few weeks against an undermanned, undermechanized, and thoroughly underprepared enemy. The war would last just over three years and end in stalemate. What started as a war of movement and maneuver would evolve into a trench struggle worthy of 1916. In terms of battlefield violence, no other conflict of the Cold War would measure up to the Korean War.

Everyone miscalculated. Korea would not be the first time, or the last, when faulty intelligence and just plain bad guesses sucked nations into a quagmire. The U.S. had withdrawn its troops from South Korea in 1949, at the same time indicating that it would not protect Chiang's remaining forces in Taiwan: The Truman administration did not hide its reluctance to become involved in armed confrontations on the Asian continent. Stalin, too, at first waffled on whether to back an invasion of South Korea. But Kim Il Sung, the leader of the North Korean puppet regime, badgered the man who was by then exalted as the veritable pontiff of the world Communist revolution: The time was ripe, he maintained, to "liberate" South Korea. In the spring of 1950, the Soviet dictator gave in. He agreed to provide Kim arms and lent him Soviet generals to orchestrate the plan of attack. They came up with a scheme straight out of the World War II Eastern Front, artillery saturation followed by a quick mechanized advance that would require no longer than a month to swallow the South. The war would be over before the U.S. even had a chance to react. Still, Stalin stressed the need to conceal the Soviet role: He did not want to give the Americans justification for intervening.

Meanwhile, Mao was preoccupied with plans to invade Taiwan that summer. Kim, the single-minded middleman, exaggerated Stalin's enthusiasm to Mao and Mao's to Stalin. Mao at last acquiesced to Kim's invasion plans, afraid that if he didn't, Stalin would deny him aid for the Taiwan invasion—and indeed, in the spring of 1950, American intelligence picked up indications that Soviet air force planes were deploying on the Chinese coast. But both the Pentagon and General Douglas MacArthur's headquarters in Tokyo discounted evidence of a North Korean build-up along the 38th Parallel.

When the invasion did come, however, the Americans pulled themselves together with a dispatch that caught the two Communist titans by surprise. The U.S. has never taken kindly to blindside attacks. How Washington reacted so quickly, and how it took advantage of the Soviet absence at the U.N., is the story that James Chace and Caleb Carr tell here. (In the process, Truman would order the U.S. Seventh Fleet to patrol the Taiwan Strait, thus preventing a Communist landing on Taiwan —or a Nationalist attempt to return to the Chinese mainland—as long as the Korean War lasted.) Though the Truman administration was certain that Stalin was behind the North Korean attack, it deliberately muted blame. Regional wars were one thing; global ones were quite another, to be avoided at all costs. As Dean Acheson, the secretary of state, mused to Charles Collingwood of CBS in September 1950, "The whole idea that war was inevitable seems to me to be completely wrong and very vicious. I remember looking back over the history of the United States not long ago and reading the terrible things that were said in the 1850s about the irrepressible conflict, talk about war being inevitable, which tends to make it so. War isn't inevitable."

These are words that a later generation might have done well to remember.

The late **JAMES CHACE** may be remembered best for his biography, *Dean Acheson: The Secretary of State Who Created the American World*. Prominent among his other eight books is *America Invulnerable: The Quest for Absolute Security from 1812 to Star Wars*, which he wrote with **CALEB CARR**. Carr is the author of two other historical studies, *The Devil Soldier* and *Lessons of Terror*, as well as four novels, *The Alienist*, *Killing Time*, *The Angel of Darkness*, and *The Italian Secretary*. His military and political writings have appeared in numerous magazines and periodicals. Carr teaches at Bard College and lives in upstate New York.

F OR THE UNITED NATIONS, the end of maintaining global peace can, under the enforcement provisions of the U.N. Charter, involve the means of making regional war. This was true of the recent large-scale multinational response to a local crisis, the Persian Gulf War; it was also true of the U.N.'s first and most famous military trial, the Korean War. Like the campaign in Kuwait and Iraq, the Korean effort was initiated as a collective response to criminally aggressive behavior; but, again, like the war against Saddam Hussein, the military action against North Korea was orchestrated by the United States. America—obsessed in 1950 with the free world's slow response to totalitarianism during the 1930s, just as in 1991 it would be haunted by its 1970s defeat in Vietnam—used the United Nations to safeguard interests it considered vital, cajoling or browbeating its allies into joining the effort. The Gulf War was an intervention that took weeks to organize, but Washington in 1950 was able to marshal a multilateral commitment and mount a forceful response to aggression in the space of just days.

In late May and early June of that year, intelligence reports stating that "somewhere across the broad globe the armed forces of some Communist power were expecting soon to go into action" reached the desk of George F. Kennan, the U.S. State Department's leading Soviet expert. Kennan had spent his life studying the Soviet Union in particular and Communist behavior generally—any report that indicated a significant move on the part of the U.S.S.R. or one of its client states was entirely too tantalizing for him to ignore. Kennan and his fellow Russian experts immediately undertook an "intensive scrutiny" of the disposition of the Soviet Union itself, and this study "satisfied us," in Kennan's words, "that it was not Soviet forces to which these indications related. This left us with the forces of the various satellite regimes, but which?"

Possibilities were discussed and discarded, and eventually, the subject of Korea came up. In 1945 that peninsula—the focus of Russian, Chinese, and Japanese ambitions during the nineteenth and early twentieth centuries—had been divided at the 38th Parallel between the forces of the United States and the Soviet Union after the surrender of Japan. The division had supposedly been for military purposes alone, each of the victorious allies assigned the task of disarming Japanese troops within its zone. But in the years since, the arrangement had taken on a political dimension: Both the Americans and the Soviets had set up client regimes under repressive strongmen.

Considering the possibility of an attack by North Korea against the southern republic, Kennan and his colleagues were informed by the Pentagon and by General Douglas MacArthur's headquarters in Tokyo that the idea was out of the question. Kennan was not comforted, for "nowhere else . . . could we see any possibility of an attack, and we came away from the exercise quite frustrated." In this state of mind, Kennan left Washington for his farm in Pennsylvania on the morning of Saturday, June 24.

That evening, W. Bradley Connors, in charge of public affairs for State's Far Eastern desk, found himself stuck in Washington. At just past eight P.M., Connors received a phone call at his apartment from the Washington bureau chief of United Press International, who said UPI's correspondent in South Korea was reporting a North Korean attack across the 38th Parallel. Would Connors care to confirm? Connors instead broke off the discussion and tried to call the American embassy in Seoul, but the switchboard was closed.

By 9:26, Connors was at his post at the State Department to receive a cable from John J. Muccio, the American ambassador in Seoul: ACCORDING KOREAN ARMY REPORTS WHICH PARTLY CONFIRMED BY [American] KMAG [Korean Military Assistance Group] FIELD ADVISOR REPORTS NORTH KOREAN FORCES INVADED ROK [Republic of Korea] TERRITORY AT SEVERAL POINTS THIS MORNING. . . . IT WOULD APPEAR FROM NATURE OF ATTACK AND MANNER IN WHICH IT WAS LAUNCHED THAT IT CONSTITUTES ALL OUT OFFENSIVE AGAINST ROK. Connors immediately got on the phone and contacted his superior, Assistant Secretary of State Dean Rusk.

Later to gain fame as secretary of state in the Kennedy and Johnson administrations, Rusk served as an intelligence officer in China under "Vinegar Joe" Stilwell during World War II. He was consistently on his guard to prevent any repetition of the errors of the 1930s. Rusk sped to the State Department after receiving Connors's call, to find that the assistant secretary for United Nations affairs, John Hickerson, and Ambassador at Large Philip C. Jessup had also been called in. The three immediately telephoned Secretary of State Dean Acheson, who was at his farm in Maryland. A forceful and independent thinker with a taste for action, Acheson shared his subordinates' alarm and ordered them to call the secretary-general of the United Nations, Trygve Lie, to inform him of the attack and schedule an emergency meeting of the Security Council for the following day.

Upon hearing Hickerson's report of the North Korean attack, Secretary-General Lie responded, "My God, Jack, this is war against the United Nations." From that moment on, American officials would do all in their power to promulgate Lie's assessment.

Rusk, Hickerson, and Jessup next got in touch with the Pentagon and began to work out possible American military responses to the North Korean attack. Meanwhile, Acheson put through a call to Independence, Missouri. President Harry S. Truman had gone home for the weekend, and when Acheson's call came, he had just finished dinner and was in his library. When Acheson told him what had happened, Truman wanted to return to the capital right away, but Acheson convinced him to wait until more was known. The secretary said he had requested an emergency Security Council session, where he hoped to obtain condemnation of the North Korean attack.

The next day in his office, Acheson was briefed on further developments. The military situation had only gotten worse, but diplomatically, the United States had already scored a victory: In an emergency session, the U.N. Security Council had passed an American-sponsored resolution calling for an "immediate cessation of hostilities" and a withdrawal of North Korean forces to the 38th Parallel—although some members had asked that the American characterization of the North Korean move be scaled down from "active aggression" to "breach of peace." The United Nations would remain in this obliging state of mind throughout the early period of the Korean War.

Passage of the resolution had been made possible by the absence of the Soviet delegate, who, Acheson assumed, was continuing a boycott of council sessions begun as a result of the U.N.'s refusal in February to admit the People's Republic of China. In reality, the Chinese issue was only part of the reason for the unusual Soviet inaction on Korea; Stalin had already decided the North Korean gambit was unlikely to pay off, and for the moment—as cables that the Russians recently declassified reveal—he wanted as little to do with it as possible. The practical effect of this Soviet inaction was historic: For the first time,

the United Nations seemed ready to vote for concrete action to counter aggression.

On the night of June 25, Truman, just returned from Independence, had
dinner with his top advisers at Blair House (the White House was being reno-
vated). He had already decided on a forceful response to the North Korean
move, which he, along with everyone else in Washington, believed had been
made with the Soviets' consent and encouragement. "If this was allowed to go
unchallenged," Truman later recalled, "it would mean a third world war, just as
similar incidents had brought on the Second World War." Truman found his
cabinet and defense advisers in complete agreement. Force, they all believed,
was the only answer to such a threat: collective force, if the U.N. could be made
to act quickly enough; unilateral force if it could not. Specifically, Dean Acheson recommended that General MacArthur be authorized to give the South
Korean army all the matériel it required, that the U.S. Air Force be directed to
cover the evacuation from Seoul, and that the Seventh Fleet be sent into the
Formosa Strait to ensure that neither Mao Tse-tung nor Chiang Kai-shek
would use the Korean hostilities as a cover for operations against his opponent.

The following day, a Monday, Acheson also suggested including direct
American air support of South Korean ground actions and additional troops
for American garrisons in the Philippines. In addition, he proposed increasing
American aid to the French in Indonesia, on the chance that Korea might be
just the first of several Communist attacks in Asia. He also recommended that
the United States sponsor a Security Council resolution calling for U.N. members to aid South Korea. Acheson, on the advice of Kennan, was betting that
the Soviets would continue to boycott the sessions.

The bet paid off. On June 27—three days after the North Korean attack—
Acheson got his resolution, and with it international sanction for military action. It was sanction that Acheson and Truman greatly prized but had not
waited for: American warplanes were already at work in the skies above Korea,
swift testament to American determination that the 1930s failure to prepare for
aggression should not be repeated.

The fighting continued to go badly for South Korea. By Thursday, June 29,
General MacArthur's personal representative in South Korea was reporting
that despite American air support, the pre-invasion status quo—the announced
goal of the United Nations—could not be restored without the deployment of
American ground forces. In typically reckless fashion, MacArthur himself vis-

ited the front, then returned to Tokyo and confirmed that without American troops, there would be disaster in Korea.

President Truman wondered whether such American intervention would not lead to a similar response on the part of one of the Communist powers; Acheson informed him that "it was State's view that while the Chinese might intervene, the Russians would not." MacArthur was asking for one brigade immediately, to be built up to two divisions. Acheson strongly urged the president to assent. On Friday morning, June 30, the decision was made: American ground forces would go to the front. As Acheson later recalled, "We were then fully committed in Korea."

One more piece of business remained. The United States succeeded in securing approval for a unified military command—five nations had pledged to contribute contingents to the Korean action—under a person of its choosing. The next day MacArthur got the job and was presented with the U.N. flag that had been used in peacekeeping operations in the Middle East.

The cost would be heavy for the U.N. forces that went to South Korea's aid, but (as in the Persian Gulf War) it would be heaviest for the United States, which supplied half the allied ground troops and almost all the air and naval forces: Washington spent some $15 billion in Korea and lost thirty-four thousand dead. The cost to the North and South Koreans, as well as the Communist Chinese, was much higher. But by the end of the summer of 1953, the goal of reversing North Korea's aggression had been realized. And on a larger scale, the United Nations had demonstrated that for the sake of maintaining global peace it was willing to make war on a truly world-class level—provided, of course, that the world's richest power was willing to foot much of the cost in money and lives.

Truman Fires MacArthur

DAVID McCULLOUGH

In the history of the Cold War—in the entire history of American arms, for that matter—few personal showdowns have been quite so freighted with consequence as the confrontation between Harry S. Truman and Douglas MacArthur. How often do two such dominating figures find themselves on a collision course from which neither is willing to veer? On the one hand, there was Truman, the artillery captain of World War I, the accidental president, the surprise victor of the election of 1948, whose decisions at the start of the Cold War would define the West's diplomatic and military policies for the next four decades. On the other, there was MacArthur, a fighting division commander in 1918, a Medal of Honor winner, the supreme commander of Allied forces in the southwest Pacific during World War II, the master of the operational art turned benevolent autocrat who had presided over the reconstruction—and democratization—of Japan, who had led the U.N. forces in Korea. This American Kitchener was a genuine hero, but then (although people did not recognize it at the time) so was Truman. The two men distrusted each other at long distance: MacArthur had not set foot in the United States since 1937. They would meet only once, and then for a few morning hours in the Pacific, at Wake Island on October 5, 1950. "Mr. Prima Donna, Brass Hat, Five Star MacArthur," Truman had once noted in his diary. "Don't see how a country can produce such men as Robert E. Lee, John J. Pershing, Eisenhower, and Bradley and at the same time produce Custers, Pattons, and MacArthurs." The feeling was mutual.

It was the crisis of the Korean War and MacArthur's repeated acts of insubordination that brought on the ultimate confrontation. He was a man no one dared to challenge until it was almost too late. As the disaster of the summer of 1950 changed to the triumph of Inchon and then disaster again, and a third world war loomed, Truman would come to one of the most difficult decisions of his presidency.

———

DAVID McCULLOUGH is one of the most deservedly popular historians of our time. His *Truman*—from which the following account is excerpted—won the National Book Award and the Pulitzer Prize for biography; *The Path Between the Seas,* his description of the building of the Panama Canal, won a National Book Award for history. His other books include *The Johnstown Flood, The Great Bridge, Mornings on Horseback,* and, most recently, *John Adams,* which earned him his second Pulitzer Prize for biography. Millions know him as the host, and often the narrator, of television shows such as *The American Experience.* The past president of the Society of American Historians, McCullough has also won the Francis Parkman Prize and the Los Angeles Times Book Award.

IT WAS, IN MANY RESPECTS, one of the darkest chapters in American military history. But MacArthur, now in overall command of the U.N. forces, was trading space for time—time to pour in men and supplies at the port of Pusan—and the wonder was the North Koreans had been kept from overrunning South Korea straightaway. Despite their suffering and humiliation, the brutal odds against them, the American and Republic of Korea units had done what they were supposed to, almost miraculously. They had held back the landslide, said Truman, who would rightly call it one of the most heroic rearguard actions on record.

In the first week of July, MacArthur requested thirty thousand American ground troops, to bring the four divisions of his Eighth Army to full strength. Just days later, on July 9, the situation had become so "critical" that he called for a doubling of his forces. Four more divisions were urgently needed, he said in a cable that jolted Washington.

The hard reality was that the army had only ten divisions. In Western Europe there was just one, and as former British prime minister Winston Churchill had noted in a speech in London, the full Allied force of twelve divisions in Western Europe faced a Soviet threat of eighty divisions. The NATO allies were exceedingly concerned lest the United States become too involved in distant Korea. Years of slashing defense expenditures, as a means to balance the budget, had taken a heavy toll. For all its vaunted nuclear supremacy, the nation was quite unprepared for war. But now, in these "weeks of slaughter and heartbreak," that was to change dramatically and with immense, far-reaching consequences.

On Wednesday, July 19, first in a special message to Congress, then in an address to the nation, Truman said the attack on Korea demanded that the United States send more men, equipment, and supplies. Beyond that, the realities of the "world situation" required still greater American military strength. He called for an emergency appropriation of $10 billion—the final sum submitted would be $11.6 billion, or nearly as much as the entire $13 billion military budget originally planned for the fiscal year—and announced he was both stepping up the draft and calling up certain National Guard units.

"Korea is a small country thousands of miles away, but what is happening there is important to every American," he told the nation, standing stone-faced in the heat of the television lights, a tangle of wires and cables at his feet. By their "act of raw aggression . . . I repeat, it was raw aggression," the North Koreans had violated the U.N. Charter, and though American forces were making the "principal effort" to save the Republic of South Korea, they were fighting under a U.N. command and a U.N. flag, and this was a "landmark in mankind's long search for a rule of law among nations."

As a call to arms, it was not especially inspirational. Nor did he once use the word "war" to describe what was happening in Korea. But then neither was there any question about his sincerity, nor was he the least evasive about what would be asked of the country. The "job" was long and difficult. It meant increased taxes, rationing if necessary, "stern days ahead." In another televised address at summer's end, he would announce plans to double the armed forces to nearly three million men. Congress appropriated the money: $48.2 billion for military spending in fiscal 1950–51, then $60 billion for fiscal 1951–52.

Was he considering use of the atomic bomb in Korea? Truman was asked at a press conference the last week of July. No, he said. Did he plan to get out of Washington anytime soon? No. He would stay on the job.

That Truman was less than fond or admiring of his Far Eastern commander, Douglas MacArthur, was well known to his staff and a cause of concern at the Pentagon. Truman's opinion in 1950 seems to have been no different from what it had been in 1945, at the peak of MacArthur's renown, when, in his journal, Truman had described the general as "Mr. Prima Donna, Brass Hat," a "play actor and bunco man." The president, noted his press aide Eben Ayers, expressed "little regard or respect" for MacArthur, calling him a "supreme egotist" who thought himself "something of a god." But working with people whom one did not like or admire was part of life—particularly the politician's life. Firing the five-star Far Eastern commander would have been very nearly unthinkable. John Foster Dulles told Truman confidentially that MacArthur should be dispensed with as soon as possible. Dulles, the most prominent Republican spokesman on foreign policy and a special adviser to the State Department, had returned from a series of meetings with MacArthur in Tokyo, convinced the seventy-year-old general was well past his prime and a potential liability. Dulles advised Truman to bring MacArthur home and retire him before he caused trouble. But that, replied Truman, was easier said than done. He reminded Dulles of the reaction there would be in the country, so great was MacArthur's "heroic standing." Nonetheless, at this stage Truman expressed no doubt about MacArthur's ability. If anything, he seemed to have been banking on it.

By the first week in August, American and ROK forces, dug in behind the Naktong River, had set up the final defense line to be known as the Pusan Perimeter, a thinly held front forming an arc of 130 miles around the port of Pusan. On the map it looked like a bare toehold on the peninsula. On the ground the fighting went on as savagely as before. But the retreat was over. At his briefing for the president on Saturday, August 12, in his customary, dry, cautious way, Omar Bradley, the chairman of the Joint Chiefs of Staff, described the situation, for the first time, as "fluid but improving."

Truman's special assistant Averell Harriman, meanwhile, had returned from a hurried mission to Tokyo, bringing the details of a daring new MacArthur plan. Harriman had been dispatched to tell the general of Truman's determination to see that he had everything he needed, but also to impress upon him Truman's urgent desire to avoid any move that might provoke a third world war. This was Truman's uppermost concern, and there must be no misunderstanding. In particular, MacArthur was to "stay clear" of Chiang Kai-shek. Truman had instructed Harriman to tell MacArthur that the Chinese Nationalist leader, now on Formosa, must not become the catalyst for a war with the Chinese Communists.

MacArthur had no reservations about the decision to fight in Korea, "absolutely none," Harriman reported to Truman at Blair House. MacArthur was certain neither the Chinese Communists nor the Soviets would intervene. MacArthur had assured Harriman that of course, as a soldier, he would do as the president ordered concerning Chiang Kai-shek, though something about his tone as he said this had left Harriman wondering.

Of greater urgency and importance was what Harriman had to report of a plan to win the war with one bold stroke. For weeks there had been talk at the Pentagon of a MacArthur strategy to outflank the enemy, to hit from behind, by amphibious landing on the western shore of Korea at the port of Inchon, two hundred miles northwest of Pusan. Inchon had tremendous tides—thirty feet or more—and no beaches on which to land, only seawalls. Thus an assault would have to strike directly into the city itself, and only a full tide would carry the landing craft clear to the seawall. In two hours after high tide, the landing craft would be stuck in the mud.

To Bradley it was the riskiest military proposal he had ever heard. But as MacArthur stressed, the Japanese had landed successfully at Inchon in 1904, and the very "impracticabilities" would help ensure the all-important element of surprise. As Wolfe had astonished and defeated Montcalm at Quebec in 1759 by scaling the impossible cliffs near the Plains of Abraham, so, MacArthur said, he would astonish and defeat the North Koreans by landing at the impossible port of Inchon. But there was little time. The attack had to come before the onset of the Korean winter exacted more casualties than the battlefield. The tides at Inchon would be right on September 15. Truman made no commitment one way or the other, but Harriman left Blair House convinced that Truman approved the plan.

By early August, General Bradley could tell the president that American strength at Pusan was up to 50,000, which, with another 45,000 ROKs and small contingents of U.N. allies, made a total U.N. ground force of nearly 100,000. Still, the prospect of diverting additional American forces for MacArthur's Inchon scheme pleased the Joint Chiefs not at all. Bradley continued to view it as "the wildest kind" of plan.

Then, on Saturday, August 26, the Associated Press broke a statement from MacArthur to the Veterans of Foreign Wars, in which he strongly defended Chiang Kai-shek and the importance of Chiang's control of Formosa: "Nothing could be more fallacious than the threadbare argument by those who advocate appeasement and defeatism in the Pacific that if we defend Formosa we alienate continental Asia." It was exactly the sort of dabbling in policy that MacArthur had assured Harriman he would, as a good soldier, refrain from.

Truman was livid. He would later say he considered but rejected the idea of relieving MacArthur of field command then and there and replacing him with Bradley. "It would have been difficult to avoid the appearance of demotion, and I had no desire to hurt General MacArthur personally."

But whatever his anger at MacArthur, to whatever degree the incident had increased his dislike—or distrust—of the general, Truman decided to give MacArthur his backing. "The JCS inclined toward postponing Inchon until such time that we were certain Pusan could hold," remembered Bradley. "But Truman was now committed." On August 28, the Joint Chiefs sent MacArthur their tentative approval.

In time to come, little would be said or written about Truman's part in the matter—that as commander in chief he, and he alone, was the one with the final say on Inchon. He could have said no, and certainly the weight of opinion among his military advisers would have been on his side. But he did not. He took the chance, made the decision for which he was neither to ask nor to receive anything like the credit he deserved.

In the early hours of September 15—it was afternoon in Washington, September 14—the amphibious landing at Inchon began. As promised by MacArthur, the attack took the enemy by total surprise; and as also promised by MacArthur, the operation was an overwhelming success that completely turned the tables on the enemy.

The invasion force numbered 262 ships and 70,000 men of the X Corps, with the 1st Marine Division leading the assault. Inchon fell in little more than a day. In eleven days Seoul was retaken. Meantime, as planned, General Walton Walker's Eighth Army broke out of the Pusan Perimeter and started north. Seldom in military history had there been such a dramatic turn in fortune. By September 27 more than half the North Korean Army had been trapped in a huge pincer movement. By October 1, U.N. forces were at the 38th Parallel and South Korea was under U.N. control. In two weeks it had become an entirely different war.

In Washington the news was almost unbelievable, far more than anyone had dared hope for. The country was exultant. It was a "military miracle." A jubilant Truman cabled MacArthur: I SALUTE YOU ALL, AND SAY TO ALL OF YOU FROM ALL OF US AT HOME, "WELL AND NOBLY DONE."

For nearly three months, since the war began, the question had been whether U.N. forces could possibly hang on and survive in Korea. Now, suddenly, the question was whether to carry the war across the 38th Parallel and destroy the Communist army and the Communist regime of the North and thereby unify the country. MacArthur favored "hot pursuit" of the enemy. So did the Joint Chiefs, the press, politicians in both parties, and the great majority of the American people. And understandably. It was a heady time; the excitement of victory was in the air. Virtually no one was urging a halt at the 38th Parallel. "Troops could not be expected . . . to march up to a surveyor's line and stop," said Secretary of State Dean Acheson.

Truman appears to have been as caught up in the spirit of the moment as anyone. To pursue and destroy the enemy's army was basic military doctrine. If he hesitated or agonized over the decision—one of the most fateful of his presidency—there is no record of it.

The decision was made on Wednesday, September 27. MacArthur's military objective now was "the destruction of the North Korean Armed Forces"—a very different objective from before. He was authorized to cross the 38th Parallel, providing there was no sign of major intervention in North Korea by Soviet or Chinese forces. Also, he was not to carry the fight beyond the Chinese or Soviet borders of North Korea. Overall, he was free to do what had to be done to wind up the war as swiftly as possible. George Marshall, now secretary of defense, told him to "feel unhampered tactically and strategically," and when MacArthur cabled, "I regard all of Korea open for military operations," no one objected. Carrying the war north involved two enormous risks—intervention by the Chinese, and winter. But MacArthur was ready to move, and after Inchon, MacArthur was regarded with "almost superstitious awe."

At the end of the first week of October, at Lake Success, New York, the United Nations recommended that all "appropriate steps be taken to ensure conditions of stability throughout Korea," which meant U.N. approval for proceeding with the war. On October 9, MacArthur sent the Eighth Army across the 38th Parallel near Kaesong, and on the following day, Truman made a surprise announcement: He was flying to an unspecified point in the Pacific to confer with General MacArthur on "the final phase" in Korea.

It was the kind of grand, high-level theater irresistible to the press and the American public. Truman and MacArthur were to rendezvous, as was said, like the sovereign rulers of separate realms journeying to a neutral field attended by their various retainers. The two men had never met. MacArthur had been out of the country since 1937. Truman had never been closer to the Far East than San Francisco.

The meeting place was a pinpoint in the Pacific—Wake Island, a minuscule coral way station beyond the international date line. The presidential expedition was made up of three planes: the *Independence* with Truman and his staff, physician, and Secret Service detail; an Air Force Constellation carrying Harri-

man, Dean Rusk, and Philip Jessup from the State Department, Army Secretary Frank Pace, Jr., and General Bradley, plus all their aides and secretaries, as
well as Admiral Arthur Radford, commander of the Pacific Fleet, who came on
board at Honolulu; and a Pan American Stratocruiser with thirty-five correspondents and photographers. General MacArthur flew with several of his staff,
a physician, and John Muccio, the American ambassador to South Korea.

As a courtesy, Truman had let MacArthur choose the place for the meeting,
and for the president, Wake Island meant a flight across seven time zones, a full
round trip from Washington of 14,425 miles, while MacArthur had only to
travel 4,000 miles from Tokyo and back. Events were moving rapidly in Korea,
Truman would explain, "and I did not feel that he [MacArthur] should be away
from his post too long."

To many the whole affair looked like a political grandstand play to capitalize
on the sudden, unexpected success of the war and share in MacArthur's Inchon
glory on the eve of the off-year elections in November. The president had been
out of the headlines for some time, it was noted. Now he was back, and for
those Democrats in Congress who were up for reelection, it was "the perfect
answer to prayer and fasting." MacArthur himself, en route to Wake Island, appeared disgusted that he had been "summoned for political reasons." In fact,
the idea for the meeting had originated with the White House staff as "good
election year stuff," Charlie Murphy remembered, and at first Truman had rejected it for that very reason, for being "too political, too much showmanship."
Apparently it was only after being reminded that Franklin Roosevelt had made
just such a trip to meet with MacArthur at Hawaii in 1944 that Truman
changed his mind. He appears to have had second thoughts, even as he flew the
Pacific. "I've a whale of a job before me," he wrote on the plane. "Have to talk
to God's right-hand man tomorrow. . . ."

The importance of the occasion, like its drama, centered on the human
equation, the vital factor of personality. For the first time the two upon whom
so much depended, and who were so strikingly different in nature, would be
able to appraise each other not at a vast distance, or through official communiqué, or the views of advisers only, but by looking each other over. As Admiral
Radford commented at the time, "Two men can sometimes learn more of each
other's minds in two hours, face to face, than in years of correct correspon-
dence." Truman, after returning, would remark simply, "I don't care what they
say. I wanted to see General MacArthur, so I went to see him."

Also what would be largely forgotten, or misrepresented by both sides in time to come, after things turned sour, was how the meetings at Wake Island actually went, and what the president and the general actually concluded then, once having met.

Truman's plane put down at six-thirty A.M. on Sunday, October 15, just as the sun rose from the sea with spectacular brilliance, backlighting ranks of towering clouds. The single airstrip stretched the length of the island.

MacArthur was there waiting. Later, MacArthur would be pictured deliberately trying to upstage Truman by circling the airstrip, waiting for Truman to land first, thus putting the president in the position of having to wait for the general. But it did not happen that way. MacArthur was not only on the ground, he had arrived the night before and was at the field half an hour early.

As Truman stepped from the plane and came down the ramp, MacArthur stood waiting at the bottom, with "every appearance of warmth and friendliness." And while onlookers noted also that the general failed to salute the president, and though Truman seems to have been somewhat put out by MacArthur's attire—his open-neck shirt and "greasy ham and eggs cap" (MacArthur's famed, gold-braided World War II garrison cap)—the greeting between them was extremely cordial.

MacArthur held out his hand. "Mr. President," he said, seizing Truman's right arm while pumping his hand, which experienced MacArthur watchers knew to be the number one treatment.

"I've been waiting a long time meeting you, General," Truman said with a broad smile.

"I hope it won't be so long next time, Mr. President," MacArthur said warmly.

Truman was dressed in a dark blue double-breasted suit and gray Stetson. In Honolulu, he had outfitted his whole staff in Hawaiian shirts, but now he looked conspicuously formal, entirely presidential, and well rested, having slept during most of the last leg of the flight.

For the benefit of the photographers, he and MacArthur shook hands several times again, as a small crowd applauded. Then the two men climbed into the backseat of a well-worn black two-door Chevrolet, the best car available on the island, and drove a short distance to a Quonset hut by the ocean, where, alone, they talked for half an hour.

According to Secret Service Agent Henry Nicholson, who rode in the front seat beside Floyd Boring, the driver, Truman began talking almost immediately about his concern over possible Chinese intervention in Korea. Nicholson would distinctly recall Truman saying, "I have been worried about that."

At the Quonset hut, according to Truman's own account in his *Memoirs*, MacArthur assured him that victory was won in Korea and that the Chinese Communists would not attack. When MacArthur apologized for what he had said in his Veterans of Foreign Wars statement, Truman told him to think no more of it, he considered the matter closed—a gesture that so impressed MacArthur that he later made a point of telling Harriman. What more was said in the Quonset hut is not known, since no notes were taken and no one else was present. But clearly the time served to put both men at ease. Each, to judge by his later comments, concluded that the other was not as he had supposed.

About seven-thirty they reemerged in the brilliant morning sunshine and again drove off, now to a flat-roofed, one-story pink cinder-block shack, a Civil Aeronautics Administration building close to the beach where the Japanese had stormed ashore in 1941. Beyond the beach, blue Pacific rollers crashed over the dark hulks of two Japanese landing boats.

Some seventeen advisers and aides were waiting in a large, plain room. Truman, setting a tone of informality, said it was no weather for coats, they should all get comfortable. He sat in his shirtsleeves at the head of a long pine table, MacArthur on his right, Harriman on the left, the rest finding places down the table or against the walls. MacArthur, taking out a briar pipe, asked whether the president minded if he smoked. Everyone laughed. No, Truman said, he supposed he had had more smoke blown his way than any man alive.

The meeting proceeded without formal agenda, and as MacArthur later wrote, no new policies or war strategies were proposed or discussed. But the discussion was broad-ranging, with MacArthur doing most of the talking, as Truman, referring only to a few handwritten notes, asked questions. As so often before, MacArthur's performance was masterful. He seemed in full command of every detail and absolutely confident. The time moved swiftly.

MacArthur had only good news to report. The situation in Korea was under control. The war, "the formal resistance," would end by Thanksgiving. The North Korean capital, Pyongyang, would fall in a week. By Christmas he would have the Eighth Army back in Japan. By the first of the year, the United Nations would be holding elections, he expected, and American troops could be withdrawn entirely very soon afterward. "Nothing is gained by military occupation. All occupations are failures," MacArthur declared, to which Truman nodded in agreement.

Truman's first concern was keeping it a "limited" war. What were the chances of Chinese or Soviet intervention? he asked. "Very little," MacArthur said.

> Had they interfered in the first or second months it would have been deci-
> sive. We are no longer fearful of their intervention. . . . The Chinese have
> 300,000 men in Manchuria. Of these probably not more than 100,000 to
> 125,000 are distributed along the Yalu River. They have no Air Force. Now
> that we have bases for our Air Force in Korea, if the Chinese tried to get
> down to Pyongyang there would be the greatest slaughter.

The Russians, MacArthur continued, were a different matter. The Russians had an air force in Siberia and could put a thousand planes in action. A combination of Chinese ground troops and Russian airpower could pose a problem, he implied. But coordination of air support with operations on the ground was extremely difficult, and he doubted they could manage it.

The support he had been given from Washington was surpassing, MacArthur stressed. "No commander in the history of war," he said, looking around the table, "has ever had more complete and adequate support from all agencies in Washington than I have." How soon could he release a division for duty in Europe? Bradley wished to know. By January, MacArthur assured him.

Dean Rusk, concerned that the discussion was moving too fast, passed Truman a note suggesting he slow down the pace. Too brief a meeting, Rusk felt, would only fuel the cynicism of a press already dubious about the meeting. Truman scribbled a reply: "Hell, no! I want to get out of here before we get into trouble."

As to the need for additional U.N. troops, MacArthur would leave that for Washington to decide. It was then, at about 9:05, that Truman called a halt. "No one who was not here would believe we have covered so much ground as we have been actually able to cover," he said. He suggested a break for lunch while a communiqué was prepared. But MacArthur declined, saying he was anxious to get back to Tokyo and would like to leave as soon as possible—which, to some in the room, seemed to border on rudeness. "Whether intended or not," wrote Bradley, "it was insulting to decline lunch with the President, and I think Truman was miffed, although he gave no sign."

"The communiqué should be submitted as soon as it is ready, and General MacArthur can return immediately," Truman said. The conference had lasted one hour, thirty-six minutes.

In later studies, some historians would write that Truman had traveled extremely far for not much. But to Truman, at the time, it had all been worth the effort. He was exuberant. He had never had a more satisfactory conference, he told the reporters present. Tony Leviero of *The New York Times* described him beaming "like an insurance salesman who had at last signed up an important prospect."

The communiqué, which MacArthur read and initialed, stressed "the very complete unanimity of view" that had made possible such rapid progress at the conference table and called MacArthur "one of America's great soldier-statesmen." At the airstrip, in a little ceremony just before boarding his plane, Truman said still more as he honored MacArthur with a Distinguished Service Medal. He praised MacArthur for "his vision, his judgment, his indomitable will and unshakable faith," his "gallantry and tenacity" and "audacity in attack matched by few operations in history."

The whole spirit of Wake Island was one of relief and exhilaration. The awful bloodshed in Korea, the suffering, was all but over; the war was won. If MacArthur said there was "very little" chance of the Chinese coming in, who, after Inchon, was to doubt his judgment, particularly if what he said confirmed what was thought in Washington? If Truman and MacArthur had disliked or distrusted each other before, they apparently did so no longer. If the conference had accomplished that alone, it had been a success.

They said good-bye in the glaring sunshine of midday at Wake Island, as Truman boarded the *Independence*.

"Good-bye, sir," MacArthur said. "Happy landing. It has been a real honor talking to you."

It was their first and their last meeting. They never saw each other again.

November through December 1950 was a dreadful passage for Truman. Omar Bradley was to call these sixty days among the most trying of his own professional career, more so even than the Battle of the Bulge. For Truman it was the darkest, most difficult period of his presidency.

That Chinese troops had come into the war was by now an established fact, though how many there were remained in doubt. MacArthur estimated thirty thousand, and whatever the number, his inclination was to discount their importance. But in Washington concern mounted. To check the flow of Chinese troops coming across the Yalu, MacArthur requested authority to bomb the

Korean ends of all bridges on the river, a decision Truman approved, after warning MacArthur against enlarging the war and specifically forbidding air strikes north of the Yalu, on Chinese territory.

Another cause of concern was MacArthur's decision, in the drive north, to divide his forces, sending the X Corps up the east side of the peninsula, the Eighth Army up the west—an immensely risky maneuver that the Joint Chiefs questioned. But MacArthur was adamant, and it had been just such audacity, after all, that had worked the miracle at Inchon.

With one powerful, "end-the-war" offensive, one "massive comprehensive envelopment," MacArthur insisted, the war would be quickly won. As always, he had absolute faith in his own infallibility, and while no such faith was to be found at the Pentagon or the White House, no one, including Truman, took steps to stop him.

Bitterly cold winds from Siberia swept over North Korea, as MacArthur flew to Eighth Army headquarters on the Chongchon River to see the attack begin. "If this operation is successful," he said within earshot of correspondents, "I hope we can get the boys home for Christmas."

The attack began Friday, November 24, the day after Thanksgiving. Four days later, on Tuesday, November 28, in Washington, at 6:15 in the morning, General Bradley telephoned the president at Blair House to say he had "a terrible message" from MacArthur.

"We've got a terrific situation on our hands," Truman told his staff a few hours later at the White House, having waited patiently through the routine of the morning meeting. The Chinese had launched a furious counterattack with a force of 260,000 men, Truman said. MacArthur was going over on the defensive. "The Chinese have come in with both feet."

Truman paused. The room was still. The shock of what he had said made everyone sit stiff and silent. Everything that had seemed to be going so well in Korea, all the heady prospects since Inchon, the soaring hopes of Wake Island, was gone in an instant. But then Truman seemed to recover himself, sitting up squarely in his high-backed chair. "We have got to meet this thing," he said, his voice low and confident. "Let's go ahead now and do our jobs as best we can."

"We face an entirely new war," MacArthur declared. It had been all of three days since the launching of his "end-the-war" offensive, yet all hope of victory was gone. The Chinese were bent on the "complete destruction" of his army.

"This command . . . is now faced with conditions beyond its control and its strength."

In further messages MacArthur called for reinforcements of the "greatest magnitude," including Chinese Nationalist troops from Formosa. His own troops were "mentally fatigued and physically battered." The directives he was operating under were "completely outmoded by events." He wanted a naval blockade of China. He called for bombing the Chinese mainland. He must have the authority to broaden the conflict, MacArthur insisted, or the administration would be faced with a disaster.

That same day, November 28, at three o'clock in the afternoon, a crucial meeting of the National Security Council took place in the Cabinet Room— one of the most important meetings of the Truman years. For it was there and then, in effect, with Truman presiding, that the decision was made not to let the crisis in Korea, however horrible, flare into a world war. It was a decision as fateful as the one to go into Korea in the first place, and it stands among the triumphs of the Truman administration, considering how things might have gone otherwise.

General Bradley opened the discussion with a review of the bleak situation on the battlefield. Vice President Alben Barkley, who rarely spoke at such meetings, asked bitterly why MacArthur had promised to have "the boys home for Christmas"—how he ever could have said such a thing in good faith. Army Secretary Pace said that MacArthur was now denying he had made the statement. Truman warned that in any event they must do nothing to cause the commander in the field to lose face before the enemy.

When Marshall spoke, he sounded extremely grave. American involvement in Korea should continue as part of a U.N. effort, Marshall said. The United States must not get "sewed up" in Korea, but find a way to "get out with honor." There must be no war with China. That was clear. "To do this would be to fall into a carefully laid Russian trap. We should use all available political, economic and psychological action to limit the war."

"We can't defeat the Chinese in Korea," said Acheson. "They can put in more than we can." Concerned that MacArthur might overextend his operations, Acheson urged "very, very careful thought" regarding air strikes against Manchuria. If this became essential to save American troops, then it would have to be done, but if American attacks succeeded in Manchuria, the Soviets would probably come to the aid of their Chinese ally. The thing to do, the "imperative step," said Acheson, was to "find a line that we can hold, and hold it." Behind everything they faced was the Soviet Union, "a somber consideration." The threat of a larger war, wrote Bradley, was closer than ever, and it was this, the dread prospect of a global conflict with Russia erupting at any hour, that was on all their minds.

The news was so terrible and came with such suddenness that it seemed almost impossible to believe. The last thing anyone had expected at this point was defeat in Korea. The evening papers of November 28 described "hordes of Chinese Reds" surging through a widening gap in the American Eighth Army's right flank, "as the failure of the Allied offensive turned into a dire threat for the entire United Nations line." The whole Eighth Army was falling back. 200,000 OF FOE ADVANCE UP TO 23 MILES IN KOREA read the banner headline across *The New York Times* the following day. The two calamities most dreaded by military planners—the fierce Korean winter and massive intervention by the Chinese—had fallen on the allied forces at once.

What had begun was a tragic, epic retreat—some of the worst fighting of the war—in howling winds and snow and temperatures as low as 25 degrees below zero. The Chinese not only came in "hordes" but took advantage of MacArthur's divided forces, striking both on their flanks. The Eighth Army under General Walton Walker was reeling back from the Chongchon River, heading for Pyongyang. The choice was retreat or annihilation. In the northeast the ordeal of the X Corps was still worse. The retreat of the 1st Marine Division—from the Chosin Reservoir forty miles to the port of Hungnam and evacuation—would be compared to Xenophon's retreat of the immortal ten thousand or Napoleon's withdrawal from Moscow.

"A lot of hard work was put in," Truman would remember of his own days in Washington. And, as Acheson would write, all the president's advisers, civilian and military, knew something was badly wrong in Korea, other than just the onslaught of the Chinese. There were questions about MacArthur's morale, grave concern over his strategy and whether on the actual battlefield a "new hand" was needed to replace General Walker. It was quite clear, furthermore, that MacArthur, the Far Eastern commander, had indeed deliberately disobeyed a specific order from the Joint Chiefs to use no non-Korean forces close to the Manchurian border.

But no changes in strategy were ordered. No "new hand" replaced Walker. No voices were raised against MacArthur. Regrettably, the president was ill-advised, Bradley later observed. He, Marshall, the Joint Chiefs, had all "failed the president." Here, in a crucial few days, said Acheson afterward, they missed their chance to halt the march to disaster in Korea. Acheson was to lament their performance for the rest of his life. Truman would never put any blame on any of them, but Acheson would say Truman had deserved far better.

General Matthew Ridgway would "well remember" his mounting impatience "that dreary Sunday, December 3," as hour after hour in the War Room discussion continued over the ominous situation in Korea. Unable to contain himself any longer, Ridgway spoke up, saying immediate action must be taken. They owed it to the men in the field, and "to the God to whom we must answer for those men's lives," to stop talking and do something. For the first time, Acheson later wrote, "someone had expressed what everyone thought—that the Emperor had no clothes on." But of the twenty men who sat at the table, including Acheson, and twenty more along the walls behind, no one else spoke. The meeting ended without a decision.

Why didn't the Joint Chiefs just send orders and tell MacArthur what to do? Ridgway asked the air force chief of staff, General Hoyt Vandenberg, afterward. Because MacArthur would not obey such orders, Vandenberg replied. Ridgway exploded. "You can relieve any commander who won't obey orders, can't you?" he said. But Vandenberg, with an expression Ridgway remembered as both puzzled and amazed, only walked away.

The next day, in another closed session, this time at the State Department, Dean Rusk would propose that MacArthur be relieved of command. But again, no one else commented.

MacArthur, meanwhile, was being taken to task by the press, as he had never been. *Time*, which had long glorified him, charged him with being responsible for one of the worst military disasters in history. An editorial in the *New York Herald-Tribune* referred to his "colossal military blunder." Unused to such criticism, his immense vanity wounded, MacArthur started issuing statements of his own to the press. He denied that his strategy had precipitated the Chinese invasion and said his inability to defeat the new enemy was due to restrictions imposed by Washington that were "without precedent."

Truman did not hold MacArthur accountable for the failure of the November offensive. But he deplored MacArthur's way of excusing the failure, and the damage his statements could do abroad, to the degree that they implied a change in American policy. "I should have relieved General MacArthur then and there," he would write much later.

As it was, he ordered that all military officers and diplomatic officials henceforth clear with the State Department all but routine statements before making them public, "and . . . refrain from direct communications on military or foreign policy with newspapers, magazines, and other publicity media." Dated December 6, the order was widely and correctly seen as directed to MacArthur.

Truman did not relieve the Far Eastern commander, he later explained, because he knew no general could be a winner every day and because he did not wish to have it appear that MacArthur was being fired for failing. What he might have done had Acheson, Marshall, Bradley, and the Joint Chiefs spoken up and insisted that MacArthur be relieved is another question and impossible to answer.

For now the tragedy in Korea overshadowed the rest. If MacArthur was in trouble, then everything possible must be done to help. "We must get him out of it if we can," Truman wrote in his diary late the night of December 2, following an intense session with Acheson, Marshall, and Bradley that had left him feeling desperately low. The talk had been of evacuating all American troops. Marshall was not even sure such an operation would succeed, should the Chinese bring in their own airpower. "*It looks very bad,*" Truman wrote. Yet bad as it was, there was no mood of panic, and this, as those around him would later attest, was principally because of Truman's own unflinching response.

The bloody retreat in Korea continued. Pyongyang fell "to overwhelming masses of advancing Chinese," as the papers reported. General Walker's Eighth Army was heading for the 38th Parallel. But Truman remained calm and steady. He wrote in his diary, "I've worked for peace for five years and six months and it looks like World War III is here. I hope not—but we must meet whatever comes—and we will."

It was Harry Truman's long-standing conviction that if you did your best in life, did your "damndest" always, then whatever happened, you would at least know it was not for lack of trying. But he was a great believer also in the parts played by luck and personality, forces quite beyond effort or determination. And though few presidents had ever worked so hard, or taken their responsibilities so to heart in time of crisis as Truman had since the start of the war in Korea, it was luck, good and bad, and the large influence of personality, that determined the course of events time and again, and never more so than in late December 1950, in the midst of his darkest passage.

Two days before Christmas, on an icy highway north of Seoul, General Walton Walker, commander of the Eighth Army, was killed when his jeep ran head-on into an ROK army truck. Walker's replacement—as requested by MacArthur and approved immediately by Truman—was Matthew Ridgway, who left Washington at once, arriving in Tokyo on Christmas Day. At his meeting with MacArthur the next morning, Ridgway was told to use his own judgment at the front. "The Eighth Army is yours, Matt. Do what you think best." MacArthur, wrote Dean Acheson later, "never uttered wiser words."

That afternoon, Ridgway landed at Taegu, and in the weeks following came a transformation no one had thought possible. Rarely has one individual made so marked a difference in so little time. With what Omar Bradley called "brilliant, driving, uncompromising leadership," Ridgway restored the fighting spirit of the Eighth Army and turned the tide of war as have few commanders in history.

Since the Chinese onslaught of November 28, the Eighth Army had fallen back nearly three hundred miles, to a point just below the 38th Parallel, and for a while Ridgway had no choice but to continue the retreat. Abandoning Seoul, Ridgway withdrew as far as Oswan, near the very point where the first green American troops had gone into action in July. Now, instead of fighting in the murderous heat of summer, they fought in murderous cold.

The mood in Washington remained bleak. MacArthur continued to urge a widening of the war—again he proposed bombing and blockading China and utilizing the troops of Chiang Kai-shek—and, as before, his proposals were rejected. Dire consequences would follow, he implied, unless policy were changed. He reported:

> The troops are tired from a long and difficult campaign, embittered by the shameful propaganda which has falsely condemned their courage and fighting qualities . . . and their morale will become a serious threat in their battlefield efficiency unless the political basis upon which they are being asked to trade life for time is clearly delineated. . . .

Truman found such messages "deeply disturbing." When a general complained about his troops' morale, observed Marshall, the time had come for the general to look to his own morale.

MacArthur called on the administration to recognize the "state of war" imposed by the Chinese, then to drop thirty to fifty atomic bombs on Manchuria and the mainland cities of China. The Joint Chiefs, too, told Truman that mass destruction of Chinese cities with nuclear weapons was the only way to affect the situation in Korea. But that choice was never seriously considered. Truman simply refused to "go down that trail," in Dean Rusk's words.

Truman also still refused to reprimand MacArthur. Rather, he treated MacArthur with what Acheson considered "infinite patience"—too much infinite patience, Acheson thought, having by now concluded that the general was "incurably recalcitrant" and fundamentally disloyal to the purposes of his commander in chief.

Truman had by now declared a national emergency, announcing emergency controls on prices and wages, and still greater defense spending—to the amount of $50 billion, more than four times the defense budget at the start of the year. He had put Charles E. Wilson, head of the General Electric Company, in charge of a new Office of Defense Mobilization; appointed General Eisenhower as supreme commander of NATO; and, in a radio and television address to the nation on December 15, called on every citizen "to put aside his personal interests for the good of the country." So while doing all he could to avoid a wider war, he was clearly preparing for one. As Marshall later attested, "We were at our lowest point."

But then, on the morning of Wednesday, January 17, Marshall telephoned Truman to read an astonishing report just in from General Joe Collins, who had flown to Korea for talks with Ridgway. "Eighth Army in good shape and improving daily under Ridgway's leadership," Marshall read. "Morale very satisfactory. . . . Ridgway confident he can obtain two to three months' delay before having to initiate evacuation. . . . On the whole Eighth Army now in position and prepared to punish severely any mass attack."

Plainly, MacArthur's bleak assessment of the situation, his forecasts of doom, had been wrong—and the effect of this realization was electrifying. As word spread through the upper levels of government that day, it would be remembered, one could almost hear the sighs of relief. The long retreat of the Eighth Army—the longest in American military history—had ended. On January 25, 1951, less than a month after Ridgway's arrival, the Eighth Army began "rolling forward," as he said.

By the end of March, having inflicted immense casualties on the Chinese, the Eighth Army was again at the 38th Parallel. Yet Ridgway's progress seemed only to distress MacArthur further. Unless he was allowed to strike boldly at the enemy, he said, his dream of a unified Korea was impossible. He complained of a "policy void." He now proposed not only to massively attack Manchuria but to "sever" Korea from Manchuria by laying down a field of radioactive wastes, "the by-products of atomic manufacture," all along the Yalu River. As so often before, his request was denied.

Talking to journalists on March 7, MacArthur lamented the "savage slaughter" of Americans inevitable in a war of attrition. When, by the middle of March, the tide of battle "began to turn in our favor," as Truman wrote, and Truman's advisers at both the State Department and the Pentagon thought it time to make a direct appeal to China for peace talks, MacArthur refused to respond to inquiries on the subject. Instead, he decried any "further military restrictions" on his command. To MacArthur, as he later wrote, it appeared that Truman's nerves were at a breaking point—"not only his nerves, but what was far more menacing in the Chief Executive of a country at war—his nerve."

Truman ordered careful preparation of a cease-fire proposal. On March 21 the draft of a presidential statement was submitted for approval to the other seventeen U.N. nations with troops serving in Korea. On March 20 the Joint Chiefs had informed MacArthur of what was happening—sending him what Truman called the "meat paragraphs" of the statement in a message that seems to have impressed MacArthur as nothing else had that there was indeed to be no all-out war with Red China. His response so jarred Washington as to leave a number of people wondering if perhaps he had lost his mind. Years afterward Bradley would speculate that possibly MacArthur's realization that his war on China was not to be "snapped his brilliant but brittle mind."

On the morning of Saturday, March 24, in Korea (Friday the 23rd in Washington), MacArthur, without warning, tried to seize the initiative in a manner calculated only to inflame the situation. He issued his own florid proclamation to the Chinese Communists—in effect, an ultimatum. He began by taunting the Red Chinese for their lack of industrial power, their poor military showing in Korea against a U.N. force restricted by "inhibitions." More seriously, MacArthur threatened to expand the war.

The enemy, therefore, must by now be painfully aware that a decision of the United States to depart from its tolerant effort to contain the war to the areas of Korea, through an expansion of our military operations to his coastal areas and interior bases, would doom Red China to the risk of imminent military collapse.

In conclusion, MacArthur said he personally "stood ready at any time" to meet with the Chinese commander to reach a settlement.

All Truman's careful preparations of a cease-fire proposal were now in vain. MacArthur had cut the ground out from under him. Later, MacArthur would dismiss what he had said was a "routine communiqué." Yet his own devoted aide, General Courtney Whitney, would describe it as a bold effort to stop one of the most disgraceful plots in American history, meaning the administration's plan to appease China.

In his *Memoirs*, Truman would write that he now knew what he must do about MacArthur.

> This was a most extraordinary statement for a military commander of the United Nations to issue on his own responsibility. It was an act totally disregarding all directives to abstain from any declarations on foreign policy. It was in open defiance of my orders as President and as Commander in Chief. This was a challenge to the President under the Constitution. It also flouted the policy of the United Nations. . . .
>
> By this act MacArthur left me no choice—I could no longer tolerate his insubordination. . . .

And yet . . . MacArthur was not fired. Truman said not a word suggesting he had reached such a decision. He sent MacArthur only a restrained reprimand, a message he himself dictated to remind the general of the presidential order on December 6 forbidding public statements that had not been cleared with Washington.

Meantime, on March 14, the Gallup Poll had reported the president's public approval at an all-time low of 26 percent. And soon there were appalling new statistics: U.N. forces had now suffered 228,941 casualties, mostly South Koreans but including 57,120 Americans.

Truman was dwelling on the relationship between President Abraham Lincoln and General George B. McClellan during the Civil War, in the autumn of 1862, when Lincoln had been forced to relieve McClellan of command of the Army of the Potomac. Truman had sent one of his staff to the Library of

Congress to review the details of the Lincoln–McClellan crisis and give him a report. Lincoln's troubles with McClellan, as Truman knew, had been the reverse of his own with MacArthur: Lincoln had wanted McClellan to attack, and McClellan refused time and again. But then, when Lincoln issued orders, McClellan, like MacArthur, ignored them. Also like MacArthur, McClellan occasionally made political statements on matters outside the military field. Truman later wrote that

> Lincoln was patient, for that was his nature, but at long last he was compelled to relieve the Union Army's principal commander. And though I gave this difficulty with MacArthur much wearisome thought, I realized that I would have no other choice myself than to relieve the nation's top field commander. . . .
>
> I wrestled with the problem for several days, but my mind was made up before April 5, when the next incident occurred.

On Thursday, April 5, at the Capitol, House Minority Leader Joe Martin took the floor to read a letter from MacArthur that Martin said he felt duty-bound to withhold no longer. In February, speaking in Brooklyn, Martin had called for the use of Chiang Kai-shek's troops in Korea and accused the administration of a defeatist policy. "What are we in Korea for—to win or to lose? . . . If we are not in Korea to win, then this administration should be indicted for the murder of American boys." Martin had sent a copy of the speech to MacArthur, asking for his "views." On March 20, MacArthur had responded— and virtually all that he said was bound to provoke Truman, as Martin well knew. Since MacArthur's letter carried no stipulation of confidentiality, Martin decided to make it public.

The congressman was right in calling for victory, MacArthur wrote, right in wanting to see Chinese forces from Formosa join the battle against Communism. The real war against Communism was in Asia, not in Europe. "There is no substitute for victory."

The letter was on the wires at once. At the Pentagon, Bradley called a meeting of the Joint Chiefs. "I did not know that Truman had already made up his mind to relieve MacArthur," he remembered, "but I thought it was a strong possibility." The Joint Chiefs, however, reached no conclusion about MacArthur.

On Friday, April 6, official Cadillacs filled the White House driveway. Marshall, Bradley, Acheson, and Harriman met with the president for an hour. Saying nothing of his own views, Truman asked what should be done. When Marshall urged caution, Acheson agreed. To the latter it was not so much a problem of what should be done as how it should be done. He later remembered:

> The situation could be resolved only by relieving the General of all his commands and removing him from the Far East. Grave trouble would result, but it could be surmounted if the President acted upon the carefully considered advice and unshakable support of all his civilian and military advisers. If he should get ahead of them or appear to take them for granted or be impetuous, the harm would be incalculable.

"If you relieve MacArthur," Acheson told Truman, "you will have the biggest fight of your administration."

Harriman, reminding the president that MacArthur had been a problem for too long, said he should be dismissed at once. "I don't express any opinion or make known my decision," Truman wrote in his diary. "Direct the four to meet again Friday afternoon and go over all phases of the situation."

He was a model of self-control. For the next several days, an air of unnatural calm seemed to hang over the White House. "The wind died down," remembered Joe Martin. "The surface was placid . . . nothing happened."

On Saturday, Truman met again with Marshall, Acheson, Bradley, and Harriman, and again nothing was resolved. Marshall and Bradley were still uncertain what to do. They were hesitating in part, according to Bradley's later account, because they knew the kind of abuse that would be hurled at them personally—an understandable concern for two such men at the end of long, distinguished careers.

On Monday, April 9, the same foursome convened with the president once more, this time at Blair House. But now the situation had changed. The Joint Chiefs had met the afternoon before and concluded that from a military point of view, MacArthur should be relieved. Their opinion was unanimous. Truman, for the first time, said he was of the same opinion. He had made his decision. He told Bradley to prepare the necessary papers.

"Rarely had a matter been shrouded in such secrecy at the White House," reported *The Washington Post* on Tuesday, April 10. "The answer to every question about MacArthur was met with a 'no comment' reply." In Tokyo, according to a United Press dispatch, a member of MacArthur's staff said meetings between the general and Secretary of the Army Pace were "going forward with an air of cordiality"—thus seeming to refute dismissal rumors. A photograph on page 1 of the *Post* showed a smiling MacArthur welcoming an even more smiling Pace at the Tokyo airport.

At the end of a routine morning staff meeting, the president quietly announced—"So you won't have to read about it in the papers"—that he had decided to fire General MacArthur. He was sure, Truman added, that MacArthur had wanted to be fired. He was sure also that he himself faced a political storm, "a great furor," unlike any in his political career. From beyond the office windows, the noise of construction going on in the White House was so great that several of the staff had to strain to hear Truman. At 3:15 that afternoon, Acheson, Marshall, Bradley, and Harriman reported to the Oval Office, bringing the drafted orders. Truman looked them over, borrowed a fountain pen, and signed his name.

The orders were to be sent by State Department channels to Ambassador Muccio in Korea, who was to turn them over to Secretary Pace, who by now was also in Korea, with Ridgway at Eighth Army headquarters. Pace was to return at once to Tokyo and personally hand the orders to MacArthur—this whole relay system having been devised to save the general from the embarrassment of direct transmission through regular army communications. All aspects of the issue thus far had been kept secret with marked success, but it was essential that there be no leaks in the last critical hours. Announcement of the sensational news about MacArthur was not to be made until the following morning.

The next several hours passed without incident, until early evening. Harriman, Bradley, Rusk, and six or seven of Truman's staff were working in the Cabinet Room, preparing material for release, when Press Secretary Joe Short received word that a Pentagon reporter for the *Chicago Tribune*, Lloyd Norman, was making inquiries about a supposed "major resignation" to take place in Tokyo—the implication being that somehow MacArthur had already learned of Truman's decision and was about to resign before Truman could fire him.

Bradley telephoned Truman at about nine o'clock to report there had been a leak. Truman, saying he wanted time to think, told Bradley to find Marshall and Acheson. Marshall, it was learned, had gone to a movie, but Acheson came to the White House immediately; he thought it would be a mistake to do anything rash because of one reporter's inquiry. As he had from the start, Acheson stressed the importance of the manner in which the general was dismissed. It was only fair and proper that he be informed before the story broke.

Meantime, something apparently had gone wrong with the transmission of the president's orders. Nothing had been heard from Muccio about their receipt. By ten-thirty Truman had decided. Short telephoned the White House to have all the orders—those relieving MacArthur, as well as those naming Matthew Ridgway his successor—mimeographed as quickly as possible.

"He's not going to be allowed to quit on me," Truman reportedly said. "He's going to be fired!" In his diary Truman recorded dryly, "Discussed the situation and I ordered messages sent at once and directly to MacArthur."

From a small first-floor study in his Georgetown home, Dean Acheson began placing calls to various officials. At the State Department, Rusk spent a long night telephoning the ambassadors of all the countries with troops in Korea. "Well, the little man finally did it, didn't he," responded the ambassador from New Zealand.

At the White House, switchboard operators began calling reporters at their homes to say there would be an extraordinary press conference at one A.M. And at one A.M. on Wednesday, April 11, Press Secretary Joe Short handed out the mimeographed sheets in the White House pressroom. Truman, in his second-floor bedroom at Blair House, was by then fast asleep.

General MacArthur learned of his recall while at lunch in Tokyo, when his wife handed him a brown Signal Corps envelope. If Truman had only let him know how he felt, MacArthur would say privately a few hours later, he would have retired "without difficulty." Where the *Tribune* reporter got his tip was never revealed. MacArthur would later testify that he had never given any thought to resigning.

According to what MacArthur said he had been told by an unnamed but "eminent" medical authority, Truman's "mental instability" was the result of malignant hypertension, "characterized by bewilderment and confusion of thought." Truman, MacArthur predicted, would be dead in six months.

TRUMAN FIRES MACARTHUR

The headline across the early edition of *The Washington Post* on April 11, 1951, was the headline everywhere in the country and throughout much of the world, with only minor variations. The reaction was stupendous, the outcry from the American people shattering. Truman had known he would have to face a storm, but however dark his premonitions, he could not possibly have measured what was coming. No one did; no one could have.

The day on Capitol Hill was described as "one of the bitterest . . . in modern times." Prominent Republicans, including Senator Robert Taft, spoke angrily of impeaching the president. The full Republican leadership held an emergency meeting in Joe Martin's office at nine-thirty in the morning, after which Martin talked to reporters of "impeachments," the accent on the plural. "We might want the impeachments of 1 or 50." A full-dress congressional investigation of the president's war policy was in order. General MacArthur, announced Martin, would be invited to air his views before a joint session of Congress.

In New York, two thousand longshoremen walked off their jobs in protest over the firing of MacArthur. A Baltimore women's group announced plans for a march on Washington in support of the general. Elsewhere, enraged patriots flew flags at half-staff, or upside down. People signed petitions and fired off furious letters and telegrams to Washington. In Worcester, Massachusetts, and San Gabriel, California, Truman was burned in effigy. In Houston, a Protestant minister became so angry dictating a telegram to the White House that he died of a heart attack.

In the hallways of the Senate and House office buildings, Western Union messengers made their deliveries with bushel baskets. According to one tally, of the 44,358 telegrams received by Republicans in Congress during the first forty-eight hours following Truman's announcement, all but 334 condemned him or took the side of MacArthur, and the majority called for Truman's immediate removal from office.

A number of prominent liberals—Eleanor Roosevelt, Walter Reuther, Justice William O. Douglas—publicly supported Truman. Further, throughout Europe, MacArthur's dismissal was greeted as welcome news. But most impressive was the weight of editorial opinion at home in support of Truman—including some staunch Republican newspapers—despite vehement assaults in the McCormick, Hearst, and Scripps Howard papers, as well as the renewed glorification of MacArthur in Henry Luce's *Time* and *Life*.

Nothing had so stirred the political passions of the country since the Civil War. At the heart of the tumult were anger and frustration over the war in Korea. Senator Kenneth Wherry had begun calling it "Truman's War," and the name caught on. People were sick of Truman's War, frustrated, and a bit baffled by talk of a "limited war." America didn't fight to achieve a stalemate, and the cost in blood had become appalling. The country wanted it over. MacArthur at least offered victory.

Except for a brief broadcast from the White House the night after his dismissal of MacArthur, Truman maintained silence on the matter. General MacArthur was "one of our greatest military commanders," he told the nation, but the cause of world peace was far more important than any individual.

MacArthur landed at San Francisco on Tuesday, April 17, to a delirious reception. He had been away from the country for fourteen years. Until now the American people had had no chance to see and cheer him, to welcome the hero home. Ten thousand were at the San Francisco airport. So great were the crowds on the way into the city, it took two hours for the motorcade to reach his hotel. "The only politics I have," MacArthur told a cheering throng, "is contained in a simple phrase known to all of you—God Bless America."

When Truman met with reporters the next day, at his first press conference since the start of the crisis, he dashed all their expectations by refusing to say anything on the subject. Scheduled to appear before the American Society of Newspaper Editors on Thursday, April 19, the day MacArthur was to go before Congress, Truman canceled his speech, because he felt it should be the general's day and did not wish anything to detract from it.

There would be "hell to pay" for perhaps six or seven weeks, he told his staff and the Cabinet. But eventually people would come to their senses, including more and more Republican politicians who would grow doubtful of all-out support for the general. Given some time, MacArthur would be reduced to human proportions. Meanwhile, Truman could withstand the bombardment, for in the long run, he knew, he would be judged to have made the right decision. He had absolutely no doubt of that. "The American people will come to understand that what I did had to be done."

At 12:31 P.M. Thursday, April 19, in a flood of television lights, Douglas MacArthur walked down the same aisle in the House of Representatives as had Harry Truman so often since 1945, and the wild ovation from the packed chamber, the intense, authentic drama of the moment, were such as few had ever beheld. Neither the president's Cabinet nor the Supreme Court nor any of the Joint Chiefs were present.

Wearing a short "Eisenhower" jacket without decoration, the silvery circles of five-star rank glittering on his shoulders, MacArthur paused to shake hands with Vice President Barkley, then stepped to the rostrum, his face "an unreadable mask." Only after complete silence had fallen did he begin: "I address you with neither rancor nor bitterness in the fading twilight of life, with but one purpose in mind: to serve my country."

There was ringing applause and the low, vibrant voice went on, the speaker in full command of the moment. The decision to intervene in support of the Republic of Korea had been sound from a military standpoint, MacArthur affirmed. But when he had called for reinforcements, he was told they were not available. He had "made clear," he said, that if not permitted to destroy the enemy bases north of the Yalu, if not permitted to utilize the eight hundred thousand Chinese troops on Formosa, if not permitted to blockade the China coast, then "the position of the command from a military standpoint forbade victory. . . ." And war's "very object" was victory. How could it be otherwise? "In war, indeed," he said, repeating his favorite slogan, "there can be no substitute for victory. There were some who, for varying reasons, would appease Red China. They were blind to history's clear lesson, for history teaches, with unmistakable emphasis, that appeasement begets new and bloodier war."

He was provocative, and defiant. Resounding applause or cheers followed again and again—thirty times in thirty-four minutes. He said nothing of bombing China's industrial centers, as he had proposed. And though he said "every available means" should be applied to bring victory, he made no mention of his wish to use atomic bombs, or to lay down a belt of radioactivity along the Yalu. He had been severely criticized for his views, he said. Yet, he asserted, his views were "fully shared" by the Joint Chiefs—a claim that was altogether untrue but that brought a deafening ovation. Republicans and most spectators in the galleries leaped to their feet, cheering and stamping. It was nearly a minute before he could begin again.

To those who said American military strength was inadequate to face the enemy on more than one front, MacArthur said he could imagine no greater expression of defeatism. "You cannot appease or otherwise surrender to Communism in Asia without simultaneously undermining our efforts to halt its advance in Europe." To confine the war only to Chinese aggression in Korea was to follow a path of "prolonged indecision."

"Why, my soldiers asked of me, surrender military advantages to an enemy in the field?" He paused; then, softly, his voice almost a whisper, he said, "I could not answer."

A record thirty million people were watching on television, and the performance was masterful. The use of the rich voice, the timing, surpassed that of most actors. The oratorical style was of a kind not heard in Congress in a very long time. It recalled, as one television critic wrote, "a yesteryear of the theater," and it held the greater part of the huge audience wholly enraptured. Work had stopped in offices and plants across the country, so people could watch. Saloons and bars were jammed. Schoolchildren saw the "historic hour" in classrooms or were herded into assemblies or dining halls to listen by radio. Whether they had any idea what the excitement was about, they knew it was "important."

"When I joined the army, even before the turn of the century, it was the fulfillment of all my boyish hopes and dreams," MacArthur said, his voice dropping as he began the famous last lines, the stirring, sentimental, ambiguous peroration that the speech would be remembered for.

The hopes and dreams have long since vanished. But I still remember the refrain of one of the most popular barracks ballads of that day which proclaimed most proudly that "Old soldiers never die. They just fade away." And like the old soldier of the ballad, I now close my military career and just fade away—an old soldier who tried to do his duty as God gave him the light to see that duty.

Good-bye.

A "hurricane of emotion" swept the room. Hands reached out to him. Many in the audience were weeping. "We heard God speak here today, God in the flesh, the voice of God!" exclaimed Republican Representative Dewey Short of Missouri, a former preacher. To Joe Martin, it was "the climaxing" of the most emotional moment he had known in thirty-five years in Congress. Theatrics were a part of the congressional way of life, Martin knew, but nothing had ever equaled this.

It was MacArthur's finest hour, and the crescendo of public adulation that followed, beginning with a triumphal parade through Washington that afternoon, and peaking the next day in New York with a thunderous tickertape parade, was unprecedented in U.S. history. Reportedly 7.5 million people turned out in New York, more than had welcomed Eisenhower in 1945, more even than at the almost legendary welcome for Lindbergh in 1927.

In fact, not everybody cheered. There were places along the parade route in New York where, as MacArthur's open car passed, people stood silently, just watching and looking, anything but pleased. In Washington, one senator had confided to a reporter that he had never feared more for his country than during MacArthur's speech. "I honestly felt that if the speech had gone on much longer there might have been a march on the White House."

Truman had not listened to MacArthur's speech, nor watched on television. He had spent the time at his desk in the Oval Office, meeting with Dean Acheson as was usual at that hour on Thursdays, after which he went back to Blair House for lunch and a nap. At some point, however, he did read what MacArthur had said. Speaking privately, he remarked that he thought it "a bunch of damn bullshit."

As Truman had anticipated, the tumult began to subside. For seven weeks in the late spring of 1951, the Senate Foreign Relations and Armed Services committees held joint hearings to investigate MacArthur's dismissal. Though the hearings were closed, authorized transcripts of each day's sessions, edited for military security reasons, were released hourly to the press.

MacArthur, the first witness, testified for three days, arguing that his way in Korea was the way to victory and an end to the slaughter. He had seen as much blood and disaster as any man alive, he told the senators, but never such devastation as during his last time in Korea. "After I looked at that wreckage and those thousands of women and children and everything, I vomited. Now are you going to let that go on . . . ?" The politicians in Washington had introduced a "new concept into military operations—the concept of appeasement," its purpose only "to go on indefinitely . . . indecisively, fighting with no mission. . . ."

But he also began to sound self-absorbed and oddly uninterested in global issues. He would admit to no mistakes, no errors of judgment. Failure to anticipate the size of the Chinese invasion, for example, had been the fault of the CIA. Any operation he commanded was crucial; other considerations were always of less importance. Certain that his strategy of war on China would not bring in the Soviets, he belittled the danger of a larger conflict. But what if he happened to be wrong? he was asked. What if another world war resulted? That, said MacArthur, was not his responsibility. "My responsibilities were in the Pacific, and the Joint Chiefs of Staff and various agencies of the Government are working night and day for an over-all solution to the global problem. Now I am not familiar with their studies. I haven't gone into it. . . ." To many, it seemed he had made the president's case.

The great turning point came with the testimony of Marshall, Bradley, and the Joint Chiefs, who refuted absolutely MacArthur's claim that they agreed with his strategy. Truman, from the start of the crisis, had known he needed the full support of his military advisers before declaring his decision about MacArthur. Now it was that full support, through nineteen days of testimony, that not only gave weight and validity to the decision but discredited MacArthur in a way nothing else could have.

Never, said the Joint Chiefs, had they subscribed to MacArthur's plan for victory, however greatly they admired him. The dismissal of MacArthur, said all of them—Marshall, Bradley, the Joint Chiefs—was more than warranted; it was a necessity. Given the circumstances, given the seriousness of MacArthur's opposition to the policy of the president, his challenge to presidential authority, there had been no other course. The fidelity of the military high command to the principle of civilian control of the military was total and unequivocal.

Such unanimity of opinion on the part of the country's foremost and most respected military leaders seemed to leave Republican senators stunned. As James Reston wrote in *The New York Times*, "MacArthur, who had started as the prosecutor, had now become the defendant."

The hearings ground on and grew increasingly dull. The MacArthur hysteria was over; interest waned. When, in June, MacArthur set off on a speaking tour through Texas, insisting he had no presidential ambitions, he began to sound more and more shrill and vindictive, less and less like a hero. He attacked Truman, appeasement, high taxes, and "insidious forces working from within." His crowds grew steadily smaller. Nationwide, the polls showed a sharp decline in his popular appeal. The old soldier was truly beginning to fade away.

Truman would regard the decision to fire MacArthur as among the most important he made as president. He did not, however, agree with those who said it had shown what great courage he had. (Harriman, among others, would later speak of it as one of the most courageous steps ever taken by any president.) "Courage didn't have anything to do with it," Truman would say emphatically. "General MacArthur was insubordinate and I fired him. That's all there was to it."

But if the firing of MacArthur had taken a heavy toll politically, if Truman as president had been less than a master of persuasion, he had accomplished a very great deal and demonstrated extraordinary patience and strength of character in how he rode out the storm. His policy in Korea—his determined effort to keep the conflict in bounds—had not been scuttled, however great the aura of the hero-general, or his powers as a spellbinder. The principle of civilian control over the military, challenged as never before in the nation's history, had survived, and stronger than ever. The president had made his point and, with the backing of his generals, he had made it stick.

The Man Who Saved Korea

THOMAS FLEMING

One has to go back almost to 1914 and the Battle of the Marne to find military fortunes that seesawed as breathlessly as those first months of the Korean War. First there was the surprise North Korean attack and the drive that penned in a battered and demoralized U.N. force and the remnants of the South Korean army in the Pusan Perimeter, that small southeastern corner of the Korean peninsula. Then came another surprise, this time an American one, the September 15 landing at Inchon, the port of Seoul, the final masterstroke of Douglas MacArthur's career, and the melting away of the North Korean army, followed by the advance to Pyongyang, the North Korean capital. A few U.N. units got as far as the Yalu River, which separated North Korea from China. The war—which Truman (in a phrase that would come back to haunt him) termed a "police action"—seemed as good as over. MacArthur predicted that the bulk of his troops would be "home in time for Christmas." That was at the end of October 1950, just four months after the fighting had begun. Suddenly, the U.N. faced a new enemy, this time Chinese "volunteers." (The Chinese Communists chose the designation in hopes of avoiding a more widespread war with the U.S.)

The story of how MacArthur misread the signs has been told many times. The immediate cause of the Chinese intervention seemed to be his decision to advance above the 38th Parallel and strike for the Yalu. (The British were antsy, afraid that the Chinese would use the attack into North Korea as a pretext to seize Hong Kong.) But apparently, Mao had taken Truman's sending of the Seventh Fleet to patrol the Straits of Taiwan as an act of war, even though its actual purpose was to prevent the broadening of hostilities. Washington, too, misread the signals. It failed to recognize the depth of Chinese resentment caused by the forestalled invasion. Mao reluctantly canceled preparations for the Taiwan invasion in August but had already begun a build-up of forces in northeast China. As his generals advised him, "One should always open an umbrella before it starts to rain." Meanwhile, Stalin, dismayed by the failure of his North Korean gamble, appealed to the Chinese for help. He also promised further military aid to the North Koreans, especially air support.

In the last days of October, the Chinese attacked, badly roughing up the American and ROK vanguard. After a few days, they abruptly withdrew, disappearing into the barren, hilly landscape. It was a warning that MacArthur failed to heed. Though some of his generals urged withdrawing to safer positions, he elected to resume his advance. On November 24, the Americans observed Thanksgiving. No effort was spared to make sure the men of the Eighth Army were served turkey dinners with all the trimmings.

The next day the Chinese attacked. It was a type of warfare that Americans had never experienced and for which they were unprepared. They were in effect facing a huge guerrilla army whose very primitiveness was its greatest strength. No wireless radio activity, movement of tanks, air reconnaissance, or sudden appearance of supply depots had warned of the Chinese approach. They lacked almost all the technological basics of modern war making. They did not advance along roads but swooped down from the hills, usually at night, announcing their coming with drums, bugles, and flutes that unsettled and paralyzed defenders. The mortar, the machine gun, and the grenade were their principal weapons, infiltration their favored tactic. Failure to anticipate, failure to adapt, failure to learn: This, the historian Eliot A. Cohen tells us, is the surest recipe for military misfortune, and the Eighth mastered the combination. In November and December 1950 it suffered one of the notable defeats in the history of American wars.

Seoul fell again; the Chinese pushed the U.N. forces back a hundred miles, and the commander of the Eighth Army died in a jeep accident. The prospect of an American Dunkirk loomed. (The mid-December evacuation of the X Corps from Hungnam, accomplished without panic or loss, was just that.) There was, to be sure, the epic withdrawal of the 1st Marine Division from the frozen Chosin Reservoir, which amounted, Martin Russ has written, to "a series of tactical victories within the overall context of a strategic defeat." In Washington and Tokyo desperation mounted. Should we drop atomic bombs on China? Unleash Chiang to invade the mainland? Blockade China? Would the Soviets choose this moment to invade Europe, using the atomic bombs that they now had? The end of 1950 had to be one of the most dangerous moments in the Cold War.

This was the situation that the new Eighth Army commander, Lieutenant General Matthew B. Ridgway, faced when he arrived in Korea the day after Christmas. Ridgway's revival of that army, Thomas Fleming writes here, became "the stuff of legends, a paradigm of American generalship." It was a leadership feat that has to be as notable as the disaster that preceded it.

THOMAS FLEMING is the author of more than forty books, including *The New Dealers' War: FDR and the War Within World War II; Duel: Alexander Hamilton, Aaron Burr, and the Future of America; Liberty!: The American Revolution; The Illusion of Victory: America in World War I;* and *Washington's Secret War: The Hidden History of Valley Forge.*

I F YOU ASKED A GROUP of average Americans to name the greatest general of the twentieth century, most would nominate Dwight Eisenhower, the master politician who organized the Allied invasion of Europe, or Douglas MacArthur, a leader in both world wars, or George C. Marshall, the architect of victory in World War II. John J. Pershing and George S. Patton would also get a fair number of votes. But if you ask professional soldiers that question, a surprising number of them will reply: "Ridgway."

When they pass this judgment, they are not thinking of the general who excelled as a division commander and an army corps commander in World War II. Many other men distinguished themselves in those roles. The soldiers are remembering the general who rallied a beaten Eighth Army from the brink of defeat in Korea in 1951.

The son of a West Pointer who retired as a colonel of the artillery, Matthew Bunker Ridgway graduated from the U.S. Military Academy in 1917. Even there, although his scholastic record was mediocre, he was thinking about how to become a general. One trait he decided to cultivate was an ability to remember names. By his first-class year, he was able to identify the entire 750-man student body.

To his dismay, instead of being sent into combat in France, Ridgway was ordered to teach Spanish at West Point, an assignment that he was certain meant the death knell of his military career. (As it turned out, it was probably the first of many examples of Ridgway luck; like Eisenhower and Omar Bradley, he escaped the trench mentality that the World War I experience inflicted on too many officers.) Typically, he mastered the language, becoming one of a handful of officers who were fluent in the second tongue of the Western Hemisphere. He stayed at West Point for six years, in the course of which he became acquainted with its controversial young superintendent, Brigadier General Douglas MacArthur, who was trying in vain to stop the academy from still preparing for the War of 1812.

In the 1920s and 1930s, Ridgway's skills as a writer and linguist brought him more staff assignments than he professed to want—troop leadership was the experience that counted on the promotion ladder. But Ridgway's passion for excellence and commitment to the army attracted the attention of a number of people, notably that of a rising star in the generation ahead of him, George Marshall. Ridgway served under Marshall in the 15th Infantry in China in the mid-1930s and was on his general staff in Washington when Pearl Harbor plunged the nation into World War II.

As the army expanded geometrically in the next year, Ridgway acquired two stars and the command of the 82nd Division. When Marshall decided to turn it into an airborne outfit, Ridgway strapped on a parachute and jumped out of a plane for the first time in his life. Returning to his division, he cheerfully reported that there was nothing to the transition to paratrooper. He quieted a lot of apprehension in the division, although he privately admitted to a few friends that "nothing" was like jumping off the top of a moving freight train onto a hard roadbed.

Dropped into Sicily during the night of July 9, 1943, Ridgway's paratroopers survived a series of snafus. Navy gunners shot down twenty of their planes as they came over the Mediterranean from North Africa. In the darkness, their confused pilots scattered them all over the island. Nevertheless, they rescued the invasion by preventing the crack Hermann Göring panzer division from attacking the fragile beachhead and throwing the first invaders of Hitler's Fortress Europe into the sea.

In this campaign, Ridgway displayed many traits that became hallmarks of his generalship. He scorned a rear-area command post. Battalion and even company commanders never knew when they would find Ridgway at their elbow, urging them forward, demanding to know why they were doing this and not that. His close calls with small- and large-caliber enemy fire swiftly acquired legendary proportions. Even Patton, who was not shy about moving forward, ordered Ridgway to stop trying to be the 82nd Division's point man. Ridgway pretty much ignored the order, calling it "a compliment."

From Patton, Ridgway acquired another command habit: the practice of stopping to tell lower ranks—military policemen, engineers building bridges—

they were doing a good job. He noted the remarkable way this could energize an entire battalion, even a regiment. At the same time, Ridgway displayed a ruthless readiness to relieve any officer who did not meet his extremely high standards of battlefield performance. Celerity and aggressiveness were what he wanted. If an enemy force appeared on a unit's front, he wanted an immediate deployment for flank attacks. He did not tolerate commanders who sat down and thought things over for an hour or two.

In the heat of battle, Ridgway also revealed an unrivaled capacity to taunt the enemy. One of his favorite stunts was to stand in the middle of a road under heavy artillery fire and urinate to demonstrate his contempt for German accuracy. Aides and fellow generals repeatedly begged him to abandon this bravado. He ignored them.

Ridgway's experience as an airborne commander spurred the evolution of another trait that made him almost unique among American soldiers—a readiness to question, even to challenge, the policies of his superiors. After the disaster of the Sicily drop, Eisenhower and other generals concluded that division-size airborne operations were impractical. Ridgway fought ferociously to maintain the integrity of his division. Winning that argument, he found himself paradoxically menaced by the widespread conclusion that airborne assault could solve problems with miraculous ease.

General Harold Alexander, the British commander of the Allied invasion of Italy, decided Ridgway's paratroopers were a God-given instrument for disrupting German defense plans. Alexander ordered the 82nd Airborne to jump north of Rome, seize the city, and hold it while the main army drove from their Salerno beachhead to link up with them. Ridgway was appalled. His men would have to fly without escort—Rome was beyond the range of Allied fighters—risking annihilation before they got to the target.

There were at least six elite German divisions near the city, ready and willing to maul the relatively small 82nd Airborne. An airborne division at that point in the war had only eight thousand men. Their heaviest gun was a 75mm pack howitzer, "a peashooter," as Ridgway put it, against tanks. For food, ammunition, fuel, transportation, the Americans were depending on the Italians, who were planning to double-cross the Germans and abandon the war.

Ridgway wangled an interview with General Alexander, who listened to his doubts and airily dismissed them: "Don't give this another thought, Ridgway. Contact will be made with your division in three days—five at the most."

Ridgway was in a quandary. He could not disobey the direct orders of his superior without destroying his career. He told his division to get ready for the drop, but he refused to abandon his opposition, even though the plan had the enthusiastic backing of Dwight Eisenhower, who was conducting negotiations with the Italians from his headquarters in Algiers. Eisenhower saw the paratroopers as a guarantee that the Americans could protect the Italians from German retribution.

Ridgway discussed the dilemma with Brigadier General Maxwell Taylor, his artillery officer, who volunteered to go to Rome incognito and confer with the Italians on the ground. Ridgway took this offer to General Walter Bedell Smith, Alexander's American chief of staff, along with more strenuous arguments against the operation.

Smith persuaded Alexander to approve Taylor's mission. Taylor and an air corps officer traveled to Rome disguised as captured airmen and met Field Marshal Pietro Badoglio, the acting prime minister, who was in charge of the negotiations. Meanwhile, plans for the drop proceeded at a dozen airfields in Sicily. If Taylor found the Italians unable to keep their promises of support, he was to send a radio message with the code word "innocuous" in it.

In Rome, Taylor met Badoglio and was appalled by what he heard. The Germans were wise to the Italians' scheme and had reinforced their divisions around Rome. The 3rd Panzer Grenadier Division alone now had 24,000 men and 200 tanks—enough firepower to annihilate the 82nd Airborne twice over. A frantic Taylor sent three separate messages over different channels to stop the operation, but word did not reach the 82nd until sixty-two planes loaded with paratroopers were on the runways warming their engines. Ridgway sat down with his chief of staff, shared a bottle of whiskey, and wept with relief.

Looking back years later, Ridgway declared that when the time came for him to meet his maker, his greatest source of pride would be not his accomplishments in battle but his decision to oppose the Rome drop. He also liked to point out that it took seven months for the Allied army to reach the Eternal City.

Repeatedly risking his career in this unprecedented fashion, Ridgway was trying to forge a different kind of battle leadership. He had studied the appalling slaughters of World War I and was determined that they should never happen again. He believed "the same dignity attaches to the mission given a single soldier as to the duties of the commanding general. . . . All lives are equal on the battlefield, and a dead rifleman is as great a loss in the sight of God as a dead general."

In the Normandy invasion, Ridgway had no difficulty accepting the 82nd's task. Once more, his men had to surmount a mismanaged airdrop in which paratroopers drowned at sea and in swamps and lost 60 percent of their equipment. Ridgway found himself alone in a pitch-dark field. He consoled himself with the thought that "at least if no friends were visible, neither were any foes." Ten miles away, his second in command, James Gavin, took charge of most of the fighting for the next twenty-four hours. The paratroopers captured only one of their assigned objectives, but it was a crucial one, the town of Sainte-Mère-Eglise, which blocked German armor from attacking Utah Beach. Ridgway was given a third star and command of the XVIII Airborne Corps.

By this time he inspired passionate loyalty in the men around him. Often it surfaced in odd ways. One day he was visiting a wounded staff officer in an aid station. A paratrooper on the stretcher next to him said, "Still sticking your neck out, huh, General?" Ridgway never forgot the remark. For him it represented the affection one combat soldier feels for another.

Less well known than his D-Day accomplishments was Ridgway's role in the Battle of the Bulge. When the Germans smashed into the Ardennes in late December 1944, routing American divisions along a seventy-five-mile front, Ridgway's airborne corps again became a fire brigade. The "battling bastards of Bastogne"—the 101st Airborne led by Brigadier General Anthony McAuliffe—got most of the publicity for foiling the German lunge toward Antwerp. But many historians credit Ridgway's defense of the key road junction of Saint-Vith as a far more significant contribution to the victory.

Ridgway acquired a visual trademark, a hand grenade attached to his paratrooper's shoulder harness on one side and a first-aid kit, often mistaken for a second grenade, on the other strap. He insisted both were for practical use, not for picturesque effect like Patton's pearl-handled pistols. In his jeep he carried an old .30-06 Springfield rifle, loaded with armor-piercing cartridges. On foot one day, deep in the Ardennes forest, trying to find a battalion CP, he was carrying the gun when he heard a "tremendous clatter." Through the trees he saw what looked like a light tank with a large swastika on its side. He fired five quick shots at the Nazi symbol and crawled away on his belly through the snow. The vehicle turned out to be a self-propelled gun. Inside it, paratroopers who responded to the shots found five dead Germans.

This was the man—now at the Pentagon, as deputy chief of staff for administration and training—whom the army chose to rescue the situation in Korea when the Chinese swarmed over the Yalu River in early December 1950 and sent EUSAK (the Eighth U.S. Army in Korea) reeling in headlong retreat. Capping the disarray was the death of the field commander, stumpy Major General Walton "Johnnie" Walker, in a jeep accident. Ridgway's first stop was Tokyo, where he was briefed by the supreme commander, Douglas MacArthur. After listening to a pessimistic summary of the situation, Ridgway asked, "General, if I get over there and find the situation warrants it, do I have your permission to attack?"

"Do what you think best, Matt," MacArthur responded. "The Eighth Army is yours."

MacArthur was giving Ridgway freedom—and responsibility—he had never given Walker. The reason was soon obvious: MacArthur was trying to distance himself from a looming disaster. Morale in the Eighth Army had deteriorated alarmingly while they retreated before the oncoming Chinese. "Bugout fever" was endemic. Within hours of arriving to take command, Ridgway abandoned his hopes for an immediate offensive. His first job was to restore this beaten army's will to fight.

He went at it with incredible verve and energy. Strapping on his parachute harness with its hand grenade and first-aid kit, he toured the front for three days in an open jeep in bitter cold. "I held to the old-fashioned idea that it helped the spirits of the men to see the Old Man up there in the snow and sleet . . . sharing the same cold miserable existence they had to endure," he said. But Ridgway admitted that until a kindhearted major dug up a pile-lined cap and warm gloves for him, he "damn near froze."

Everywhere he went, Ridgway exercised his fabulous memory for faces. At this point he could recognize an estimated five thousand men at a glance. He dazzled old sergeants and MPs on lonely roads by remembering not only their names but where they had met and what they had said to each other.

But this trick was not enough to revive EUSAK. Everywhere Ridgway found the men unresponsive, reluctant to answer his questions, even to air their gripes. The defeatism ran from privates through sergeants all the way up to generals. Ridgway was particularly appalled by the atmosphere in the Eighth Army's main command post in Taegu. There they were frantically planning how to avoid a Dunkirk.

In his first forty-eight hours, Ridgway had met with all his American corps and division commanders and all but one of the Republic of Korea division commanders. He told them, as he had told the staffers in Taegu, that he had no plans whatsoever to evacuate Korea. He reiterated what he had told Korean president Syngman Rhee in their meeting: "I've come to stay."

But words could not restore the nerve of many top commanders. Ridgway's reaction to this defeatism was drastic: He cabled the Pentagon that he wanted to relieve almost every division commander and artillery commander in EUSAK. He also supplied his bosses with a list of younger fighting generals he wanted to replace the losers. This demand caused political palpitations in Washington, where MacArthur's growing quarrel with President Harry Truman's policy was becoming a nightmare. Ridgway eventually got rid of his losers, but not in one ferocious sweep. The ineffective generals were sent home singly over the next few months as part of a "rotation policy."

Meanwhile, in a perhaps calculated bit of shock treatment, Ridgway visited I Corps and asked the G-3 to brief him on their battle plans. The officer described plans to withdraw to "successive positions."

"What are your attack plans?" Ridgway growled.

The officer floundered. "Sir—we are withdrawing." There were no attack plans.

"Colonel, you are relieved," Ridgway said.

That is how the Eighth Army heard the story. Actually, Ridgway ordered the G-3's commanding officer to relieve him, which probably intensified the shock effect on the entire corps. Many officers felt, perhaps with some justice, that Ridgway was brutally unfair to the G-3, who was only carrying out the corps commander's orders. But Ridgway obviously felt that the crisis justified brutality.

As for the lower ranks, Ridgway took immediate steps to satisfy some of their gripes. Warmer clothing was urgently demanded from the States. Stationery to write letters home, and to wounded buddies, was shipped to the front lines, and steak and chicken were added to the menu, with a ferocious insistence that meals be served hot.

Regimental, division, and corps commanders were told in language Ridgway admitted was "often impolite" that it was time to abandon creature comforts and shed their timidity about getting off the roads and into the hills, where the enemy was holding the high ground. Again and again Ridgway repeated the ancient army slogan "Find them! Fix them! Fight them! Finish them!"

As he shuttled across the front in a light plane or a helicopter, Ridgway studied the terrain beneath him. He was convinced a massive Communist offensive was imminent. He not only wanted to contain it, he wanted to inflict maximum punishment on the enemy. He knew that for the time being, he would have to give some ground, but he wanted the price to be high. South of the Han River, he assigned Brigadier General Garrison Davidson, a talented engineer, to take charge of several thousand Korean laborers and create a "deep defensive zone" with a trench system, barbed wire, and artillery positions.

Ridgway also preached defense in depth to his division and regimental commanders in the lines they were holding north of the Han. Although they lacked the manpower to halt the Chinese night attacks, he said that by buttoning up tight, unit by unit, at night and counterattacking strongly with armor and infantry teams during the day, the U.N. army could inflict severe punishment on anyone who had come through the gaps in their line. At the same time, Ridgway ordered that no unit be abandoned if cut off. It was to be "fought for" and rescued unless a "major commander" after "personal appraisal" Ridgway-style—from the front lines—decided its relief would cost as many or more men.

Finally, in this race against the looming Chinese offensive, Ridgway tried to fill another void in the spirit of his men. He knew they were asking one another, "What the hell are we doing here in this God-forgotten spot?" One night he sat down at his desk in his room in Seoul and tried to answer that question.

His first reasons were soldierly: They had orders to fight from the president of the United States, and they were defending the freedom of South Korea. But the real issues were deeper—"whether the power of Western civilization, as God has permitted it to flower in our own beloved lands, shall defy and defeat Communism; whether the rule of men who shoot their prisoners, enslave their citizens and deride the dignity of man, shall displace the rule of those to whom the individual and his individual rights are sacred." In that context, Ridgway wrote, "the sacrifices we have made, and those we shall yet support, are not offered vicariously for others but in our own direct defense."

On New Year's Eve, the Chinese and North Koreans attacked with all-out fury. The Eighth Army defenders, Ridgway wrote, "were killing them by the thousands," but they kept coming. They smashed huge holes in the center of Ridgway's battle line, where ROK divisions broke and ran. Ridgway was not surprised; having met their generals, he knew most had little more than a company commander's experience or expertise. Few armies in existence had taken a worse beating than the ROKs in the first six months of the war.

By January 2 it was evident that the Eighth Army would have to move south of the Han River and abandon Seoul. As he left his headquarters, Ridgway pulled from his musette bag a pair of striped flannel pajama pants "split beyond repair in the upper posterior region." He tacked them to the wall, the worn-out

seat flapping. Above them, in block letters, he left a message: TO THE COM-
MANDING GENERAL CHINESE COMMUNIST FORCES WITH THE COMPLIMENTS OF
THE COMMANDING GENERAL EIGHTH ARMY. The story swept through the ranks
with predictable effect.

The Eighth Army fell back fifteen miles south of the Han to the defensive
line prepared by General Davidson and his Korean laborers. They retreated, in
Ridgway's words, "as a fighting army, not as a running mob." They brought with
them all their equipment and, most important, their pride. They settled into
the elaborate defenses and waited for the Chinese to try again. The battered
Communists chose to regroup. Ridgway decided it was time to come off the
floor with some Sunday punches of his own.

He set up his advanced command post on a bare bluff at Yoju, about one
third of the way across the peninsula, equidistant from the I Corps and X Corps
headquarters. For the first few weeks, he operated with possibly the smallest
staff of any American commander of a major army. Although EUSAK's force of
350,000 men was in fact the largest field army ever led by an American general,
Ridgway's staff consisted of just six people: two aides, one orderly, a driver for
his jeep, and a driver and radio operator for the radio jeep that followed him
everywhere. He lived in two tents, placed end to end to create a sort of two-
room apartment and heated by a small gasoline stove. Isolated from the social
and military formalities of the main CP at Taegu, Ridgway had time for "uninterrupted concentration" on his counteroffensive.

Nearby was a crudely leveled airstrip from which he took off repeatedly to
study the terrain in front of him. He combined this personal reconnaissance
with intensive study of relief maps provided by the Army Map Service — "a
priceless asset." Soon his incredible memory had absorbed the terrain of the entire front, and "every road, every cart track, every hill, every stream, every ridge
in that area . . . we hoped to control . . . became as familiar to me as . . . my own
backyard," he later wrote. When he ordered an advance into a sector, he knew
exactly what it might involve for his infantrymen.

On January 25, with a thunderous eruption of massed artillery, the Eighth
Army went over to the attack in Operation Thunderbolt. The goal was the Han
River, which would make the enemy's grip on Seoul untenable. The offensive
was a series of carefully planned advances to designated "phase lines," beyond
each of which no one advanced until every assigned unit reached it. Again and
again Ridgway stressed the importance of having good coordination, inflicting
maximum punishment, and keeping major units intact. He called it "good

footwork combined with firepower." The men in the lines called it "the meat grinder."

To jaundiced observers in the press, the army's performance was miraculous. Rene Cutforth of the BBC wrote, "Exactly how and why the new army was transformed . . . from a mob of dispirited boobs . . . to a tough resilient force is still a matter for speculation and debate." A *Time* correspondent came closest to explaining it: "The boys aren't up there fighting for democracy now. They're fighting because the platoon leader is leading them and the platoon leader is fighting because of the command, and so on right up to the top."

By February 10 the Eighth Army had its left flank anchored on the Han and had captured Inchon and Seoul's Kimpo Airfield. After fighting off a ferocious Chinese counterattack on Lincoln's birthday, Ridgway launched offensives from his center and right flank with equal success. In one of these, paratroopers were used to trap a large number of Chinese between them and an armored column. Ridgway was sorely tempted to jump with them, but he realized it would be "a damn fool thing" for an army commander to do. Instead, he landed on a road in his light plane about a half hour after the paratroopers hit the ground.

M-1s were barking all around him. At one point a dead Chinese came rolling down a hill and dangled from a bank above Ridgway's head. His pilot, an ex-infantryman, grabbed a carbine out of the plane and joined the shooting. Ridgway stood in the road, feeling "that lifting of the spirits, that sudden quickening of the breath and the sudden sharpening of all the senses that comes to a man in the midst of battle." None of his exploits in Korea better demonstrates why he was able to communicate a fierce appetite for combat to his men.

Still another incident dramatized Ridgway's instinctive sympathy for the lowliest private in his ranks. In early March he was on a hillside watching a battalion of the 1st Marine Division moving up for an attack. In the line was a gaunt boy with a heavy radio on his back. He kept stumbling over an untied shoelace. "Hey, how about one of you sonsabitches tying my shoe?" he howled to his buddies. Ridgway slid down the snowy bank, landed at the boy's feet, and tied the laces.

Fifty-four days after Ridgway took command, the Eighth Army had driven the Communists across the 38th Parallel, inflicting enormous losses with every mile they advanced. The reeling enemy began surrendering by the hundreds. Seoul was recaptured on March 14, a symbolic defeat of tremendous proportions to the Communists' political ambitions. Ridgway felt "supremely confident" his men could take "any objective" assigned to them. "The American flag never flew over a prouder, tougher, more spirited and more competent fighting force than was the Eighth Army as it drove north beyond the parallel," he declared. But he agreed with President Truman's decision to stop at the parallel and seek a negotiated truce.

In Tokyo his immediate superior, General Douglas MacArthur, did not agree and let his opinion resound through the media. On April 11, Ridgway was at the front in a snowstorm, supervising final plans for an attack on the Chinese stronghold of Ch'orwon, when a correspondent said, "Well, General, I guess congratulations are in order." That was how he learned that Truman had fired MacArthur and given Ridgway the job of supreme commander in the Far East and America's proconsul in Japan.

Ridgway was replaced as Eighth Army commander by Lieutenant General James Van Fleet, who continued Ridgway's policy of using coordinated firepower, rolling with Communist counterpunches, and inflicting maximum casualties. Peace talks and occasionally bitter fighting dragged on for another twenty-eight months, but there was never any doubt that EUSAK was in Korea to stay. Ridgway and Van Fleet built the ROK army into a formidable force during these months. They also successfully integrated black and white troops in EUSAK.

Later, Ridgway tried to combine his "profound respect" for Douglas MacArthur and his conviction that President Truman had done the right thing in relieving him. Ridgway maintained that MacArthur had every right to make his views heard in Washington, but not to disagree publicly with the president's decision to fight a limited war in Korea. Ridgway, with his deep concern for the individual soldier, accepted the concept of limited war fought for sharply defined goals as the only sensible doctrine in the nuclear age.

After leaving the Far East, Ridgway would go on to become head of NATO in Europe and chairman of the Joint Chiefs of Staff under President Eisenhower. Ironically, at the end of his career, he would find himself in a MacArthuresque position. Secretary of Defense Charles E. "Engine Charlie" Wilson had persuaded Ike to slash the defense budget, with 76 percent of the cuts falling on the army. Wilson latched on to Secretary of State John Foster Dulles's foreign policy, which relied on the threat of massive nuclear retaliation to intimidate the Communists. Wilson thought he could get more bang for the buck by giving almost half the funds in the budget to the air force.

Ridgway refused to go along with Eisenhower. In testimony before Congress, he strongly disagreed with the administration's policy. He insisted it was important that the United States be able to fight limited wars without nuclear weapons. He said massive retaliation was "repugnant to the ideals of a Christian nation" and incompatible with the basic aim of the United States, "a just and durable peace."

Eisenhower was infuriated, but Ridgway stood his ground—and then proceeded to take yet another stand that angered top members of the administration. In early 1954 the French army was on the brink of collapse in Vietnam. Secretary of State Dulles and a number of other influential voices wanted the United States to intervene. Alarmed, Ridgway sent a team of army experts to Vietnam to assess the situation. They came back with grim information.

Vietnam, they reported, was not a promising place to fight a modern war. It had almost nothing a modern army needed: good highways, port facilities, airfields, railways. Everything would have to be built from scratch. Moreover, the native population was politically unreliable, and the jungle terrain was made to order for guerrilla warfare. The experts estimated that to win the war, the United States would have to commit more troops than had been sent to Korea.

Ridgway sent the report up through channels to Eisenhower. A few days later, he was told to have one of his staff give a logistic briefing on Vietnam to the president. Ridgway gave it himself. Eisenhower listened impassively and asked only a few questions, but it was clear to Ridgway that the president understood the implications. With minimum fanfare, Eisenhower ruled against intervention.

For reasons that still puzzle historians, no one in the Kennedy administration ever displayed the slightest interest in the Ridgway report—not even Kennedy's secretary of state, Dean Rusk, who, as assistant secretary of state for Far Eastern affairs in 1950–51, knew and admired what Ridgway had achieved in Korea. As Ridgway left office, Rusk wrote him a fulsome letter telling him he had "saved your country from the humiliation of defeat through the loss of morale in high places."

The report on Vietnam was almost the last act of Ridgway's long career as an American soldier. Determined to find a team player, Eisenhower did not invite him to spend a second term as chief of staff, as was customary. Nor was he offered another job elsewhere. Although Ridgway officially retired, his departure was clearly understood by Washington insiders as that rarest of things in the U.S. Army, a resignation in protest.

After leaving the army in 1955, Ridgway became chairman and chief executive officer of the Mellon Institute of Industrial Research in Pittsburgh. He retired from this post in 1960 and lived to the age of ninety-eight. He died in 1993.

When Ridgway was leaving Japan to become commander of NATO, he told James Michener, "I cannot subscribe to the idea that civilian thought per se is any more valid than military thought." Without abandoning his traditional obedience to his civilian superiors, Ridgway insisted on his right to be a thinking man's soldier—the same soldier who talked back to his military superiors when he thought their plans were likely to lead to the "needless sacrifice of priceless lives."

David Halberstam is among those who believe that Ridgway's refusal to go along with intervention in Vietnam was his finest hour. Halberstam called him the "one hero" of his book on America's involvement in Vietnam, *The Best and the Brightest.* But for the student of military history, the Ridgway of Korea towers higher. His achievement proved that the doctrine of limited war can work, provided those fighting it are led by someone who knows how to ignite their pride and confidence as soldiers. Ridgway's revival of the Eighth Army is the stuff of legends, a paradigm of American generalship. Omar Bradley put it best: "His brilliant, driving uncompromising leadership [turned] the tide of battle like no other general's in our military history." Not long after Ridgway's arrival in Korea, one of the lower ranks summed up EUSAK's new spirit with a wisecrack: "From now on there's a right way, a wrong way, and a Ridgway."

The First Jet War

DENNIS E. SHOWALTER

In Korea, jets fought jets for the first time in history. The world's first actual jet encounter took place near the Yalu River on November 8, 1950, when MiG-15s, the best and newest Soviet frontline fighters, attacked a formation of American B-29s escorted by F-80 jets. Lieutenant Russell Brown brought down the first Communist jet to be lost over Korea. "As Communist troops swept across the Yalu . . . and sliced through overextended and overconfident U.N. ground forces," Dennis E. Showalter writes here, "the MiG-15 seemed poised to reverse the course of the air war." It never did, largely because it soon came up against a fighter that was its equal, the F-86 Sabrejet. For the next two and a half years, the planes would duel over the area of North Korea south of the Yalu and bordering the Yellow Sea that U.N. pilots nicknamed "MiG Alley."

The first MiG-15 pilots were mainly Soviets and Poles. Chinese pilots did not show up until the spring of 1951, and there were never many North Koreans. (We sometimes forget how genuinely international the Korean War was.) "Incidents" may have occurred during the Cold War, but this was the only instance in those four decades and more when Americans and Russians traded shots in anger over a prolonged period. According to a CIA report in the summer of 1952, "a de facto air war exists over North Korea between the UN and the USSR." Apparently, as many as seventy-two thousand Soviet air personnel rotated in and out of Chinese airfields, those frustratingly "privileged sanctuaries" that U.N. airmen were forbidden to attack. (There were times when U.N. pilots violated this order.) The original Soviet airmen belonged to elite units that had been stationed around Moscow. Their initial mission was to intercept and destroy the B-29 bombers, propeller-driven behemoths from

World War II, that were destroying what little transportation and manufacturing infrastructure North Korea possessed, much of it in MiG Alley. But the Soviet pilots, many of whom were Eastern Front veterans, regarded Korea as an opportunity for a refresher course in aerial combat; younger men made it their finishing school. Although their MiG-15s bore the red wing stars of the Soviet air force, the pilots otherwise took elaborate precautions to conceal their identities. They dressed in Chinese uniforms, refrained as much as possible from speaking Russian in radio transmissions, and never (except through the rare mistake) flew over U.N.-held territory or over the sea. It is recorded that one MiG-15 pilot, downed behind U.N. lines, shot himself rather than be captured and interrogated. Another, who crashed in the sea and managed to swim free of his sinking aircraft, was strafed and killed by fellow pilots as a U.N. patrol boat rushed to rescue him. Stalin did not want to present the West with a pretext for starting World War III. American leaders were just as wary. Even after he learned of the Soviet involvement, President Dwight D. Eisenhower kept quiet, out of fear that conservatives in Congress might push for retaliation if they got wind of it.

Though Stalin came to believe that his unleashing of the North Koreans had been a mistake, the old man still took consolation in contemplating the huge U.N. air losses, which his lieutenants led him to believe were mostly the handiwork of his MiG-15s. The losses, as Showalter acknowledges here, were indeed great; ground fire, not the dogfights of MiG Alley, accounted for most of them. As for air battles with MiG-15s, Sabrejets actually earned a respectable advantage in kill ratio—and did even better at the end of the war, as Chinese and North Korean pilots took over from the Soviets.

Korea may have been the first jet war, but piston-driven propeller planes still had their pride of place, including some famous names out of World War II, such as YAKs, Sturmoviks, Mustangs, Corsairs, B-26 Invaders, and B-29 Superfortresses. In the last year of the Pacific War, the B-29 had ranged over the Japanese Home Islands, practically unopposed by enemy fighters. That was not the case in the Korean War when these ponderous targets were jumped by MiG-15s; they were forced to begin flying only at night. That did not prevent the B-29s from turning much of North Korea into a vast crater field. They firebombed cities like Pyongyang with napalm, something that gave Prime Minister Winston

Churchill pause. "I do not like this napalm bombing at all," he told an acquaintance, adding, "We should make a very great mistake to commit ourselves to approval of a very cruel form of warfare. . . . I will take no responsibility for it." As Stanley Sandler points out in his excellent summation, *The Korean War,* "In light of the death tolls of the Tokyo fire raids, the two nuclear bombings, and of similar raids on Pyongyang and Sinuiju, the B-29 can be said to have killed more civilians than any other aircraft in history."

American bombs may have come close to rending the social fabric of North Korea, but they did not keep supplies from the front or otherwise help to end the war. By the time a truce was signed in July 1953, the Communist armies were better fed than they had ever been and were able to lay down mass barrages that even a World War I artilleryman would not have disparaged.

In Korea, the past may have been recaptured on the ground. But in the sky, the future took shape.

DENNIS E. SHOWALTER is the past president of the Society for Military History, joint editor of the journal *War in History,* and the author of *The Wars of German Unification* and *Tannenberg: Clash of Empires.* He is a professor of history at Colorado College.

ON THE AFTERNOON OF JUNE 27, 1950, eight Soviet-built, piston-engined IL-10 attack planes of the North Korean Air Force were attacked over Kimpo Airfield by four American jet fighters, F-80 Shooting Stars. Within minutes, four of the North Korean planes were down. Lieutenants R. E. Wayne—who shot down two planes—and R. E. Dewald and Captain Raymond Schillereff had scored the first jet kills of the U.S. Air Force. But this historical milestone was not the first American victory of the air war. That same morning, five North Korean fighters had tangled with an equal number of U.S. planes and lost three of their number to an aircraft that was little more than a footnote in aviation history. The F-82 Twin Mustang, essentially two P-51 fuselages linked by a stub wing and a tail section, had been cobbled together in the aftermath of post-1945 budget cuts as an interim night fighter and long-range escort.

These two very different encounters reflected the ambiguous nature of the air war over Korea. Jet aircraft had made their first appearances during the final stages of World War II. Nazi Germany's Messerschmitt 262 jet fighter was not the potential war winner of legend. Nevertheless, it shocked the U.S. Eighth Air Force even in the small numbers the Luftwaffe finally deployed. The Allies were slow to react. Britain managed to send a single squadron of Gloster Meteors, roughly similar to the Me 262, into combat before V-E Day, but the German jet's only losses came when two of them collided while returning to base. The United States began designing and ordering jets during the war, but none came into service until after 1945. The Soviet Union was even further behind. Both superpowers depended heavily on German jet technology once it became available.

Were jets the wave of air power's future? In principle, it seemed so—until the shooting started over Korea. On the one hand, jet fighters, by now entering a second design generation represented by the swept-wing MiG-15s and F-86 Sabres, dominated the peninsula's skies whenever they were present. But at the same time, piston-engined veterans of World War II like the Mustang, the F4U Corsair, the B-26 light bomber, and the B-29 Superfortress played vital roles in the air campaign from the Pusan Perimeter to the armistice at Panmunjom. Nor were these old warhorses kept in service merely for want of more modern alternatives. The U.S. Navy's propeller-driven AD Skyraider saw its first combat in Korea. Fifteen years later, it was to play a major role in Vietnam.

The air war was complicated by politics as well as technology. For the first time in their respective histories, all four of the U.S. armed services were directly and primarily involved in the same combat zone. World War II's scope had been sufficiently broad that the U.S. Army, Army Air Forces, Navy, and Marine Corps were usually able to find enough for their aircraft to do without getting in one another's way. In Korea, doctrines and policies on the use of airpower clashed directly. At stake were the military budgets and the nature of national strategies for years, if not decades, to come.

The North Korean invasion began on June 25, 1950. U.S. transport aircraft began evacuating Americans from Seoul the next day. As South Korean defenses crumbled, U.S. ground troops were committed as well, with the first units landing on July 1. Even before their arrival, U.S. combat planes were executing the three types of missions that would define the air war: air superiority, close air support, and interdiction.

Any question of the immediate priority of driving the North Koreans from the sky was settled on June 29, when General Douglas MacArthur flew to Suwon to observe the fighting personally. Almost as if planned, four North Korean fighters tried to attack the airfield. All were shot down by Mustangs, but five-star generals seldom appreciate being used as targets. MacArthur promptly fixed control of the air as a primary campaign objective. Whether flying jets or propeller-driven planes, U.S. pilots, often seasoned in the great air battles of World War II, proved exponentially superior to their enemies. In a matter of days, the Americans virtually owned the skies over the Korean peninsula.

How could that advantage be put to best use? Since its emergence from the army's shadow beginning in the 1930s, the U.S. Air Force—which became an independent branch of the armed services in 1947—had been committed to the concept of airpower as an autonomous entity. During World War II, its energies had been focused on striking directly at an enemy's economic and psychological centers. Now Major General Emmett O'Donnell, commanding Far East Air Forces Bomber Command, recommended that North Korea be told "to stop the aggression and get back over the thirty-eighth parallel or they had better have their wives and children and bedrolls to go down with them, because there is not going to be anything left up in Korea to return to."

O'Donnell's apocalyptic rhetoric found little favor with the Joint Chiefs of Staff, who feared both having to rebuild what the Superfortresses had demolished and acquiring a reputation as aerial terrorists. President Harry Truman, adamant that fighting be confined to the Korean peninsula, was even more reluctant to risk provoking the Soviet Union and Communist China with an all-out bomber offensive.

The airmen had more immediate problems to consider. Far from intimidating the North Koreans, American ground troops had proved unable to check a retreat that seemed ready to become a disaster. As U.S. and South Korean troops pulled back in increasing disorder, everything with wings was thrown in to strike everything wearing a red star and moving south. The North Korean army was not a self-sustaining light-infantry force; it was heavily motorized, depending on trucks for logistical support. Crowded onto South Korea's limited road network, North Korean vehicles were destroyed by the thousands during the war's first months. North Korean troops went hungry; North Korean gas tanks, unfilled; North Korean weapons, empty.

Interdiction of the battlefield was complemented by an increasing emphasis on direct air support of ground troops. Even in World War II, this had not been a high institutional priority for an air force whose doctrines and commanders alike consistently warned against the risks of tying aircraft too closely to ground operations. But with the North Korean Air Force destroyed and strategic bombardment limited for reasons of national policy, MacArthur's command had a surplus of planes available to strike ground targets.

But were they the right planes? The principal aircraft initially committed to ground-support missions, the F-80 jet, had such high fuel consumption that its loiter time over Korea was restricted to a half hour. It was so fragile that it could not be deployed to primitive Korean forward bases. In the summer of 1950, a half-dozen F-80 squadrons turned in their jets for F-51s. The Mustang's liquid-cooled engine, however, made it less than an ideal fighter-bomber: Even a small-caliber bullet could inflict fatal damage. Mustang squadrons suffered over twice the losses of jet formations on similar missions. An air force firmly committed in principle to becoming all-jet responded by equipping F-80s with wing tanks, improving their strike capabilities, and insisting they were better overall fighter-bombers than their piston-engined counterparts.

An alternative position emerged when the 1st Provisional Marine Brigade began arriving at Pusan in August. From Tarawa through the Marianas to Iwo Jima and Okinawa, the experience of World War II had suggested to the Marine Corps that aircraft flown by marines and controlled by marines could save marine lives by promptly and precisely striking small targets. The brigade sent to Korea in the summer of 1950 included an organic air group with no jets but three squadrons of Corsairs, two of them fighter-bombers.

The Corsair had seen its first action over Guadalcanal in 1943, and it subsequently established a formidable reputation as a ground-support aircraft. The latest versions used in Korea, the F4U-5 and AG-1, were armed with four 20mm cannon, carried over five thousand pounds of bombs and rockets, and could absorb extremely high levels of damage. Their marine pilots delivered the mail quickly, spectacularly, and with what seemed like millimetric accuracy. Over half their strikes were within a half mile of the front lines. This was in sharp contrast to an air force whose difficulties with air–ground coordination resulted in numerous cases of friendly fire, the most notable being the napalming of a British battalion on September 23, 1950.

Air support for MacArthur's end-run amphibious landing at Inchon was a marine-and-navy show—and a showcase. The newly organized 1st Marine Division and its army stablemate, the 7th Division, enjoyed air power à la carte. Ground-control parties could summon almost at will Corsairs and Skyraiders already in orbit with full combat loads. Army general Edward Almond, in operational command of the Inchon campaign, embraced marine concepts of close support with the zeal of a convert, insisting at every opportunity to the correspondents who flocked to his headquarters that the marines and navy were light-years ahead of an air force that seemed perfectly willing to trade riflemen's lives for doctrinal purity and technical sophistication.

The air force responded by dispatching a study group to Japan. The army sent its own independent investigator, Brigadier General Gerald Higgins. Both sets of reports, based on inquiries conducted in November and December 1950, warned against tunnel vision. Close air support was making headlines in good part because of the initial success of the air-superiority campaign conducted earlier. Even more to the point, the piston-engined planes being praised so highly could not be expected to survive, much less perform, against modern aircraft and air defenses.

These conclusions reflected a major change in the nature of the air war. Despite the restrictions imposed from Washington, U.S. B-29s supported by carrier aircraft had hammered such industrial plants as North Korea possessed to the point that one bored Superfortress crew reported chasing a soldier on a motorcycle and dropping bombs on him until one finally hit. As United Nations ground troops advanced into, then across, North Korea, the bombers ranged closer and closer to the Yalu River border with Communist China, eventually striking not only targets on the Korean side of the riverbank but international bridges across the Yalu as well. China's diplomatic warnings that it would intervene unless the invasion ceased were supported by a growing concentration of aircraft across the Yalu. Mustangs and F-80s easily countered initial sorties by piston-engined YAK-9s. Then, on November 1, 1950, a forward air control plane and its F-51 escort were attacked by—but managed to escape—six jets that looked and performed like nothing ever seen over Korea. They were MiG-15s, the latest Soviet frontline fighter.

Six days later, the MiGs struck again, this time at a B-29 formation and its escort of F-80s. In history's first all-jet air battle, first honors went to Lieutenant Russell Brown, who shot down the first Communist jet to be lost over Korea. The kill reflected pilot skill and a bit of luck rather than any inherent capacities of the F-80. The U.S. jets were clearly outclassed by the MiG, a swept-wing design with a top speed of over 600 miles an hour, a ceiling of 50,000 feet, and an armament of three cannon heavy enough to shred any U.S. aircraft. It owed much of its airframe design to German technology. Its engine was based on British turbojets purchased in 1946—a decision by the newly elected Labour government that allegedly led Joseph Stalin to exclaim, "What fool will sell us his secret?" But the plane itself was archetypically Soviet: compact, simple, and so reliable that it acquired the nickname "aircraft-soldier" from its pilots. As Chinese troops swept across the Yalu in late November and sliced through overextended and overconfident U.N. ground forces, the MiG-15 seemed poised to reverse the course of the air war.

The U.S. Air Force responded with a trump card of its own. On November 8, 1950, the 4th Fighter Interceptor Wing and its F-86A Sabrejets were ordered to Korea. The F-86 had begun as a straight-wing design configuration. Converted to a swept-wing with the aid of the same German technology that contributed to the MiG, it still suffered from a plethora of teething troubles. Like the MiG, the Sabre was intended as an interceptor, not an escort or air-superiority fighter. Even with wing tanks, its combat range was only about five hundred miles, good for no longer than twenty minutes over the Yalu when flying from bases around Seoul. Its armament of six .50-caliber machine guns often did no more than chew at the tough Soviet fighters. Its operational ceiling was lower than that of the MiG, which also could climb faster. What the Sabre had was dive speed, a better gun-sight system—and pilots. The 4th Fighter Interceptor Wing included some of the world's most experienced jet pilots. Also, many were veterans of aerial combat in World War II: men like James Jabara, America's first jet ace, and Colonel Francis Gabreski, who had scored twenty-eight kills against the Luftwaffe. They were to set the measure of the air war in MiG Alley.

Almost 70 percent of the MiGs shot down in Korea fell to men at least twenty-eight years old, with the self-image of cool, calculating professionals, as opposed to the stereotypical fighter jock. Gabreski claimed his first jet kill when his flight spotted a lone MiG at ten thousand feet: "I kept on descending till I was about five hundred feet below—in his blind spot. It took three passes before the MiG went down. I remember one of the guys . . . needling me: 'Good shooting, Colonel, but he was a sitting duck.' I answered, 'I like mine easy.'"

Some MiG pilots were indeed easy targets. Chinese pilots had been training on MiGs in the Soviet Union since the start of the war, but they were so far behind their prospective opponents that they were not committed to combat until the spring of 1951. North Korea's air force began receiving MiGs in November 1950, but almost all the experienced pilots had been lost in the war's earlier weeks. Lieutenant Kum Sok No had only fifty jet hours when he tackled his first F-86s: "Suddenly I heard the staccato of machine-gun bullets. We had wandered into the middle of the [dispersed] Sabre groups by mistake. . . . The fight was over in an instant. . . . [My] formation was badly scattered, so I turned and raced thankfully the forty miles toward home." From the days of the Fokker monoplane in 1915 to the air war over Iraq in 1991, novices have told similar stories—if they survived the experience.

From the beginning, then, the burden of the air war over the Yalu was borne by the Soviet air force. Records and reminiscences made available since the end of the Cold War describe MiG formations sent to China as early as February 1950, but their pilots did not initially expect to take part in the Korean fight-

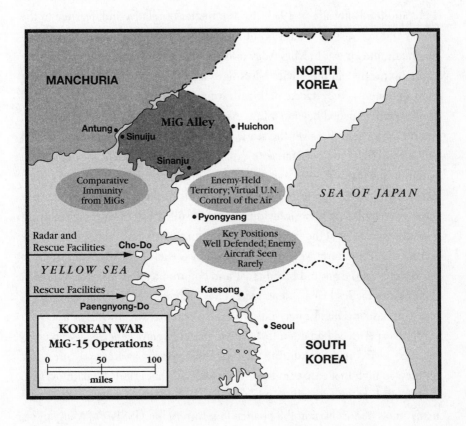

MANCHURIA

NORTH
KOREA

MiG Alley

Antung •   • Huichon
• Sinuiju

Sinanju

Comparative
Immunity
from MiGs

Enemy-Held
Territory; Virtual U.N.
Control of the Air

SEA OF JAPAN

• Pyongyang

Key Positions
Well Defended; Enemy
Aircraft Seen
Rarely

Radar and
Rescue Facilities   Cho-Do

YELLOW SEA

Rescue Facilities

Paengnyong-Do

Kaesong

• Seoul

SOUTH
KOREA

KOREAN WAR
MiG-15 Operations

0   50   100

miles

ing. Some Russians were selected for Korean service. Others were asked to volunteer. Little encouragement was necessary, however, at least in the war's initial stages. Like their American counterparts, Soviet pilots were willing, often eager, to test themselves and their planes.

Senior Soviet officers have stated that their main objective was to shoot down bombers; engaging Sabrejets was only a means to an end. In practice, Korea offered a golden opportunity to learn state-of-the-art fighter-jet tactics against first-rate opposition. Moreover, in contrast to the Royal Air Force in 1940 and the Luftwaffe in 1943, it was a matter of relative indifference to the Soviet air force just how many bombs fell on North Korean targets. Almost immediately, the air war in MiG Alley took on the qualities of a personal duel.

By no means did the Soviet pilots have a free operational hand. Like their U.S. opponents, they faced politically imposed restrictions. Enemy aircraft could not be pursued beyond a line extending from Pyongyang to Wonsan, in the northeast. Combat over the sea was likewise forbidden, another reflection of the Soviet Union's reluctance to expand the war by accident. Soviet participation in the war was a top state secret, and preserving secrecy may have been a factor in the decision to rotate complete units through the combat zone, as opposed to replacing pilots individually. As a result, every six weeks or so meant a set of newcomers at the bottom of the learning curve. Base and maintenance facilities in Manchuria were primitive even by Soviet standards. Mountainous terrain limited the ground-based radar and communications systems on which their fighter tactics heavily depended. They suffered, too, from a training system emphasizing flight safety rather than risk-taking. Meanwhile, those with wartime experience had often lost what Colonel Evgeny Pepelyaev, who commanded a MiG regiment during the war, calls "combat awareness." Stress levels grew so high that entire units were affected. Colonel Boris Abakumov, who scored five F-86 kills, recalls that in October 1951, "our medical board offered many pilots of our division the chance to return to the USSR. . . . Many pilots who left had to be given medical aid" for physical and emotional stress.

The U.S. Air Force had sent a wing of F-84 Thunderjets to Korea along with the Sabres, but this straight-wing design was so far out of the MiG-15's performance league that its original escort mission rapidly gave way to ground support, in which the plane was very successful. The best jet available to British and Australian pilots was the Gloster Meteor, obsolescent since the late 1940s. The Sabres stood alone.

For a year the MiGs faced a single wing, the 4th, with only two of its three squadrons actually deployed in Korea: a theoretical strength of fifty planes. Maintenance problems under the inadequate conditions of a still-developing airfield network around Seoul, combined with operational wear and tear, kept increasing numbers of F-86s on the ground. Meanwhile, the original first team of MiG killers was beginning to rotate home. New blood was reaching the squadrons—pilots such as Second Lieutenant Jim Low, who shot down his fifth MiG six months after graduating from flight school. But not every youngster was a Jim Low. Replacements also included an increasing number of recalled reservists, men in their thirties whose reflexes had slowed and whose killer instincts were often dormant, when not atrophied. Colonel Harrison Thyng took command of the 4th on November 1, 1951. After evaluating his command and its mission, he sent a direct message to the air force chief of staff, Hoyt S. Vandenberg: "I can no longer be responsible for air superiority in northwest Korea."

On October 22, though, Vandenberg had ordered another seventy-five Sabres to Korea, including some of the new E versions. A wing of F-80s, the 51st, converted to Sabres. The 4th received its third squadron. The odds were still not even, but the balance stabilized, despite maintenance problems that in January 1952 put 45 percent of the Sabres in Korea out of action. By the fall of 1951, the Soviet, Chinese, and Korean MiG inventories totaled over five hundred, but not all of them were on the front line. Lieutenant General Georgy Lobov, who commanded the 64th Fighter Corps in 1952, has insisted that at that stage of the war, "the total strength of our aircraft did not exceed the strength of the Americans' [Sabre] Wings."

Technically, the MiG and Sabre remained remarkably well matched. The F-86E featured a more reliable engine than its predecessor. The F-86F, which reached MiG Alley in the summer of 1952, had a redesigned wing that significantly improved its ceiling and maneuverability. On the other side, the MiG-15 bis, which had begun reaching the front a year earlier, incorporated a number of minor technical improvements over the original version. Still, for practical purposes, the adversaries' principal characteristics were unchanged. The MiG had a higher ceiling and a faster rate of climb; the Sabre was more maneuverable and could dive more rapidly. While pilots on both sides praised their respective mounts, few were willing to bet their lives on the technical superiority of one aircraft over the other. Pilot skill, tactics, and luck were the crucial determinants of success.

Nor were Sabre pilots averse to stacking the deck with what amounted to a pattern of violating Manchurian airspace, sometimes in hot pursuit of fleeing or damaged MiGs, at other times coming in from the Sea of Japan to evade enemy radar and secure the advantage of height against MiGs as they took off. This behavior was subject to condign punishment if discovered officially, but it continued throughout an air campaign that essentially stalemated by mid-1951.

U.S. bombers and fighter-bombers kept striking targets in MiG Alley; Soviet pilots, reinforced by increasing numbers of Chinese and North Koreans, maintained an effective defense. B-29s still carried the war into MiG country, but by October 1951 their loss and damage ratios had grown so high that the Superfortresses switched from daylight raids to night operations. Nevertheless, MiG-15 night interceptors proved such a threat to the lumbering four-engine bombers that specialized jet night fighters, air force F-94s and navy F3Ds, were used increasingly as escorts. These straight-wing planes' exponentially superior electronics—a critical factor in night flying—made up for inferior speed and maneuverability relative to the MiG.

The results of the bombing were, however, marginal. To tip the balance required either an infusion of strength or a widening of the combat zone to degrees neither side was willing to risk. General Carl Spaatz, a World War II hero, grumbled that the debacle of 1950 might not have happened if "the air power could have gotten into play, and gone in to a depth of two or three or four hundred miles back." General O'Donnell thought that "for a very small cost in casualties we could have really hit them hard and perhaps even stopped them." But air strikes across the Yalu remained forbidden by both the Truman and the Eisenhower administrations.

The MiGs stayed in a defensive role as well, making no effort to contest most of North Korea's airspace. That task was left to another technical anachronism in the first jet war. Polikarpov PO-2s—canvas-covered biplanes whose ancestors had been respected even by the Wehrmacht—had flown night raids since the start of the war; in 1951 these became systematic. These "sewing machines" defied radar and challenged the naked eye. Their slow speed and high maneuverability made them difficult targets, and cannon shells occasionally passed through wings and fuselages without exploding. Often dismissed as merely a nuisance, PO-2 raids—which concentrated on airfields—disrupted sleep, disturbed operational routines, and occasionally destroyed or damaged badly needed aircraft. Corsairs that were adapted for night operations, and later specialized night fighters, piston-engined and jet-propelled, took to the air against these pests; however, until the war's end, "Bedcheck Charlie" remained a feature of Korea's night skies, insouciantly defying both old and new U.S. technologies.

As the Sabres held the ring in MiG Alley, the air war took on new forms. Close air support made perhaps its greatest contribution of the war in November 1950, when the Chinese sledgehammer sent MacArthur's overextended forces reeling south. Artillery positions were overrun; guns could not find targets. But fighter-bombers filled the gaps. In particular, the 1st Marine Division's withdrawal from the Chosin Reservoir was covered all the way by marine pilots determined to see that as many foot soldiers as possible, whatever their uniforms, got out of the Chinese meat grinder. Marines climbing steep and icy slopes to cover the roads below went in behind a screen of bombs, rockets, and cannon shells—not always but often enough for their presence to send the message "Hold on! You're not alone! We'll be back!" Some strikes came in so low that mortar rounds arched across their flight paths. A veteran marine sergeant major remarked of those airmen that "it was as though part of them was right there on the ground with the riflemen."

Despite its achievements, the marine air-ground team did not survive the retreat from Chosin. Continued air force insistence on integrating marines into an overall air-support system culminated on December 11, 1950, when it was announced that in the future, marine pilots would be available to the entire Eighth Army. The reorganization was more cosmetic than substantive. Misdirected air strikes continued to plague ground operations; for example, on April 24, 1951, a marine Corsair napalmed D Company of the Royal Australian Regiment. Differences among the services on the best and most practical ways of supporting ground operations remained unresolved. On one occasion the commander of the 1st Marine Division said he wanted marines supporting his riflemen, or no air cover at all.

Ground-support technology improved as the war progressed. Proximity-fused bombs became standard issue. Some experiments were made with radar-guided bombs. Ground-control parties were increased in number and given improved communications equipment. But as the front stabilized and the Chinese and North Koreans constructed increasingly elaborate defensive systems, air strikes of any kind diminished in effectiveness. Deep dugouts were far harder to destroy than troops maneuvering in the open. Enemy antiaircraft also was more effective in defending fixed targets.

Forbidden to cross the Yalu, less and less effective in ground fighting, the airmen turned to interdiction: isolating the battle zone by choking off supplies and reinforcements. Killing men on the move seemed a promising alternative to trying to demolish bunkers. Later in the year, aircraft embarked on a round-the-clock campaign against Chinese and North Korean lines of communication. Initially given the suitably warlike name Operation Strangle, it targeted primarily roads and railroads, in particular their vulnerable points: bridges and tunnels.

The raids were flown by a mixed bag of piston-engined planes and second-line jets. A few F-51s continued on operations as late as January 1953, but F-80s and F-84s carried most of the air force's load. Piston-engined B-26 light bombers were usually restricted to night missions and survived to the end of the war, less for acceptance of their intrinsic value than because the air force lacked an effective jet counterpart. The marines' Corsairs were supplemented by increasing numbers of F9F Panther jets, used as attack planes. Since the war's first days, the navy had been mounting what amounted to interdiction raids into North Korea from its *Essex*-class carriers, combining Corsairs and Skyraiders with Panthers and F2H Banshee jets in strikes against ground targets. While the air force might have been ready to abandon piston-engined combat aircraft, the navy continued to see a place for propellers in modern war. In particular, the AD Skyraider achieved a formidable reputation for accuracy, carrying capacity, and survivability. Its four-ton payload was four times that of an F-80 or an F-84. Over a decade later, ADs were a standard part of carrier air wings.

Whatever the nature of the aircraft involved, their effect was limited. Certainly the interdiction campaign affected the Chinese and North Korean ability to mount and support anything more than local offensives. On the other hand, gasoline, rations, and ammunition continued to get through to the front as troops and civilians worked nonstop to keep open the routes south. General Matthew Ridgway put it best when he said there was "no such thing as choking off supply lines in a country as wild as Korea." Camouflage, discipline, and an increasingly effective antiaircraft umbrella were as important as terrain. Contemporary U.S. reports stressed the enemy's use of human and animal transport. In fact, most supplies were moved at night by trains and trucks that remained hidden by day and defied the best efforts of jets and propeller planes alike to stop them.

Instead, aircraft losses mounted. Some 350 planes were destroyed and another 300 damaged, almost all by ground fire, in an operation that provided neither the glamour of jousts over MiG Alley nor the gratification of directly assisting beleaguered ground troops. In that context, rescuing downed pilots became as important for morale as for honor. Extraordinary efforts were made to bring out anyone still alive. A typical incident occurred in June 1952, when marine colonel Robert Gaither went down over North Korea. While he, in his own words, "played hide and seek for the next four or five hours," Corsairs and Skyraiders harassed his pursuers with strafing runs. When their fuel was spent, according to Gaither, "everyone who was heading south, including Air Force and I believe some South Africans, swung by to expend any available ammunition." A navy helicopter crew located Gaither at dusk, lifted him in a sling, and headed for the coast. With marine Corsairs clearing the way, the helicopter brought Gaither to safety, despite taking hits that almost brought it down as well.

Not all the stories were heroic. Korean women and children played a significant role in moving supplies and working on repair gangs. How did pilots react to strafing these noncombatants? A series of interviews conducted in late 1950 and early 1951 suggested that no more than 10 percent of the pilots involved believed the air force should avoid such targets. Over 60 percent felt that "we don't like it, but we do it because we have to." Regulars and volunteer reservists, officers with no World War II experience, and those who wanted the air force as a career took the lead in willingness to strafe civilians when ordered to do so.

These side effects of interdiction may have contributed to the decision to modify and then abandon the relatively indiscriminate approach of Operation Strangle. Instead, beginning in the summer of 1952, the air campaign emphasized mass attacks against specific targets such as command and communications centers, warehouse complexes, dams, and power plants. These objectives were selected with a view to damaging civilian morale, too: Warning leaflets were frequently dropped in advance of raids, in an effort to minimize noncombatant casualties while disrupting public order.

This dual approach reflected political and military concerns. The refocused bombing campaign was designed to encourage China and North Korea to conclude an armistice and to convince the Soviet Union to put pressure on its clients. The strikes did major material damage. Pyongyang was gutted. In one two-day operation, over 90 percent of North Korea's electric-power capacity was reported knocked out. Chinese and Soviet technicians were brought in to repair the damage, which affected northeast China as well as Korea. The political consequences of the raids were less favorable. World headlines attacked

American "terror bombing." As much to the point, by the end of 1952 reconnaissance reports showed nothing much left to bomb except for political purposes. But the Communists' eventual decision to conclude the armistice on July 27, 1953, was, like the initial invasion three years earlier, a political decision whose parameters ultimately lay outside U.S. control.

The historian D. Clayton James has described Korea as the refighting of World War II on a reduced scale. Yet its air operations prefigured the spectrum of technological, doctrinal, and operational issues that in practice have governed the uses of airpower ever since. Without question, the spectacular duels over MiG Alley established the jet mythology in public opinion, and within the air force. U.S. pilots claimed kills at an eight-to-one ratio, a level of achievement found nowhere else in a war that was at best a standoff. The fighting over the Yalu also seemed to confirm the exponential superiority of Western pilots over their Communist counterparts—a qualitative edge vital to subsequent military planning, given the inability of NATO and the United States to match their principal adversaries in sheer numbers of ground troops.

Korean War legacies were so strong that in the early stages of the air war over North Vietnam, when U.S. kill ratios in air-to-air combat stabilized at lower levels (about two and a half to one), concern over a presumed decline in American effectiveness led to a drastic overhauling of training, tactics, and design. Such programs as Red Flag and Top Gun, and such aircraft as the F-15, owe a good deal to images established during the MiG–Sabre war of the early 1950s. It is ironic that recently released information from the former Soviet Union reduces the number of MiG kills to something under 400, as opposed to the 792 originally claimed; admitted Sabre losses are slightly over 100, resulting in an actual kill ratio of only about three and a half to one, when victories scored by other aircraft are factored in. In other words, the efficiency of today's U.S. fighter force is based in part on response to a legend.

The general focus on jet technology and jet tactics fostered by the Korean experience contributed to a misunderstanding of the actual, as opposed to the theoretical, nature of war over the next half century. U.S. doctrine and planning focused on nuclear Armageddon at one end, insurgency and counterinsurgency at the other. Korea, an intermediate, conventional war, seemed either an anomaly or an anachronism. Instead, America's major military commitments since 1950 have involved adversaries with no meaningful economic targets. Their hardware has been imported, not manufactured—and usually imported from third parties politically immune to military action. Their infrastructures have not been sensitive to air attack at levels or within time spans acceptable to U.S. policy makers and U.S. public opinion.

The doctrines for fighting such wars have lagged significantly behind the technologies involved. Not until Operation Desert Storm were air superiority, interdiction, and close air support integrated in a comprehensive campaign, which left a devastated Iraq wide open to General Norman Schwarzkopf's hundred-hour ground offensive. In that sense, perhaps, the legacy of Korea has finally been established: the first in a long series of politically structured, mid-intensity conventional conflicts that have decisively shaped international relations in the second half of the twentieth century.

"Murderers of Koje-do!"

LAWRENCE MALKIN

Once the Korean War settled down to what Lawrence Malkin aptly characterizes here as an "enervating military stalemate," no issue caused the U.N. truce negotiators at Panmunjom more glacial torment than the prisoner-of-war question. The dispute over the fate of the 130,000 captives in U.N. prison stockades, as well as that of the 13,000 Western POWs in camps along the Yalu, not only postponed an armistice for fifteen months but came close to torpedoing one altogether. Should POWs have a choice about whether they should be repatriated? Too many American and British veterans of World War II had unsettling memories of the forcible repatriation of Soviet prisoners in Germany, when former captives faced with the prospect of Stalin's gulags or his executioners jumped to their deaths from the boxcars carrying them into the Soviet zone.

Both sides, of course, were pursuing ideological ends, and both treated POWs as pawns in an ideological struggle. As MacArthur put it in September 1950, when total victory seemed in sight: "Treatment of P.O.W.s shall be directed toward their exploitation for psychological warfare purposes." He actually established a pilot program, patterned on successful postwar reeducation schemes in Germany and Japan, in which five hundred North Korean prisoners were to be instructed in the values of democracy and prepared for citizenship in a nation that was about to be reunified. Meanwhile, the Communists, mindful of how many U.N.-held prisoners would probably choose to remain in South Korea or, if they were Chinese, defect to Taiwan, refused to compromise. Voluntary repatriation was a propaganda defeat in the making. They determined to transform the POW issue into a propaganda setback for the U.N. comparable to the first retreats of 1950 or the disintegration of the Eighth Army. It did not hurt that the Americans inadvertently created the conditions that handed the Communists the triumph for which they had schemed. The generals in charge of operations in this strangest of wars failed to grasp that, as the historian Stanley Sandler has written, "Communist POWs were simply soldiers on a different battlefront."

Malkin tells the story of Koje-do, an ordinarily obscure island off the southwest coast of Korea that briefly contended for the attention of the world. The evacuation of seventy thousand North Korean and Chinese prisoners to Koje-do had originated in the desperate circumstances of the first winter of the war. The U.N. authorities wanted to make sure the prisoners didn't escape and join Communist guerrillas behind the retreating U.N. forces. Lacking the manpower to run the island camps effectively—there was one MP for every 188 prisoners instead of the optimum one to twenty—the Eighth Army simply allowed the POWs to run their own affairs. The North Koreans began to smuggle intelligence officers into batches of new captives. They took charge of the compounds and were apparently in direct contact with Panmunjom. "Behind the wire," the historian Callum A. MacDonald tells us, "camp life was shaped not by military discipline but by political struggle."

In May 1952, Koje-do erupted, an explosion that was carefully orchestrated and designed to humiliate those in charge of the camps. In a war that nobody won, the prisoner dispute would disprove MacArthur's maxim that there was no substitute for victory.

LAWRENCE MALKIN, himself a frontline veteran of Korea, was a prizewinning correspondent for the Associated Press, *Time,* and the *International Herald Tribune.* He is the author of *The National Debt* and has collaborated with Paul Volcker and Anatoly Dobrynin on their memoirs. Malkin is currently writing a book on history's greatest counterfeit: 130 million fake British pounds printed under Nazi orders by Jewish concentration-camp prisoners during World War II. He divides his time between New York City and Majorca.

F OR FORTY YEARS OF THE COLD WAR, whenever the American military actually fought a hot war of any importance, it was bedeviled by the
dilemma of how to deal with prisoners of war. The truce ending the Korean
War was delayed for well over a year by political posturing about the fate of
tens of thousands of Chinese and Korean prisoners who refused to return to
Communism in their homelands. The Communists adroitly turned this co-
nundrum into a second front by harassing their captors at the Koje Island
prison camp off the peninsula's southern coast. American generalship was utterly confounded by a sharp political engagement in the midst of an enervating
military stalemate. The allied truce negotiators judged the additional fifty
thousand casualties that their side suffered during the protracted talks to be
wildly disproportionate to what they regarded as a dubious principle of free
choice, which, after all, was being accorded to soldiers who only recently had
been trying to kill their own troops. The negotiators' political masters, whatever the righteousness of their original motives, seem to have insisted on continuing to fight for the principle in order to salvage some moral victory from
the humiliating battlefield stalemate inflicted on them by what they contemp-
tuously regarded as an uncivilized Asian horde.

The Nixon administration also converted the U.S. prisoners in Vietnam into
a domestic political issue, enabling it to display some token of victory through a
class of heroes who could be celebrated upon their return. It never seemed odd
that their heroism was based on suffering and not conquest, and this may have
eased the pain of the only major defeat the United States ever suffered against
foreign arms. But it also helped delay for years the solution of our most domes-
tically divisive war by extending and politicizing the insoluble problem of the
missing in Vietnam. This envenomed the tragedy, and it still poisons our polit-

ical debate; even as late as the 1992 political campaign, it became an issue through the history of H. Ross Perot's personal attempts to redeem missing Americans by a variety of methods, including outright ransom.

Although the decline of Communism removes for the time being the threat of ideological empires that cannot bear the sting of mass defection, the problem will not go away. The use of human captives as political pawns has merely reemerged in an age-old form—hostage-taking. It has been turned into a heartbreaking game of cat and mouse by cruel appeals through the international media. Politicians can no more disable this tactic than could the stalwart World War II generals in Korea, many of whom were endlessly befuddled by what one 1952 intelligence summary described as "a new area of total war."

But not entirely new. The ur-event in this recurring drama took place at the end of World War II, when Stalin demanded and received from the Allies the forceful repatriation of thousands of Soviet soldiers who had been taken prisoner by the Germans—some to fight alongside them. The sense of horror turned to personal revulsion and guilt after the worst fears of the officers who handed them over were confirmed and many Russians were exiled, imprisoned, or executed, sometimes all three. For years afterward, Soviet commanders reminded their men that this would be their eventual fate if they surrendered. This memory seemed to dominate American minds, from President Harry Truman on down, when prisoners began falling into the hands of American troops fighting in Korea under the United Nations flag. More than 130,000 were in Allied prison camps by January 1951, six months before the Communists asked for negotiations. To support Allied insistence on voluntary repatriation, teams began screening the captives. To the amazement of the U.N. command and the embarrassment of the Communists, the ratio of those polled who refused repatriation ran at about four to one before the process was suspended under a combination of invective at the Panmunjom truce talks and obstruction by the Communist leadership inside the prison camps.

If the wise policies of World War II had been followed, the prisoners would have been transferred out of Korea to the United States, or at least to Okinawa. That was what General Douglas MacArthur recommended to Washington, but he never got a reply. The principal arguments against it were cost, political sensitivity in Japan about the status of Okinawa, and the unspoken fact that a stateside transfer of prisoners would constitute an admission that the conflict was more than a temporary "police action." As the numbers became unmanageable and even threatening behind the wavering front lines, the prisoners were shifted south to holding camps near Pusan, where the South Korean civilians who had been impressed into North Korean service units were separated from the Korean and Chinese soldiers.

I have always felt that retaliation was the real reason the Communists did not treat our own prisoners better. The captured Asian troops, many of whom had fought with more discipline and determination than their American opponents, were regarded by most ordinary soldiers with whom I served in Korea, and by altogether too many officers, as subhuman "gooks," which is what they were usually called. They were therefore deemed unworthy of the civilized treatment accorded less than a decade earlier to white European prisoners. They were crowded into improvised prison space at four times the level prescribed in U.S. federal penitentiaries, and given little to do except dig drainage ditches and organize parties for the removal of their own excrement. They were beaten by military police, although this occasional brutality nowhere approached the murderous barbarity the North Koreans practiced on Allied captives in the north. In fact, that brutality was matched in the Allied POW camps only by the North Korean prisoners' enforcement of their own internal discipline, which was essential to their high command's strategy of holding out against the principle of voluntary repatriation.

The now-obscure episode that crystallized the incompatibility of the Communists' subtle political tactics with the classical American military strategy of victory by overwhelming firepower took place on the small fishing island of Koje off the southern coast of Korea. Koje-do (the Korean suffix signifies an island) is about half again as large as Martha's Vineyard. Two rock-strewn valleys on its northern coast were hastily converted into a tented outdoor Alcatraz for seventy thousand Chinese and North Korean captives in January 1951.

"The first blunder was the camp design," wrote Edward Hymoff, an International News Service correspondent, after a visit. "Instead of small compounds, easily policed, it was decided for ease and economy to make them fewer and bigger. The result was a sprawling series of mammoth, 100-acre compounds enclosed by double fences of barbed wire with a single sally-port gate system and guard towers at the corners. With this incredibly bad planning, all pretense of prisoner control was foredoomed."

The compounds were originally designed to hold from 700 to 1,200 men each, but about 5,000 were soon jammed into each one. Space between them was later filled to confine more prisoners, saving on the number of guards but making their task more dangerous because thousands of prisoners could be mobilized quickly for protests, strikes, and riots by orders shouted across the barbed wire from one enclosure to another. The guards, green recruits led by officer misfits sent down from the front with no knowledge of Chinese or Korean, often left their posts to trade souvenirs, cigarettes, or sex with the camp-follower town of eight thousand that had sprung up around the perimeter. Several were murdered. At night the small guard force feared it could easily be overwhelmed, and so it largely retreated to barracks, in effect leaving the camp under control of the prisoners. Their Communist commanders imposed brutal discipline on recalcitrants, who would be found in the morning stomped to death, with rib fragments causing fatal internal bleeding; choked by cotton forced down their throats; or hanging from the barbed-wire fences. One nonlethal method of discipline was to tie a prisoner to a tent pole by his testicles and then dump his head in water.

In this idleness and overcrowding, rebellion would have festered even without an ideological spur. Each compound developed its own arsenal, which was described by Colonel William R. Robinette, one of the Koje commandants:

> In each GI shoe, there is an eight-inch sliver of steel. These had been sharpened into knives. Twenty lengths of barbed wire made a club, wired together and with a cloth handle. One of Koje's many stones, put into a sock, made a deadly blackjack. They made pikes out of Army tent poles, sharpening the pin at the end. They even made mock weapons out of wood—replicas of machine guns, automatic rifles, and M-1's painted black with soot from the camp incinerator, their bayonets covered with tinfoil from American chewing gum or cigarette wrappers.

As so often happens, local commanders on the ground were either unwilling or unable to understand the grand political strategy of both sides. Brigadier General Paul Yount, the commander in Pusan, was grandiosely engaged in constructing a courthouse that was to be the port city's largest building; it was intended to be the site of military trials to punish the camp's prisoner leadership as war criminals, just as if the Koreans were Nazis and this was to be their Nuremberg.

Various people sent to Koje-do to investigate late in 1951 found what amounted to a scandal. One of them was John E. Murray, then a major and secretary to the general staff of the Pusan Logistical Command, who reported that the administration of the camp was slapstick and slipshod. He tried to alert Eighth Army Headquarters in Seoul of the explosive situation, but there he ran up against General James Van Fleet's chief of staff, who was partly deaf and never quite seemed to understand what they faced. As the ranking army commander in Korea, Van Fleet himself counseled patience lest any sharp reaction provoke a riot that might sabotage the truce talks, which he believed would soon end the war.

Early in 1952, Washington prohibited Koje-do commanders from judicial prosecution to enforce discipline: So much for Yount's mini-Nuremberg. But Truman and his advisers were divided on much more than that. The Joint Chiefs of Staff at first hungered for the propaganda victory that would come from public mass defections by the Communist prisoners, but they realized this posed a risk that the Communists might end the talks and hold on to the Allied prisoners as pawns. Army Secretary James M. Lovett argued for a straight exchange to avoid spinning out the talks and threatening the welfare of U.S. prisoners. Secretary of State Dean Acheson also backed a straight exchange under the Geneva Convention, which would get the far smaller number of American GIs back sooner. But it was too late for mere legalism, and Truman himself recognized that. In 1951 he ordered General Matthew Ridgway to demand "some major concessions" preventing the forced repatriation of prisoners. In a lengthy public statement defending the diplomatic behavior of the United Nations, he declared with Trumanesque forthrightness, "We will not buy an armistice by turning over human beings for slaughter or slavery."

On the ground, the Communists thought of victory more than of honor and had their tactics well coordinated. They viewed the prison camps as a mere extension of the battlefield, which included the worldwide battle for public opinion. Charges of germ warfare were a principal weapon, and U.S. prisoners were threatened and tortured—"brainwashed" was then the popular term—to make statements admitting they had conducted it, mainly from the air. The most notorious confession came from a senior marine pilot, Colonel Frank H. Schwable, who had been put in a hole outdoors and left in his own filth for six months before he cracked.

On Koje-do, most compound commanders were North Korean intelligence officers who had been smuggled through the lines, surrendering as enlisted captives. The overall political commissar was Pak Sang Hyong, a Korean raised in the Soviet Union who had served as a staff officer and interpreter to Russian troops occupying North Korea after World War II. He was a close associate of

Nam Il, the chief truce negotiator at the Panmunjom talks, and the two worked together, passing reports and instructions back and forth through underground channels, the existence of which American officers found hard to believe. Pak had made his way via the POW process to Koje-do disguised as a private soldier; he was equal in rank to Nam Il, but American intelligence never identified him. Another high-ranking North Korean officer was Colonel Lee Hak Koo, who had surrendered in the summer of 1950 in full uniform with red piping and Russian pistol, claiming to have lost his Communist faith. He became the military commander inside the barbed wire on Koje-do. Under the leadership of Pak and Lee, the die-hard compounds of the camp had acquired a terrible potential for embarrassing its hosts.

The prisoners provided ample warning of their commitment. Their ideological activity was shouted out in slogans and posters, including drawings of the Soviet and North Korean dictators, Joseph Stalin and Kim Il Sung. They demonstrated for better conditions, drilled with homemade rifles, and forcibly resisted United Nations screening, to the point of murdering those who wavered. In the compounds they controlled, riots on command slowed down the U.N. process of screening out anti-Communist prisoners from the hard core. When the leader of Compound 62 declared that screening was unnecessary because all 5,600 prisoners demanded to be returned to North Korea, the 3rd Battalion of the American 27th Infantry Regiment was sent to subdue them on February 18, 1952.

As more than a thousand prisoners in Compound 62 ran yelling from their tents brandishing improvised weapons and throwing rocks, the men of the 27th hurled grenades and finally opened fire. Fifty-five inmates were killed outright; twenty-two more died in hospitals. One GI was killed and thirty-eight wounded. When the infantrymen returned to the front line shortly afterward in a supposedly secret transfer, they were greeted by Communist loudspeakers blaring at them, "Welcome, murderers of Koje-do!" It was, to say the least, unnerving; I know, because I was in the 15th Infantry on the flank.

More to the point was the opening the incident created for Nam Il at the truce talks. At Panmunjom he railed at the U.N. negotiators: "The fact now placed before the people of the world is that in spite of your barbarous measures, you violated the will of the captured personnel of our side. Thousands of them would rather die than yield to your forcible retention." In fact, the Allied command had begun to retreat quietly. In a message on April 29, Ridgway cautioned the Joint Chiefs of Staff that resumption of forced screening would demand "brutal" repression and asked them to assume that those who refused to be screened had in effect accepted repatriation. The parlous security at the camp was confirmed early in May by a visit from Colonel Robert T. Chaplin, provost marshal of the Far East command. Chaplin's report prompted Ridgway to warn Van Fleet of the need to tighten control. Van Fleet's response was to complain that Chaplin had been sent to inspect over his head without the protocol of first informing Eighth Army Headquarters.

The Koje uprising had resulted in the appointment of Brigadier General Francis T. Dodd as camp commander on February 20, but with conflicting orders. Ridgway told Van Fleet to maintain tight control, while Van Fleet told Dodd to "go easy" on the prisoners and keep them quiet because the armistice was near. This muddle had been a major factor in turning the camp into what Dodd's predecessor, Colonel Maurice J. Fitzgerald, called a "graveyard of commanders"—a new one almost every month, even before Fitzgerald had taken over the previous September.

In May 1952 the political and military elements collided dramatically in a way that none of the principal actors could have foreseen—not just Dodd and Van Fleet but Ridgway himself. At the precise moment of the climax, he was in the process of handing over his Far East command to another celebrated World War II leader, General Mark W. Clark, and trying to avoid the stain on his glittering reputation before he became commander of the North Atlantic Treaty Organization forces in Europe.

Dodd, an imposing West Pointer with a fine combat record, was anxious to decrease tensions in the camp. He circulated freely, talking to the Communist leaders and fatuously trying to win their cooperation. He went unarmed as a show of goodwill—and to avoid having his weapon seized and used against him. But because the Communists had already gained such mastery over their own compounds that neither guards nor officers had been allowed to enter them for months, Dodd easily fell into their trap. In a prisoners' dry run, Lieutenant Colonel Wilbur Raven, the commanding officer of the camp's military police guards, had actually been seized and held briefly, but this did not alert either officer to a plot. Nam Il himself had set it up, through bamboo-telegraph orders, to strengthen his negotiating hand at Panmunjom.

On the evening of May 6, members of a work detail from the hard-core Compound 76 complained to Raven that they had been beaten by the guards, and they asked to see Dodd. As an inducement, they agreed to be fingerprinted, thus assisting him in his program of positively identifying all prisoners. Just after two P.M. on May 7, Dodd arrived and started talking, as was his custom, at the unlocked sally port of the compound. The subject moved from food to politics to the truce negotiations, but however amicable the discussion may have seemed, the two officers refused the prisoners' invitation to enter the compound. A work detail carrying tents for salvage approached the gate, which was opened for them. The prisoners drew closer to Dodd and Raven to continue the discussion—and then jumped them. As the prisoners pulled at him, Raven held fast to a post. But before any guards could reach Dodd, he was dragged into the compound and placed in a specially prepared tent divided into a two-room suite. The prisoners quickly raised a banner, also prepared in advance: WE CAPTURE DODD. AS LONG AS OUR DEMAND WILL BE SOLVED, HIS SAFETY IS SECURED. IF THERE HAPPEN BRUTAL ACT SUCH AS SHOOTING, HIS LIFE IS IN DANGER. Within hours, a field-telephone line from camp headquarters was connected to Dodd's quarters in the prison compound, and tortuous negotiations for his release commenced.

No more vulnerable moment could have been chosen, and it was impossible that the Communist planners did not know that Dodd's kidnap coincided with the transfer of command from Ridgway to Clark. The new commander arrived in Tokyo almost at the moment Dodd was being seized on Koje-do, thus making for confusion through equivocal responsibility. The memoirs of the two generals make it easy to imagine the almost farcical relationship between them as they juggled this international incident in the hope that the onus for it might land on the other.

At first, Ridgway writes, he "was determined to work out a solution to this prickly matter myself, along with Van Fleet, and not toss it, on such short notice, onto General Clark's dinner plate." Nevertheless, Ridgway took himself on a final inspection tour of Korea on May 8, four days before he was to hand over command to Clark, and he asked Clark to fly with him to Korea. Only when they were aloft did he let Clark in on what was happening. According to Clark's memoirs, Ridgway, addressing him by his middle name as his intimates did, confided, "Wayne, we've got a little situation over in Korea where it's reported some prisoners have taken in one of the camp commanders, General Dodd, and are holding him as a hostage. We'll have to get into that situation when we arrive at Eighth Army Headquarters [in Seoul] and find out what the score is."

Clark likened himself to someone who was "walking into something that felt remarkably like a swinging door." But what really astounded him was that the prisoner uprising was "something for which I had no preparation whatever. Although I had been briefed in Washington on every conceivable subject, this was the first time I had ever heard of Koje or the critical prisoner of war problems that existed behind our lines."

He was to hear more, much more. At Seoul, Ridgway directed Van Fleet in writing to establish order, using tanks if necessary to "shoot and to shoot with maximum effect." Ridgway was ready to sacrifice Dodd, who, he argued, had accepted mortal risks when he took up the profession of arms. "In wartime," he wrote later, "a general's life is no more precious than the life of a common soldier. If, in order to save an officer's life, we abandoned the cause for which enlisted men had died, we would be guilty of betraying the men whose lives had been placed in our care." Brave words after the fact, especially when Ridgway, in later reports to Truman and testimony to Congress, could not bring himself to take any blame as supreme commander. "In my view," he stated, "the whole situation had been ineptly handled by the responsible officers in Korea."

When Van Fleet arrived at Koje-do, he delayed attacking the compound until heavy armor arrived from the mainland. Meanwhile, negotiations to save Dodd were under way through Brigadier General Charles F. Colson, a staff officer suddenly vaulted into command of the Koje camp. It was not the mere seizure of Dodd that was at issue, but what the Communists could make of it. Under the direction of Pak, the political commissar, a statement in fractured English was proposed in which the U.N. command would agree to stop using "poison gas, germ weapons, experiment object of A-Bomb"—and, to stop screening prisoners for repatriation. After several days of exchanging drafts with the Communists to determine their price for Dodd's release, Colson signed a statement assuring that in the future, "the prisoners of war can expect humane treatment" and promising that after Dodd's release, "there will be no more forcible screening" of any prisoners. Dodd was released May 11. The next day Ridgway turned over his command to Clark.

Colson had no idea that his words would be used against the Allies in negotiations or in press and propaganda the world over to undercut the last remaining principle for which the Allied troops were fighting: the right of voluntary repatriation. Clark later overrode a court of inquiry that largely exonerated Dodd and Colson. He appointed his own court, which demoted each to colonel. They were then exiled to rear-echelon jobs in Japan, and their military careers were effectively ended. General Yount, the Pusan base commander, received a reprimand for not keeping closer surveillance over the negotiations, although it is hard to see why he was brought in except to increase the number of scapegoats for the omissions of higher headquarters. Clark wrote later that he would have "let them keep that dumb son of a bitch Dodd, and then go in and level the place."

In the denouement, that is more or less what happened, although happily for Dodd, he was well out of the way. On May 13, wasting no time, Clark sent in Brigadier General Haydon "Bull" Boatner, assistant commander of the 2nd Division and an old China hand who had served in World War II under Vinegar Joe Stilwell. He spoke Chinese fluently, understood the Asian sense of hierarchy and face, and was not an especially nice man. John E. Murray, whose warnings had gone for nothing, recalled years later in his own retirement as a major general that Boatner's large round face with its thin lips "always looked like he was ready to spit." Boatner was not very smart, either. As Major General Thomas Watlington remarked in a letter to Murray, "I have known three 'Bulls' in the Army, and all were nicknamed not for their size but their brains. I cannot truthfully say that Boatner is the most stupid of the three, for comparison of superlatives is not easy."

But Boatner did not have to be particularly smart; he merely had to know precisely what his orders were and carry them out efficiently. Clark told him he was "to regain control of the rebellious prisoners on Koje and maintain control thereafter." His policy was sharply enunciated after he received a demanding message from one prisoner compound. "Prisoners of war do not negotiate," Clark shouted at a surprised subordinate. Boatner quickly set about building stronger, smaller prison enclosures, each holding between 500 and 1,000 men, as International Red Cross representatives had previously recommended in vain. To start the transfer, he baited the Chinese prisoners by expressing amazement that they would take orders from Koreans, who were descendants of their former slaves. Meanwhile, he received reinforcements in the form of paratroopers of the 187th Regimental Combat Team, one of the best battle-tested units in Korea. Clark later wrote, "Staff planning for this operation was done as carefully as for any orthodox military campaign. We knew by this time that the Communist POWs were active combatants and had to be dealt with as soldiers, not as prisoners in the traditional sense."

In an initial feint, Boatner sent infantrymen and tanks to pull down the Communist signs and banners in several compounds, demonstrating that he intended to regain control. On June 10 he massed his forces directly against the enemy command, ordering Colonel Lee to assemble the prisoners of his Compound 76 in groups of 150 for transfer to new quarters. They rallied with home-made barbed-wire clubs and flails, tent-pole pikes, and Molotov cocktails made from hoarded cooking gasoline. Half an hour after the first order, disciplined troops of the 187th advanced, using concussion grenades, tear gas, bayonets, and their fists, but not firing a shot. The first prisoners were hauled from the trenches, and hundreds more were moved out by riot tactics. After Patton tanks trained their guns on the last holdouts, they gave up; Colonel Lee was dragged away by the seat of his pants to solitary confinement for the remainder of the war. The remaining compounds were broken up, and little more was heard from Koje-do thereafter, although the issue of forced repatriation continued to the last.

A year later, when peace was finally imminent, South Korean president Syngman Rhee tried to block an armistice that would not give him the entire country. Once again, the prisoners were the markers in his gamble. Just after midnight on June 18, South Korean guards opened the gates of camps holding about thirty-five thousand North Korean POWs. They vanished into the night with the help of South Korean soldiers, who led them to hiding places and fed them. Only about nine thousand hard-core Communist POWs refused to leave, insisting on repatriation. To Rhee's chagrin, the Communist side shrugged off his provocation. An armistice was signed on July 27, 1953, leaving North and South split along the battle line, which became a demilitarized zone.

The armistice provided for a complex process of what was called "explana-tion" by representatives of both sides to persuade prisoners to remain or go home. But inside the barbed wire, the prisoners had chosen up sides long be-fore, and there was no going back. LSTs brought the North Korean prisoners from Koje to Inchon on August 13, where they boarded trains for the exchange point at the demilitarized zone. The windows had been covered with wire mesh, and the Communists were warned against revealing themselves along the route. Nevertheless, they cut up their underwear, turned it into North Korean flags using dye hidden in their caps, pulled off the windows' mesh pro-tection, and waved the improvised red-and-blue banners out the train win-dows—to an angry shower of stones thrown by schoolchildren along the route. North Korean female prisoners trashed their railroad car by smashing the win-dows, slashing the seat covers, urinating on the upholstery, and then, as they left, defecating in the aisle.

Defiance marked every moment of the North Koreans' return. At the demilitarized zone, Communist Red Cross officials urged the prisoners to get rid of the uniforms that their captors had provided. They stripped themselves naked except for their Communist caps, GI shoes, and breechclouts made from towels. Snake-dancing, singing, and yelling, they were loaded onto trucks for the exchange point, whereupon they began throwing away their shoes along the dusty road to the North and repatriation.

These antics proved the futility of the exercise to the man who had conducted it, Vice Admiral C. Turner Joy, the chief Allied truce negotiator. One of his main objectives in holding out against forced repatriation had been the hope that Communist regimes would be so gravely embarrassed by mass defections that they would be undermined. "I regret to say this does not seem to have been a valid point," the admiral later remarked drily. "Whatever temporary loss of prestige in Asia Communism suffered from the results of 'voluntary repatriation' has long since been overtaken by Communism's subsequent victory in the area."

He spoke too soon. If there is any military lesson in all of this, and indeed in the Korean War itself, it comes from turning on its head General MacArthur's famous dictum: "There is no substitute for victory." The prosperity of South Korea today, the visible crumbling of the regime in the North, and China's fundamental turn toward a market economy prove that there is a substitute: constancy of purpose, patience, and avoiding the chimera of mistaking propaganda victories for real ones. Commanders win when they recognize that tactics and politics are simply different sides of the same strategic coin, and then, as Clark did, take the political measure of their opponents. By applying just the right amount of force, to bluff and stiff his opponents and then wait them out, he proved a far better Cold War general than he ever was in World War II. It is a military lesson that holds good in any war, hot or cold.

Strategic View: The Meaning of Panmunjom

ROBERT COWLEY

The early 1950s were an interval of mixed—and missed—historical signals. The Korean War, the most potentially explosive confrontation of the decade, had frozen along trench lines that might not have seemed out of place on the Great War's Western Front. Increasingly displeased with the sterile results of the Korean standoff, the American public waited in vain for some small frisson of hope to emerge from the hutments of Panmunjom, where negotiations for an armistice had consumed over a year without result. It was no wonder that Dwight D. Eisenhower's stunning statement on October 24, 1952, " I shall go to Korea," clinched his campaign for the presidency. Eisenhower didn't say what he would do there or exactly how he intended to wrap up the conflict; the simple words seemed enough. And, once elected, he did go. He looked around with his trained general's eye, noting that "small attacks on small hills would not win this war." A big offensive might produce big gains, but it might also bring in Soviet troops and tanks. Better to leave matters as they were and try to resusitate the Panmunjom negotiations. He stayed away from the place on purpose.

Then fate, in the form of actuarial probability, gave Eisenhower the advantage he needed a month and a half after he had taken office. On March 5, 1953, Stalin died, succumbing to a stroke in his fortresslike dacha outside of Moscow. The Pope of World Communism had been seventy-three. Even as he had lain unconscious, the struggle for succession began. The man who briefly emerged on top was Georgi Malenkov, but as the months passed, his hold on power became increasingly shaky. Malenkov spoke hopefully of "peaceful coexistence" with the West and made noises about a summit conference. Eisenhower stalled. He and his secretary of state, John Foster Dulles, feared that the Soviets might use it as a platform for blocking the rearmament of West Germany.

The bare-knuckled infighting for political supremacy continued behind the walls and closed doors of the Kremlin. Almost unnoticed, the rise of Nikita Khrushchev began. Lavrenti Beria, the man who had engineered Stalin's Great Terror and who had later presided over the successful creation of a Soviet atomic bomb, was himself arrested and accused of having been a British spy for thirty years. He confessed, of course, and was executed before the year was out.

Stalin's death and the leadership turmoil in Moscow did release the peace process from the frigid grasp of the old dictator. He had viewed Korea as a learning experience for the Chinese, and, as he cabled Mao, the war "shakes up the Truman regime in America and harms the military prestige of the Anglo-American troops." As for the North Koreans, they "have lost nothing, except for casualties. . . ." His successors were eager to achieve better relations with the West, at least in the short term, and there seemed no better place to start than Korea. They pressed their new determination on the Chinese and North Koreans, both of whom were, by this time, more than willing to make a deal. Their combined casualties were appalling, probably more than 1.5 million, three times what the U.N. had suffered. The Communist side also feared that Eisenhower might authorize the use of atomic weapons. The possibility was discussed in Washington, and rejected, though the U.S. Air Force apparently did drop dummy atomic bombs over North Korea. The Soviets took our nuclear arsenal seriously. "They must be scared as hell," Eisenhower once remarked about the new Soviet leaders.

That was the background of the armistice that was eventually agreed upon at Panmunjom. Did that armistice, as so many claimed at the time, mark the end of the first war that the U.S. lost? The following essay takes an entirely different view.

ROBERT COWLEY is the founding editor of *MHQ: The Quarterly Journal of Military History*. He has edited three previous anthologies, *No End Save Victory*, about World War II; *With My Face to the Enemy*, about the Civil War; and, most recently, *The Great War*. He has also edited three volumes of the *What If?*™ series. Cowley lives in Connecticut and Rhode Island.

FIVE DECADES HAVE PASSED since July 23, 1953, when the armistice agreement that ended the Korean War was signed at Panmunjom. No wild celebration attended the event, only a hushed and sullen sourness. In the rain the night before, North Korean carpenters had erected a makeshift building for the ceremony. They had deliberately left only a single entrance at the north end, which meant that the United Nations delegation would have had to march a few symbolic yards through Communist territory. The commander of the U.N. forces, General Mark W. Clark—"Wayne" to his close associates—insisted on a second, southern entrance; it was hacked through at the last minute.

Promptly at ten A.M., the opposing delegations, two men on each side, entered the room and sat down at tables placed side by side. Two years, seventeen days, and 575 meetings had led up to this moment in the artificial settlement in no-man's-land. The U.N. signers, studiedly casual, wore open shirts; their North Korean opposites, full-dress uniforms buttoned to the neck. Nobody spoke. Documents were exchanged for signing. Then everyone stood up and, without a word, a glance, or a handshake, filed out their respective doors. The whole ceremony had taken exactly twelve minutes. "I cannot find it in me to exult in this hour," Clark said later, forever bitter that he would be remembered as the first U.S. commander in his country's history to preside over an armistice without victory.

But the significance of Panmunjom had eluded Clark. Korea had been a new kind of war, a war that neither side could afford to lose—or to win. Victory, as Douglas MacArthur had learned to his sorrow, was too dangerous to risk. That went for the Communist side as well. In an effort to unify Korea, they had originally overplayed their hand—a hand that Mao Tse-tung, at Stalin's urging, once more overplayed when he sent in Chinese "volunteers" that first autumn.

The war had to end close to where it had begun on June 25, 1950, on an irregular line that slanted through the 38th Parallel at Panmunjom. As if to provide a parenthetical symmetry, rain had fallen that first morning, too.

I should admit at the outset that I did not fight in the Korean War. I was a freshman in college the spring before it ended, and I managed to preserve my student status—barely—through a test administered all over the country one balmy Saturday morning in May 1953. Every male who received a grade of 77 or better would escape the draft as long as he remained in college; a postcard informed me that I had scored a 78. But unlike Vietnam a decade later, most of us were prepared to serve. I still have acquaintances, a little older than I, who experienced the terror of night patrols in the wide no-man's-land between hillside trench systems, or who flew as observers in Cessna L-19s, calling in targets. (They always flew with a metal plate under their seat cushion, to protect their private parts from ground fire.) One of my closest friends, a former infantryman in the 25th Division, will talk about everything except his wounding in 1952. To them, Korea is hardly a forgotten war.

Byron Hollinshead, with whom I worked for fifteen years, served as a marine. The problem, he says, is less that Korea is forgotten now than that it seemed to be forgotten at the time. "Today in Iraq when guys get killed, it's front-page news. We had big battles, and they made the second section."

"Overlooked" would probably be a more precise word than "forgotten." The Korean War does not deserve to be remembered merely as a cliché. Historians explain it away as a conflict lacking myths, as if wars should be ranked by their Olympian attractions. What about the left hook out of nowhere at Inchon—or the Stonewall Jackson–like surprise of the American Eighth Army by the Chinese in November 1950? Or the anabasis of the marines from the Chosin Reservoir, a fighting retreat worthy of Xenophon? Or the stand by the British and Belgians of the 29th Brigade the following April at the Imjin River? Weren't they epic enough?

You can tick off other features of Korea that are worth remembering. It was, to begin with, truly coalition warfare: Twenty-two nations participated in varying degrees in the U.N. "police action" (we could use some of them in Iraq today). Japan, so recently our mortal enemy, experienced an economic renaissance, which owed much to the American need for an untouchable base of operations. President Harry S. Truman integrated our armed forces, a true milestone for the United States. There were notable firsts. The first war in which massive nuclear retaliation was brandished as an overt threat. The first jet war. The first war in which helicopters played a part. The first war whose outcome hinged on the fate of prisoners of war—remember the phrase "brainwashing"?—a dispute that delayed the armistice by fifteen months and cost the U.N. side an estimated fifty thousand casualties.

From a strictly military point of view, the Korean War was a tactical and operational draw. Clark was right in that sense. But in strategic terms, most of which were not evident at the time, it was ultimately a defeat for the U.S.S.R. and, to a lesser extent, for Communist China. Drawn battles often produce undrawn results. When the French and British fleets broke contact after the Battle of the Capes in 1781, neither victory nor defeat was discernible. But the lack of British initiative left Lord Cornwallis's army trapped at Yorktown, making American victory in the Revolutionary War inevitable. Gettysburg was at once a tie and a huge Confederate defeat. The Germans may have sunk more British ships than they lost at Jutland in 1916, but the High Seas Fleet never again emerged from its home bases.

So, too, had the Cold War stalemated by 1950. The wave of Communism had reached its high-water mark. After the success of the Marshall Plan, the failure of the Berlin blockade and the Greek civil war, and the creation of NATO and an independent West Germany, Stalin sought to turn the momentum of the Cold War once more in his favor. Gambling on the forced reunification of Korea before Japan resumed her place as a Pacific power, he had backed (albeit with misgivings) the invasion of South Korea by his North Korean puppet, Kim Il Sung. Truman's unexpected response not only saved South Korea and strengthened Japan but also blocked a planned Communist assault of Taiwan. The U.S. could then use the not so covert involvement of the U.S.S.R. in the Korean War as a pretext for excluding the Soviets from the peace settlement with Japan—and went on to forge a defensive alliance with its former enemy. (To this day, the Russians have still not signed a peace treaty with Japan; the disposition of four small islands in the Kuriles, taken by the Soviets in 1945, has hindered relations between the two countries for almost sixty years.)

But momentum was not all that Stalin and his heirs lost. The invasion of Korea would have lasting repercussions on the other side of the globe. Both sides repeatedly misread the intentions of the other. Washington viewed the North Korean and Chinese invasions as the prelude to a similar Soviet attack in Europe. America backed what Stalin feared most: the rearmament of West Germany and the creation of a West German army, the Bundeswehr—which automatically strengthened NATO as a force capable of slowing a Soviet advance. Presumably, American nuclear bombs would do the rest. The Communist bloc (which included China) might have the operational advantage of fighting on interior lines. But meanwhile, the West was gaining the strategic upper hand by fencing it in with an interlocking network of defensive alliances. Moreover, Truman made the decision to station American troops permanently in Europe. Between 1950, when the North Koreans invaded, and 1951, he quadrupled the defense budget and doubled the size of the armed forces to almost three million. It was the beginning of an arms race that did not end until the beginning of the 1990s—a race that, once started, the Soviets could never win. You can make a persuasive argument that as a result of Korea, the Soviets lost the Cold War.

In the twentieth century, there were four turning points in an off-and-on conflict that was, in a sense, a continuous war. The first was 1914 and the beginning of World War I. The second was the dropping of two atomic bombs on Japan in 1945, the end of World War II, and the beginning of the Cold War the next year. The third was the collapse of the Soviet empire in 1991 and the end of the Cold War. To those we must add a fourth, the Korean War. It made the Cold War a global phenomenon and led to the militarization of Asia and Europe. (You might almost think of it in historical terms as the "deep" Cold War, in the same sense that we talk of astronomical deep space or geological deep time.) American military might and the huge defense industry that supported it expanded exponentially. The free world (or what passed for it) would not be caught flat-footed by another Communist invasion, as it had been in Korea. To quote the British journalist and historian Martin Walker, "Washington and Moscow alike were learning to operate in a new strategic environment in which the need to prevent a crisis from expanding into full-scale war was more important than any local victory. The Cold War . . . was becoming an institution."

Korea brought about the change and set the pattern for the next four decades. That was the ultimate meaning of Panmunjom.

III

THE DEEP COLD WAR

The Truth About Overflights

R. CARGILL HALL

It was only after an antiaircraft missile brought down Francis Gary Pow-ers's U-2 photo reconnaissance plane over the Urals on May 1, 1960, and the Soviet premier Nikita Khrushchev demolished the Paris summit con-ference two weeks later that the world began to learn about American overflights of the U.S.S.R. As far as most people knew, those overflights had been made only by U-2s, beginning in 1956. But in fact, U-2 aerial reconnaissance was a continuation of a secret effort that had been going on since the early 1950s. Not until the last ten years has the true story begun to surface. As R. Cargill Hall, a noted air force historian, writes, "Since the dissolution of the Soviet Union fragmentary accounts have ap-peared. Too frequently, however, they have turned on misperceptions and questionable interpretations. Armed with a few interviews and still fewer archival records from the Cold War, authors have provided Oliver Stone–like conspiracies." When Hall's "The Truth About Overflights" appeared in *MHQ* in 1997, it was the first authoritative discussion of the subject. Hall knew, and was trusted by, many of those who had flown on overflight missions—and who, decades later, were willing to speak out at last.

The initiation of overflights was a direct reaction to the invasion of South Korea and the entrance of Communist China in the war. American political and military leaders viewed the sequence of events as a possible prelude to an attack of Western Europe and even raids on the U.S. by bombers armed with Russia's newly developed atomic weapons. Early in December 1950, Truman noted in his diary, "It looks like World War III is here. I hope not—but we must meet whatever comes—and we will."

On December 16, he proclaimed a state of national emergency. Shortly after, he authorized selective overflights.

The West had merely the vaguest notion of Soviet strengths and intentions; overflights might give some shape to them. The rigid security of Stalin's Russia made intelligence gathering on the ground all but impossible. "For all the money spent on espionage," a CIA official later admitted, "nobody knew a helluva lot about what was happening in Moscow." The Strategic Air Command (SAC) wasn't even sure where prime targets were located. And there was the frightening prospect of Soviet long-range bombers massing on Siberian air bases close to Alaska. Were they actually preparing to strike American targets? A one-way suicide flight could reach Chicago or Detroit. What one B-47B reconnaissance plane discovered, after flying over more than a thousand miles of Siberia, would provide the answer—and would convince Washington that overflights were the quickest and most reliable way to close the intelligence gap.

Unbelievably, miraculously, until the missile hit Powers's U-2, not a single plane that penetrated Soviet airspace was brought down. But spy missions that were technically not overflights were not always so fortunate. All through the Cold War, aircraft of the Peacetime Airborne Reconnaissance Program (PARPRO) flew along the dangerous margins of the Soviet and Chinese empires, taking photographs of air and naval bases, as well as other military installations and radar and communications equipment. From the beginning, those so-called ferrets took losses. Sometimes, in the predictably foul weather, they would stray too close to the Soviet coast—or MiGs brought them down beyond the forty-mile limit that the Soviets had established. Hall estimates here that between 1946 and 1991, when the Soviet Union dissolved, some 170 aircrewmen died or disappeared into Soviet prisons, where they were interrogated and then apparently executed. As he makes clear, their missions should not be confused with actual overflights, which in every case had to receive presidential authorization. Unlike the ferrets, there was nothing routine about overflights.

It is not surprising that the Soviets had ferrets of their own, including the giant four-engine Tu-95 turboprop, nicknamed "the Bear," which had a range of four thousand miles and could stay aloft for twenty-four hours. Bears regularly flew along both coasts, though they were careful to stay beyond a fifty-mile limit. American jets took to escorting them, and aircrewmen would jovially wave to one another. No Soviet spy plane was ever shot down, as well they might have been if they had ventured too close to the continental U.S. As far as is known, the Soviets never attempted overflights, and perhaps with good reason. President Eisenhower once said that nothing would cause him to "request authority to declare war" sooner "than violation of our air space by Soviet aircraft."

Until Powers's ill-fated mission, all the overflights may have gotten through, but it was a tale of increasingly close calls. Firefights actually took place. This is another case in which Soviets traded shots in anger with American and British pilots. (One overflight veteran kept a chunk of fuselage holed by a cannon shell and had it framed: It now hangs in his California home like a piece of nonobjective art.) After Hall's article appeared, a former RAF pilot, Squadron Leader John Crampton, fleshed out in a letter the account of his hair-raising experience flying over Kiev in the spring of 1954:

I had seen a lot of flak in my time—during the last year of World War II over France and Germany as a bomber pilot. But I saw nothing like that Russian effort. It was brilliant! . . . Every shell burst simultaneously rather as if there had been one master shell—the light or sound seemed to detonate the others. And all the shells went up together in the same split second, and formed this sharply defined "firepath" about 400 feet wide and a mile long. Astonishing. Frightened the life out of me.

Crampton got away—somehow—and as he escaped across the Ukraine, he was able to photograph many of his remaining targets. The U-2, which could reach an altitude of seventy thousand feet, was harder to bring down, and it would take the Russians almost four years to do so. The plane would get the credit for revealing many of the military secrets of the Soviet Union. The earlier overflights were totally forgotten—on purpose. But their accomplishments had been considerable. They allowed the West, in the words of the eminent Cold War scholar John Lewis Gaddis, "to shift reconnaissance out of the realm of espionage altogether." What they learned about Soviet offensive and defensive capabilities would have a profound effect on the conduct of the Cold War.

––––––––

R. CARGILL HALL is chief historian (emeritus) of the National Reconnaissance Office in Washington, D.C.

DURING THE FIRST HALF of the 1950s, before the introduction of the U-2, the United States and its allies sent military aircraft on secret reconnaissance flights over the Soviet Union. They flew over Siberia and behind the Ural Mountains; photographed cities such as Stalingrad, Murmansk, and Vladivostok; and on occasion were engaged by Soviet interceptors. Not a single plane was lost. These were never rogue operations. Between 1951 and 1956, Presidents Truman and Eisenhower and Prime Minister Churchill periodically and on a case-by-case basis authorized these military overflights of the U.S.S.R. and other "denied territory." The risks were great, but so were the intelligence payoffs.

Even today many of the men who took part in the missions (and who were sworn to secrecy) are reluctant to talk about them. Since the dissolution of the Soviet Union in 1991, fragmentary accounts have appeared. Too frequently, however, they have turned on misperceptions and questionable interpretations. Armed with a few interviews and still fewer archival records from the Cold War, authors have provided Oliver Stone–like conspiracies. Some have alleged that the missions were the sole responsibility of the commander in chief of the Strategic Air Command, General Curtis LeMay—who, they charge, sought through overflights to blackmail the Soviet Union or provoke it into starting World War III. To quote one account, he "had apparently begun raising the ante with the Soviet Union on his own, covertly and extralegally."

Other writers have confused presidentially authorized overflight missions with a related aerial reconnaissance effort that operated near Soviet territory but without overflight authorization. The latter missions, which began before 1950 and continued throughout the Cold War, were known as the Peacetime Airborne Reconnaissance Program, or PARPRO. By combining the two different activities, Richard Rhodes could claim in *Dark Sun*, his history of the making of the hydrogen bomb, that "the Soviet Union shot down at least twenty planes during overflights with the loss of an estimated one to two hundred U.S. airmen."

A few words of definition are necessary here. In using the term "overflight," I mean a flight by a government aircraft that, expressly on the direction of the head of state, traverses the territory of another state in peacetime without that other state's permission. PARPRO aircraft did not possess overflight authorization, although a few of them did stray into Soviet territory or over the Soviet Union's territorial waters; some were shot down. Even today almost all of the pertinent records about overflights remain unexhumed, but those already found, as well as the recollections of surviving participants, do provide a broad outline of this most clandestine Cold War enterprise. The true story, so far as it can now be determined, is more dramatic and its dimensions larger than anything recently alleged. The only conspiracy that exists is the conspiracy of silence.

The Cold War began in 1946–47 with the unraveling of the World War II alliance against the Axis powers. Anxious to preserve the independence of Western Europe in the face of a perceived military threat, Western leaders sought to determine the size, composition, and disposition of Soviet forces arrayed behind the Iron Curtain. Late in 1946, Army Air Forces aircraft began flights along the borders of the Soviet Union and its satellite states. These PARPRO missions collected electronic and photographic intelligence, but their intelligence coverage was limited to peripheral regions. Before long, commanders of the new United States Air Force (USAF), formed by the National Security Act of 1947, sought permission to conduct direct overflights of Soviet territory, especially those regions in Siberia closest to Alaska.

The Joint Chiefs of Staff (JCS), however, after consulting with the director of Central Intelligence and the secretaries of defense and state, consistently denied these requests. Indeed, in 1948, after the Soviet foreign ministry vigorously protested the intrusion of American "bombers" over Soviet territorial waters, the Department of State restricted PARPRO missions approaching Soviet borders to standoff distances of no closer than forty miles. Overflights remained out of the question. In receipt of one request for such a mission from Strategic Air Command (SAC) headquarters in Omaha, Nebraska, in October 1950, the

USAF director of intelligence, Major General Charles P. Cabell, replied that he would have to recommend against it. But, Cabell added, "[I am] looking forward to a day when it becomes either more essential or less objectionable."

That day, in fact, was close at hand. International tensions had increased significantly in late 1949, when the Soviet Union exploded a nuclear device and Communist forces swept to victory in China. But perhaps the greatest shock for Western leaders occurred in June 1950, when North Korea launched a surprise attack on South Korea. In November 1950, a few weeks after Cabell wrote to SAC headquarters, Chinese military forces joined the Korean War. The sequence and pace of these events caused American political and military leaders to believe that their Soviet counterparts might launch an attack against Western Europe, possibly along with a surprise aerial attack on the United States.

With United Nations forces in North Korea in full retreat, President Truman issued a proclamation of national emergency on December 16, 1950, and called numerous National Guard units to active duty. A short time later, in an unannounced decision made after a review conducted by the JCS, the president approved selected overflights of the Soviet Union to determine the status of its air forces in those regions of Siberia closest to this country, as well as in the maritime provinces closest to Korea.

The Soviet region of greatest military concern was the Chukotskiy Peninsula, directly across the Bering Strait from Alaska. Russian Tu-4 bombers, essentially carbon copies of the B-29, equipped with nuclear weapons and massed on airfields on the peninsula, could make devastating one-way flights to attack American cities. In December 1950, Truman authorized two deep-penetration overflights of this region; to accomplish them, the JCS and USAF headquarters selected for modification the fourth B-47B off the Boeing assembly line. This newest of SAC bombers, an air-refuelable swept-wing aircraft powered by six jet turbine engines, would be equipped with special compasses, autopilot equipment, a high-latitude directional gyro system for flight in the Arctic, and a special pod for installation in the bomb bay that contained a number of cameras. The B-47B "Stratojet," which carried a crew of three (pilot, copilot, and bombardier-navigator), could reach a full speed of 448 knots (516 mph) and a ceiling of about 41,000 feet.

The command pilot that SAC selected for this mission was Colonel Richard C. Neeley, a B-47 test pilot. Late in July 1951, Neeley and his crew flew the aircraft to Eielson AFB near Fairbanks, Alaska. On August 15, while awaiting clear weather in Siberia and authorization to proceed, Neeley was awakened from a nap in the barracks by a telephone call: His aircraft was burning on the ramp. He stepped outside to see a pillar of smoke and flame in the direction of the runway. Boeing technical representatives had been practicing a single-point fueling of the tanks over the bomb bay when a float valve stuck. Fuel rushed through an overflow vent onto a wing and swirled down onto a power cart below; an electric spark ignited the spill. While the wreckage still smoldered, orders to conduct the overflight mission arrived. Neeley notified SAC headquarters of the disaster; forty years later, he still remembered the four-word return telex message: FIX RESPONSIBILITY AND COURT-MARTIAL! (Since a mechanical malfunction was involved, there was no court-martial.) It was a year before a U.S. aircrew would make an attempt to overfly the eastern U.S.S.R.

Meanwhile, Truman had initiated talks with British Labour prime minister Clement R. Atlee and his foreign minister, Ernest Bevin. Concerned that the United States might use atomic weapons in the Korean conflict, Atlee had visited Truman in Washington at the end of 1950. At that time or shortly thereafter, the two leaders had apparently agreed on a joint aerial reconnaissance program to overfly the European U.S.S.R.; it is not clear whether Truman made concessions on the use of atomic weapons, but it seems likely. Whether Atlee actually intended to approve any overflights is not known; in any event, he would not be around to make the decision. In October 1951 the British reelected as prime minister their wartime leader, the Conservative Winston Churchill.

In the spring of 1951, the RAF formed a secret "Special Duty Flight" of three aircrews to fly North American Aviation RB-45C reconnaissance aircraft. Led by RAF squadron leader John Crampton and his navigator, Flight Lieutenant Rex Sanders, the British airmen flew from England to Barksdale AFB in Louisiana to begin formal flying training in the RB-45C, under the presumed disguise of British-American air refueling trials. Late in the fall of 1951, the RAF aircrews returned with four American aircraft (one acting as a spare) to Sculthorpe Royal Air Force Base in Norfolk, where a detachment of SAC RB-45Cs was already stationed. Lieutenant Colonel Marion C. ("Hack") Mixson arrived in March 1952 to command the SAC detachment, to which Crampton's Special Duty Flight was attached. In the weeks that followed, Mixson, Crampton, and Sanders dealt with the British Air Ministry at the highest levels. In approving the mission, Churchill took a breathtaking political risk. In the 1950s the House of Commons was divided in its attitude toward the Soviet Union: Many in the

Labour Party were sympathetic in varying degrees to Britain's former ally. If any of the RB-45Cs had been brought down, the resulting outcry probably would have led to Churchill's unseating as prime minister. But balanced against this was the need of Western intelligence to acquire radar-scope photographs of specific military installations.

After a trial nighttime flight to the east of Berlin on March 21 to measure the state of Soviet air defense, the first overflight mission was approved and briefed. On the night of April 17–18, 1952, in absolute radio silence, three RB-45Cs repainted in RAF colors took off from Sculthorpe, were air-refueled, and entered the Soviet Union simultaneously at different locations. Flying at about thirty-five thousand feet, the planes proceeded on separate tracks. As each RB-45C crossed the border—into the Baltic states in the north, Belorussia in the center, and the Ukraine in the south (the mission Crampton and Sanders flew)—the Soviet air defense system sprang into action, and Allied intelligence listened in. For all of the fighters that scrambled into the night sky, however, none found the British in the dark, and they returned safely to base. The information they brought back was crucial. In the event of war—which, in the 1950s, seemed likely—SAC had to destroy the U.S.S.R.'s Long-Range Air Force at the outset to prevent it from striking targets in Western Europe and the United States. All three overflights photographed LRAF bases, as well as nearby air defense bases.

The Special Duty Flight disbanded shortly thereafter, though in October it was reformed at Sculthorpe. Training for a second mission began. But in early December the impending mission was canceled. For Churchill, the risking of his political future in one covert overflight had perhaps proved enough. On December 18, John Crampton and Hack Mixson led the Special Duty Flight of four RB-45Cs back across the Atlantic Ocean, landing at Ohio's Lockbourne AFB as snow was falling. Through the gloom, base maintenance personnel who approached the aircraft stared in disbelief at the U.S. Air Force bombers still decked out in British livery.

Back in the United States, the air force, in collaboration with the navy, already had begun to probe eastern Siberia's coastal radar sites and airfields through shallow penetration overflights. Directed by the JCS in 1952, these secret missions depended on the navy Lockheed P2V-3W, a two-engine unpressurized aircraft that possessed a top speed of 300 knots (345 mph) and a service ceiling of 32,000 feet. The novel P2V-3W, equipped with a ventrally mounted APS-20 radar beneath the aircraft, was employed primarily as a submarine hunter-killer. This aircraft was modified with an experimental electronics suite that filled the nose: It could identify, locate, and home in on radars and communications equipment over a wide range of frequencies.

Piloted by Commander James H. Todd with Lieutenant (jg) Richard A. Koch as copilot, the P2V-3W flew out of the Kodiak Island, Alaska, naval base and, in March 1952, conducted test missions against radars of the Alaskan Air Command. It then began overflights of the Siberian coast, leading an air force RB-50 (an improved version of the B-29) that photographed the Soviet radar sites and airfields.

Between April 2 and June 16, 1952, the two planes flew eight or nine missions. They maintained the strictest secrecy, without radio communications of any kind, even on takeoff and landing. They managed to locate and photograph Soviet installations from the Kamchatka Peninsula in the south all the way north through the Bering Straits to Wrangel Island. They were, according to Koch, daytime missions, which were normally launched from Kodiak or Shemya in the Aleutian Islands. The P2V-3W flew at fifteen thousand feet, with its crew on oxygen, and the RB-50 followed above and behind it. Flying inland about fifteen to twenty miles from the Soviet coastline, the navy aircraft used special direction-finding equipment to locate installations for the camera-laden RB-50.

In Alaska, only the aircrews—the admiral commanding Fleet Air Alaska, the general commanding the Alaskan Air Command, and their deputies for intelligence—knew of these missions. Recovery bases varied according to the mission. In one instance late in the evening, the Navy P2V-3W, intercepted by F-94s, landed in radio silence before nonplussed personnel in the control tower at Ladd AFB, Alaska (the RB-50 had presumably gone on to its home base). Immediately surrounded by gun-wagging security police, the navy aircrew members were forced to throw their identity tags onto the tarmac. The exhausted aviators remained under guard and confined onboard their aircraft for several hours until a "higher authority" could be found to vouch for them.

On two of these overflight missions, Soviet MiG-15s intercepted the American aircraft: once over the Bering Strait near the St. Lawrence Islands, and once over Soviet territory, when the fighters scrambled from a snow-covered runway. In each instance, Koch recalled, the MiG-15s flew alongside, inspected and photographed the U.S. planes, but did not attack. (At this time there was apparently a tacit gentleman's agreement between the air forces of the two nations not to initiate hostile action.) Shortly after these shallow overflight missions terminated in mid-June 1952, the navy recalled the crew and their P2V-3W to the continental United States. The crew members neither asked nor were told where the "take" from their missions went—or of any results produced.

Whatever the intelligence product of the air force/navy peripheral overflights of Siberian shores in the spring, by the summer of 1952, American military and political leaders had new cause for concern. By listening in on Russian shortwave broadcasts, signals intelligence had learned that the Soviet air force had begun staging Tu-4 bombers in large numbers at airfields at Dikson on the Kara Sea; at Mys Shmidta on the Chukchi Sea; and at Provideniya on the Chukotskiy Peninsula at the Bering Strait. Moreover, U.S. intelligence suspected that World War II airfields deep inside Siberia, used for staging American lend-lease aircraft bound for Soviet forces on the Eastern Front, might also have been upgraded to accommodate these four-engine bombers. If loaded with the nuclear weapons then believed available to them, any unusual concentration of these bombers represented a real threat.

Officials in the Department of Defense and the CIA again sought permission to photograph air bases in Siberia through deep-penetration aerial overflights. On July 5, 1952, headquarters advised SAC to modify two B-47B bombers for a special photoreconnaissance mission over "unfriendly areas," in the event it was requested. On August 12, Secretary of Defense Robert A. Lovett delivered to President Truman memoranda from General Omar N. Bradley, chairman of the Joint Chiefs of Staff, and General Walter Bedell Smith, director of the CIA, requesting two reconnaissance overflights of Siberia. After discussion, the president approved a "northern run" between Ambarchik and the Chukotskiy Peninsula, but disapproved as too dangerous a "southern run" over Provideniya southwestward past Anadyr to Magadan, returning eastward over the Kamchatka Peninsula. His approval of a single overflight, Truman told Lovett, was contingent on the concurrence of "appropriate officials of the State Department." Secretary of State Dean Acheson must have concurred, because on August 15, USAF headquarters issued instructions for the mission.

For this flight, SAC modified two B-47Bs from the 306th Bombardment Wing at Florida's MacDill AFB. Colonel Donald E. Hillman, the deputy wing commander, was selected to plan the mission and pilot the primary aircraft. The mission was assigned the highest of security classifications; only the commander of SAC, General Curtis E. LeMay, and his directors of operations and intelligence knew the details. In the field, initially only Major General Frank Armstrong, commander of the 6th Air Division at MacDill (and responsible for executing the project), and Hillman knew of it. It should be emphasized that in this instance, as in all others involving overflights, LeMay took his orders from above.

On September 28, 1952, the two modified B-47Bs, accompanied by two KC-97 tankers, flew from MacDill to Eielson AFB. Hillman remained as command pilot of the primary aircraft, with Majors Lester E. Gunter, copilot, and Edward A. Timmins, navigator. Colonel Patrick D. Fleming piloted the backup aircraft, with Majors Lloyd F. Fields, copilot, and William J. Reilly, navigator. With word of good weather over Siberia, General Armstrong authorized takeoff early on October 15, 1952. After meeting the KC-97 tankers in the area of Point Barrow, Alaska, the B-47s received full loads of fuel, and the mission proceeded.

Fleming and his crew photographed and mapped Wrangel Island, located about a hundred miles from the Siberian mainland, and then flew to the communications area over the Chukchi Sea and took up station, flying a racetrack pattern. Maintaining radio silence, Hillman continued on course past Wrangel Island, then turned southwest toward the Soviet coast. Making landfall close to noon, Timmins switched on the cameras as the aircraft swung south for a short period, and then turned eastward and flew back toward Alaska, through the heart of Siberia. The weather, which had been bright and clear throughout the flight, changed after the B-47 crossed the coast. Scattered clouds appeared, and occasional haze at the ground obscured viewing of the surface for the remainder of the flight.

By now, after burning off fuel, Hillman's aircraft had become light enough to be able to fly above 40,000 feet and well over normal cruising speed, at approximately 480 knots (552 mph). After two of five target areas had been covered and photographs of the forbidden landscape below had been taken, warning receivers on board told the crew that the aircraft was being tracked by Soviet radar. Gunter swiveled his seat 180 degrees to the rear to control the plane's only defensive armament, the tailguns. A few minutes later, he advised Hillman that he had Soviet fighters in sight, below and to the rear, climbing desperately to intercept them. But the fighters had scrambled too late to catch up to the B-47, and it flew eastward unopposed.

The aircraft completed photographing the remaining three areas in eastern Siberia without encountering any more fighters. It passed over Egvekinot, then over Provideniya, and turned northeast, exiting Soviet territory at the coast of the Chukotskiy Peninsula. Hillman flew his B-47 straight back to Fairbanks, landing at Eielson well after dark. A few minutes later, Fleming's backup B-47 touched down. Altogether, the mission spanned seven and three quarter hours in the air; the primary B-47 had made a 3,500-mile flight and overflown some 1,000 miles of Soviet territory.

Technicians immediately developed the film. The photographs would belie the presence of massed Tu-4 bombers in Siberia. Messages intercepted soon after revealed that the Soviet regional commander had been sacked and that a second MiG regiment was to be moved into the area. As for the Americans, members of both aircrews received the Distinguished Flying Cross.

By that same fall, Communist and U.N. forces had reached a virtual military stalemate at the 38th Parallel in Korea. Indeed, the Korean conflict had provided President Harry Truman the legal rationale for overflights of the Soviet Union. The U.S.S.R., an unannounced co-belligerent, supported Chinese and North Korean forces with military aircraft operating from sanctuaries in the Soviet Far East. Under international law, when engaged in a United Nations peace enforcement operation, the U.S. could claim the right to overfly such sanctuaries under Chapter VII of the U.N. Charter. But as early as 1950, even before the outbreak of hostilities, a pair of special drop-tank and camera-equipped RF-80As began reconnaissance missions, in an effort to determine the composition of Soviet air forces in the Far East. Between March and August they periodically flew around—and later, directly over—Sakhalin and the Kurile Islands and the Soviet mainland near Vladivostok.

These Far East Air Forces (FEAF) tactical reconnaissance aircraft operated from Yokota Air Base near Tokyo. After the outbreak of the Korean conflict, a detachment of three SAC RB-45Cs performed occasional deep-penetration overflights of North Korea, the Soviet maritime provinces, and the People's Republic of China. In December one of these aircraft was apparently lost to MiG fighters over North Korea, near the Yalu River, leaving only two aircraft to continue the missions. Although details are wanting, these RF-80As and RB-45Cs unquestionably penetrated Soviet territory before Colonel Hillman's B-47B overflight almost two years later.

In October 1952 two RB-45C crews replaced their compatriots in the detachment at Yokota Air Base. Led by Captain Howard S. (Sam) Myers, Jr., they continued deep-penetration overflights in the Far East. Besides missions over

North Korea, other overflight missions, though few in number, focused on mainland China, Sakhalin Island, the Kamchatka Peninsula, and the Vladivostok area. For example, on the night of December 17–18, 1952, Myers and his two-man crew flew RB-45C number 8027, which was painted entirely black, to avoid detection by searchlights, from Yokota across the Sea of Japan. They coasted inland a few miles south of Vladivostok; the Soviet city was well lit and clearly visible off the right wing tip at thirty-five thousand feet. They continued on three hundred miles to targets of interest in the neighborhood of Harbin, Manchuria. After collecting radar-scope photographs of airfields and other military and industrial installations in the area, they returned via South Korea. The two RB-45Cs continued to fly reconnaissance missions until April 1953.

The extreme secrecy that surrounded these flights increased, if that was possible, during 1953. It was a time of leadership change in both the Soviet Union and the United States. Stalin died, and Dwight D. Eisenhower succeeded Harry Truman as president. The former supreme commander of Allied Expeditionary Forces in Europe during World War II fully appreciated the value of strategic overflight reconnaissance that might alert American leaders to a potential nuclear surprise attack (both countries had now exploded hydrogen devices). But if the Korean Armistice that he engineered in July ended hostilities, it also eliminated any legal justification for overflights of the Soviet Union and Communist China. Eisenhower weighed the importance of strategic reconnaissance to national security and the precedent set by President Truman against the political risks of continuing overflights in peacetime, in violation of international treaties to which the United States was a signatory. His choice seemed clear. He determined to continue the overflights as part of the Sensitive Intelligence Program (SENSINT).

In the Far East after July 1953, overflights of the Soviet maritime provinces launched from Japan employed new reconnaissance fighter aircraft—RF-86Fs and RF-100s—and B-57A Canberra bombers converted to photoreconnaissance aircraft. (Overflights of the People's Republic of China devolved largely on the air force of the Republic of China based on Taiwan.) Most, but not all, of the FEAF reconnaissance fighter missions between 1953 and the end of 1956 were shallow-penetration overflights. One deep-penetration daytime overflight, however, is known to have surveilled the city of Harbin in Manchuria, in the People's Republic of China.

Major Robert E. "Red" Morrison piloted another unusually deep-penetration overflight in a reconnaissance fighter in 1955. Morrison had assumed command of the 15th Tactical Reconnaissance Squadron, composed of RF-86Fs stationed at Komaki Air Base, just west of Nagoya. These RF-86s had had their guns removed and their weight and balance adjusted. Each one was equipped with four drop tanks (two 200-gallon and two 120-gallon) that extended their range significantly, and each mounted two aerial cameras featuring a distortionless telephoto lens that adjusted automatically to the pressure and temperature variations inherent in high-altitude photography. Mounted on either side of the pilot's seat, the two cameras photographed the earth in a near-panoramic overlapping swath. Blisters outboard on the fuselage accommodated the film magazines. A wide-area mapping camera looked at the earth vertically from a position beneath and just forward of the pilot's seat.

Morrison's detachment of eight pilots received overflight orders exclusively from officers at FEAF headquarters. There, only four commanding officers and an intelligence officer knew of these missions. Morrison and his squadron conducted nine overflights between April 1954 and February 1955. Normally, four aircraft would take part in daytime missions; they flew at altitudes of 45,000 to 48,000 feet, and always when atmospheric conditions precluded telltale contrails. (Though radar tracked the American fighters, Soviet interceptors could not "see" them to attack. By this time, the old gentleman's agreement had long since faded.) Airfields represented the principal reconnaissance targets, and Morrison and his compatriots overflew Vladivostok, Sakhalin Island, and Sovetskaya Gavan, Dairen, and Shanghai.

The last and longest of these missions, a two-ship flight with Morrison in command, occurred on February 19, 1955. Instead of a shallow horseshoe route over a coastal target, it was directed well into the Soviet mainland to photograph the airfield in Khabarovsk, a city located alongside the Amur River on the border of the U.S.S.R. and Manchuria. As the two aircraft climbed to altitude over the Sea of Japan, Morrison's wingman signaled mechanical problems and turned back. The flight leader pressed on, releasing the last two of his wing tanks as he approached altitude at the Soviet coast. But one of the two tanks did not separate, and the additional weight and drag prevented the aircraft from reaching its peak altitude. To complicate matters further, the pre-flight weather briefing had estimated winds aloft that did not match those encountered, and at the appointed navigational moment, Morrison looked out to find no target in sight.

Fortunately, the Amur River could be seen, and as he flew along it, Morrison homed on a broadcast from the Khabarovsk radio station. With the city in view, he performed a maneuver well known to World War II tactical reconnaissance pilots: he first rolled 90 degrees to port, then reversed the process and rolled in similar fashion to starboard, thereby obtaining a clear view of the earth beneath and ahead of his aircraft, permitting adjustment in the line of flight that would bring the RF-86 directly over the airfield. As he completed these maneuvers and turned on the cameras, the airplane shuddered. The last drop tank, its markings of origin carefully filed off, separated from the wing and whistled downward over Khabarovsk. Though short on fuel, Morrison returned safely to Chitose Air Base on Hokkaido, plunged through a break in the overcast, and landed. The airplane was so light, he recalled, he had difficulty forcing it down onto the runway. As his RF-86 turned off Chitose's concrete ribbon and onto the asphalt apron, its fuel expired and the engine flamed out.

Back on the other side of the world in the spring of 1953, Prime Minister Winston Churchill had reconsidered strategic overflight reconnaissance after word reached Western intelligence of a formidable Soviet missile program under way at a base called Kapustin Yar, near Stalingrad. Once again, Churchill approved an overflight. This time the RAF and the USAF collaborated to squeeze a large, oblique-looking camera into the aft fuselage of a standard RAF B-2 twin-engine Canberra bomber. This bomber could not be air-refueled; but, stripped of all excess weight and with its bomb bay filled with fuel tanks, the aircraft possessed a range sufficient for it to fly at high altitude from Germany across the southern U.S.S.R., and then swing south to Iran.

The British assigned the name Project ROBIN to this effort, which consisted of two or three shallow-penetration missions over the Eastern bloc satellite states preparatory to the main event. Approved by the prime minister, the key mission was flown in late August 1953 from Giebelstadt in West Germany, near the East German border. The Canberra was tracked by Soviet radar almost from the moment of takeoff. Happily for an RAF aircrew flying in broad daylight, accurate radar tracking did not prevent various elements of the Soviet air defense system from performing a Three Stooges routine for Stalin's heirs in the Kremlin. In the face of an air defense system on full alert, the "unidentified" aircraft, operating at 46,000 to 48,000 feet altitude, remained untouched. With its hundred-inch focal-length camera peering obliquely out the port side, it flew doggedly east past Kiev, Kharkov, and Stalingrad to its target, Kapustin Yar.

In spite of frantic commands and radar vectoring, Soviet fighter aircraft could not see the airplane above them and did not successfully intercept the plane until it approached Kapustin Yar. Though they managed to hit the British machine, it flew on, and the fighters lost sight of it again. Damage to the aircraft, however, introduced vibration, which adversely affected the optics performance of the camera. Pictures of Kapustin Yar furnished to the USAF and CIA were blurred and of poor quality; they apparently revealed little. The Canberra turned southeast to follow the Volga River. It escaped and managed to land safely in Iran. Its near-loss ended any further British thoughts of daytime strategic reconnaissance overflights of the western U.S.S.R.

But the flight had unexpected results. Seven years later, on August 5, 1960, *The Philadelphia Inquirer* carried an account of the mission by a Soviet defector who had served in 1953 as an air defense radar officer: "During the [Canberra] flight all sorts of unbelievable things happened. . . . In one region, the operator accidentally sent the Soviet flights west instead of east; in Kharkov, the pilots confused the planes [aloft] and found themselves firing at each other."

The result was a major purge. Many generals and officers were removed from their posts. One general was demoted to the rank of lieutenant colonel and committed suicide. Other personnel were sent to punishment battalions.

However discouraging the outcome of the Canberra's daytime flight to Kapustin Yar, the British and Americans soon agreed on another group of nighttime strategic reconnaissance overflights of the western U.S.S.R. (By this time the USAF had transferred its RB-45Cs from SAC to the Tactical Air Command [TAC], and General LeMay no longer played a direct role in the missions.) At Sculthorpe RAFB, the RAF's Special Duty Flight re-formed with most of the same crews from the 1952 overflight missions; they were once again led by Squadron Leader John Crampton and Squadron Leader Rex Sanders. RAF Bomber Command's chief scientist, "Lew" Llewelyn, worked to improve the pictures produced by the cameras that filmed images on the radar scopes. In late April the RAF aircrews learned that the mission plan was virtually identical to the one flown in 1952, except that the third aircraft would make a deeper penetration of southern Russia.

The Special Duty Flight executed the mission on the night of April 28–29, 1954. The primary targets again involved bases of the Soviet Long-Range Air Force. The RB-45Cs again were repainted in RAF colors, and Crampton and Sanders again took the southern run, but it did not go so easily for them this time. As their airplane approached Kiev—and while Sanders tended the radar—Crampton was startled to see a highway of bursting flak about 200 yards before him at exactly his own altitude, 36,000 feet. Briefed to return if the security of the flight was compromised, he hauled the airplane around on its star-

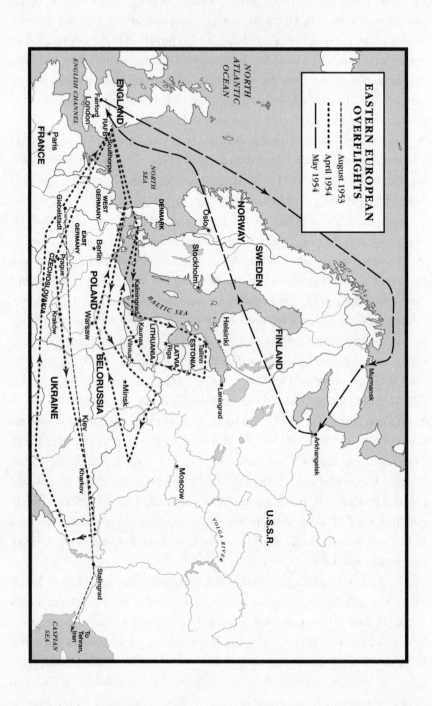

EASTERN EUROPEAN
OVERFLIGHTS

- - - August 1953
.... April 1954
——— May 1954

board wing tip, until its gyro compass pointed west, and descended to thirty-four thousand feet to avoid the flak, which was set to explode at a fixed altitude. He cut short the mission. Nonetheless, the return track took the aircraft close to many of the remaining targets, which Sanders photographed as they passed. When the RB-45C met up with its tanker over West Germany, the refueling boom refused to stay in the aircraft receptacle. Fearing that it might have been damaged by the flak over Kiev, Crampton landed near Munich to refuel. Meanwhile, the other two flights covered their routes without misadventure, though numerous fighters were sent up after them. A few weeks later, in early May, the RAF Special Duty Flight disbanded for the last time.

By now Western leaders had been alerted to the existence of a new Soviet Myacheslav-4 jet-turbine-powered intercontinental bomber (NATO code-named "Bison"). With the number of Bison bombers and nuclear weapons believed to be growing, the region of greatest concern in the U.S.S.R., and about which the least was known, was the Kola Peninsula in extreme northwest Russia, above the Arctic Circle. Intercontinental bombers positioned here could fly foreshortened routes over the North Pole to attack targets in America—and also could easily strike targets in Great Britain. A daytime photographic mission was called for. Whether the British agreed or not, Eisenhower approved one of his own.

In mid-April 1954, SAC—on instructions from the JCS—dispatched a detachment of RB-47Es to the Fairford RAF base near Oxford. The RB-47E mounted in its nose and bomb bay the same type of cameras carried in the RB-45C. On May 8 three aircrews were briefed separately for a secret mission to be conducted in radio silence near the Kola Peninsula in the northern region of the U.S.S.R. Two crews were instructed to turn back at a certain coordinate; unbeknownst to them, the third crew was instructed to fly on into Soviet territory and photograph nine airfields over a six-hundred-mile course from Murmansk south to Arkhangelsk, then southwest to Onega, at which point the aircraft would head due west to the safety of Scandinavia.

The aircrew named to fly this deep-penetration overflight consisted of Captain Harold Austin, pilot; Captain Carl Holt, copilot; and Major Vance Heavilin, navigator. When these men took off from Fairford early on May 8, 1954, they were quite unaware that they followed by one week the nighttime flight of the three RB-45Cs over the western-central Soviet Union. Soviet air defenses still reverberated from that futile exercise. After a refueling off southern Norway, and at the designated departure point about a hundred miles north of Murmansk, two of the three aircraft turned back. Austin's pressed on. Two non-plussed aircrews watched over their shoulders as a comrade receded from view toward the Soviet mainland. It is a tribute to SAC's remarkable standards of professional training that the two aircrews did not break radio silence but, as briefed, returned to base.

Austin's aircraft coasted in over the Kola Peninsula at Murmansk, at noon, at 40,000 feet altitude, and at 440 knots (506 mph) airspeed. Heavilin turned on the radar cameras, along with the suite of cameras in the nose and bomb bay. The weather, Austin recalled, was crystal-clear; it was one of those days when "you could see forever." Before they left the Murmansk area, a flight of three MiG fighters joined them, apparently confirming the identity of the intruder. As they approached airfield targets at Arkhangelsk, six more MiGs arrived, now intent on destroying the American aircraft. Cannon tracers flew above and below the RB-47E; the interceptors could not stay steady at that altitude, and their aim was poor. A running gun battle ensued as Austin finished covering his targets and turned toward Finland. As he banked the plane, a MiG struck from above, and the aircraft took a cannon shell through the top of the port wing, knocking out the intercom. Holt had fired the tail gun, but it jammed after the first burst. Nevertheless, he kept the MiGs at a safe distance long enough to reach the Finnish border.

Austin's RB-47E, with its cameras and film, succeeded in reaching Fairford after another refueling over the North Sea. The photographs reassured Western leaders that long-range bombers were not deployed on the Kola Peninsula. For their extraordinary aerial feat, the aircrew members each received *two* Distinguished Flying Crosses, though the SAC commander, General LeMay, made it plain that he would rather have decorated them only with a Silver Star. That award, however, required the approval of a board in Washington whose members were not cleared to know about SENSINT overflights.

If such reconnaissance overflights were to continue at a reasonable risk, another kind of airplane was required, one that operated above all known Soviet air defenses. A few months later, in November 1954, President Eisenhower approved Project Aquatone, a secret air force–CIA effort directed to build a jet-powered glider that could fly at altitudes in excess of seventy thousand feet, far above Soviet air defenses. So the U-2 was born.

There was at least one further overflight of the Soviet Union launched from Great Britain. In March 1955 a nighttime USAF mission led by Major John

Anderson followed routes and overflew targets that were nearly identical to those of earlier RAF flights: Three RB-45Cs took off from the Sculthorpe RAF base, flew east at thirty thousand feet, and simultaneously crossed the frontiers of Czechoslovakia, Poland, and the Baltic States—though this time the Ukraine track was farther to the south. The mission objective, as before, involved radar-scope photography of Soviet military installations and cities for Allied target folders. Soviet fighters again scrambled into the night sky but, even with ground radar vectoring, could not locate the reconnaissance aircraft in the darkness. All of the RB-45Cs returned safely, landing in West Germany. These crew members, too, received Distinguished Flying Crosses.

That reconnaissance overflight mission preceded by a few months the Four-Power Summit Conference held in Geneva, Switzerland, in July 1955. There President Eisenhower, in an unannounced disarmament proposal, would call for mutual Soviet and Western overflights, eventually called "Open Skies." At the time, the U-2 aircraft was about to begin flight trials in Nevada. Although Soviet officials rejected the Open Skies proposal, the president had determined to employ the U-2 in daytime missions over the western Soviet Union to assay the number of bombers in the Soviet Long-Range Air Force—a number, USAF leaders insisted, that surpassed the number of such bombers in the air force inventory.

But the fragile U-2 was not air-refuelable. Even though its unrefueled radius of action was anticipated to be substantial, around 3,400 miles, when launched from England or West Germany, it would be unable to fly far beyond the Ural Mountains and return in safety. And it was not designed to operate in the snow and ice of Arctic bases. For American intelligence, the U.S.S.R.'s vast Arctic territory, stretching 3,500 miles from the Kola Peninsula in the West to Wrangel Island in the East, remained largely terra incognita—and the U-2 appeared unable to explore it.

Between March 30 and May 7, 1955, shortly before the summit conference convened, the Strategic Air Command conducted Project Seashore, again on instructions from the JCS. Four RB-47Es, specially modified with the side-looking hundred-inch focal-length cameras like those carried by the Canberra, teamed with four RB-47Hs to fly PARPRO missions from Eielson AFB, Alaska, along Siberia's northern and eastern shores. The resulting intelligence of increased aerial forces in the region caused the nation's leaders to consider over-flights of Russia's entire northern slope that would locate and identify air defenses as well as the disposition of aerial forces there. In early February 1956, President Eisenhower terminated Project Genetrix, the launching of high-altitude photoreconnaissance balloons that would drift across the U.S.S.R. In the four preceding weeks, SAC had launched 516 of them from Western Europe and Turkey. Those that succeeded in crossing the U.S.S.R. released their gondolas by parachute, the gondolas being recovered in midair by C-119 cargo aircraft near Japan. But so many were shot down by Soviet air defenses, or were otherwise lost, that only forty-four were retrieved. At the same time, Eisenhower approved an air force project to fly SAC reconnaissance aircraft over and around the Soviet far north, mapping it completely, photographically and electronically.

The Strategic Air Command's Project Homerun overflights—unknown to all but a few until now—were launched from Thule, Greenland, between March 21 and May 10, 1956. During that seven-week period, RB-47E photo reconnaissance aircraft and RB-47H electronic reconnaissance aircraft flew almost daily over the North Pole to reconnoiter the entire northern slope and interior portions of the U.S.S.R., from the Kola Peninsula to the Bering Strait. It was a 3,400-mile round trip. The special SAC detachment formed for this operation included, with spares, sixteen RB-47Es of the 10th Strategic Reconnaissance Squadron, Lockbourne AFB, Ohio; five RB-47Hs from the 343rd Strategic Reconnaissance Squadron from Forbes AFB, Kansas; and two full squadrons of some twenty-eight KC-97 tankers. All of these aircraft shared Thule's single ten-thousand-foot snow-and-ice-covered runway; all of them took off, refueled over the North Pole, and landed in complete radio silence.

The air base, located 690 miles north of the Arctic Circle on North Star Bay, is thirty-nine miles north of the nearest human habitation, the Eskimo village of Thule. The aircrews typically deplaned in temperatures of 35 degrees below zero (in an era when windchill factors were unheard of), in a region devoid of vegetation and covered in snow, at a time of year when darkness ruled nearly twenty-four hours a day. Maintenance crews and flight crews alike were quartered in what looked like railroad refrigerator cars, down to the levered door handles. Toilets operated via the "armstrong" flush system—hand-pumped. After receiving Arctic clothing, including fur-lined parkas and mukluks, the crews spent the first week in Arctic survival training and practicing Arctic flight operations: takeoffs and landings on ice-covered runways, navigating over the Pole, and air refueling in radio silence.

Planners had divided the Soviet Arctic into three basic sectors, spanning a

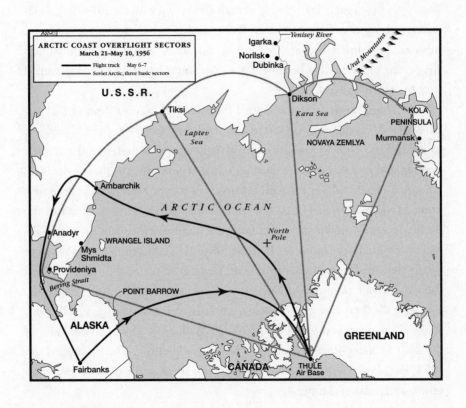

ARCTIC COAST OVERFLIGHT SECTORS
March 21–May 10, 1956

Flight track   May 6–7
Soviet Arctic, three basic sectors

Igarka

Yenisey River

Norilsk
Dubinka

Ural Mountains

U.S.S.R.

Tiksi

Dikson

Kara Sea

KOLA
PENINSULA

*Laptev
Sea*

NOVAYA ZEMLYA

Murmansk

Ambarchik

ARCTIC OCEAN

*North
Pole*

Anadyr

WRANGEL ISLAND

Mys
Shmidta

Providetiya

Bering Strait

POINT BARROW

ALASKA

GREENLAND

Fairbanks

CANADA

THULE
Air Base

total of 3,500 miles. The first extended eastward from the Kola Peninsula to Dikson on the Kara Sea; the second extended from Dikson to Tiksi on the Laptev Sea; and the third from Tiksi to the Bering Strait. The RB-47s normally flew in pairs, often with an E (photoreconnaissance) and H (electronic reconnaissance) model teamed, in a normal wing formation. Because one tanker was required for each bomber, the KC-97s operated in a similar fashion. Each flight of one or more reconnaissance aircraft over the North Pole to the Soviet Union, whatever the number in it, was counted as a mission. About four or five missions were flown each day, rotating aircraft and crews, with the RB-47Es and Hs always arriving over Soviet territory during daylight. The aircrews for different missions were briefed separately, and no one knew where their compatriots were going or asked what became of the film and electronic recordings turned in at the end of the day.

The Thule missions photomapped the island of Novaya Zemlya (or "Banana Island," as the aircrews referred to it) and its atomic test site. They flew in behind the Ural Mountains and down rivers, reconnoitering the timber, mining, and nickel smelting industries in the region. Siberia, they discovered, remained mostly wilderness, with few roads or towns. Most of the Thule missions, however, operated but a few miles inside Soviet territory all across the Arctic, locating, identifying, and photographing the infrequent radar stations and air bases. They confirmed that the Soviet Union's northern regions were poorly defended against enemy aircraft: Only on three or four occasions did Russian aircraft attempt to intercept missions, never successfully. At Thule, Brigadier General Hewitt T. Wheless, commander of the 801st Air Division, directed the operation along with Colonel William J. Meng, commander of the 26th Strategic Reconnaissance Wing at Lockbourne, which supplied the RB-47Es. Major George A. Brown served with them as the project operations officer and mission planner.

The Thule missions drew down in early May 1956, beginning with the RB-47Hs' departure for Lockbourne AFB. Before the RB-47Es followed them, they conducted the so-called massed overflight. In a single mission flown on May 6 and 7, six RB-47Es took off from Thule, flew over the North Pole, and entered Siberia in daylight near Ambarchik. Flying abreast, they proceeded south at forty thousand feet, with engines operating at full power. The aircraft turned eastward and, while photomapping the entire region, exited the U.S.S.R. over

Anadyr on the Bering Strait. The RB-47Es recovered at Eielson AFB, Alaska, and the next day returned over the North Pole to Thule.

In his retirement years, General Curtis LeMay more than once referred erroneously to a massed overflight of Vladivostok. In Tom Coffey's book *Iron Eagle*, based on interviews with the general, LeMay declared, "I flew the entire SAC reconnaissance force over the Siberian city of Vladivostok." But later writers have conveniently forgotten—or ignored—his words at the end of this accounting: "It wasn't my idea," he said. "I was ordered to do it." Whether LeMay altered and exaggerated the account for effect or for reasons of his own, we will probably never know.

Reflecting on the Thule missions collectively, Brigadier General William Meng recalled, "They were conducted in complete radio silence. One word on the radio, and all missions for the day had to abort. But that never happened; not one mission was ever recalled. Altogether, we flew 156 missions from Thule." Throughout the entire operation, Meng might have added, with maintenance crews working in subzero temperatures on exposed aircraft, and with aircrews operating from the ice- and fog-covered runway, not a single person or airplane was lost in an accident or to Soviet action. To this day, the SAC Thule missions remain one of the most incredible demonstrations of professional aviation skill ever seen in any military organization at any time.

In Washington, D.C., on May 28, 1956, President Eisenhower met with top administration officials to discuss, among other things, a protest of the American overflights of Soviet Arctic territories. In attendance, beside Eisenhower's military assistant, Colonel Andrew Goodpaster, were Allen Dulles, director of the CIA; Admiral Arthur M. Radford, chairman of the JCS; General Nathan F. Twining, air force chief of staff; and Undersecretary of State Herbert Hoover, Jr. The Soviet note, dated May 14, had been delivered to the American embassy in Moscow (but, for whatever reason, did not mention specifically the massed overflight of Anadyr). Twining advised that the Thule operation had been shut down a few days before the note was received. The president said he wanted to encourage the Soviet leadership to move in peaceful directions: The American response must be carefully drawn. Hoover read a proposed draft to which, apparently, all agreed. The next day, May 29, the Department of State presented to the Soviet embassy a note explaining that "navigational difficulties in the Arctic region may have caused unintentional violations of Soviet air space, which, if they in fact had occurred, the Department regretted."

A few months later, on July 4, 1956, a U-2 took off from West Germany and flew a first mission over the western U.S.S.R. It, too, drew a sharp Soviet protest a few days later. Because the overflights threatened a rapprochement between the superpowers, the president had become increasingly uncomfortable approving American violations of Soviet airspace. But administration leaders, according to the president's science adviser, James Killian, viewed the high-flying single-engine U-2 as far less menacing than a multiengine reconnaissance bomber. Eisenhower determined to continue U-2 overflights, especially after a mission on July 5 provided intelligence about the number of Soviet long-range aircraft that all but ended the "bomber gap" controversy. In the fall, a newly-appointed chairman of the JCS, former air force chief of staff General Nathan Twining, nonetheless urged the president to approve another military overflight of Soviet territory with a new reconnaissance aircraft.

This aircraft was the air-refuelable Martin RB-57D-0, a single-seat photo-reconnaissance version of the RAF Canberra bomber, built under British license. The lightweight long-winged aircraft, powered by two Pratt & Whitney J57 jet engines, possessed a combat speed of 430 knots (495 mph) and could reach an altitude of some 64,000 feet. Because it flew faster than the U-2 and almost as high, Eisenhower was persuaded that the machine would escape Soviet detection. He approved a mission to fly three RB-57Ds over separate targets in the maritime region near Vladivostok.

Three RB-57D-0s deployed to Yokota Air Base in Japan in early November 1956. This detachment flew the mission on December 11, a bright, clear day. They entered the maritime region simultaneously from three different locations near Vladivostok and overflew three different targets. Contrary to air force hopes, the bombers were picked up on Soviet radar, and MiG-17s scrambled to intercept them, but the Americans were out of reach. In the exposed film returned to the intelligence community, the fighters were clearly visible, pirouetting in the thin air beneath the bombers. The resulting protest on December 14 left no doubt about the capabilities of Soviet air defenses to detect and identify aircraft:

On December 11, 1956, between 1307 and 1321 o'clock, Vladivostok time, three American jet planes, type B-57, coming from . . . the Sea of Japan, south of Vladivostok, violated the . . . air space of the Soviet Union. . . . Good weather prevailed in the area violated, with good visibility, which precluded

any possibility of the loss of orientation by the fliers during their flight. . . .
The Government of the Soviet Union . . . insists that the Government of the
U.S.A. take measures to punish the guilty parties and to prevent any future
violations of the national boundaries of the U.S.S.R. by American planes.

Four days after the Soviet note was delivered, an exasperated president met
with Secretary of State John Foster Dulles to consider the embarrassing situation and decide on a course of action. Under the circumstances, Dulles had to
say that it would be difficult for the country to deny the RB-57 overflights. But
Eisenhower would not consent to such an admission. Instead, he instructed
Colonel Goodpaster to relay an order to Secretary of Defense Charles Wilson,
JCS chairman General Nathan Twining, and CIA director Allen Dulles: "Effective immediately, there are to be no flights by U.S. [military] reconnaissance
aircraft over Iron Curtain countries." With the sole exception of the Cuban
Missile Crisis, U.S. military overflights of the U.S.S.R. and other Iron Curtain
countries ceased for the remainder of the Cold War—though CIA overflights
would be authorized periodically.

When President Eisenhower ended U.S. military overflights of Iron Curtain
countries, this clandestine effort disappeared entirely from view and almost entirely from memory. Though few of the pertinent documents can be located
now, and despite the passing of almost all those who shaped the policy, military
overflights have an important place in the postwar evolution of strategic overhead reconnaissance.

By the time Eisenhower approved the building of the U-2 in late 1954,
peacetime strategic overflight reconnaissance had become a firm national policy. Meanwhile, the platforms from which to conduct it moved to ever higher
altitudes: from military aircraft to high-altitude balloons, from the U-2 to the
SR-71—a supersonic aircraft that could fly at altitudes above eighty thousand
feet—and ultimately, from airspace into outer space with robotic reconnaissance satellites. After military fighters and bombers, every one of these
remarkable technical advances was evaluated, approved, and first funded for
development by one American president: Dwight Eisenhower. By the time
Eisenhower left office in 1961, the intelligence produced by overhead reconnaissance had eliminated the supposed gaps in weaponry between the superpowers. Once American leaders could meet a real rather than an imagined
Soviet threat, they could hold the size of the military establishment to reasonable limits. The resulting defense savings amounted to billions of dollars.

In the mid-1950s, American military and political leaders worked with virtually no reliable intelligence information on Soviet military preparations and capabilities. Thanks to strategic overflight reconnaissance, their successors dealt with a surfeit of such information, almost all of it reliable. That transformation turned first on the sacrifices of American airmen who flew in the SENSINT program. They knew of the risks they took and accepted them in the interests of national security. Altogether, between 1946 and 1991, some 170 U.S. Air Force and Navy aircrew members were lost to Soviet attacks on PARPRO missions. Remarkably, among all of the American flights that intentionally overflew Soviet and Chinese territory on White House orders, none was lost until a Soviet antiaircraft rocket knocked Francis Gary Powers's U-2 out of the sky on May 1, 1960. But that is another story.

The Berlin Tunnel

GEORGE FEIFER

Berlin, as George Feifer remarks here, was "ground zero of the clash between East and West." It was like an island washed by the unfriendly seas
of Communism; but until the erection of the Berlin Wall in 1961, the
borders between the three Allied zones of the city and the Soviet remained open. The East needed the products and hard currency of the
West. People moved back and forth, more from east to west: All through
the 1950s well over a hundred thousand a year chose to flee East Germany, the so-called German Democratic Republic, or simply the GDR.
Both sides took advantage of this relative openness in another way. Espionage became a trade as ordinary as haberdashery or milk delivery, and
almost as respectable. The divided city, said a CIA operative, was a place
where "everyone was a spy, and the spies were spying for everyone."
Berlin, the historian David Clay Large adds, was "postwar Europe's capital of espionage. Some eighty spy agencies and their various front organizations, disguised as everything from jam exporters to research
institutes, worked the city." (It was a novelist's paradise, and Cold War
fiction became a literary genre all its own.)

Berlin may have given Allied intelligence services one of their few
windows on the East, but the panes were too often distorted and mist-
enshrouded. The farther from the city one traveled, the more difficult
it was to pick up the information needed to gauge the potential of the
Soviet threat. The U.S.S.R. was all but impenetrable to Western espionage, as were its satellites. (As has been pointed out, that impenetrabil-
ity explained the need for overflights.) What was the Soviet capability
for offensive action, not only against Berlin and West Germany but also
against Western Europe itself? How much was the GDR contributing

to the Soviet nuclear program? After the anti-government riots that had spread across East Germany in June 1953, how strong did anti-Communist sentiment remain? Could it still be exploited?

The spy game became even more risky thanks to moles in the British Secret Intelligence Service (SIS) and the West German Foreign Intelligence Service. Between 1953 and 1955, they betrayed the West's spy network in the Soviet bloc and for a time almost eliminated it. Several hundred Allied agents were rounded up, not a few of whom were executed. Meanwhile, the GDR cut telephone links between East Germany and the West, suspended bus and tram service between the two Berlins, and closed the frontier with West Germany. With its barbed wire, watchtowers, minefields, and control points, *die Grenze*—"the border"—became a genuine iron curtain, an uncrossable corridor 858 miles long. None of these measures stopped the flow of refugees, which included many of East Germany's youngest and best-educated citizens, a true brain drain (as well as a sizable number of Stasi, the GDR secret police organization that, per capita, was larger than the Nazi Gestapo).

If the Soviets continually outdid the West in spycraft and the brutal and distasteful exercise of counterintelligence, its adversaries had the edge in matters technological. Technology could be the equal of any number of well-placed spies: Witness the success of overflights. That brings us to the Berlin tunnel, among the most spectacular, if short-lived (eleven months and eleven days), intelligence contrivances of its time. The tunnel was the brainchild of one of the outsize (in every sense) characters of the Cold War—the CIA station chief in Berlin, William King Harvey, a hard-drinking, womanizing gun nut who had earned a deserved reputation as an imaginative case officer. Harvey recognized that there was much intelligence mileage to be had in the tapping of phone lines. As one CIA man remembered, pinpointing a notable limit of Communist technology, "When the Soviet commandant in Bucharest or Warsaw called Moscow, the call went through Berlin." Overhead lines, which the KGB favored, were virtually inaccessible, but buried cables were another matter. The CIA discovered that signal cables ran along a road just on the other side of the border from the American sector. But how to reach them? Harvey's solution was to dig a tunnel that would be stuffed with the most advanced listening devices and would end in a tapping chamber next to the cables. Its model was a similar but far more modest tunnel that the British had dug in that other Cold War espionage capital, Vienna. Operation Silver, as it was called, had produced a great amount of useful information about Soviet arms and intentions; this tunnel would be Operation Gold. "Harvey's Hole" would work beyond the wildest imaginings of its creators. But would it, really? The argument still goes on. The project was so important that it had to be kept secret from most CIA agents. But the Soviets, as it turned out, had an even bigger secret of their own.

GEORGE FEIFER is the author of eight books on Russia, including *Justice in Moscow, Moscow Farewell,* and *Red Files*. Since his first visit in 1959, he has lived in Moscow on and off extensively. Feifer spent 1962, the year of the Cuban Missile Crisis, as a graduate exchange student studying Soviet criminal law at Moscow University. He is currently writing an account, from both the American and Japanese sides, of Commodore Perry's opening of Japan.

HARVEY'S HOLE, the Cold War's most daring espionage exploit, crowned the legend inspired and courted by its namesake. William Harvey, a former FBI specialist in Soviet counterintelligence operations, switched to the CIA in 1947 after failing to uphold J. Edgar Hoover's standards for his agents' personal comportment. Harvey's Hole was a tunnel dug in 1953 from a secret site near the border of Berlin's American and Soviet sectors, then boldly into Communist territory to tap communication cables there. The visionary undertaking ended in high success and abysmal failure. Although Harvey was a kind of misbegotten John Wayne, the story, like many about espionage at the highest levels, is too complex and ambiguous for that kind of movie.

Not that the setting was less than ideal. Throughout the 1950s, the Cold War was most intense in divided Berlin. After the 1948–49 Soviet blockade failed to force the United States, Great Britain, and France from their sectors, the old German capital—with the world's largest, most prestigious CIA station a stone's throw from the world's largest concentration of Soviet troops—remained ground zero of the clash between East and West. It was as if the proximity of the nemesis pumped both sides' adrenaline into the torn city from throughout the planet.

Berlin's KGB station was so critical that its chief was one of the huge agency's deputy chairmen. General Yevgeny Pitovranov, who occupied the position during the tunnel's conception and construction, happened to be a model officer. The well-educated, low-key professional had served as the chief of Soviet foreign intelligence. He had few vices, not even an interest in acquiring coveted German consumer goods, an activity that preoccupied some of his subordinates. While the general lived very modestly in the Soviet compound, his opposite number, William King Harvey, followed his 1952 appointment as the CIA station chief by choosing a magnificent, heavily fortified villa. The flamboyant Harvey and the temperate Pitovranov made a curious contrast.

Like all legends, "Big Bill" prompted exaggeration. The outsize thirty-seven-year-old drank up to five martinis before raising a fork to his lunch, and he seemed immune to criticism for sometimes making an afternoon spectacle of himself. The staff at BOB (Berlin Operations Base), as the station was called, held him in half-admiring, half-nervous awe. He always kept loaded revolvers there: three or four in his desk and two on his person, rotated daily from among his collection. Racks of firearms lined the walls, and thermite bombs atop the safes would instantly destroy the files within if the Soviets invaded, as expected. During his Berlin heyday, a beer-hall waitress politely handed Harvey a pistol that had fallen from his pocket. He never checked his heaters in restaurants because "When you need 'em, you need 'em in a hurry." Actually, he had no such need in Berlin, thanks to a scrupulously observed understanding that KGB and CIA officers didn't shoot one another. Still, Harvey required all new BOB personnel to draw a weapon.

To some extent, the man merely reflected the times; CIA Cold Warriors were hardly alone in fearing the Communist peril. The Doolittle Report commissioned by President Eisenhower would warn in 1954, during the tunnel's construction, that America confronted "an implacable enemy whose avowed objective is world domination by whatever means and at whatever cost." No rules mattered in such a struggle, the authors contended. "Hitherto acceptable norms of human conduct do not apply. If the United States is to survive, long-standing American concepts of 'fair-play' must be reconsidered." Harvey himself might have written the report's appeal for more espionage to "subvert, sabotage, and destroy our enemies." As it was, ranking American visitors to BOB headquarters were buoyed by a rousing delivery of his signature speech about "protecting the United States against its enemies." Startled Europeans tended to see the passionate lover of pearl handles and battle hyperbole as dangerously half-cocked himself: the archetypal anti-Communist cowboy.

John Kennedy approved. The young president and Ian Fleming fan would speak of the pear-shaped Harvey, with his bulging eyes and froglike voice, as a kind of American James Bond. Actually, the "memorably bizarre figure"—as described by Evan Thomas's account of CIA all-stars, *The Very Best Men*—occupied the opposite end of the manly-beauty spectrum from braw Bond. That aside, the comparison was not outrageous. Harvey took pains to broadcast his relish for whiskey and guns. The son of a small-town Indiana lawyer cultivated his macho Texan image because he believed it helped him get results. Something clearly did. He was known as a superb case officer who combined astute hunches with careful legwork in running his cases—usually potential new sources of information. More street-smart than academically analytical, he had a sure sense of the human frailties that often led people to involve themselves in spying. Uncommon ability to identify and mesh every relevant detail bolstered his excellence in operations.

The anti-elitist Harvey was chosen to head BOB—the CIA's most critical station—fresh from sniffing out Kim Philby as an arch KGB spy in Washington, while other Americans were still inviting the upper-crust British traitor to their clubs. But he'd had so little administrative preparation for a post of BOB's importance, and he so differed from his Ivy League predecessors, that his case officers saw their new boss as "a creature from another planet."

The stakes were huge. Would Moscow succeed in dominating Europe by dislodging the bone in its throat called West Berlin? Would there be war? Would the information filched by the other side give it a decisive advantage? The espionage players were certain that Europe's fate hung in the balance, especially after a series of Berlin confrontations, including the blockade, that were more suggestive of real war than any cold variety. Post-Communism studies have established that both sides were convinced the other was itching to invade. The Americans particularly feared that the Soviet onslaught would fall on NATO's embryonic European defenses. To counter the vastly superior Communist forces, information about them, and about Moscow's intentions, became more vital than ever.

Berlin's unique features put it on the front line of Cold War espionage. It was an island surrounded by Soviet-bloc territory. The only land access to its Western sectors was through a hundred miles of East Germany, which often harassed Berlin-bound traffic, under Moscow's direction. Still, East and West could mix on the island as nowhere else. Before the erection of the Berlin Wall in 1961, freedom of movement throughout the city created a gap in the Iron Curtain. The city was a rare operational asset for both sides because all Germans, and their respective Cold War allies, could make normal social contact with one another there. Among them, squads of spies, "illegals," informers, double agents, and accomplices crossed back and forth between the hostile sectors, controlling agents who were spying, lying, stealing, secretly photographing, deceiving, and working to thwart their opposite numbers who were doing the same.

Big Bill envisioned something better. Interception of the enemy's radio traffic had recently all but ceased because Soviet communications had switched to more secure means. The lost source of information had to be replaced—but almost certainly not by raiding the scrupulously patrolled Soviet lines strung on telephone poles. However, Harvey knew about Operation Silver, in which British intelligence had tapped underground lines at the Soviet army's Vienna headquarters. He wanted to try something similar but far more ambitious in Berlin. It would be called Operation Gold.

Among the plentiful myths that would spring up about the tunnel were those suggesting that the idea first came from Reinhard Gehlen, the famous founder of West Germany's Intelligence Service, or from the U.S. Army's intelligence section (G-2). In fact, the project's father was Harvey, even before he took up his Berlin post. Indeed, it was his inspiration to tap underground Soviet cables that explained the appointment, startling to CIA veterans, of the then obscure, non-German-speaking staff officer as BOB's chief.

Harvey directed the first step while still in Washington: learning where the enemy cables were, and what traffic each one carried. He brought in a communications specialist fluent in German and supervised a powerful effort to recruit East Germans who had access to the cable network's routings. Since no BOB officer personally ventured into East Berlin, that had to be done by instructing BOB's covert agents when they visited West Berlin. An official of an East Berlin post office procured bulky books with details of cable traffic. An operative dubbed the *Nummer Mädchen,* or "numbers girl," provided comprehensive data from the cards maintained in her classified post office switching room, where orders were executed designating cables for specific Soviet traffic. A prominent East German lawyer specializing in international postal usage would arrive impeccably dressed for an elaborate dinner in his honor at a West Berlin safe house. The highly conservative guest would then begin by lowering his trousers and ripping adhesive tape from his buttocks to remove cards onto which the operations of communications switching offices had been copied. Slowly, laboriously, with time-consuming checks to ensure that the information from various sources agreed, new and old East German operatives helped BOB form a picture of the Soviet network.

The intricate undertaking was made yet more difficult by Harvey's determination to hide it from all but three top CIA officers in Germany. A handful of selected BOB officers worked on matters related to Operation Gold, but without knowing the purpose of their assignments and unable to give them their full

time because emergencies kept sidetracking them. The just-founded Hauptver-
waltung Aufklärung, or Main Intelligence Directorate, of the GDR (German
Democratic Republic)—which would become notorious under Markus Wolf,
the "man without a face"—had recruited an important agent who had been
providing BOB information from his position in an East German foreign exchange bank. The BOB officer running that case was also in charge of developing agents in East German telecommunications, so his time and attention
were split. Another major distraction came when Soviet and East German intelligence kidnapped Walter Linse, a leader of a CIA-supported "Free Jurists'
Committee" that attempted to defend East Germans from Soviet and East German oppression.

Those and other urgent new tasks did not dent Harvey's iron resolve to preserve the project's secrecy. He did not mention Operation Gold to David Murphy when the latter was appointed BOB's deputy base chief in 1954. (Murphy
is coauthor of *Battleground Berlin: CIA vs. KGB in the Cold War.*) Murphy's
briefing, which came only after he arrived in Berlin, was further delayed while
he worked to recruit Boris Nalivaiko, a highly knowledgeable veteran of the
KGB's Berlin station. That compound was known as Karlshorst, for the district
where it was located.

Some three thousand people, including Soviet military guards and signals
personnel, inhabited Karlshorst's tightly fenced square mile. In BOB's cramped
Target Room, a dozen miles away, the "targets" were KGB officers, such as
Nalivaiko, who occupied or had occupied critical positions in the Soviet compound. Paucity of information about possible candidates made exhausting
work of choosing which ones might be worthy of a campaign to turn them. Col-
lating scraps of meticulously gathered information about the Soviets' duties
and habits, BOB officers tried to connect their names and ranks with faces on
photographs, some taken from a disguised truck parked just outside Karlshorst.
Other photos came from a nearby retail photo shop whose proprietor made
BOB an extra set of prints when the Soviets came in to develop their family
snapshots. The fond aim in the Target Room was to identify, select, and finally
recruit Karlshorst personnel by uncovering and exploiting their vulnerabilities.

It was a daunting task. Intense professionalism, reinforced by the extreme
wariness of officers who knew the penalty for slips, rendered futile BOB's recruitment efforts with Nalivaiko and every other KGB officer in Berlin. Endlessly coached to avoid both East and West Germans as possible "imperialist"

agents, KGB officers were also ceaselessly watched by the security specialists of various Soviet agencies, buttressed by swarms of colleague-informers. Over 95 percent of the social contacts between Soviets and East Germans reported to BOB were for quick commercial sex. GDR counterintelligence investigated meetings of longer duration, of which there were few.

The KGB's powerful defenses heightened Harvey's zeal for the tunnel gamble. He and the handful of senior officials who knew about the plan were able to shape it more precisely after a BOB source in the GDR's Ministry of Post and Telecommunications provided copies of maps showing the locations of Berlin's cable traces. In the spring of 1953 an intrepid BOB agent in an East Berlin telephone office, working in the dead of night, patched Soviet lines to a West Berlin circuit long enough for BOB to record them. The tapes confirmed that the Soviets were making ample use of the underground cables, and that the material being transmitted was of great interest.

The overwhelming majority of BOB officers, who knew nothing about the tunnel, kept to their normal duties, which included a ceaseless hunt for information from new volunteers or targets. Soon one of the best of the former would be an anonymous man never seen by anyone in BOB. The mysterious benefactor would use a West Berlin letter drop for secret written notes, some warning of KGB penetrations of Western intelligence services. He would sign his messages "Sniper." Valued as the notes were, Harvey could not have imagined the Sniper's eventual effect on Operation Gold.

The big questions for Harvey in late 1952 and early 1953 were where to start and end the tunnel, and how to disguise the digging. More tests and precious additional information from East German telecommunications files and technicians' reports indicated that the most promising cables—numbers 150, 151, and 152—lay along a highway called Schönefelder Chaussee, which led to Karlshorst. They included a high-frequency line that linked Moscow with Soviet military headquarters in Wunsdorf, twenty miles south. With Harvey often traveling to other European cities for technical consultation about construction, designs were drawn to gouge a shaft fully six feet in diameter to the cables. Big Bill posed as a diplomat so that he would have immunity if something happened, by accident or intent, to bring down his plane during his frequent flights over East Germany. All other BOB personnel were supposedly members of Berlin's American military garrison.

Harvey supervised the writing of a report to CIA director Allen Dulles, who loved the project and formally approved it. In October 1952, Harvey flew to London for highly secret meetings with specialists from the British Secret Intelligence Service (SIS). Thanks to their greater expertise and experience, British technicians would plant the actual taps at the tunnel's end. After experiments in England and New Mexico to test soil conditions, ground was broken in August 1953.

No quick summary can do justice to the imaginative solutions and ardent exertions that went into the construction. The tunnel began below a massive semiunderground warehouse near the southern end of the border between the American and Soviet sectors. That was another Harvey brainchild: a structure specially built to hide the 3,100 tons of earth that would be excavated—and to provide cover, since the cupola-topped warehouse was disguised as a radar intercept station, the logical need for which would not arouse Soviet suspicions. The impostor radar facility had ramps along which trucks laden with earth could roll to the cavernous basement. From five yards below it, the tunnel would burrow nine hundred yards to the border, then another nine hundred to the cables.

The ceaseless war of espionage aboveground continued to serve as a spur. Following the kidnapping of Walter Linse, the GDR began arresting other members of the Free Jurists' Committee. That, together with generally tightened Soviet security, made BOB's communications with its agents in the East even more difficult, inspiring the tunnel staff to solve their design and construction problems.

When the diggers, from a carefully chosen unit of the U.S. Army's Corps of Engineers, broke though a wall beneath an old house, the contents of a cesspool drenched them. To avoid the attention likely to be aroused if foul-smelling clothing were sent to local laundries, an underground washer and dryer were installed. At the same time, the listening and recording devices—such as demodulation equipment to separate carrier channels in the Soviet cables and amplifiers for each line—were chosen or specially designed, then coordinated. Only personnel aware of the tunnel were admitted to the warehouse. Harvey and his closest colleagues avoided observation by visiting in closed trucks. Daily logs registering all movement of personnel and vehicle traffic near the site were scrutinized for pattern changes. Microphones for detecting intruders were placed along the border fence. Overlooking the tunnel's line to its target, a concealed observation post in the warehouse was manned around the clock. Following a trip to Washington by Harvey to obtain approval, plastic explosives were planted for collapsing the tunnel in an emergency without causing a surface explosion.

The tunnel's construction, like its conception, was a dazzling display of CIA creativity and enterprise, technological expertise, and resourcefulness in overcoming myriad problems. It also seemed to exhibit superb ability to maintain the highest degree of security in the world's most difficult environment for it, where armies of spies and double agents reported every rumor to debriefers of the eighty-odd secret service agencies. Normally, Berlin was an intelligence sieve where "everyone was a spy, and the spies were spying for everyone," as a colleague of Harvey's described the city those seven years before the building of the Wall. Preserving the secrecy of so large and complex a project in those conditions seemed a demonstration of operational brilliance. Despite East Germany's vigilant police state, despite ardent surveillance by the KGB and Stasi, its near-paranoiac, Gestapo-like East German offspring, the digging proceeded undetected.

The caricature of the hard-drinking, gun-toting "Pear," as Harvey's agents had nicknamed him, held true in its narrow way. Colleagues called luncheon at his suburban villa "trial by firewater": Dry martinis were poured and sipped from noon to the serving of the meal four hours later. But his labors to give birth to the tunnel while heading Europe's largest, most active CIA station were remarkable. The project quivered with his huge energy and ability to inspire his subordinates. His work discipline and nose for potential trouble had never been more impressive. His creative single-mindedness fused with his passion and talent for thinking of every detail.

Construction was completed in February 1955. The great "hole" ran beneath Schönefelder Chaussee and ended at its far shoulder. During the following month, the British experts dug a vertical shaft up to near ground level, then built a small tap chamber for the equipment that had to operate near the cables. The first of three taps was in place in May.

An ingenious new KGB technique of placing wires filled with pressurized air inside their cables had convinced the Soviets that their high-frequency lines were virtually immune to tapping. Those devices registered the most minute sag in the current, inevitable when the most sophisticated device bugs a line.

But they were defeated by an even cleverer SIS installation of minute, specially designed amplifiers on each of the several hundred telephone wires inside the three cables: a critical contribution of British expertise.

Recording began as soon as the first tap was installed, while taps on the remaining two cables were safely placed during the following three months. Eureka! Triumph!

BOB now slaked its thirst on a continuous flow of information from one of the juiciest outposts of Soviet intelligence. Some 500 communications channels were active at a given time, enabling continuous recording of an average of 28 telegraphic and 121 voice circuits, the former producing some 4,000 feet of Teletype messages daily. Hour after hour, hundreds of machines in the warehouse recorded every scrap of conversation and every telegram—about troop dispositions, personnel changes, tactical and strategic plans. Sorted and analyzed, much of it was considered immensely valuable. Much later, Markus Wolf, often called the greatest modern spymaster, would marvel at this "intelligence man's dream," which was no less a delight for military planners.

> The Americans could pick up conversations about weapons acquisitions, shortages, technical deficiencies, and code names for newly developed weapons technology between the defense ministry in Moscow and East Berlin base in Karlshorst. . . . They could also listen in on operational planning and the arguments over the constant budget difficulties plaguing the Soviet military.

The wide-ranging usefulness of the taps was unintentionally confirmed when an army cook at the warehouse misread a road sign and drove toward East Germany's Frankfurt an der Oder instead of his intended destination, Frankfurt am Main in West Germany. BOB had decided not to prohibit car travel by the operation's nonsensitive personnel, believing that to do so while other American servicemen were free to use their cars might prompt suspicion. Although the cook knew nothing about the tunnel, clever interrogation might reveal helpful, albeit unwittingly given, information.

East German border guards indeed took the lost driver into custody, prompting an American alert. But tunnel monitors captured live East German reports about the incident, allowing BOB a sigh of relief when it became apparent that the secret of secrets wasn't suspected.

West Berlin (American Sector of Occupation)

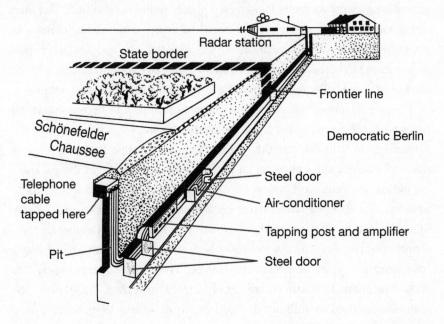

The mass of new intelligence simplified BOB's hitherto daunting task of cross-checking information provided by its Soviet and East German agents. Analysis of the cables' river of Soviet orders and chatter made it easier to determine who were false defectors and double agents—a maddeningly difficult task in the pre-tunnel days. Before the taps were placed, BOB had recruited a KGB plant posing as a Soviet code clerk; the KGB had gone so far as to invent a special military unit where "the clerk" supposedly worked. It was now much harder to fool BOB, and easier to spot clues about planned KGB and East German operations.

With the Target Room's files much expanded by a new wealth of professional and personal details on potential KGB recruits, it was also much easier to craft campaigns against them. Tunnel material, rich in facts, hints, and gossip about KGB personnel, then meshed with reports from covert agents in the field, was especially helpful for corroborating the bona fides of BOB's Soviet and East German agents.

As before, extreme security measures were scrupulously observed. The underground tap room was cleverly insulated. The wood of the tunnel's floor had been chosen to muffle sound, which was further stifled by sandbags. Cable transmissions were monitored and recorded only in the warehouse, rather than in the tap room, from which noises might be heard above. As in submarines under depth-charge attack, total silence was essential. Aboveground, every possibly relevant field report, especially about Karlshorst communications activity, was painstakingly checked for hints of a Soviet inkling about the operation.

There were none, but American whispers, too, had to be prevented. So many tape reels were needed for recording the talk and telegrams that BOB felt it necessary to stifle the curiosity of the officer responsible for flying some of them to Washington. Let in on an invented explanation—that the packages contained uranium ore from an East German plant that BOB was trying to monitor—the flattered officer never again mentioned the vital "secret." Every other day, the Royal Air Force flew a much heavier cargo to London for transcription and analysis. By any measure, the feat was greater than anyone might have dreamed, apart from exultant Harvey. The remarkable yield—50,000 reels of magnetic tape with recordings of 368,000 Soviet and 75,000 East German conversations—continued during the early months of 1956, aiding almost every facet of BOB's work just when ever stiffer Soviet security elsewhere was thwarting it, and inspiring new initiatives suggested by the highly confidential Soviet traffic. Harvey's Hole had cost the United States more time and money than any other intelligence operation in Germany, but no investment in nerves and resources appeared to pay off more lavishly. Nothing better demonstrated the skill and value of American espionage or undermined its detractors' arguments.

"A cold, wet spring," goes a German saying meant to buoy the spirit in the long rainy season, "fills the peasants' barns and barrels." That old bromide from less tense times little comforted East German communication engineers in the spring of 1956. The wetness troubled them more than the cold. So much rain fell on central Germany during the third week of April that faults affected major telephone and telegraph circuits. Some underground cables developed electrical shorts.

Both sides in the murky struggle of wits and dirty tricks tended to cheer at news of any difficulty for the other. But BOB's reaction to the distressed East German cables was quite the opposite. After reaping the precious harvest from its tapped cables for nearly a year, the prospect of even a temporary suspension caused concern.

Apart from Soviet commanders' complaints of disturbances on their lines, nothing else seemed unusual in the flow of Russian and German chatter. When the threat of serious interruptions seemed to ease, BOB personnel breathed easier—until shortly after midnight on the night of April 21–22. Armed with nightscopes, the watch at the warehouse observation post detected some fifty men on the Soviet side of the sector border, just beyond Schönefelder Chaussee. They were near the tap chamber, digging at close intervals. Leaving his dinner party the instant the BOB switchboard informed him, Harvey rushed to the warehouse. The work party discovered the chamber's top at two A.M.; by then the BOB cable monitors were picking up the diggers' live speech. Informed of the find, General Pitovranov urged caution in case the site had been mined. Within an hour, the Soviets spied the tap cables leading down to a trapdoor of tempered steel separating the chamber from the tunnel. As Harvey watched through night vision binoculars, the monitors also recorded the diggers' excitement over their unexpected find. "Hey!" exclaimed one. "This cable's tapped!" The work party, it appeared, had been assembled to deal with the vexing moisture problems on the lines.

If all good things must end, the termination of Operation Gold, coming just when it was in full, fruitful swing, seemed spitefully premature. Predictably, the Russians tried to turn their accidental discovery into a propaganda triumph. In a loud campaign trumpeting Socialist heroism, they claimed the work party had found the tunnel's steel door open, permitting them to surprise Americans manning the recording machines. Catching sight of the dauntless diggers, the astonished CIA culprits dropped their coffee and fled into the tunnel.

Ex-KGB officers continue telling that tale today, but BOB's tapes make nonsense of it. It took the discoverers some fourteen hours to blowtorch their way through the steel door to "their" long-empty half of the tunnel. Accompanied by a film crew, the Soviets entered its main body at 2:20 P.M. on April 22. Harvey sent an aide to request authorization from General Charles Dasher, the U.S. Army's Berlin commander, to destroy the shaft with the planted charges. The general, at a yacht club reception for the visiting army chief of staff, denied the request because Harvey couldn't guarantee that no one, particularly no Russians, would be hurt. But Harvey ordered sandbags and barbed wire installed midtunnel, precisely below the border between the Soviet and American zones. YOU ARE NOW ENTERING THE AMERICAN SECTOR, read a handwritten cardboard sign. At three P.M., when the Americans heard the cautious footsteps moving through the tunnel toward them, Big Bill was fully in his element. He cocked the bolt on a .50-caliber machine gun that had been set up behind a barbed-wire barrier. The bolt made a loud, distinctive click. The footsteps stopped; the explorers scurried back.

The Soviets' hoped-for propaganda coup would not have succeeded in any case. Western media acclaim for the operation's technical brilliance drowned out rare objections about unscrupulous eavesdropping. One newspaper praised the tunnel achievement as a "striking example of the Americans' capacity for daring undertakings." Even the aggrieved parties inadvertently joined in the chorus of praise. In a formal protest to the U.S. Army command in Europe, the Soviet military command in Germany noted that the expensive tunnel structure and equipment were "executed thoroughly, with a view to long use." Markus Wolf would be less coy: "It was a perfectly designed underground listening post."

But no compliment could compensate for the rotten luck delivered by the April downpours. Or so it seemed for nearly five years.

The mysterious Sniper defected to the West after sending his vital secret messages for three years. On the tense day in January 1961 when the prized source finally appeared at BOB's headquarters, he turned out to be Lieutenant Colonel Michal Goleniewski, former deputy chief of Polish military counterintelligence. The colonel was not entirely sound of mind: His delusions included a conviction that he was heir to the imperial Russian throne. But his "business" reports were distinctly more rational. Safe in the West, he identified hundreds of Polish and Soviet agents.

One was George Blake, an unequivocally trusted officer of Great Britain's Secret Intelligence Service. In London seven years earlier, Blake—as no less than secretary of the planning committee—had attended the first CIA/SIS meeting about the project's conception. He was a KGB agent. The Soviets had code-named him "Diomid" after recruiting him in North Korea, where he was interned for three years following the Communists' 1950 capture of Seoul.

Was nothing sacred? At sixteen, brave Blake had been a courier for the anti-Nazi resistance in Holland, his homeland. After a terrifying pickup by the Gestapo, the principled, reticent teenager was smuggled to Spain and imprisoned there, on general suspicion. Eventually released, he made his way to Britain and served in the Royal Navy. Later recruited by the SIS, he was posted to South Korea under diplomatic cover. His background and service made him one of the SIS's most admired members.

As Diomid, however, Blake had passed the minutes of the CIA/SIS meeting, together with a tunnel map that he'd sketched, to his Soviet control in London. That secured his status as the best Soviet mole in the West: The KGB knew the tunnel plan before the first shovel scratched the ground!

The Soviets were actually far cleverer than their hype about their diggers' chance heroism suggested. The tunnel's faked "find" was actually part of a campaign to prevent the CIA and SIS from suspecting Blake. As soon as Karlshorst's chief learned of the super-secret project in 1955, he began preparations to stage its supposedly accidental discovery. Working with a KGB specialist in eavesdropping flown in from Moscow—a colonel who would lead the "work party"—he developed plans for the find to be made by a fictitious Red Army signals unit on a routine detail. Moscow orchestrated tactics and timing. Nikita Khrushchev himself chose a date for staging the exposé—the eve of the general secretary's first visit to London—that promised maximum diplomatic and propaganda value. He also ordered that the culprits be nabbed in the act, which may account for the Soviet boasts of catching American personnel with their earphones on.

The Soviet theater totally fooled BOB until the Sniper fingered Blake those five years later. (He had not been uncovered through an investigation by MI-6, the British counterpart to the FBI, prompted by a 1959 Sniper warning of a Soviet mole in the SIS, possibly code-named "Diamond.") The consummate traitor had been protected with great skill.

Soviet security outdid BOB's. No member of Soviet counterintelligence in Berlin had the slightest knowledge of the tunnel. The KGB's top command instructed Blake to reveal his information to no one, including KGB officers. As late as the summer of 1955, only three people in Moscow Central's First Chief Directorate (for foreign intelligence) knew his identity and of Operation Gold's existence. More humiliating for BOB, its extraordinary measures for protecting the tunnel's secrecy had all been for nothing.

Did that futility apply to the operation as a whole? Was the huge effort to record, transcribe, translate, categorize, cross-reference, and evaluate the sea of tapped material also for nothing? Or worse than nothing: Did the Soviets, as several agents later claimed, feed the taps with massive disinformation? Operation Gold seems cut to the current fashion of dismissing most espionage as a scandalously exorbitant con. Writing after examining the archives on their respective sides, many experts—from Markus Wolf to John le Carré to Phillip Knightley—concluded that the tunnel's practical value in the Cold War was extremely limited. In that view, the massive tunnel adventure can be seen as a telling display of the futility of espionage in general and the CIA's efforts in particular.

Former BOB officers disagree, as might be expected. Recovering from the Sniper's seemingly crushing revelations, they continued to sing the tunnel's praises. Denying that they were duped by disinformation fed through it, they cited selected Soviet evidence to bolster their rebuttal. In general, they say, the tunnel treasury—1,750 intelligence reports by September 1958, based on 90,000 translated messages or conversations—was a huge asset even two years after the taps were shut down. In 1957, for example, an East German BOB operative fired from her housekeeping job for General Pitovranov (during a Soviet security campaign to eliminate German employees) managed to land another job in Karlshorst, this one for East Germany's counterintelligence chief, General Karl Linke. The production of "Frau K," as she was called, swelled because Linke was much less meticulous about not taking home official documents than the extremely security-minded Pitovranov. Tunnel material contained the necessary elaboration and corroboration for the files Frau K managed to copy. The same applied to the offerings of BOB's star source, Lieutenant Colonel Pyotr Popov of Soviet Military Intelligence. Popov supplied invaluable information, especially after his fortuitous transfer to Karlshorst, also in 1957. Without the explanation, enhancement, and interpretation made possible by the tunnel material, his reports on the Soviet compound would have been far less valuable. (Caught in the act, Popov would be executed for treason in 1960, despite a KGB plea to spare his life.)

Operation Gold also braced the defense against the Soviet crusade to force the Western Three from Berlin. Unless the Allies accepted East German control over access to the Western sectors, warned Nikita Khrushchev in a 1958 ultimatum, he would sign a separate peace treaty with the GDR, ceding it control of that access as a sovereign nation. That move would have gravely jeopardized the Western presence in Berlin. The tunnel material's rich details of Soviet undercover operations in West Berlin were critical to Washington's winning counterattack.

American enthusiasts are convinced that the cables continued transmitting massive quantities of sensitive material even after the First Chief Directorate knew it was being tapped. Baffling as that might seem to laypeople, the reason makes impeccable sense to spies. Changing communication practices and procedures to negate the taps would have required orders to hundreds of Soviet personnel: an operation of a size that would have tipped off BOB, whose search for the leak may have uncovered Blake. To protect its secret that it knew the American secret—thus shielding Blake as an intelligence source—the First Directorate willingly compromised other KGB departments, together with fellow intelligence services and the Soviet army in Germany. Not even General Pitovranov was told about the tunnel until Blake's reassignment, in a normal rotation, from London to Berlin's SIS station.

Whether some disinformation was leaked into the torrent of genuine stuff coursing the cables may never be known. Whether it's true, as Markus Wolf believes, that his side never would have discovered the tunnel without Blake's tip-off is also a moot question. But Operation Gold does reveal some of espionage warfare's ironies. George Blake would not have been prosecuted without a confession; too little hard evidence against him could be found. "Come on, George," a skilled British interrogator kept baiting the arrested traitor. "We know why you did it. It was for the money." Finally, Blake was provoked. "No, not for money. I never got a penny! I did it for the ethics." What ethics? Imprisoned in North Korea, Blake had taken the initiative in serving Moscow by asking to speak to a Russian officer. Before his posting to Seoul under British diplomatic cover, he'd been assigned to take a Cambridge professor's course on the menace of Communism, which attracted the introverted young man instead of repelling him. Communist sermons—all for one and one for all; a need for the people to own the means of production because they are more important than property—echoed the moral lessons his devoutly Lutheran mother had taught him as a boy. Thus a course on Communism's dangers triggered his conversion.

There was more irony in the fate of the tunnel itself. Although it was "blown" from the beginning, the Soviets couldn't blow up the American operation until it had served its purpose for Soviet, as well as American, intelligence. Thus ended a classic modern spy story, illustrating the dividends and the waste of major operations and the sometimes strange rules of the game, which some participants are beguiled into playing for itself, with little wisdom about the national interest.

After sentencing to forty-two years in prison—a year, some say, for each British agent sent to death because of his treason—George Blake escaped from Wormwood Scrubs, London's maximum-security prison, in 1966. His method remains secret; he himself remains unrepentant. Britain's most wanted criminal—whose parents named him after King George V, Britain's monarch at the time of his birth—lives a quiet life in Moscow as a Middle East expert for the Russian Republic's successor to the KGB.

Not long after leaving BOB in 1959, Bill Harvey began working directly for John Kennedy. The stylish young president placed "America's James Bond" in command of ZR/Rifle, a new CIA program for developing the capability to perform assassinations anywhere in the world. Thus Harvey would run "wet" operations for the man with whom he shared a claim of never going a day without enjoying a woman. Fidel Castro was among the first targets. Drinking more than ever, Big Bill negotiated with Mafia mobsters who made attempts to kill the Cuban leader in the early 1960s.

Then he incurred Bobby Kennedy's wrath—not, as was then supposed, because the Cold War cowboy took it upon himself to send sabotage teams into Cuba during the possibly calamitous Cuban Missile Crisis of 1962. His offense was open rebuke of the Kennedys during a supremely tense Cabinet meeting at the height of that crisis. Referring to the CIA-sponsored invasion of Cuba some eighteen months earlier, Harvey expressed the fury of much of the intelligence community over Kennedy's refusal to provide air support for the ill-trained anti-Castro brigade facing disaster at the Bay of Pigs. "If you hadn't fucked up in the first place," he was said to have informed the president, "we wouldn't be where we are now." Beyond their hearing, he called the Kennedy brothers "fags" and "fuckers."

"Exiled" to Rome, Harvey guzzled before, during, and after bizarre episodes involving revolvers—one pointed at a policeman who stopped him for speeding—and on trips to relive his glory in Berlin. A handful of CIA colleagues attended the legend's funeral in 1976. Some remembered the gold medals the CIA had awarded them two decades earlier, for what the agency then believed was the Cold War's greatest espionage coup.

The Invasion of Cuba

DINO A. BRUGIONI

Most published accounts and studies of the Cuban Missile Crisis tend to concentrate almost exclusively on the debates and decisions of the Kennedy White House during those harrowing days of late October 1962. Since that time, however, major aspects of the crisis, strangely overlooked, have come to light. One is the preparation for war, against both Cuba and the Soviet Union, that took place in a period just short of two weeks and turned southern Florida into a D-Day–like staging area. The result would prove to be the largest short-term mobilization of men and equipment since World War II—exceeded in size only by Desert Storm and the invasion of Iraq. The plans for the invasion of Cuba, which came close to happening, were mostly unknown at the time; even now the exact tactical details of Operational Plans 312-, 314-, and 316-62 remain classified. Fortunately for the world, the trains (as well as the planes and ships) could be stopped, and were. This would not be another 1914.

Dino A. Brugioni, who worked at the time of the crisis for the National Photographic Interpretation Center (NPIC) of the CIA, was a key member of the team that, on October 15, confirmed the presence of Soviet surface-to-surface missiles in Cuba. Here he tells the story, as it unfolded day by increasingly tense day, of the preparations to invade Cuba and destroy the missile sites if the Soviets—in the person of their leader, Nikita Khrushchev—had refused to back down. If the operation developed with unbelievable swiftness and was for the most part efficient, remember that in 1962 the U.S. armed forces had reached a Cold War peak of morale and readiness. And in this case they would have been meeting a threat, not half a world away as they did in Korea or Vietnam, but a hundred-odd miles off their own shores. Still, that extraordinary mobilization did not come off without some typically American glitches.

The Cold War would pivot on the Cuban Missile Crisis. This would be the ultimate confrontation between West and East. It was, as John Lewis Gaddis has written:

> the only episode after World War II in which *each* of the major arenas of Soviet-American competition intersected: the nuclear arms race to be sure, but also conflicting ideological aspirations, "third-world" rivalries, relations with allies, the domestic political implications of foreign policy, the personalities of individual leaders. The crisis was a kind of funnel . . . into which everything suddenly tumbled and got mixed together. Fortunately no black hole lurked at the other end, although new evidence confirms how easily one might have.

DINO A. BRUGIONI is a renowned authority in the analysis of aerial photography and is a founder of the National Photographic Interpretation Center of the CIA. He is the author of *Eyeball to Eyeball: The Inside Story of the Cuban Missile Crisis,* from which this article was adapted. He has also written *Photo Fakery: The History and Techniques of Photographic Deception and Manipulation.* Brugioni lives in rural Virginia.

October 15–16, 1962. Throughout the summer of 1962, the CIA had maintained close surveillance over the heavy volume of Russian shipping exiting the Baltic and Black seas bound for Cuba. The dramatic increase in Soviet cargoes and the arrival of numerous "technicians" at Cuban ports became a paramount intelligence concern. A U-2 mission over the island on August 29 revealed that the Soviets were constructing an islandwide SA-2 surface-to-air-missile (SAM) defense network. Soon after, the discovery of Komar guided-missile patrol boats and coastal cruise-missile sites to defend against an amphibious landing alerted the U.S. government to more sinister possibilities.

The emerging picture of a Soviet military build-up in Cuba particularly worried John McCone, director of the Central Intelligence Agency. Of the SA-2 missiles, he stated: "They're not putting them in to protect the cane cutters. They're putting them in to blind our reconnaissance eye." McCone insisted that the number of U-2 flights over Cuba be increased, and he expressed to top policy makers his concern that the Soviets might introduce offensive missiles in Cuba. On September 4 and 13, President Kennedy issued warnings to the Soviets that "the gravest issues" would arise if they installed surface-to-surface missiles (SSMs) in Cuba. In official statements and high-level meetings with U.S. officials, the Soviets stated emphatically that they would not deploy offensive weapons in Cuba.

On Monday, October 15, interpreting a U-2 mission flown over Cuba the day before, NPIC discovered two medium-range ballistic missile (MRBM) sites under construction in the San Cristóbal area. When the president was briefed on October 16, he ordered the island completely covered by U-2 missions. Interpreting the photographs that these flights brought back, the center found four additional MRBM sites and three intermediate-range ballistic missile (IRBM) sites under construction. (The MRBMs could reach just beyond Washington, D.C.; the IRBMs could hit all parts of the United States except the extreme Northwest.) NPIC also spotted four mobile Soviet combat groups.

General Maxwell D. Taylor, chairman of the Joint Chiefs of Staff, saw the secret Soviet move into Cuba with nuclear missiles as a major effort to change the strategic balance of power. It was an attempt to erase in one stroke the U.S. nuclear superiority to the Soviets. That superiority, according to a top-secret estimate, was at least seven to one. (In meetings with Americans in Moscow in 1989, Soviet officials stated that the ratio was closer to fifteen to one—or greater—in favor of the United States.) Taylor and the other members of the JCS recommended a preemptive air strike, an airborne assault, and an invasion to wipe out the missile bases. As Dean Acheson, then a senior adviser with the National Security Council (NSC), put it—and Taylor agreed—one does not plan a military operation of the magnitude of the Soviets' with the expectation that it will fail.

The NSC debated three courses of action: a "quarantine" (actually a block-ade) of Cuba, air strikes against the missile sites, and an invasion. The president chose the quarantine. At the same time, preparations were set in motion for the alternatives. Acheson began to press for a declaration of war against Cuba. He wanted to make it plain to the Soviets that "their bayonets had struck steel in-stead of mush."

To the intelligence community, the Soviet-Cuban venture had the Khrush-chev stamp: a gamble—bold, large, premeditated, but not carefully thought through. That gamble would become a colossal Soviet blunder. Militarily, as General Taylor would remark, the Soviets chose the wrong issue and the wrong battlefield.

JCS contingency plans for air strikes, a quarantine, and the invasion of Cuba had been completed by the summer and were known as Operational Plans 312, 314, and 316, respectively. Practice for these operations had already been scheduled to take place with an amphibious brigade landing exercise from October 15 to 20 on Vieques Island, off Puerto Rico. At the last moment the ex-ercise had been canceled because of bad weather. But thousands of marines were still on their ships, ready for a real landing.

During the same period, the U.S. Army and U.S. Air Force were engaged in exercises called "Three Pairs" and "Rapid Roads" in central Texas. Units of the 82nd Airborne Division, the attacking force, were waiting at the James Con-nally Air Force Base at Waco, Texas, when ordered to return to their home base, Fort Bragg, North Carolina. The Tactical Air Command (TAC) fighters that were to support the 82nd Airborne were sent to airfields in Florida. The 1st Armored Division, which was to be the aggressor force in the exercise, was told to return to base at nearby Fort Hood and await orders.

October 17–19. The JCS, through Admiral Robert Lee Dennison, commander in chief of Atlantic (CINCLANT), began alerting naval Task Forces 135 and 136 to head for the Caribbean. Commanding officers were told to round up their men as inconspicuously as possible. Task Force 135 consisted of two attack carrier groups built around the nuclear-powered U.S.S. *Enterprise* and the U.S.S. *Independence*, along with fifteen screening destroyers. It was to proceed to positions off the southern coast of Cuba. Task Force 136, the blockading force, consisted of the aircraft carrier *Essex* and cruisers *Newport News* and *Canberra*, along with an underway replenishment group and nineteen destroyers. The quarantine line was marked by twelve destroyers on an arc five hundred miles from Cape Maisí.

Lieutenant General Hamilton Howse, commanding general of the Strategic Army Command (STRAC) and the XVIII Airborne Corps at Fort Bragg, ordered the commanders of the 101st Airborne Division, the 1st Infantry Division, the 2nd Infantry Division, the 1st Armored Division, and the 82nd Airborne Division to report to his headquarters immediately. He briefed them on October 19, a Friday, with aerial photos provided by NPIC and ordered them to bring their commands to full alert status.

The 82nd and 101st Airborne divisions stationed at Fort Bragg and at Fort Campbell, Kentucky, were alerted for immediate movement to intermediate staging areas in southern Florida. The 1st Division at Fort Riley, Kansas, and the 4th Division at Fort Lewis, Washington, were also alerted for possible movement. The 2nd Division at Fort Benning, Georgia, would be moved to New Orleans for embarkation. The 1st Armored would be sent to Fort Stewart, Georgia. The commanders assembled their staffs and gave detailed instructions for the movement of men and matériel from their commands to Georgia or Florida.

One of the first priorities was to establish an impenetrable air-defense umbrella over forces gathering in Florida. Just ninety miles and five minutes of jet flying time from Havana, Key West would become one of the principal bases of the crisis. Rear Admiral Rhomad Y. McElroy, the Key West commander, cleared Key West International Airport and the nearby U.S. naval air station at

Boca Chica of all utility and support aircraft in order to accommodate the navy and marine strike, reconnaissance, and defense aircraft that had already begun arriving from bases along the East Coast. Naval Squadron VF-41, transferred to Key West from Oceana, Virginia, on October 6, was already patrolling along the Florida Keys and the north shore of Cuba. All leaves were cancelled at the base.

Meanwhile, military aircraft of all types, from fighters to reconnaissance planes packed with computers and sophisticated listening equipment, began to converge on other Florida air bases. By the evening of October 19, hundreds of fighters were lined up wing tip to wing tip, ready for action.

Army air-defense battalions, equipped with Hawk and Nike Hercules SAMs, were given the highest priority for rail, air, and truck movement. From as far away as Fort Lewis, equipment was moved south to defend the Florida airfields that were most vulnerable to Cuban attack. The Hawk surface-to-air missiles battalion at Fort Meade, Maryland, was ordered to proceed posthaste by road to Key West. The loading was quickly accomplished, but it was evident that there had been little regard for weight or orderliness in the packing of the equipment. The unit selected U.S. Highway 1 as the fastest route to Florida. As the convoy moved through Virginia, a state highway patrolman noticed that a number of trucks appeared to be overloaded. He signaled the convoy to follow him to the weighing station. There his suspicions were confirmed. The military officers protested vehemently that they had an important defense mission to perform in Florida—they couldn't yet say what it was—and that precious time was being wasted. The patrolman remarked that military convoys were always in a hurry. He calmly proceeded to write out a warning to the U.S. Army to be more careful in future loading of convoys.

October 20–21. The great mobilization was under way. Ammunition and supplies were moving by rail and road from all parts of the country. Truck after truck left the Letterkenny Ordnance Depot in Chambersburg, Pennsylvania, and began to roll to Florida loaded with ammunition. Several ordnance plants were placed on three-shift, seven-day weeks to produce the 20mm strafing ammunition required for the fighter aircraft. The war plans called for the use of napalm as well as conventional ammunition. Hundreds of napalm drop tanks began arriving at the naval and tactical airfields, where they were stacked, according to one observer, like "mountains of cordwood." Ammunition for naval gunfire against Cuban installations was also shipped to bases in Florida. Food rations came from such inland storage depots as Bonner Springs, Kansas. Army boat units, which would be needed for an invasion, were ordered to go to Fort Lauderdale and Port Everglades in Florida.

Military hospitals—especially those along the East Coast, previously devoted primarily to treating service dependents—were prepared to receive war casualties. Blood supplies were monitored, and troops not involved in the movement to Florida were asked to give blood. One hospital unit was sent to Florida on chartered buses. Presuming that this movement was another exercise, the buses had stopped at several liquor stores along the way. When it arrived in Florida, the unit itself was a casualty.

Billeting of the troops arriving in Florida was already becoming a problem. At some airfields, the bachelor officers' and enlisted men's quarters were operated on the "hot bunk" principle: Three men would be assigned to each bunk, with someone sleeping in it at all hours. Mess halls remained open around the clock. Later, after the president announced that missiles were in place in Cuba, the owner of the Gulfstream Park at Hallandale, Florida, invited the army to bivouac some of the troops of the 1st Armored Division at the racecourse. The army accepted, and soon military police were placed at all entrances; parking lots became motor pools, and the infield was used for storage and mess. Troops were billeted on the first and second floors of the grandstand. Weapons and duffel bags were stacked next to the betting windows. Church services were held in the photo-finish developing rooms.

According to Contingency Plan 316, the 82nd and 101st Airborne divisions would be the first to land on Cuba. Large numbers of transport aircraft would have to be diverted to support the operation; more than eight hundred Lockheed Hercules flights would be needed to execute the invasion plan. Plans for deployment of the airborne divisions had been rehearsed and tested again.

Drops would be made at altitudes of 700 to 900 feet. Airborne commanders knew conducting military operations on Cuba in October would not be easy. It was the season of rain and hurricanes, clouds and high winds, certainly not the best jump weather. Some drop zones would be in valleys containing sugarcane fields and cattle ranches. By the end of October, the cane fields would reach their maximum heights of seven to ten feet. The cane stalks not only posed a landing hazard for the parachutists but also presented problems in rallying and maneuvering—and provided the Cubans with sites that were ready-made for conducting guerrilla operations and harassing the airborne troops.

Those troops were issued a number of instructions about the treatment of any prisoners. They were specifically told that "Sino-Soviet bloc personnel" were to be carefully handled and taken into protective custody. At this point the United States was still trying its utmost to avoid a direct confrontation with the Soviet Union.

To assure proper interrogation of prisoners of war, Spanish-speaking military intelligence personnel were assigned to both division and regimental head-quarters. Crash courses on interrogation techniques were offered to the air-borne divisions. Prisoners of war were one thing, but it soon developed that the State Department had no specific plan for the handling of Cuban refugees. Although there were generalized plans for the occupation and a military gov-ernment, there was no detailed plan for the recruitment of indigenous Cuban administrators. Nor were there plans to prevent starvation, disease, or civil un-rest. When asked whether it had the funds to deal with such likely calamities, the State Department replied that "none had been budgeted." This enormous potential for trouble would never really be solved, and other matters were more pressing.

One of the first issues President Kennedy raised during the crisis had been whether U.S. dependents at the Guantánamo Bay U.S. Naval Station on the southeastern end of Cuba should be evacuated. At the time there were more than 2,800 women and children living on the base. The navy had strong feel-ings that the Soviets and Cubans might regard removal of the dependents as a sign of weakness rather than a matter of practicality. More to the point, it also might tip them off that the United States knew about the missiles, and the Soviets and Cubans could respond by upgrading their military and naval de-fenses. But Secretary of Defense Robert S. McNamara had insisted that the dependents be removed. It had not yet been established that McNamara was reflecting the president's views. In an attempt to convince McNamara of the value of keeping the dependents at Guantánamo, the assistant secretary of defense for international security affairs, Paul Nitze, and the Second Fleet commander, Admiral Alfred G. Ward, met with him. Ward was in charge of the blockade and the navy's role in any invasion. Nitze pointed out various rea-sons why it would be inadvisable to pull out the American civilians. After lis-tening patiently, McNamara stood up and said, "Mr. Secretary, you have your instructions to get the dependents out of Guantánamo Bay. Please carry out those instructions."

Shortly after eleven A.M. on October 21, the Sunday-morning routine at Guantánamo was interrupted by phone calls and messengers hurrying to the buildings where families were housed. Each family was told to pack one bag per person and be prepared to evacuate within fifteen minutes' notice. Loading on aircraft and naval vessels was completed before four P.M. At this point the Cuban military threat was spelled out in only the most general way.

If the Cubans thought the Americans were showing signs of weakness by evacuating service dependents from Guantánamo, they were soon to see an impressive display of strength as cargo aircraft began landing on the airfield. By the evening of the next day, 3,600 marines and 3,200 tons of equipment had been airlifted by the Material Air Transport Service. In a glaring overestimate of U.S. strength, Soviet intelligence reported that "the garrison had been increased from 8,000 to 18,000 personnel from the 2nd Marine Division, and reinforced by 150 tanks, 24 antiaircraft missile systems and 70 recoilless guns. The number of airplanes had been increased to 120." The actual U.S. defense force deployed to Guantánamo, including men and equipment already in place, comprised 5,750 marines, a Hawk missile battery, 155 tanks, several battalions of 105mm artillery pieces, three gunfire support ships, two marine air-attack squadrons, and a patrol squadron. Two aircraft carriers were in the area to render support.

The Guantánamo reinforcement was largely a deception, and it worked. While the United States regarded this as a defensive operation, the Soviets and Cubans saw the "uninterrupted intensive reconnaissance along Cuban shores and approaches" as proof that Guantánamo was "actively being prepared as a bridgehead for military operation." But for the moment, the marines' function was to secure the Guantánamo defensive perimeter; once fighting started, it was to handle the Cuban artillery dug in on the surrounding hills. Only when the main amphibious and airborne forces established themselves on the island would the marines consider moving out.

Kennedy had originally intended to make his speech to the nation that evening, but politics dictated that he inform Congress first, and it proved impossible on such short notice to round up everyone who was out campaigning.

October 22. This was the day, a Monday, when the Cuban Missile Crisis became public. Planes had been dispatched to bring back ranking senators and congressmen. Even so, their briefing took place little more than an hour before the president's speech, and there was considerable anger that he had waited until the last minute to inform them. Just before Kennedy went on the air at seven P.M., U.S. jet fighters scrambled into the sky from bases in Florida. The action was termed an airborne alert—a precautionary measure "in the event of a rash action by the Cubans." Not just the Cubans: As the president made clear, any offensive action by the Cubans would be considered an offensive action by the Soviet Union.

As Kennedy was speaking, the secretary of defense placed the entire U.S. military establishment on Defcon (defense condition) 3 status (Defcon 5 was all normal; Defcon 1 meant war). In accordance with JCS directives, Strategic Air Command (SAC) B-47 bombers were dispersed to more than thirty predesignated civilian airfields in the United States. At two SAC bases in Spain, three in Morocco, and three in England, B-47 bombers were loaded with nuclear weapons and prepared for takeoff. Simultaneously, a massive airborne alert was begun by U.S.-based B-52 bombers and KC-135 tankers. The B-52s were loaded with nuclear weapons and ordered to fly under continuous command control, either far out over the Pacific, deep into the Arctic, or across the Atlantic and the Mediterranean. There the planes would wait for instructions either to proceed to the Soviet Union or to return to their home bases. In addition, fighter-bombers at American bases in England, France, Italy, Germany, Turkey, South Korea, Japan, and the Philippines were placed on alert and armed with ordnance, including nuclear, for striking targets in the Soviet Union or in Eastern Europe.

There were three intercontinental ballistic missile (ICBM) systems in the SAC inventory at the time: Atlas, Titan I, and Titan II. A fourth system, the solid-fuel Minuteman, would enter the inventory during the later days of the crisis. There were also 60 Thor IRBMs in England, 30 Jupiter IRBMs in Italy, and 15 Jupiters in Turkey. Late in the evening General Curtis LeMay, chief of staff of the air force, notified McNamara that 91 Atlases and 41 Titans were being readied for firing. Nine missile-carrying submarines capable of firing 144 Polaris missiles had left their bases and taken up stations in the North Atlantic. Matador and Mace cruise missiles deployed in tactical wings were brought to combat status in West Germany; they could strike strategic targets in Eastern Europe.

Fifteen minutes before the president's address, the nation's railroads were also put on alert. The Pentagon asked the Association of American Railroads for the immediate use of 375 flatcars to move air-defense and air-warning units to Florida. That evening the 1st Armored Division began the 1,100-mile trek from Texas to an intermediate staging base at Fort Stewart. This division alone would require 3,600 flatcars, 190 gondola cars, 40 boxcars, and 200 passenger cars. In all, over 5,000 men, 15,000 vehicles, and thousands of tons of supplies would be loaded on 38 trains, some up to 150 cars long. At the height of the crisis, normal rail movement in the Southeast practically came to a halt. Another 10,000 men would be airlifted in 135 commercial flights.

October 23. The president authorized the use of low-level aerial photoreconnaissance and of the navy's F8U Crusaders; later, air force RF-101 Voodoos began flying from Florida at treetop level over the Cuban missile sites. The low-altitude photography, transferred immediately to Washington for analysis, added a new dimension to NPIC's reporting. Each piece of missile equipment could be identified precisely and its function in the missile system determined. Rather than taking the interpreter's word, as they had with the U-2 photography, policy makers now could see clearly what the interpreters had seen and were reporting.

October 24. The JCS ordered Defcon 2—maximum alert before war with the optimum posture to strike either Cuba or the U.S.S.R. or both. With this change of status, 1,436 U.S. bombers loaded with nuclear weapons and 134 ICBMs were now on constant alert: One eighth of the bombers were in the air at all times, and aircrews were waiting near the rest of the bombers, prepared for takeoff on a moment's notice.

Both the White House press secretary and the news desk at the Pentagon were being besieged by reporters demanding to know more about the reported build-up for an invasion of Cuba. Although the president felt that the Washington press would exercise control in reporting military information, he was appalled by reports that local television crews throughout the United States had stationed themselves near military bases and were making public the sort of details that would never have been leaked during World War II and the Korean War.

Kennedy decided that a nationwide reporting guideline had to be established for the news media, and he asked the Department of Defense to draft it. While he made it clear he was not imposing censorship, he did want to restrict information on the deployment of forces, degrees of alert, defenses, dispersal plans, vulnerabilities, and air- and sea-lift capabilities.

Late that evening, the president called McNamara to confirm when U.S.

forces would be ready to invade Cuba. The secretary replied, "In seven days." When Kennedy pressed him on whether all the forces would be well prepared, McNamara replied that they would be "ready in every respect in seven days": Wednesday, October 31, Halloween.

October 25–26. Photo interpreters at NPIC had identified four camps suspected of housing Soviet armored combat groups. All were in the vicinity of the missile sites, which would tend to indicate that their main function was to protect them. But other intelligence analysts had maintained that they were simply camps where Cubans were being trained to handle Soviet arms—or that they were temporary equipment transfer points, places where, as one U.S. general put it, "The Cosmoline was removed." NPIC kept insisting that these were more likely to be Soviet combat facilities, since the equipment observed was parked in neat formations, characteristic of the Soviet army, rather than in the haphazard ones typical of Cuban installations. That equipment, of the most sophisticated recent vintage, included T-54 tanks, assault guns, tactical rocket launchers, antitank weapons, and personnel carriers. It wasn't until October 24 that the intelligence community agreed with the photo interpreters that these were Soviet installations and that they did house combat troops, as many as 1,500 each.

The next day a low-altitude reconnaissance aircraft brought back absolute confirmation. At the Santiago de las Vegas installation, Soviet ground-force-unit symbols and insignias were seen implanted in the flagstone and flowers in front of garrison areas. One unit proudly displayed the Elite Guards Badge, the Soviet equivalent of the U.S. Presidential Unit Citation. These four camps were quickly targeted, and ordnance, including nuclear, was selected for their destruction in the event of an invasion.

That day, too, the continuing Soviet denial that offensive missiles were in Cuba was exposed as a lie when Adlai Stevenson, the U.S. ambassador to the United Nations, confronted the Soviet ambassador with aerial photographs of the missile sites during a Security Council meeting.

Throughout the crisis, President Kennedy was concerned that an American move on Cuba would provoke a countermove by the Soviets on Berlin. Close watch of Soviet forces was maintained in the Soviet Union and East Germany, but there was no indication of preparations for offensive action. The Soviets were obviously concerned that any such indication might provoke a first-strike response by alerted U.S. forces. Soviet U.N. ambassador Valerian Zorin told a group of neutral African and Asian U.N. delegates that "The Americans are thoroughly mistaken if they think we shall fall in their trap. We shall undertake nothing in Berlin, for action against Berlin is just what the Americans would wish."

Khrushchev's overall behavior during this week appeared unsure and erratic. He continued to lie about the missiles after their presence had been established beyond doubt. Even as he attempted to pacify the United States, his soldiers at Cuban bases were working frantically to bring the missiles to operational status. After ordering his ships to turn around, he threatened to run the blockade using submarines. He threatened to fire missiles but took no overt offensive action that might cause the United States to further increase its alert status. U.S. military leaders knew that Khrushchev could be ruthless when desperate. The JCS was wary of what direction the crisis would take, determined, as Admiral Ward later put it, not to be "the Kimmels and Shorts of this generation"—a reference to Admiral Husband Kimmel and Major General Walter Short, who were relieved of their commands after the Japanese surpised them at Pearl Harbor.

To ensure the success of possible amphibious landings in Cuba, Ward decided that exercises should be conducted in Florida in as realistic a manner as possible. A number of projected landing areas in Cuba were at or near resort areas, so Hollywood Beach, near Fort Lauderdale, was selected to simulate the Havana beach area. In the predawn chill, the sea off Fort Lauderdale was rough, and it was late morning before the marines climbed down nets from the ships offshore into the bobbing personnel landing craft. The bigger landing ship tanks (LSTs) prepared to move toward the shore to disgorge tanks and armored personnel carriers.

The littoral behind the landing zone, situated along the central portion of Hollywood Beach, was dense with hotels, motels, restaurants, and bars. By the time the men and equipment hit the beach, sunbathers had already gathered under their umbrellas. The tanks, armored personnel carriers, and infantrymen soon joined the crowd on the narrow beach. Instead of obeying the instructions of a forward observer who was installed on the roof of a jai alai court, some of the marines began fraternizing with bikini-clad girls on the beach; others posed for tourists' cameras in their combat gear; an even greater number headed for the bars. Admiral Ward later characterized the exercise as about the closest thing to the Keystone Kops that he had ever seen. He never reported the Hollywood Beach fiasco to his superiors, instead emphasizing that the landing exercises the same day at Hutchinson Island, Fort Pierce, and near Fort Everglades had gone as planned.

At six P.M. on the twenty-sixth, the White House began to receive transmission of a long, rambling polemic from Khrushchev—which did, however, give a glimmer of hope. The Soviet premier hinted that he was prepared to withdraw his missiles if Kennedy would agree not to invade Cuba.

October 27. This was the day that would be referred to as "Black Saturday" by both the president and members of the National Security Council. Khrushchev remarked that "a smell of burning hung in the air."

Just before ten A.M., Soviet personnel fired an SA-2 surface-to-air missile and downed a U-2 reconnaissance plane flown by Major Rudolf Anderson, who was killed. The order to fire was apparently given by General Igor D. Statsenko, commander of the Soviet forces in Cuba. The intelligence community could come up with no reason why the Soviets, who had been tracking the U-2 flights, would select this moment to down one. Most feared that the Soviets were escalating the crisis.

JCS Contingency Plan No. 312 directed CINCLANT to be prepared to strike a single SA-2 SAM site, or all Cuban SAM sites, within two hours of a U-2 shootdown. The established policy, agreed to by the president, was that any SAM site that fired at a U-2 was to be immediately neutralized. Sixteen armed F-100 Super Sabre fighters stood by at Homestead Air Force Base in southern Florida on thirty-minute alert to attack any firing SAM site.

When word that Anderson had been shot down reached General LeMay, he ordered the F-100s readied to strike. The White House, realizing that there was a standing order for this operations procedure, frantically contacted LeMay and asked if the fighters had been launched. LeMay replied that they were being readied. He was admonished not to launch the fighters until he received direct orders from the president. Angered, LeMay hung up. "He chickened out again," he said. "How in the hell do you get men to risk their lives when the SAMs are not attacked?" When an aide said he would wait at the phone for the president's order, LeMay disgustedly replied, "It will never come!"

The crisis had entered a new phase. A fragile and volatile situation existed that could explode into a major conflict with little or no warning. The CIA now believed that all the MRBM sites in Cuba were operational. Pilots returning from low-altitude flights reported that antiaircraft weapons were firing on them. Analysis of the aerial photography revealed that antiaircraft weapons were being installed around the MRBM sites. There was also a desperate effort by the Soviets to camouflage and conceal those sites. And hundreds of trenches were being dug to protect them from ground assault.

That afternoon the Executive Committee of the NSC (ExCom) discussed what retaliatory action should be taken. It decided that, beginning the next morning, all low-flying reconnaissance aircraft would have armed escorts. That afternoon, too, McNamara ordered twenty-four troop-carrier squadrons of the air force reserve, along with their associated support units, to active duty. Besides paratroopers, these squadrons would drop supplies to the ground units that would be placed ashore in an invasion of Cuba. And LeMay announced to McNamara that 1,576 bombers and 283 missiles stood poised to strike the 70 principal cities of the Soviet Union.

In the evening the CIA briefed the president in depth on the startling events of the day. Kennedy had already responded to Khrushchev's message of the previous evening with the suggestion that he would be willing to make a pledge not to invade Cuba if the Soviets met his conditions. But Kennedy decided it was time to deliver an ultimatum. The president's brother, Attorney General Robert Kennedy, was sent to meet with Soviet ambassador Anatoly Dobrynin, warning him that the United States had to have a commitment by the next day that the missiles would be removed, or the United States would remove them by force.

At that moment in Florida, 156 tactical aircraft were ready to strike Cuba. They were backed up by almost 700 more strike planes that were on the ground or at sea. The air force and the navy were prepared to conduct continuous air strikes until all the SAM, MRBM, and IRBM sites, as well as the Cuban Air Force, had been destroyed. If an invasion of Cuba were ordered, a total of 1,190 sorties could be flown the first day.

U.S. planning for the invasion of Cuba and possible war against the Soviet Union was now going so well that the date had been moved forward: It could come as early as Tuesday, October 30. Military leaders openly admitted, however, that an invasion of Cuba would be as bloody as Korea. The estimate of total U.S. casualties for the first few days of the combined airborne and amphibious operation was about 1,000 a day. The invasion would be opposed by 75,000 Cuban regular troops, 100,000 militia, and 100,000 home guards—not to mention Soviet personnel, then estimated at 22,000. (The Soviets later maintained that there were almost 40,000 personnel in Cuba at the height of the crisis.)

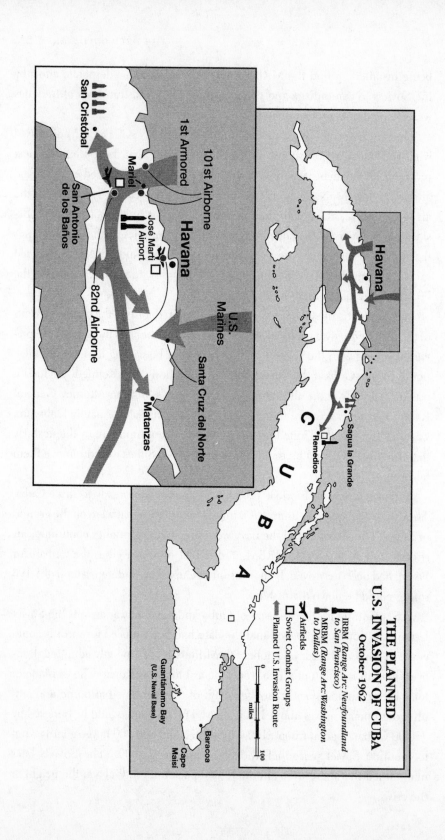

THE PLANNED
U.S. INVASION OF CUBA
October 1962

IRBM *(Range Arc: Newfoundland to San Francisco)*
MRBM *(Range Arc: Washington to Dallas)*
Airfields
Soviet Combat Groups
Planned U.S. Invasion Route

miles
0   100

C U B A

Havana
Sagua la Grande
Remedios
Guantánamo Bay
(U.S. Naval Base)
Cape
Maisí
Baracoa

San Cristóbal
1st Armored
101st Airborne
San Antonio
de los Baños
Mariel
José Martí
Airport
Havana
82nd Airborne
U.S.
Marines
Santa Cruz del Norte
Matanzas

The aerial and naval bombardment of the island would begin early Tuesday morning. The 82nd Airborne Division would be dropped farther inland than the 101st. The 82nd's objective was to seize the San Antonio de los Baños military airfield and the José Martí International Airfield just outside Havana. The 101st would also take the military airfields at Mariel and Baracoa, along with the port of Mariel. There would be airdrops of humanlike dummies to confuse the enemy. These would not be ordinary dummies: They would be armed with recorded tapes to create the sounds of firefights.

There were a total of ten battalions of marines afloat in the vicinity of Cuba. They would come ashore at a number of famous beaches on Cuba's northern shore between Havana and Matanzas and link up with the 82nd Airborne Division. (The Soviets and Cubans suspected the invasion would come ashore at these beaches and had deployed cruise missiles along the coast; they also had dug defensive trenches along those beaches.) Once the beaches and the port of Mariel were secured, the 1st Armored Division would come ashore. They would move along the major highways and isolate Havana; then they would head for the missile sites. Other units of the 1st Armored would strike southward to cut the island in half.

October 28. That morning at nine o'clock Washington time, the U.S. Foreign Broadcast Intercept Service, while listening to Radio Moscow, began picking up an extraordinary message: It was an open letter from Khrushchev to Kennedy. The Soviets were clearly so alarmed by the speed with which events were moving that they elected to bypass the usual method of sending such a high-level message. Even in the time it would take to encode, decode, translate, and deliver the message, the crisis might have escalated out of control and the invasion might already have begun. So the Soviets decided to broadcast Khrushchev's letter to the president on the radio. "The Soviet government," the message read, "has ordered the dismantling of bases and the dispatch of equipment to the USSR. . . . I regard with respect and trust the statement you have made in your message . . . that there would be no attack or invasion against Cuba."

Less than forty-eight hours remained before the invasion was set to begin.

U.S. military leaders greeted the end of the crisis with relief. No one relished the prospect of heavy casualties, not to mention the threat of nuclear war. The main responsibility now fell on the intelligence community to monitor the dismantling of the missile sites and verify the removal of the missiles from the island. "The military posture of the United States," Admiral Ward noted in his diary a week later, on November 4, "continued to be one of increased readiness." Ships carrying twelve thousand marines from the West Coast were on their way, while sizable units of the 2nd Marine Division remained at sea off Florida. Air force and army units were poised for an assault, as were the carriers *Enterprise* and *Independence*.

But by now only Fidel Castro remained belligerent. He threatened to fire on the U.S. reconnaissance planes. Anastas Mikoyan, the first deputy secretary, was dispatched from Moscow to pacify the Cuban leader. When Castro told him that the Cuban people were prepared to fight as they had at the Bay of Pigs, Mikoyan replied, "You won't have a ragtag brigade against you this time. You will have the full might of U.S. forces. If you want to fight, you can fight— but alone." Mikoyan tightened the screws. He threatened to return immediately to Moscow and cut off all economic aid to Cuba. Grumbling, Castro backed down.

After the Soviet missiles had been removed from Cuba, but before the troops assembled in the southeastern United States were disbanded, Maxwell Taylor wanted the president to see firsthand the military machine that had been gathered for the projected invasion. On November 26, accompanied by the JCS and the chairman of the House Armed Services Committee, Kennedy arrived at Fort Stewart and reviewed just one of the three brigades of the 1st Armored Division. He looked on, incredulous, at the armor arrayed before him. That incredulity only grew as he traveled south that day, ending up on a pier at the Key West naval base. At Fort Stewart he recited a poem, supposedly found in a British sentry box at Gibraltar:

> God and the soldier all men adore,
> In time of danger and not before.
> When the danger is past,
> And all things righted,
> God is forgotten and the old
> Soldier slighted.

The president added, "The United States forgets neither God nor the soldier upon which we now depend."

But three decades later, we have almost forgotten the great invasion that never happened—forgotten it, perhaps, because we never really knew how awesome it would have been.

EPILOGUE

Surprises—and for the U.S., the discovery of missiles in Cuba was one—have a way of generating more surprises, not all of them pleasant. What might have happened if American troops had invaded Cuba? American troops probably would have gone in on Tuesday, October 30, had Khrushchev and Kennedy not made their last-minute deal over the previous weekend. Since Cuba was too far from the Soviet Union to be reinforced by conventional means, the only sure protection for the Russian troops on the island was tactical nuclear weapons, in the form of twelve short-range *Luna* rockets (or FROGS, as they were known in the U.S.) that carried a two-kiloton charge. Their effect on a Cuban beach or an invasion flotilla just offshore would have been awesome. "Assuming that the *Luna* was aimed to detonate in the air," the historians Aleksandr Fursenko and Timothy Naftali write,

> at an optional height of 600 feet above the ground, just one of these missiles would produce a huge fireball about 31 miles from the launch site. At the epicenter of the blast, there would be 100-mile-an-hour winds and a crater 130 feet in diameter and 130 feet deep. Any tank or armored personnel carrier within 500 yards would be destroyed. Unprotected human beings 1,000 yards from the blast site would probably die immediately as a result of the dramatic increase in air pressure, but those unfortunate enough to survive the explosion and the winds would suffer a painful death by radiation poisoning within two weeks.

Robert McNamara, then the secretary of defense, later described the *Luna* missiles as "the most dangerous element of the entire episode."

For all America's technological supremacy from the air, intelligence on the ground remained flawed (and still is). Estimates indicated that there were only 10,000 Soviet troops in Cuba; there were 42,000, many of them belonging to crack combat units. A mere 10,000 presented little problem. Plus, the American troops preparing for the invasion were not given the tactical nuclear weapons they normally would have carried. The planners, understandably, did not want to risk escalation, especially if the invasion force came up against Soviet detachments, as it surely would. Khrushchev had originally given his commanders in Cuba oral authorization to use tactical nuclear weapons if an invasion began and they were unable to reach Moscow "to confirm permission." But once Kennedy had announced the discovery of missiles in Cuba, the Soviet premier rescinded the order: Neither tactical nor strategic weapons could be fired without Moscow's explicit approval. This assumed, and it was a perilous assumption, that Soviet commanders would not take matters into their own hands, as they did when they ordered SAM antiaircraft missiles to shoot down Major Rudolf Anderson's U-2. The Soviet submarines that ranged around the island presented a similar danger. Many of them were armed with nuclear-tipped torpedoes; their captains were authorized to fire them if their hulls were breached. And what if a couple of IRBMs had escaped American bombs long enough to be armed, fueled, and launched toward the continental U.S.? That ultimate nuclear resort would have invited American retaliation in kind. Curtis LeMay's SAC bombers would have been heading for the U.S.S.R.; ICBMs would have lifted off from their underground silos. That, of course, is the worst-case scenario.

Nor can the potentially influential role of Fidel Castro be dismissed: He was another wild card. As he said at the 1992 Havana conference on the Cuban Missile Crisis:

> You want me to give you my opinion in the event of an invasion with all the troops, with 1,190 sorties [by American planes]? Would I have been ready to use nuclear weapons? Yes, I would have agreed to the use of nuclear weapons. Because, in any case, we took it for granted that it would become a nuclear war anyway, and that we were going to disappear. . . . I would have agreed, in the event of the invasion that you are talking about, with the use of tactical nuclear weapons. . . . I wish we had had the tactical weapons. It would have been wonderful. . . . The closer to Cuba the decision of using a weapon effective against a landing, the better.

There is no telling how elite troops, with pride and revolutionary principles at stake, would have acted in a moment of desperation—presumably after they had run through their *Lunas*. "We were all ready and willing to fight to the very last man," General Anatoly I. Gribkov, the former head of the Warsaw Pact, who had been in Cuba, said at the same Havana conference. "We didn't just plan an initial resistance. We even decided that if it proved necessary—if large tracts of the island were occupied—we would form guerrilla units in order to continue defending the interests of revolutionary Cuba. I'm using the very words that we used in 1962. That's the way we were then. We did not have anywhere to withdraw to. No retreat was possible."

There were other possibilities, of course, as Gaddis has pointed out. "Perhaps the Americans would have refrained from pressing the attack, thereby allowing the Russians a graceful exit. Perhaps Khrushchev would have tolerated Castro's overthrow and the Red Army's humiliation. Perhaps Kennedy still would have cut a deal. Perhaps—but all sides are fortunate, in retrospect, not to have had to rely upon these counterfactuals becoming fact."

Let us speculate that the invasion had gone smoothly, that the Soviets had refrained from firing their *Lunas*, and that the island had been overrun in reasonably short order. American military planning can be spectacular in the short term. But no firm plans had been made for the future of Cuba when a successful invasion had been completed. It was a potential source for trouble, as it has been in Iraq. Let us finally recall Brugioni's prescient sentences: "Although there were generalized plans for the occupation and a military government, there was no detailed plan for the recruitment of indigenous Cuban administrators. Nor were there plans to prevent starvation, disease, or civil unrest. When asked whether it had the funds to deal with such likely calamities, the State Department replied that 'none had been budgeted.'"

Twilight Zone in the Pentagon

THOMAS B. ALLEN

The simulation of battle through war games, Thomas B. Allen observes, has probably existed as long as organized warfare itself. The games go back at least as far as that dim past that saw the creation of the Asian go, the Hindu *chaturanga*, and chess, which with its king, queen bishop, knight, castle, and peasant pawn mimicked the conditions of medieval warfare. In 1797 a German tactician named Georg Venturini invented *kriegsspiel*—"war game"—which was played in military schools, its 3,600 squares representing the territory along the border with northern France; the rules of play were set out in a sixty-page book that, with time, increased in size. In 1824, watching his junior officers play *kriegsspiel*, the chief of the Prussian General Staff commented, "It's not a game at all! It's training for war."

Under Rear Admiral Alfred Thayer Mahan, the esteemed strategist who headed the Naval War College in Newport, RI, "naval *kriegsspiel*" became part of the school's curriculum. It still is, although it has evolved from the days when blue-water encounters were played out on huge checkerboards. War games, both military and naval, came to utilize computers, although in the Vietnam years, they began to fall out of favor. Vice Admiral Hyman G. Rickover, known as "the father of the nuclear submarine," criticized computer-based systems analysis in war games. "On a cost effectiveness basis," he told a congressional hearing in 1966, "the colonists would not have revolted against George III. . . . Computer logic would have advised the British to make terms with Hitler in 1940." Rickover went on to note that "A war, small or large, does not follow a prescribed 'scenario' laid out in advance. If we could predict the sequence of events accurately, we could probably avoid war in the first place."

This was the time of the Vietnam War, and the army colonel and military historian Harry G. Summers, Jr., recounted a story that had circulated in 1969, as the Nixon administration was taking over. All the vast data on North Vietnam, from population and gross national product to number of tanks and size of its armed forces, had been fed into a computer. The computer was then asked, "When will we win?"

The computer needed only a moment to answer: "You won in 1964."

Much preferred these days is a simpler form of war gaming that emphasizes the decisions people must make under the extreme conditions of war. Until the Cold War ended, players would be assigned to a U.S. Blue Team and a Soviet-bloc Red Team, with a Control Team presenting the opening scenario, fielding questions, or presenting new ones. The control team also does its best to prevent players from manipulating reality. For example, navy players often decline to sink aircraft carriers. Mark Herman, a well-known game creator, told Allen that there are "three words that do not belong in the military lexicon: unsinkable, unbreakable, and indestructible." All the participants sit at a long table; the windowless walls are decorated with maps. "The important aspect of any war game is the players," Herman said, adding that if you put the right ones at the table, they may come up with scenarios that are both realistic and useful. Games last as long as four or five days, from eight in the morning until four in the afternoon. (The Soviets were also fierce war gamers, although because of rigid distinctions between politicians and the military, civilians ordinarily did not participate, so their games tended to be more strictly tactical in nature.)

Allen has compared war games to autopsies: "They have great value in showing the living why certain actions can be fatal." In a game, expensive lessons can come cheaply. One participant recalled a game in which a high-ranking official got so caught up in the terrors of crisis management that he suddenly rose from the table and threw up in a wastebasket. That was during the Vietnam era, a time when such people had every right to feel queasy.

The article that follows describes what surely has to be one of the most bizarre war games ever played. It took place at the beginning of December 1962, a little over a month after the Cuban Missile Crisis ended (but two years before most people took our involvement in Vietnam seriously). That week, you might say, a group of "fresh and uninhibited" celebrity minds entered the Fifth Dimension in Room 1D-957 of the vast Pentagon basement.

———

THOMAS B. ALLEN has written on a wide variety of military subjects. His books include War Games and Remember Pearl Harbor. He is coauthor, with Norman Polmar, of World War II: America at War; Why Truman Dropped the Atomic Bomb on Japan; and Spy Book: The Encyclopedia of Espionage. His most recent book (with Paul Dickson) is The Bonus Army: An American Epic. Allen lives in Bethesda, Maryland.

A S ROD SERLING USED TO SAY, "There is a fifth dimension beyond that which is known to man. It is a dimension as vast as space and as timeless as infinity. It is an area we call the Twilight Zone." And once, in real life, the popular television dramatist took the Pentagon into *The Twilight Zone*.

Imagine, if you will, Serling in Room 1D-957 in the basement of the Pentagon for five days at the end of 1962, at the invitation of the Joint Chiefs of Staff. He and other civilians have been asked to participate in a series of games in which they are developing secret scenarios of America's future. Urged on by high-ranking military officers, the civilians are producing their own Twilight Zone: The Soviet Union conquers the United States; in a face-to-face confrontation with Nikita Khrushchev, President Barry Goldwater poises his finger over a nuclear button. But sometimes their fantasies are eerily prophetic: The president is impeached; the shah of Iran is toppled and flees into exile.

Besides Serling, the Olympians (as game reports call them) include Milton Caniff, the creator of the comic-strip hero Steve Canyon; John Ford, the Oscar-winning director whose classics included movies set in every American conflict from the Revolution to World War II; mystery writer Harold Q. Masur; and representatives from organized labor and industry. All the players have signed nondisclosure statements and have been told to say, if asked why they are in Washington, simply that they are "attending a conference." The games are highly secret, as is the existence of the Joint War Games Control Group of the Joint Chiefs of Staff, which manages the games. Serling and the others have been invited to the Pentagon to play Olympiad 1-62, a series of politico-military war games that start on Monday, December 3, 1962, and end on Friday, December 7—a date that seems a bit freighted with irony.

Such policy-planning games, imported from academia early in the Kennedy administration, still go on today. The players in these games usually are military officers and middle-level or high-ranking civilian officials drawn from the Department of Defense, the Department of State, the Central Intelligence Agency, and the White House.

In a typical war game, the thirty to thirty-five players are divided into player and Control Teams. Each team is put in a room that contains little more than a long table, chairs, and equipment for viewing videotapes. On the walls are maps (usually the sort published by the National Geographic Society) and whatever printed material needs to be displayed. A video camera, attached near the ceiling, is aimed at the table.

The basic game scenario—"believable; real and projected world tensions, activities, and policies," according to a Pentagon description—sets up a crisis situation, generally a year or more in the future. The staff may work as long as six months developing the basic scenario. Researchers often go overseas to interview U.S. ambassadors, senior military commanders, and experts on the region that is the setting for the scenario. They may even gather information on the performance of specific weapons—"to the trench level."

The final scenario is in two parts: a "world scene," usually presented documentary-style on a video screen; and the "crisis," in written form. The world scene—maps, clips of news broadcasts—thrusts the players into the future and lays out the situation in which the crisis is taking place. The staff strives to make the video presentation realistic. "We get support from the Defense Communications Agency, which as a matter of course records all the news programs, and they save that, and we can go and raid those clips," says a Pentagon briefing officer. "The world scene creates synthetic history to bring participants forward. We project into the future to change history a little bit and to get participants away from current-day policy restraints and let them freewheel."

Players are assigned to a U.S. Blue Team or a Soviet-bloc Red Team, with a Control Team presenting the scenario—typically, a description of a potential crisis just over the horizon—and running the game. Control might be represented by a military officer from the War Games Control Group or an Ivy League professor of political science.

The game does not move rapidly. It can last four days, from about eight in the morning to about four in the afternoon, with occasional overtime. A typical move takes three or four hours to make and report to Control. "When they begin to address the new situation, time is stopped. The four hours fit on one tick of the clock," the briefing officer says. "There are no late-breaking news flashes, no démarche from the Soviets. The reason is because we want them to achieve consensus and discuss the policy aspects of it. We don't want them to prove how they can respond with the right actions."

Olympiad was different, for its principal players were merely civilians with imaginations. And they played not one game over three or four days, as was usual, but four separate games, each seemingly designed to stimulate extreme reaction among the participants.

Assassinations of world leaders, for example, occur frequently in the Olympiad scenarios. Most of the assassinations are the work of the scenario writers, but sometimes they originate with the players. (For some time, I was told, assassinations had become quite the vogue in game playing.) West German chancellor Konrad Adenauer is poisoned. Soviet agents posing as anti-Gaullists kill French president Charles de Gaulle in one scenario and gravely wound him in another. Indian prime minister Jawaharlal Nehru and British prime minister Harold Macmillan are also assassinated. Serial regicide, in a Pentagon-sponsored game eleven months before the assassination of President Kennedy, undoubtedly helps to explain why the Department of Defense kept Olympiad 1-62 classified as top secret for over a quarter of a century.

But even when a game is pried from the Department of Defense through the Freedom of Information Act, the document bears the "sanitizing" black streaks of a Pentagon censor who blots out the names of the speakers in war-game dialogue. The words of players are not attributed lest rash comments during a game come back to haunt them.

The same courtesy was extended to the Olympians. So although a slip of the censor's pen revealed that Serling and Caniff were on the Blue Team, there is no way of knowing who said what. Nor are there any authors' credits for the initial scenarios or the teams' reactions to the events in the scenarios. What emerges from the released report on Olympiad is a series of anonymous interlocking narratives. But when compared to records of other games, Olympiad stands out as unique. There can be no doubt of the credits:

Produced by the Pentagon
Dramatization by Rod Serling
Directed by John Ford
Starring Steve Canyon

The Olympians warm up on three relatively routine games: negotiations for a disarmament treaty; simultaneous crises in Berlin and Cuba; and turmoil in the Middle East. The games introduce the Olympians to a world in which the United States is threatened by Communists around the globe. (Playing the third warm-up game, the Blue Team decides to explode a nuclear bomb a hundred miles off the Soviet coast as a warning. The game report notes that the Olympians did not balk at any action "even though it means full-scale nuclear war.") The crucial fourth game, dubbed DAFT (for "decade after"), departs from the Blue-Red team format; instead, the Olympians are asked to respond to three scenarios that might have come straight out of the Twilight Zone. Each scenario breaks off at a crucial moment. The Olympians must produce an ending that will help guide planners of U.S. strategy in the decade ahead.

The first scenario envisions America's defeat in a nuclear war in the early 1970s. Enraged, one of the players says, "The real reason why we lost the war was the failure of the President." Criticism of President Kennedy punctuates the scenarios. Those same scenarios had circulated among Kennedy's military and civilian policy planners but had not been played. "I tried unsuccessfully for several months to get anyone to use them," an anonymous Control tells the Olympians. "You were a heaven-sent opportunity."

As the first scenario opens, NATO has begun to crack following 1963 elections of Communist governments in France and Italy. West Berlin mayor Willy Brandt (who really would become chancellor of West Germany in 1969) makes a deal with East Germany, and a united Germany is reborn.

The scenario continues:

Desperate conferences between England, Canada and the U.S. ended when England agreed to withdraw all troops from the European Continent, but insisted on the free passage of U.S., Canadian, and English troops and equipment to their homelands. The ensuing evacuations resembled Dunkirk; women and children were flown out, minus nearly all personal possessions; every available ship was pressed into service to evacuate the streams of military convoys converging on the western European ports, through crowds of jeering or crying people.

The United States and Canada, expecting a Soviet nuclear attack, evacuate all cities. Soviet missiles knock out early-warning radar and then destroy Detroit, Pittsburgh, Seattle, San Francisco, Los Angeles, and other U.S. cities.

Khrushchev telephones the U.S. president, unnamed but presumably Kennedy, to say: "This is not nuclear blackmail. This is it. Only one-quarter of my force was launched. If you retaliate, I'll wipe out the rest of the U.S." The president, who has sent Strategic Air Command bombers on retaliatory strikes, calls them back and agrees to negotiate with Khrushchev.

But, says the scenario, "two squadrons of B-52s, either through communication garble or madly enraged, pushed on—delivering 100 megatons on Moscow, Minsk, and Pinsk." The Soviets answer this Steve Canyonesque mutiny with another wave of missiles. The United States sues for peace.

Soviet troops and officials arrive in the United States, which is divided for occupation. The old Confederacy states east of the Mississippi, plus Kentucky and Tennessee, are turned over to Castro. Texas, New Mexico, and Arizona are put under control of Mexico, which is a Communist nation. Alaska and Hawaii are directly annexed by the Soviet Union, along with the states of the Pacific Northwest. The Northeast and Midwest as far as the Rockies are largely a nuclear wasteland and are occupied by Soviet troops until a puppet government is set up.

The Cuban Confederacy, as it is called, gives American blacks new status as Cuban "blood brothers." There are wholesale executions of whites in the Orange Bowl. But in this scenario there is hope—at least for the white Americans—for within a year, a "strongly organized underground of firm discipline" and "growing power" challenges the rule of the Cubans and the blacks. The new organization calls itself the Centennial Ku Klux Klan.

In the Democratic Peoples Federation of Mexico, "Spanish-speaking Americans of intelligence and standing" become local officials. In the Democratic Republic of Mid-America, an underground movement called the Sons of Liberty II has developed ray guns that can "stop nuclear and internal-combustion engines, paralyze or kill life, and possibly influence weather." But freedom for them and all other Americans is only a dream. *The End.*

"Too downbeat," one of the Olympians, presumably John Ford, says of this scenario, adding: "I'm not buying it for a motion picture. . . ." Another brushes aside the dismal vision. Americans, he declares, "are not going to quit, and we are going to have arms all over that are hidden." We must begin caching arms right now, the Olympians urge as they quickly veer from the hypothetical future to a present threatened by the enemy "at our doorstep."

No weapon, an Olympian passionately declaims, "is better than the hand or the heart of the man who carries it. We urge that while one American lives who can pull a trigger, it is his duty to do so." Only two months before, Khrushchev had been caught putting Soviet missiles in Cuba. Most Americans believed that Kennedy had won the nuclear showdown with Khrushchev, but the DAFT scenarios reflect a fear that Khrushchev's bold move in Cuba was far more significant than his retreat. The futures presented to the Olympians are haunted by nuclear confrontations even more ominous than the real Cuban Missile Crisis. The United States is imperiled on every side. Besides the Soviets, with their missiles, there is also "the indistinct shadow of the sleeping Chicom giant . . . a menace that needed to be chained."

Caught up in this vision, the Olympians make recommendations that seem more suited to the 1962 present than the 1972 future. They want "subterranean armories of small arms scattered throughout the country and available to any civilian population." They suggest that the United States go beyond its shores to set up "great secret armories." The Olympians want missile-equipped submarines hidden in the Antarctic and remote "super-secret bases" manned by covert troops "who can retaliate" from overseas if "we are shot down in the street." They advise the immediate building of "basic vaults of production units" to preserve vital apparatuses, such as communications equipment, along with the ingredients and blueprints for manufacturing nuclear weapons. Resistance forces, aware of these caches, then can make their own nuclear bombs to use against the Soviet occupiers.

To stave off this looming conquest, the Olympians say, American youth must be taught that "in case of enemy invasion," everyone is "expected to carry on the fight," from "the ash cans of the lower East Side of New York to the apple orchards of Oregon." Special Forces and the CIA should "arm those who are with us behind the iron and bamboo curtains." And America must prepare to "mercilessly introduce biological and meteorological warfare" against our enemies.

To preserve civilization, the Olympians create a new form of citizenship—"Canambrian," which encompasses the people of the United States, Canada, Great Britain, Ireland, and Australia. Canambrian citizenship could even be extended to Latin Americans, as long as there are "educational safeguards."

The second DAFT episode, weaving domestic politics with world affairs, opens in August 1963, when "the shamed representatives of the new African states went into virtual hiding" at the U.N. because "most Caucasians south of the Sahara to the Union of S. Africa had been wiped out in a gruesome cannabalistic [sic] orgy of Inter-tribal MauMau murder more shocking than anything in history."

The U.S. ambassador to the U.N. (then Adlai Stevenson) "introduced only an insipid motion of censure against the responsible African governments." So "the U.S. Congress, Press and public, surfeited with our namby-pamby reactive policy (dubbed 'shrinkmanship' by ex-governor Tom Dewey), blew up."

Congress demands U.S. withdrawal from the U.N. and impeaches the president. In the new Cabinet, United Auto Workers leader Walter Reuther is secretary of state and Teamster boss Jimmy Hoffa is secretary of labor. (In real life, Hoffa, just convicted of jury tampering, was the major target of Attorney General Robert Kennedy's investigation of labor racketeering.) General Matthew B. Ridgway is recalled to active duty to head the new War Department as the one chief of staff. The scenario abolishes the office of the Joint Chiefs—the game's sponsor.

Under a resolute new president (presumably Lyndon Johnson), the U.S. Air Force destroys Cuba for no apparent reason. Panama and Puerto Rico jointly become the fifty-first state. All foreign aid is stopped. Taiwan is "turned over to Japan, with the concurrence of China." American technicians help China build nuclear weapons. "Senator Wayne Morse made an impassioned plea for liberalism, claiming neutralism was really only isolationism, but retired, visibly shaken by his colleagues' roaring boos."

Europe, with both NATO and Eastern bloc troops withdrawn, forms United Western Europe. A Syrian Muslim known as Saladin II forges a new Saracen empire that encompasses the Arab world. "The Mid-African continent was again 'Darkest Africa,' practically out of touch with the rest of the world, consumed by inter-tribal battles."

Saladin, backed by the Soviet Union and China, conquers Israel. Senator Jacob Javits of New York, a firm supporter of Israel in real life, is mocked in the scenario, which has him demanding that "the United States immediately invade the Saracen Empire and restore a free Israel stretching from the Suez to the Dardanelles." Only one nation, the Dominican Republic, offers asylum to Israeli refugees. The Saracens take over Israeli nuclear facilities and manufacture small weapons so that individual Arabs are able to carry nuclear bombs into the cities of the West.

When the Olympians respond to DAFT II, laughter greets one remark: "The Kennedy dynasty has been broken." In that post-Kennedy America, fallout shelters and domed cities guarantee the nation will survive even with "tens of millions of casualties from a massive nuclear attack." U.S. scientists are working on "a global satellite-borne anti-ballistic missile boost and mid-course intercept system" that uses laser beams to stop enemy missiles. And the Saracens who are toting nuclear bombs will be detected by "cheap portable fluoroscopes for surveillance in guarding against suitcase weapons."

The Olympians also come up with a "substitute for aid funds": an antifertility powder that can be secretly slipped into a needy nation's drinking water "if it is to our advantage somewhere to check the growth of a population."

The Olympians revise the U.S. educational system. Old-fashioned patriotic messages are emphasized: "It's a wonderful thing to have the hackles of your neck come up when you see the Stars and the Stripes in front of you." All high-schoolers of a certain IQ are required by law to go to college or trade school. A national physical-fitness program will "make a potential Ranger out of every American boy and out of all American girls that are willing to go for it." At the age of eighteen or nineteen, "this lad can be a Ranger just by putting on the uniform." Then, say the Olympians, "we . . . give them their practice in using knives."

DAFT III, the wildest of all, focuses directly on the man who is the commander in chief of all the military men in the Pentagon's Room 1D-957. In 1964 the Democratic Party,

> committed to the candidacy of President Kennedy, could not inject any suspenseful counter to the battle royal joined between the Republican prospects. . . . Then, suddenly, . . . the Southern Democrats and Conservative Republicans agreed to hold a non-partisan convention in Dallas in September to discuss "National policy and the threat of the 'far left' to American existence."

President Kennedy is reelected in 1964, but his running mate is Nelson Rockefeller. Vice President Lyndon Johnson has resigned and is running as the presidential candidate for the newly organized Constitutional Democrats party; Johnson's running mate is Barry Goldwater.

In his second term, President Kennedy drives up the national debt and launches several apparently meaningless small-scale wars in which 34,407 U.S. servicemen are killed and 107,743 wounded. Robert McNamara continues as secretary of defense, but his Pentagon is caricatured as a building full of record-keeping machines and civilians concerned with motion studies and management analyses. Steve Canyon's beloved Strategic Air Command is put under civilian control.

In the 1968 election, Goldwater defeats Rockefeller, and subsequently, he meets Khrushchev at summit conferences in Moscow and Washington. The two leaders cease competitive aid to other nations, embargo military arms exports to China and Africa, and agree to negotiate a peace treaty. In November 1969, Goldwater and Khrushchev meet again in Moscow, along with leaders of Warsaw Pact and NATO nations.

At a grand ball in the Kremlin,

As the music of the Moscow symphony swelled, and the Bolshoi Ballet began its intricate and beautiful symbolism of Swan Lake, a disheveled sub-minister rushed in to Khrushchev and whispered something. The Premier, almost apoploctic [sic], removed his shoe and began beating on the arm of his chair. The music stopped. Khrushchev shrieked, "I've been betrayed! The capitalist war mongers have started a revolution in Hungary! It is supported by the Chinese from Albania, and aided by the traitorous Yugoslavs, who proclaim that they are going to restore the old Austro-Hungarian Empire with the help of the West!"

In the stunned silence that followed, communists and westerners edged apart; women fainted; into the ballroom came burp gun-carrying Red Army soldiers in field uniforms. In a wild rage, Khrushchev pointed at President Goldwater, "You have gone too far," he hissed. "This time the American dogs are not in their kennels. They are here in my house. Remember Beria's death; declare yourselves now, before you die!"

The Olympians react to this cliff-hanger by finishing the scene: President Goldwater—"his white hair gleaming, his black tortoise shell glasses shining"—takes from a briefcase a black box manufactured by Westinghouse (one of whose executives is an Olympian). On the box are rows of buttons, including four labeled *Homeland China, Albania, Hungary, Yugoslavia*. Other buttons are labeled *Total Destruction by Nuclear Devices, Partial Destruction by Conventional Means, Temporary Immobilization by Nerve Gas*. (An Olympian later explains that in playing out their game, they had Kennedy secretly approve the development of earth-orbiting satellites "containing nerve gases, permanent death-dealing chemicals, nuclear and conventional weapons.")

Goldwater shows the black box, which controls the satellites, to Khrushchev and says, "Mr. Chairman, as you can see, the capabilities for stopping the reported actions lies [sic] between the choices you see before you, and I now offer you, as a gesture of good faith, the opportunity of choosing the method of ending the circumstances which have caused your gore [sic] to rise."

The report does not say which button Khrushchev selects.

The gaming ended on the afternoon of December 7 with Paul Nitze, assistant secretary of defense for international security affairs, speaking to the Olympians. War games like this are important, he says. "We've done what you've just been doing: gone through several Berlin war games, several disarmament war games. . . . We're going to read with interest the results of the work you've done."

Nitze was not just being polite. Politico-military simulations were considered so important for policy planners that the lengthy reports were sent directly to Nitze and other high-ranking officials. During the game, the Olympians heard from General Maxwell D. Taylor, chairman of the Joint Chiefs of Staff; General Earle G. Wheeler, army chief of staff; General Curtis E. LeMay, air force chief of staff; and Admiral C. V. Ricketts, vice chief of naval operations.

The chiefs' remarks are not recorded in the Olympiad report, but the words of a Pentagon general are. He tells the Olympians that this game "is the initial effort to get some fresh and uninhibited minds from the leading walks of American life in here to add fresh ideas to the Department of Defense in the effort to enhance our U.S. interests."

We know that the Pentagon has continued to enter the Twilight Zone of imaginary futures on the march toward Vietnam, toward Star Wars, toward whatever still lies beyond. The Joint Chiefs of Staff and commanders of U.S. forces use computer-run games for contingency planning. These games, somewhat more tuned to reality than those played out by the Olympians, have included scenarios based on the potential fall of the Marcos regime in the Philippines and a possible U.S. invasion of Nicaragua. Grenada was gamed long before the actual invasion. But because of the secrecy shrouding the games, we do not know the identities of other "fresh and uninhibited minds" who may have been summoned to Room 1D-957 and asked to help construct the American future.

The Right Man

VICTOR DAVIS HANSON

For a figure of archetypical menace in the Cold War, it would be hard to beat General Curtis E. LeMay, his eternal cigar jutting pugnaciously from the right corner of his mouth. In its most dangerous years, he came to personify the merchant of death, the liberal nightmare of the American military. Part of his malign image was of his own making, and he probably could have cared less. "LeMay spoke too candidly and wrote too much," Victor Davis Hanson notes in his striking reassessment of LeMay's career. He was almost too quotable. The man who turned the Strategic Air Command into a justifiably feared offensive instrument once said, "There are only two things in the world, SAC bases and SAC targets." Another time he said that the only foolproof antisubmarine system was "to boil the ocean with nukes." As for Cuba: "Fry it." Or North Vietnam: Bomb it "back into the Stone Age." Not surprisingly, LeMay became the object of antiwar sport, W. C. Fields brandishing a nuke. Indeed, Buck Turgidson and Jack D. Ripper, two characters in Stanley Kubrick's memorable send-up, *Dr. Strangelove*, seem almost a composite of the man. LeMay's reputation may never recover from those twin portrayals. But his detractors could never give him credit for what he was, a sure-handed tactician and unsentimental realist who happened to be one of the great captains of American history: a Ulysses S. Grant of the air, as it were.

LeMay's reputation could rest on his World War II record alone. In Europe in 1943, he developed new formations and tactics that dramatically increased the potency of the Allies' strategic bombing campaign and reduced its losses. In the Pacific in 1945, heading the XXI Bomber Command and, later, the Twentieth Air Force, he soon recognized that high-altitude bombing of Japan was not working. He stripped down his B-29s and sent them in low, making them in effect giant dive-bombers. He dumped incendiary bombs on Japan's major cities, which were built largely of wood. The two atomic bombs dropped in August were merely the strategic offensive taken to an extreme—and they worked. As the Japanese emperor Hirohito said, he did not want his nation "reduced to ashes." LeMay's campaign against Japan is the single instance in which a sustained air offensive ended a war. (Curiously, at the time, he objected to the dropping of the bombs, maintaining that incendiary raids would have done the job as well—a position that was noteworthy in view of his later advocacy of nuclear weapons.)

"I suppose if I had lost the war," LeMay once confessed, as if no one else mattered, "I would have been tried as a war criminal." And then he added, "All war is immoral, and if you let that bother you, you're not a good soldier." The cost in lives was terrible, but LeMay's air campaign ultimately saved lives, Allied and Japanese. We had to use the bomb. Time was running out. The projected American-led invasion would have been unimaginably bloody, despite what revisionist historians say. But the abrupt end of the Pacific War would have enormous, if not often considered, ramifications for the Cold War. It kept the Soviets out of the Japanese home islands. They were cobbling together an invasion of the northernmost island, Hokkaido, two months before we were ready to launch Operation Olympic, our invasion of the south island, Kyushu. If the Soviets had succeeded in making a landing, they would have had legitimate claim to the island, a significant (and no doubt troublemaking) role in the formal surrender preparations, and a zone of a partitioned Tokyo. Just think of the Cold War twists of a Berlin in the Pacific. To what extent would a Soviet presence have slowed the reconstruction of Japan? Or influenced our decision in 1950 to intervene in Korea, using Japan as a base? We have Curtis LeMay to thank for ending the war when it did end.

He was just thirty-nine in 1945, and he would play, if anything, an even greater role in influencing the direction the Cold War took. In 1948 he was the principal designer of the Berlin Airlift, originally nicknamed "LeMay's Coal and Feed Company." He was soon transferred home to head SAC, which he turned into a strategic deterrent all its own, and one that the Soviets were unable to match until the coming of the ICBM. His

B-29s turned much of North Korea into a moonscape, but he chafed at Washington's refusal to allow him to extend the bombing to China, where the real targets lay. (Loose cannon that he was, he did not order overflights of China and Russia, as some historians have maintained: Only the president could do that.)

He never hid his feelings: We should have taken out the U.S.S.R. while we had the chance, which was in the 1950s. "There was, definitely, a time when we could have destroyed all Russia (I mean by that, all of Russia's capability to wage war) without losing a man to their defenses," he said in his memoirs. He was that confident of SAC. His words could take on an eerie eloquence, as they did in a speech he delivered at the Naval War College in 1956: "Between sunset tonight and sunrise tomorrow morning the Soviet Union would likely cease to be a major military power or even a major nation. . . . Dawn might break over a nation infinitely poorer than China—less populated than the United States, and condemned to an agrarian existence perhaps for generations to come."

LeMay was eventually made chief of staff of the air force, the position he held during the Cuban Missile Crisis. Privately, he believed that JFK behaved like a coward, that we should have exercised a first-strike option. The Sunday morning after the two Ks cemented their deal, the president summoned his military chiefs to the Cabinet Room to inform them. LeMay pounded the table, his cigar no doubt clenched in his teeth. "It's the greatest defeat in our history, Mr. President. . . . We should invade today!" For the rest of his life, he remained convinced that we had "lost" the Cuban Missile Crisis—and, indeed, the entire Cold War.

***

VICTOR DAVIS HANSON retired last year as a professor of classics at California State University, Fresno, and is now a fellow at the Hoover Institution at Stanford University. He has written on subjects ranging from Greek military and rural history to the history of warfare and contemporary agriculture. His books include *The Western Way of War, Fields Without Dreams, Carnage and Culture, The Soul of Battle, Ripples of Battle*, and a history of the Peloponnesian War, *A War Like No Other*. He writes a weekly column for the *Chicago Tribune* and is writing a novel set in ancient Greece about the freeing of the Helots. He still lives on the farm outside Fresno where he grew up.

N DR. STRANGELOVE, Stanley Kubrick's 1964 black satire about a nuclear Armageddon, George C. Scott portrays the chairman of the Joint Chiefs of Staff, gum-chewing, jingoistic, right-wing nut General Buck Turgidson. Along with his wing commander, General Jack D. Ripper (the cigar-chomping Sterling Hayden), Turgidson welcomes the chance to unleash the nuclear firepower of America's bombers in the final showdown against the "Russkies." Both Turgidson and Ripper, of course, bear some uncanny resemblances to General Curtis E. LeMay, who at the time was serving on the Joint Chiefs in his role as chief of staff of the U.S. Air Force.

LeMay had clashed continually with Secretary of Defense Robert S. McNamara and the chairman of the Joint Chiefs of Staff, General Maxwell Taylor, over the so-called missile gap and limitations on the use of American strategic power during the Cold War—especially during the Cuban Missile Crisis and early in the Vietnam War (1961–65). The unpredictable LeMay was supposedly quoted at one Pentagon strategy session on Cuba as saying, "Now we've got him [the Russian Bear] in a trap, let's take his leg off right up to his testicles. On second thought, let's take off his testicles too." Buck Turgidson likewise brags about catching "the Commies with their pants down" in a war that General Ripper says is "too important to be left to the politicians."

Nor has more recent history been kind to LeMay, the air force general most readily identified with the American strategic arsenal during the first two decades of the Cold War. For example, in Richard Rhodes's *Dark Sun: The Making of the Hydrogen Bomb*, LeMay is depicted as a hothead who tried his best to provoke a nuclear conflagration during the Cuban Missile Crisis. In Rhodes's opinion, LeMay felt that our nuclear forces (otherwise a "wasting asset") ideally should be used in a preemptive attack on the Soviet Union, a move that Rhodes believes would have resulted in "historic omnicide."

Once described as "a rogue elephant barging out of a forest," LeMay spoke too candidly and wrote too much. His method of argumentation and counsel was both undiplomatic and often theatrical; Maxwell Taylor remarked that LeMay "would jam that damn cigar in his mouth and place a chip on his shoulder and parade through the halls of the Pentagon looking for a fight." So, despite his substantial experience and proven record of success, LeMay is now remembered too often for his outrageous one-liners ("Well, maybe if we do this overflight right, we can get World War III started"), which seemed to confirm that for years a scary dinosaur from World War II had America's atomic weapons under his operational command. No wonder he ended up a near-recluse, reluctant to appear publicly or grant interviews, still bitter over the crude and simplistic portrayal of him in the popular media during the 1960s.

LeMay was an obvious and easy target for caricature. After President Lyndon Johnson successfully portrayed Republican candidate Barry Goldwater as a trigger-happy nuclear warmonger in the 1964 campaign, and with disenchantment growing over the stalemate in Vietnam, the American public began to grow leery of the power—and intentions—of the country's Cold Warriors. In addition, in 1965, LeMay had at last published his memoirs (*Mission with LeMay*), which confirmed the hearsay and innuendo that had circulated about him for years. For once, in fact, the official record was far more inflammatory than the rumor and gossip of any liberal journalist. Of the existing "no-win" policy against the North Vietnamese, LeMay scoffed, "My solution to the problem would be to tell them frankly that they've got to draw in their horns and stop their aggression, or we're going to bomb them back into the Stone Age. And we would shove them back into the Stone Age with Air power or Naval power—not with ground forces." LeMay's "back into the Stone Age" became an often repeated and embarrassing part of the discourse about the war. Further, LeMay's experience in dealing with Japanese kamikazes in World War II, and his later concern over the human-wave attacks by North Korean and Chinese Communists, appeared in print as racist advice on how to win another Asian war:

> Human attrition means nothing to such people. Their lives were so miserable here on earth that there can't help but be a better life for them and

all their relatives in a future world. They look forward to that future world with delight. They're going to have everything from tea-parties with long-dead grandfathers down to their pick of all the golden little dancing girls in Paradise.

Because of LeMay's theatrics and frequently uncouth pronouncements, most critics missed the fact that his advocacy of a strategic air campaign against military targets in North Vietnam—dockyards, ports, power plants, railroads, factories, and irrigation facilities—might have been more successful, as well as less devastating to civilians in the long run, than the actual policy of carpet-bombing the south. Because LeMay was his own public relations nightmare, most forgot that he had deplored the use of tactical fighter-bombers in occasional haphazard strategic roles, while—against his wishes—his beloved strategic B-52 bomber fleet was used tactically, resulting in slaughter without harming the enemy's infrastructure.

As for the fictional General Buck Turgidson's eagerness to push the nuclear button ("only 10 to 20 million killed, tops"), LeMay himself had written nearly as much in his 1965 autobiography:

> There was, definitely, a time when we could have destroyed all of Russia (I mean by that, all of Russia's capability to wage war) without losing a man to their defenses. . . . It would have been possible, I believe, for America to say to the Soviets, "Here's a blueprint for your immediate future. We'll give you a deadline of five or six months"—something like that—"to pull out of the satellite countries, and effect a complete change of conduct. You will behave your damn selves from this moment forth."

LeMay's nuclear fascination was in evidence as late as a 1984 interview, in which the seventy-eight-year-old retired general still lamented his inability as commander of America's strategic air forces to gain unquestioned access to nuclear weapons "and to take some action on my own" if—as Buck Turgidson puts it in *Dr. Strangelove*—"the normal chain of command has been disrupted."

In 1968, when he ran for vice president on George Wallace's third-party ticket, LeMay published the polemical *America Is in Danger*, which in part outlined a strategic air campaign against Red China. On occasion, he quoted Dr. Edward Teller—the model for Dr. Strangelove himself—about the advantages of nuclear proliferation. "One could also question the basic premise," LeMay added, "that stability itself is always desirable."

LeMay's physical appearance only enhanced his hard-nosed reputation: a burly physique, thick hair combed straight back, bushy black eyebrows, a barrel chest bedecked with air medals, binoculars slung around his neck, the huge cigar perennially stuck out of one side of his mouth, occasional sunglasses—a cartoonist's dream, which ever since has provided the stereotype of the Pentagon's top brass. An avid big-game hunter and sports-car enthusiast, he was frequently photographed with elephant, buffalo, and bear trophies as well as souped-up racing cars. This was no technocrat, no West Point academician controlling our nation's nuclear bomber fleet, but a general more comfortable behind the wheel of a fully loaded bomber. Indeed, LeMay ended his autobiography with his favorite last order as he boarded his bomber: "Crank her up, let's go."

All this has made it difficult for the historian to separate LeMay's public bluster from his actual record as an air force general. Like many others, I accepted without question Kubrick's caricature of LeMay and considered him a reckless and one-dimensional military mind with little concern for human lives, civilian or military, the enemy's or those of his own men.

I also had some personal, anecdotal information about General LeMay, and it confirmed the image of a no-holds-barred, bombs-away hyperpatriot. During World War II, my father had flown on thirty-four missions (and was credited with two destroyed Japanese fighters) in a B-29 attached to the 504th Bomb Group, stationed with the 313th Bombardment Wing on the island of Tinian as part of LeMay's XXI Bomber Command. My father's stories of the firebombing of Japanese cities seemed to tell of indiscriminate attacks on the civilian population and a reckless use of American aviators. By taking their magnificent precision bombers (which were theretofore targeting strictly military and industrial targets) from the near safety of 30,000 to 35,000 feet to fly as little more than huge dive-bombers at 5,000 to 7,000 feet and occasionally lower, LeMay seemed bent on a deliberate sacrifice of aviators' lives simply to deliver more ordnance. That Hiroshima and Nagasaki were both nuked under LeMay's command and, with his support, rounded out the crude stereotype.

Still, I have been intrigued by my father's failure to criticize LeMay directly, when it would have been so easy for him to do so. Despite his horrific stories of B-29s overloaded with napalm and blowing up on takeoff, of low-flying bombers shredded by flak and their eleven-man crews sent spiraling into a self-generated inferno over Tokyo, of the smell of burning Japanese flesh wafting through the bomb-bay doors, he never equated that barbarity with LeMay. On the contrary, he seemed to think that the carnage below his plane and the sacrifice of his friends in the air—twelve of sixteen B-29s in his 398th Squadron crashed, were shot down, or were never heard from again—had been necessary to win the war and save, not expend, lives. And despite his lifelong Democratic Party credentials, my father spoke highly of LeMay even in the midst of the general's entry into controversial right-wing politics. Increasingly, I have wondered why he bore affection for such a seemingly unaffectionate personality.

To review the career of Curtis E. LeMay is to chronicle the growth of the U.S. strategic air force. To review his behavior and conduct in the military is to understand the American character itself, its mettle in wartime and its naïveté and impudence during the peace. No other American bore more responsibility for the development of strategic air power from 1944 to 1965, a twenty-one-year period that saw the strategic fleet develop from a force of often ineffectual propeller-driven bombers into the most powerful airborne arm the world had seen. LeMay's role was decisive at all levels—operational, tactical, and strategic—and characterized throughout by decisive judgment, aggressive leadership, and unquestioned personal courage. Anywhere American bombers were deployed, LeMay was not far away; often he was in the cockpit. (By the end of his career, LeMay was certified to fly—and flew—seventy-five types of military aircraft, ranging from strategic and tactical bombers to tankers, cargo planes, fighters, civilian transports, and helicopters.)

In 1937, after nine years in the U.S. Army Air Corps, First Lieutenant LeMay was attached to the 2nd Bombardment Group, which was the first unit to fly the new B-17 bomber. LeMay's crews trained on it for the next four and a half years, until the United States entered World War II. In April 1942, Colonel LeMay was assigned to the Eighth Air Force, and he took command of the 305th Bombardment Group, comprising thirty-five B-17s. Although he was only thirty-five years old, no other American had more experience with the B-17; in fact, LeMay was the only pilot in his entire group to have flown the bomber at all. "I gave them a ride in a B-17 before we went overseas so they could shoot at a target as we flew across the desert at a hundred feet," he later recounted in his autobiography. "That was it. That's what we went to war with.

They were not only a rabble, but I didn't have any confidence in their commander—me! I had never commanded anything."

But in little over a year, after leading many of the daylight missions over
Europe himself, LeMay was made brigadier general. By March 1944, as a
major general, he had taken command of an entire air division (266 B-17s and
B-24s) and flown on some of the most dangerous air battles of the war, including the Schweinfurt-Regensburg raids. Although not yet forty, he had developed a reputation for organizational skill in creating professional, effective
forces ex nihilo.

In August 1944 he was ordered to the Pacific theater to take over the XX
Bomber Command, as part of the army's new strategic air campaign against
Japan. This force, based in China and India, was understaffed and its novel
B-29s still unproved; LeMay was largely frustrated in his attempt to destroy
strategic Japanese industries on a wide scale. But in January 1945 he went to
the newly conquered Mariana Islands and assumed command of the consolidated strategic forces of the XXI Bomber Command, a force far different from
the B-29 squadrons he had commanded the year before in Asia. The new bases
on Guam, Tinian, and Saipan were easily supplied by the navy, relatively safe
from enemy attack, completely autonomous, and not surrounded by hostile native populations, while the B-29s themselves were gradually being freed from
engineering flaws and early mechanical problems. Both crews and planes were
arriving in increasing levels, and fighter squadrons of P-47s and P-51s were
being assembled to escort the planes over Japan. In addition, the capture of Iwo
Jima in February created a safe base for damaged B-29s on their return trip
from Tokyo. Finally, LeMay's predecessor, Brigadier General Haywood S.
Hansell, Jr., had devised the foundation—infrastructure, command organization, tactical approach—of an effective bombing command during his three-
month tenure. Unfortunately for Hansell, the inclement weather over Japan
—the jet stream and thunderclouds that tossed planes wildly in random directions—and the enormous distances involved for the new planes and crews had
meant a failure to achieve the dramatic results demanded by Washington from
the corps's orthodox reliance on high-altitude, precision bombing.

It was here, with a radical change in tactics, that LeMay gained fame as he
methodically engineered the destruction of most of the urban areas of Japan.
But for six weeks after he arrived on Guam, LeMay did little to change his predecessor's tactical and strategic practices. The huge bombers, after all, had

been created to fly well above Japanese fighters at 30,000 to 35,000 feet. From there, equipped with radar and protected by twelve .50-caliber guns whose turrets could be synchronized, the bombers' well-trained eleven-man crews could supposedly attack industrial targets accurately and with impunity.

In reality, that was rarely true. The bombers' unreliable engines overheated during the strenuous effort to reach high altitudes while overloaded with enormous bomb loads of twenty thousand pounds. Mechanical difficulties and adverse weather reduced the number of bombers that could reach the target. Often under 5 percent of the bombs dropped on Japan were landing within a thousand feet of the designated target. Further, until Iwo Jima was captured, bombers were crashing into the ocean in increasing numbers on their long way back to the Marianas.

LeMay knew that if aircraft losses continued to rise and Japan's infrastructure remained largely viable, he, too, would be relieved of command. But he also was aware of some preliminary and successful trials with low-level incendiary attacks at night. The E. I. du Pont company had produced a new substance known as napalm that ignited and engulfed with flame anything it came in contact with. And in December 1944, B-29s had burned out over 40 percent of the Japanese supply facility at Hankow, China. So the challenge for LeMay was to expand on that early, promising, and harrowing evidence—in the process, refuting the entire tradition of precision bombing, dismissing much of his own experience gained in the daylight air war over Germany, contradicting the previous training of his own bomber crews, ignoring the original design intent of the B-29, and committing a democratic United States to a policy that would guarantee the incineration of thousands of noncombatants.

By early March, LeMay had finalized his plan for low-level nighttime fire-bombing; planes would fly in low, below 10,000 feet—sometimes, if need be, down to 5,000, even if "flesh and blood can't stand it." At that level, a number of advantages immediately accrued. The B-29s could fly singly beneath the cloud cover and not be subject to the jet stream. Strain on the engines would be minimized, as planes would not have to labor to reach thirty thousand feet and fly in tight formation. Reduced fuel consumption meant no auxiliary gas tanks, permitting increased bomb loads. Japanese antiaircraft battalions were accustomed to high-level attacks, so there were few 40mm and 20mm rapid-firing smaller batteries that were so effective below ten thousand feet. Although the Japanese could send up formidable fighters during day raids, they possessed few planes that were effective at night. And by flying over Japan under the cover of darkness, the returning bombers would be in the vicinity of Iwo Jima in daylight, easing the challenge of forced landings and ditchings.

LeMay also ordered most guns and ammunition removed, to save weight and reduce accidental firing on friendly planes in the night. He felt that initial losses to enemy fighters would be more than offset by the destruction of factories and refineries, which would ensure an end to most fighter and flak resistance in the near future. And so, for the inaugural fire raids, the bombers flew in essentially unarmed—until declining crew morale and increasing fighter resistance mandated a return to defensive capability. Still, by war's end, LeMay's missions were becoming progressively safer for his crews. By July 1945 the loss per mission was 0.03 percent, and LeMay could boast that the final incendiary raids over Japan had become the safest air assignment of the war.

Most important, LeMay realized that the Japanese cities were far more densely populated than European urban centers, and built largely of wood. Because industrial production was often decentralized in smaller, family-run factories, the idea of simply torching the entire urban core not only was practicable but also made strategic sense. Even if thousands of civilians were killed in the process—"I suppose if I had lost the war, I would have been tried as a war criminal," LeMay said later—the general felt his plan would shorten the war and avert an American invasion of Japan, thus saving lives on both sides. Besides, he reasoned, Japan had started the war and had a record of atrocity, including routinely torturing and beheading downed American fliers: Of the roughly 5,000 B-29 crewmen of the Twentieth Air Force shot down during the war, approximately 200 were found alive in Japanese camps after the war.

The decision to go in low was entirely LeMay's. In a preview of LeMay's future operational style, he did not notify his immediate superior, General Henry "Hap" Arnold, of his radical redeployment of the B-29s. He reasoned, "If it's all a failure, and I don't produce any results, then he can fire me." He also ignored the fierce opposition of subordinates, some of whom called the plan suicidal.

On March 9, 1945, a trail of 334 B-29s, four hundred miles long, left the Marianas. Preliminary pathfinders had seeded napalm over Tokyo in the shape of an enormous fiery X to mark the locus of the target. Planes flew over in small groups of three, a minute apart, most at not much over five thousand feet. Five-hundred-pound incendiary clusters fell every fifty feet. Within thirty minutes, a 28 mph ground wind sent the flames roaring out of control as temperatures approached 1,800 degrees. The fire lasted four days.

No single air attack in the history of conflict had been so devastating. We will never know the exact number of people incinerated; officially, 83,793 Japanese died outright and 40,918 were injured. Nearly 16 square miles were obliterated, 267,171 buildings destroyed, and 1 million Japanese left homeless; one fifth of Tokyo's industrial sector and nearly two thirds of its commercial center no longer existed.

The planes returned with their undercarriages seared and the smell of human flesh among the crews, yet only fourteen bombers had been lost and forty-two damaged. And the March 9 raid was only the beginning of LeMay's incendiary campaign. Suddenly, all of Japan lay defenseless before LeMay's unforeseen plan of attack. Quickly, he increased the frequency of missions, at one point sending his airmen out at the unheard-of rate of 120 hours per month each—the Eighth Air Force in England had flown a maximum of 30 hours per month—as they methodically burned down Tokyo, Nagoya, Kobe, and Osaka within ten days before turning to smaller cities. LeMay's supply of incendiaries posed the one real obstacle to his plan of attack: His ground crews now simply unloaded the bombs at the dock and drove them right over to the bombers, without storing them in arms depots.

In between fire raids, his B-29s dropped high explosives on industrial targets and aerial mines into harbors and ports, which eventually helped to shut down nearly all the maritime commerce of Japan. By war's end, LeMay's forces had wiped out 175 square miles of Japan's urban area in sixty-six cities. A million Japanese had died, more than 10 million were left homeless, and the country ceased to exist as a modern industrial nation.

Although it is often stated that the two atomic bombs prompted the Japanese to sue for peace, their own leadership cited LeMay's far more lethal fire attacks as the real incentive. As Prince Fumimaro Konoe put it, "The determination to make peace was the prolonged bombing by the B-29s." LeMay, who strongly supported dropping the atomic bombs, concluded, "The war would have been over in time without dropping the atomic bombs, but every day it went on we were suffering casualties, the Japanese were suffering casualties, and the war bill was going up."

By August 1945, LeMay had destroyed urban Japan, yet he had more planes and men under his command than ever. By November, he would have had 2,500 operational B-29s, with 5,000 more on order. Together with the 3,692 B-17s that were to be based on Okinawa as part of the redeployed Eighth Army Air Force, and the 4,986 B-24s that were already being transferred from Europe, the Americans were planning the systematic destruction of Japanese society through the weekly use of more than 12,000 bombers. With the additional transference of Britain's Royal Air Force, including four-engine Lancaster VII heavy bombers, more than 15,000 heavy aircraft soon would have been operational. A force of that magnitude might have dropped over 500,000 tons of bombs each month, far above the 34,402 monthly average dropped by B-29s on Japan between May 1 and August 15, 1945. Surely, dropping the two atomic bombs was the correct decision—not so much because it circumvented an American invasion of Japan but because it abruptly ended LeMay's bomber crusade, which would have slaughtered millions of Japanese, a campaign he had warned the recalcitrant Japanese about through preliminary leaflet droppings. Had LeMay been given another year of bombing, the American assault would have found Japan a vast crematorium.

LeMay's career in the 1950s and 1960s is essentially the history of America's venture into the potential for nuclear-equipped strategic bombing and the general use of tactical airpower in the hot spots of the Cold War. A string of commands and crises followed his victories in the Pacific. From 1945 to 1947, he headed the U.S. Army Air Forces research-and-development program and facilitated the transition to jet bombers and in-flight refueling. In 1947 he took command of all American air forces in Europe and directed the Berlin Airlift. (At one point, the highest-ranking U.S. Air Force commander in Europe flew in a load of coal himself. He explained, "In those early days I had to make several runs to see how things were going.") When American strategic forces were considered inadequate to meet a potential Soviet response, LeMay was sent back to Washington in late 1948 to reorganize the Strategic Air Command. Shocked by the poorly trained crews and the absence of regulation, he concluded of his forces' first practice mission under his command, "Just about the darkest night in American military aviation history. Not one airplane finished that mission as briefed. *Not one.*"

Quickly, he brought in his trusted generals from the Pacific bombing campaign over Japan, and by the outbreak of the Korean War in 1950, the United States had developed a formidable striking force under LeMay's command. Accident rates plummeted from sixty-five per hundred thousand hours flown to a mere three. LeMay's forces dropped nearly as many bombs on Korea as on Japan. It is too often forgotten that thousands of North Korean civilians were killed directly or indirectly as a result of these missions; in three months during the first summer of the war, *all* assigned targets in North Korea were considered eliminated, the B-29 campaign was therefore called off as essentially completed, and the bombers were used only haphazardly thereafter against strategic sites. "We killed off—what—twenty percent of the population," LeMay wrote of all bombing between 1950 and 1953, arguing that strategic bombing over China and restricted portions of North Korea would have made that carpet attack on civilians unnecessary. But after the winter of 1950–51, with the entry of China, the American restriction on targets near the Chinese border, and the appearance of Soviet MiG-15 jets, the B-29 strategic campaign over Korea became marginal: Their targets were now off-limits and the planes too vulnerable. The protocols of unlimited bombing against the enemy, which had brought America success in World War II, no longer applied in a world of nuclear weapons. LeMay's worst postwar nightmare had materialized: America's strategic assets were either prevented from actively engaging the enemy or given the unheroic, dangerous, unpopular, and inevitably inconclusive role of tactical bombing of ground troops. LeMay realized that 169,676 tons dropped on Japan in 1944 and 1945 had destroyed the enemy's ability to resist; 167,000 tons dropped on North Korea between 1950 and 1953 had not. Worse still, when bombers were used wrongly, it discredited the entire doctrine of victory through strategic airpower.

LeMay, forever the absolutist, believed in unchanging rules of military doctrine and felt that new geopolitical conditions did not alter the need to destroy utterly the enemy's infrastructure from the air, whatever the threat of Soviet intervention. The Pentagon's stricture on strategic bombing of North Korea and China ensured that LeMay's bombers, unlike their use against Japan, would not be able to resume their proper mission and thus win the war outright. LeMay later wrote:

> That wasn't what the B-29s were trained for, nor was it how they were intended to perform. The B-29s were trained to go up there to Manchuria and destroy the enemy's potential to wage war. They were trained to bomb Peking and Hankow if necessary. They could have done so. The threat of this impending bombardment would, I am confident, have kept the Communist Chinese from revitalizing and protracting the Korean War.

Although LeMay was never allowed "to turn SAC loose with incendiaries" over the major industrial areas of China and Korea, he continued to expand the Strategic Air Command during the increased tensions of the Cold War. When he arrived, the air force did not have even systematic reconnaissance, much less a list of strategic targets in the Soviet Union and China. By 1957, when LeMay left SAC to become vice chief of staff of the U.S. Air Force, he had created an enormous organization that was capable of reaching every industrial center in the Soviet Union. In all, 224,014 people and 2,711 aircraft had been under his direct control at SAC, and he was eyeing command of the navy's intercontinental-missile program. (He supposedly had a model of a Polaris submarine *with a SAC insignia* displayed in his command hallway.) "There are only two things in the world," LeMay purportedly boasted at the time, "SAC bases and SAC targets."

While LeMay has often been condemned as trigger-happy and bellicose during his tenure at SAC, the command was perhaps a paradoxical one. LeMay—who inaugurated the command's motto, "Peace Is Our Profession"— was ordered to create a strategic air force of nuclear bombers formidable enough to deter Soviet aggression; yet, should he ever use one of his nuclear bombers in an actual attack, his entire command would be considered a failure, and its leader little more than a butcher who had sent millions to a nuclear crematorium. LeMay saw the paradox, quite unabashedly referring to his bombing command as enforcing a Pax Americana through a "Pax Atomica." To entrust to the most aggressive and successful bomber commander in our nation's history the task of creating an offensive bomber force that should never be used was fraught with irony from the beginning, and but a glimpse of LeMay's growing dilemma to come.

Between 1957 and 1965, he was vice chief and then chief of staff of the U.S. Air Force, overseeing the creation of America's nuclear ballistic-missile force and the modernization of its manned-bomber fleet. At this point, according to most critics, LeMay's previous energy and eccentric bellicosity for the first time posed grave risks for the nation and the world at large. While acknowledging the general's record in deterring Soviet airpower in crises involving Berlin, China, and the Middle East, the critics have pointed out that such aggressiveness was precisely the wrong temperament for someone who was to oversee America's nuclear arsenal. There is much in the LeMay record to bear out this criticism. "We must RACE!" he wrote, advocating enormous increases in nuclear weaponry and advances in new bomber technology, oblivious that "the arms race" was becoming a catchphrase for the danger and expense of a seemingly endless, pointless strategic competition with the Soviets. Throughout the

Kennedy and Johnson administrations, as air force chief of staff, LeMay battled repeatedly over the restrictions placed on his command during the Cuban Missile Crisis and the war in Vietnam:

> Always I felt that a more forceful policy would have been the correct one for us to embrace with the Russians, and in our confrontation of their program for world Communism. In the days of the Berlin Air Lift I felt the same way. . . . I can't get over the notion that when you stand up and act like a man, you win respect . . . though perhaps it is only a fearful respect which leads eventually to compliance with your wishes. It's when you fall back, shaking with apprehension, that you're apt to get into trouble. We observed Soviet reaction during the Lebanon incident and during the Cuban incident. Each time when we faced the Russians sternly we've come out all right. It's only when we haven't stood up to these challenges that things went sour.

During the tense days of October 1962, LeMay repeatedly demanded offensive action ("city-busting") against the Soviet Union: "If there is to be war, there's no better time than the present. We are prepared and 'the bear' is not." Of Cuba ("a side-show"), he remarked simply, "Fry it." Throughout the Cuban Missile Crisis, he specifically urged a comprehensive plan of open reconnaissance flights over Cuba, guarded by armed fighter escorts; around-the-clock readiness of SAC nuclear bombers targeted at the Soviet Union; and the eventual use of nuclear weapons against Cuba. To LeMay, the thought of a small Caribbean state only ninety miles off the coast of Florida threatening the security of the United States, when the latter possessed overwhelming military superiority over both Cuba and its patron, was unthinkable and dangerous. As American officials hesitated, LeMay worried that even a blockade of Soviet armaments to Cuba was an admission of weakness, especially if monitored by United Nations inspectors. Far better, he urged, to send the fleet to Havana, circle the skies overhead with SAC bombers, and then order Fidel Castro to allow U.S. military officers to inspect the Soviet-installed nuclear missile sites. LeMay shocked Attorney General Robert Kennedy, who wanted to know the capability of SAC bombers in a possible conventional strike against Cuban installations; when the president's brother asked how many of LeMay's planes carried nuclear weapons, the general said, "All of them." In disbelief, Robert

Kennedy asked, "How many of them could carry conventional weapons?" LeMay answered, "None of them."

To LeMay, incrementalism encouraged provocation, and only the ability and clear intent to face off the Soviets would ensure a cessation of their presence near the Americas. Of the peaceful final resolution to the Cuban crisis, LeMay scoffed that it was "the greatest defeat in our history." He thought the secret trade-off of American Jupiter missiles in Turkey for Soviet weapons in Cuba, and the clear impression that the United States would not, when pushed, use its strategic assets against a Soviet Union inferior in nuclear power, meant that the Soviets would be free to continue to aid Cuba and meddle in Latin America. In short, he felt the United States had gained the international reputation of an enormously powerful state that could not or would not act. Central to LeMay's brinkmanship was the belief that the Soviet Union either would not attack American interests or would be annihilated before its bomber fleet could reach the United States and its allies. LeMay was mostly correct: The Soviets probably would have backed off, and had they not, he probably could have caught their bombers and missiles on the ground. But "mostly" and "probably" were not guarantee enough in a new world in which a single surviving warhead might mean the loss of hundreds of thousands of Americans. Whatever LeMay's astute reading of human nature and his confidence in his superb bombers, he could not ensure the absolute safety of the American citizenry in the ensuing inferno—and it is not clear that he always understood this.

What, then, are we to make of this strange Curtis E. LeMay, this trigger-happy Buck Turgidson in the flesh? We can begin by realizing that both LeMay's military success and public relations catastrophes evolved from a frank, often brutal, but ultimately realistic assessment of human and hence national behavior. LeMay's bleak summation of human character was entirely Thucydidean, nearly echoing the historian's famous dialogue between the Athenians and their doomed foes on the island of Melos in 415 B.C., in which he lays out the bleak, timeless realities anytime the strong confront the weak. LeMay wrote:

> In all candor the strong and the rich are seldom popular. They are sometimes feared and sometimes resented. But they are usually respected. Anyone who seeks an absolute end to the possibility of war might as well resign from the human race. Pacifists with their perennial utopian quests can

harm the human race as much as conquerors. . . . There can be no doubt that the believed strength of an enemy's defenses and his counterattack capability have always been a deterrent to war. Unless we start to win the wars we get into, we may find ourselves overextended around the world on several frontiers, fighting equivocal wars. To maintain such vast military forces America would become an armed camp with all our sons being drafted for these endless foreign wars. God forbid!

For all his hyperbole and failure to grasp the dilemma of nuclear warfare—in which America demanded absolute, rather than near, invulnerability—LeMay's assessment of Soviet intentions and the need to achieve overwhelming strategic superiority seems, after the collapse of the Cold War, more rather than less correct. His distrust of the numbers crunchers in Robert McNamara's Pentagon ("so-called thinkers") was often based on the premise that it was amoral for bureaucrats to send Americans into a war they could not win—and that those who did so had not tasted fire. Given McNamara's own confessional, LeMay's program for ending the war may have even been the more humane one, political issues aside, in the sense that an early and comprehensive campaign against all strategic targets in Hanoi and Haiphong would have saved more lives on both sides in the long run. LeMay's idea that guerrilla fighters and irregular armies could not be stopped with piecemeal use of American ground troops, but only through massive air attack on their ultimate sources of supply, seems in hindsight more logical than lunatic. LeMay, remember, thought entirely in a military sense: Airpower could be successful only when the enemy's entire infrastructure was strategically targeted. If politicians worried about subsequent escalation of hostilities, LeMay would counter that any overwhelming military deterrence precluded enemy options and hence made all-out war less rather than more likely. Current American defense doctrine of the need for overwhelming force in cases of intervention is beginning to appear more rather than less in line with LeMay's earlier advice.

Nor does LeMay's innate skepticism about idealistic but inexperienced technocrats without battle experience seem shallow. For example, he worried about the young Harold Brown—who, in 1980 as secretary of defense in the Carter administration, was to oversee the flawed and undermanned raid into Iran to try to free the American hostages in Tehran. LeMay concluded that Brown was naive and utopian and could be dangerous in his misguided view of the nature of war. In anger, LeMay correctly ridiculed Brown's dictum that the air force was to use "the minimum force available to attain those ends. We are trying to minimize our own casualties, the casualties of our allies. We are even trying to minimize the casualties of our adversaries." In LeMay's eyes, minimizing "the casualties of our adversaries" inevitably meant prolonging war—and increasing our losses.

While it is easy to quote the garrulous LeMay to his detriment, and to find examples in which he may have exceeded authority, his subservience to civilian control was never really in doubt. Much of his rhetoric now seems to have been intended for in-house bickering over budgetary appropriations, designed to advance the extreme position in hopes that the ultimate compromise might satisfy his insatiable need for more bombers. Moreover, his public lectures and writings echo a common theme: Decisive, massive use of force—especially airpower—can shorten, even circumvent, war, thus saving more lives than it costs. LeMay had no faith in the United Nations as a preventive force, and he urged the United States to act alone or with its NATO allies according to its own interests and military capability.

If, like Sophocles' Ajax—who finds his heroic code outmoded and unappreciated in a more complex and nuanced world—we find the LeMays of our country at times dangerous, surely uncouth, and always embarrassing, we must realize that theirs is the baggage that often comes with unsurpassed courage and a willingness to step forward to take on the burden of defense in war's darkest hours. Men of that temperament organize massive armadas, create air forces ex nihilo, and cannot and should not be caged within established bureaucracies where the necessary business is maintenance, not construction; peace, not war; conciliation, not assault. In peace, of course, we want men of education, prudence, and manners guiding our military. But in times of war, as we have learned from both the fire raids over Japan and the standoff with the Soviets, we have often been served far better by the improbable emergence of warriors like Curtis E. LeMay, who somehow can find, organize, and lead men into the inferno. In the darkest hours of the Cuban Missile Crisis, President Kennedy acknowledged this: "It's good to have men like Curt LeMay and Arleigh Burke commanding troops when you decide to go in. But these men aren't the only ones you should listen to when you decide whether to go in or not." By his careful use of "only," Kennedy acknowledged the value even of LeMay's blunt and often extreme advice.

Like Grant and Patton, the LeMays can do what Lincoln called "the terrible arithmetic," and so understand that the American way of war is to throw vast amounts of men and matériel into the fire in order to end, not prolong, the killing. They know battle for what it is, so have no illusions that even a democracy must sometimes go to war wholeheartedly and therefore kill—thousands of the enemy if need be—to survive. Their legacy is that while being branded bellicose, they have saved more lives than they have taken. Their tragedy is that their brutal success in war produces a peace uneasy with their continued presence, and that their continued ardor asks us to make sacrifices we cannot and should not make. Just as they have come out of nowhere, so, too, when their foul business is done, should they disappear into the dark recesses that they inhabit. LeMay himself seemed to concede this: "I had blood upon my hands as I did this, but not because I preferred to bathe in blood. It was because I was part of a primitive world where men still had to kill in order to avoid being killed, or in order to avoid having their loved Nation stricken and emasculated."

Embattled and caricatured in his later years, LeMay understood his own Sophoclean dilemma. Many of his reckless pronouncements, as chilling as they sound today, were more likely the final proud bluster of an epic figure onstage who would rather perish in his absolute code of good and evil than change to meet the necessities of a far more nuanced and complex world for which he was so poorly suited in both comportment and speech. That he was not secretary of defense during the Cold War was wise; that he was even chief of staff of the U.S. Air Force with nuclear weapons under his command was cause for legitimate concern; that he commanded our bombers against Japan was a stroke of fortune for us all. And so now I tend to agree with my father that he had survived the war largely because of the daring and genius of the loudmouthed, cigar-chewing General Curtis E. LeMay.

IV

VIETNAM:
THE LONG GOOD-BYE

Calamity on the R.C. 4

DOUGLAS PORCH

The historian George G. Herring opens his notable study, *America's Longest War,* with a scene that in retrospect is suffused with an unforgettable (but almost forgotten) poignance. The date was September 2, 1945, the same day that representatives of the Japanese government signed a formal surrender agreement on the battleship *Missouri.* At Hanoi that day, the former cabin boy Ho Chi Minh, wearing a faded khaki suit and rubber sandals, proclaimed the independence of Vietnam from French rule.

As Herring writes:

[H]e borrowed liberally from Thomas Jefferson, opening with the words, "We hold these truths to be self-evident. That all men are created equal." During independence celebrations in Hanoi later in the day, American warplanes flew over the city, U.S. Army officers stood on the reviewing stand with Vo Nguyen Giap [the commander of the still-insignificant Viet Minh army] and other leaders, and a Vietnamese band played the "Star Spangled Banner." Toward the end of the festivities, Giap spoke warmly of Vietnam's "particularly intimate relations" with the United States—something, he noted, "which it is a pleasant duty to dwell upon."

For several months Ho's Communist front organization, the Viet Minh—which translates roughly as the "Vietnamese Independence League"—occupied the government headquarters in Hanoi. But France was determined to hold on to Indochina, which comprised not only Vietnam but also Cambodia and Laos. Vanguards of the French army, helped by British occupation forces that had taken responsibility for accepting the Japanese surrender south of the 17th Parallel, drove the Viet Minh out of the area then known as Cochin China, centered around Saigon. The U.S. gave tacit approval to the French reoccupation of its richest colony. Our backing of nationalist movements in Southeast Asia, which FDR had advocated before his death, would have to wait. The threat of a Communist takeover in France kept the U.S. from interfering in its colonial affairs. The risk of alienating, and perhaps losing, a key nation in the Western alliance was one the Truman administration did not want to take.

The French attempted to negotiate with the Viet Minh, which all the while continued to build up strength. The talks went nowhere. "Their own stubbornness," the journalist and historian Bernard Fall writes, "and their unwillingness to see the situation as it was" doomed the half-hearted French overtures. To Indochina, the appeal of nationalism, stiffened by Communist discipline, was becoming irresistible. Part of the genius of Communism, especially in colonial nations, was that this system of ultimate repression seemed forever on the side of liberation.

Out of frustration, the French abandoned political means in favor of military ones. In November 1946 a French cruiser shelled Haiphong, Indochina's biggest port, killing an estimated six thousand and setting off, in Herring's words, "a war which in its various phases would last nearly thirty years." Between 1946 and 1949, the French, who lacked both the manpower and the necessary weight of modern weaponry, struggled in vain to smother the Viet Minh rebellion. All attempts to pin down and destroy the Viet Minh in set-piece battles failed. Whenever their losses threatened to become insupportable, Giap's men simply faded into the jungle that covered more than half of Indochina. For France, this *guerre sans fronts* soon proved a gamble as foolhardy as the Communist decision to invade South Korea. As Ho expressed it in a neat parable: "If ever the tiger pauses, the elephant will impale him on his mighty tusks. But the tiger will not pause, and the elephant will die of exhaustion and loss of blood."

Whatever chance the French had of pulling out a face-saving victory, or even of achieving a measure of stabilization, ended when the Chinese Communists arrived on the borders of Indochina in November 1949. Now Giap could train Viet Minh recruits in safe bases across the Chinese border. By this time Viet Minh regulars and guerrillas numbered in the hundreds of thousands. The French might control an area by day; the Viet Minh, by night. In fact, the Viet Minh held about two thirds of the country. The French, meanwhile, were losing about a thousand men a month trying to win it back.

The Soviets recognized the Viet Minh at the end of January 1950. France may have been saved, but the U.S. was openly afraid that all of Southeast Asia was about to fall to the Communists, and pledged economic and military aid to the beleaguered French. (There was a quid pro quo: French support for the rearmament of West Germany.) In April 1950, two months before the invasion of South Korea, Truman's National Security Council cautioned that further "extension of the area under the domination of the Kremlin would raise the possibility that no coalition adequate to confront the Kremlin with greater strength could be assembled." A line was being drawn in the undergrowth; it may already have been too late.

On October 1, Giap's troops attacked the French border forts strung out along the road called the Route Coloniale 4, just south of the border with China. The battles, which Douglas Porch recounts here, would last two weeks and would result in France's worst colonial disaster—ever. The loss of the R.C. 4 would happen within days of another Communist border triumph: the invasion of Korea by Chinese "volunteers." The difference was that the French, unlike the Americans, never had the strength to bounce back. Nor did they possess a soldier of the stature of Matthew Ridgway.

DOUGLAS PORCH, one of America's most prominent military historians, is the author of such books as *The French Foreign Legion; The French Secret Services: From the Dreyfus Affair to the Gulf War;* and *The Path to Victory: The Mediterrean Theater in World War II.* He is a professor of national security affairs at the Naval Postgraduate School in Monterey, CA.

A SMALL GLAZED TILE inconspicuously set in a corner wall of the French Foreign Legion's retirement home at Puyloubier, in the South of France, bears the inscription "R.C. 4." Hardly noticed by the old men who shuffle past it while conversing in most of the languages of Europe, it is a memorial that seems out of place among the umbrella pines and vineyards that crowd the foot of Mont Sainte-Victoire. But it is a reminder of a forgotten battle that had repercussions undreamed of forty-five years ago.

In the long and bloody conflict that churned Indochina between 1946 and 1975, the struggle along the road known as the R.C. 4 was eclipsed in the public mind by later confrontations, such as those at Dien Bien Phu and Khe Sanh. However, the contest between the French and the Viet Minh to dominate the strategic highway—a contest that climaxed in October 1950 with what is often referred to as the Battle of Cao Bang—must count among that dreary war's most significant. For the first time, the Viet Minh commander Vo Nguyen Giap resoundingly demonstrated his ability to crush a large European force in a set-piece battle. On the R.C. 4, Giap grasped the strategic initiative in his war against the French, and he never relinquished it. The ghost of the R.C. 4 haunted subsequent French attempts to defeat Giap's main-force units in the highlands of Tonkin, Vietnam's northernmost province. Indeed, the climactic battle at Dien Bien Phu in 1954 was, in a very real sense, an attempt by the French to avenge their defeat on the R.C. 4. Unfortunately for them, the French demonstrated at Dien Bien Phu that they had done nothing to correct the serious shortcomings glaringly revealed in the savage battle on the Chinese frontier four years earlier.

Traveling northeast from Hanoi, the R.C. 4 stretches through a flat, cultivated land of rice paddies before it plunges into the mountains separating the rich Tonkin Delta from the Chinese frontier near the border garrison of Lang Son. Lang Son straddles what in 1950 was one of the most important road junctions in Indochina. From the north, the old Mandarin Road, a traditional invasion route, ran from China's Kwangsi Province through the "Gates of China" to the Tonkin Delta beyond. This was intersected at Lang Son by the R.C. 4, which began at Mong Cai near the Gulf of Tonkin and paralleled the Chinese frontier.

From Lang Son, the R.C. 4 ran northwest, a ribbon of road that twisted, rose, and tumbled through a turmoil of jagged limestone ridges and high needles of jungle-covered rock, linking the delta with the strategic posts of That Khe, Dong Khe, and finally, Cao Bang some sixty miles distant. From Cao Bang, another road, the R.C. 3, curved south through Bac Kan and Thai Nguyen back to Hanoi. It was joined by the area's third major road, the R.C. 2, which ran northwest to the Chinese border at Lao Cai.

These villages were military camps, fortified citadels rising out of rural communities where the only permanent buildings were often churches. They had been inserted in narrow valleys carved out of the rock by rivers bloodred with the clay of the terraced rice fields on their banks. These remote approaches were traditionally utilized by brigands and opium smugglers who were willing to travel the miles of almost trackless jungle that stretched to the south toward the Tonkin Delta or west toward Laos.

By 1950 this frontier region had become infested with another formidable enemy—the "Viet Minh," short for the Vietnam Independence League founded by Ho Chi Minh in 1941. During World War II, the American Office of Strategic Services (OSS) had supplied Ho's movement with arms to use against Japanese troops who had established an uneasy joint rule with the Vichy French in Indochina. However, the Viet Minh carefully avoided tackling the Japanese, who, on March 9, 1945, launched surprise attacks on the unprepared French garrisons, capturing, butchering, or dispersing most of them. That the French could be defeated and driven out of Indochina did not escape the Viet Minh, and soon after the Japanese surrendered in August 1945, the Viet Minh emerged in Hanoi to proclaim the Democratic Republic of Vietnam.

However, Ho's initial political victory rested upon foundations too narrow to maintain. The Viet Minh forces numbered perhaps thirty thousand men at the time, and though this figure doubled by the following year, they were poorly armed and trained. French forces began to disembark at Saigon as early as September 1945 and by February 1946 numbered fifty-six thousand men. Furthermore, Ho Chi Minh found it expedient to invite the French to return to the northern part of the country to replace rapacious Chinese Nationalist troops assigned to occupy Tonkin under the Yalta Agreement. "It is better to sniff French dung for a while than eat China's all our lives," Ho replied to critics of his decision to allow 15,000 French troops north of the 16th Parallel in return for the departure of almost 180,000 Chinese Nationalist soldiers.

At the end of 1946, growing tensions between the Viet Minh and the French finally erupted into open conflict. On November 23, French warships opened fire on Haiphong, the port city of Hanoi, after the Viet Minh refused to relinquish control of it. On December 19 the Viet Minh rejected French demands that they disarm, instead withdrawing their forces to the mountains of Tonkin behind a barrage of diversionary attacks against French targets in Hanoi. The war was on.

In the early phase, the Viet Minh's greatest strength was patience. Ho and his military commander, Giap, plotted a war of *longue duree*, based on Mao Tse-tung's theories of revolutionary warfare. According to Mao, revolutionary war passes through three phases. In the first, the superior strength of the enemy force causes the revolutionaries to avoid decisive combat and to fall back on a strategy of small-scale raids and attacks. In the second phase, the guerrillas build their strength and achieve rough parity with the enemy; their commanders are able to mix conventional and guerrilla actions to keep the enemy off balance. The final phase occurs when the enemy—like a bull confused, badly bloodied, and exhausted by the matador—is forced onto the defensive. When this happens, the revolutionaries move to a general counteroffensive that culminates in victory.

For the first years of the war, Giap concentrated on small-unit operations. The logical French response was to strike at the Viet Minh while they were weak, in an attempt to "decapitate" the leadership and disorganize the fledgling army. But French operations, while enjoying some success, failed to inflict decisive damage on an elusive foe. Meanwhile, the 1949 Communist victory in China initiated a series of events that produced a decisive turn in the war, for China gave Giap a sanctuary in which to train brigade—and eventually division-size—forces. After the summer of 1950, these were well supplied largely with American arms collected on the battlefields of Korea.

The posts along the R.C. 4 were now on the front line of the conflict. Isolated and vulnerable, many of their satellites were little more than log bunkers that would not have looked out of place on the American frontier three quarters of a century earlier. As early as 1948, Giap had begun to pressure the convoys that supplied the garrisons, and soon there was a murderous struggle to keep these posts alive.

A sergeant of the Third Regiment of the Foreign Legion later described one such attack to French journalist Lucien Bodard. It had occurred at a point where the road passed through a narrow gorge.

First, the Viets paralyzed the convoy. Mines blew just behind the leading armored cars, separating them from the trucks. As soon as this happened, a dozen impregnable machine guns, perched on the limestone cliffs above, opened fire, enfilading the entire column. Then a hailstorm of grenades came down. Regulars, hidden elbow to elbow on the embankment which dominated the roadway, threw them with precision, a dozen per vehicle. It was a firestorm. Trucks burned everywhere, completely blocking the way.

As the Viet Minh attacked, the legionnaires jumped from their trucks and climbed the embankment through a surging tide of Vietnamese. There the legionnaires grouped to defend themselves. "The Viets proceeded methodically," the sergeant continued:

The regulars went from truck to truck picking up the abandoned arms and supplies, then they fired the vehicles. Others attacked the French who still fought on the embankment. The coolies finished off with machetes the wounded who had fallen on the roadway or at the bottom of the bank. It was hand to hand everywhere. There were hundreds of individual fights, hundreds of reciprocal exterminations. In this slaughterhouse, the political commissars, very calm, directed the work, giving orders to the regulars and the coolies which were immediately executed. . . . The Red officers circulated in the middle of the battle, crying in French, "Where is the colonel? Where is the colonel?" They were looking for Colonel Simon, commander of the *Troisieme etranger*, the man who had a bullet in his head—a bullet lodged there from years ago. . . . He was in the convoy and Giap had ordered that he be taken alive.

I was in the part of the convoy which was destroyed. I was on the embankment with several legionnaires. We defended ourselves furiously there for a half hour, then we were overrun. I escaped into the forest. I hid in a thicket fifty yards from the road. Just next to me I heard several shots. It was legionnaires who blew their brains out. They had been discovered by the Viets. They didn't find me.

I don't know how this nightmare finished. It seems that Colonel Simon succeeded in assembling around him a hundred of his men. Formed in squares, they fought off the Viet waves with grenades for hours. Three hours later, reinforcements arrived—heavy rescue tanks. A few minutes before one heard the noise of their tracks, the Viets had beat it. At the beginning, to attack, they had blown the bugle charge. They gave the signal for the retreat by a new bugle call. They disappeared into the jungle in perfect order, unit after unit. Special formations of coolies took their killed, their wounded, as well as all the booty they had picked up.

We were masters of the battlefield. The road was a cemetery, a charnel house. The convoy was nothing but a tangle of disemboweled corpses and burned-out machines. It already stank. The survivors reassembled. They cleared the road and collected the dead and wounded. The convoy, or what was left of it, departed.

That night, upon reaching Cao Bang, they all drank themselves into oblivion.

As casualties mounted on the road that the legionnaires had already baptized the *route de sang* or the *route de la mort*, the French began to wonder if this string of isolated outposts was worth the blood and treasure required to secure them. In May 1949 the government dispatched the army chief of staff, General Georges Revers, to Indochina to report his opinion. Revers returned to recommend, among other things, that these posts be evacuated, a recommendation endorsed by the *Comite de defense nationale* on July 25. The commander in chief in Indochina, General Roger Blaizot, made preparations to withdraw from the R.C. 4 in September.

At this point two things occurred to postpone an evacuation order that was already dangerously overdue. The first was one of those bizarre scandals with which French politics appear to abound. On September 18 a fight broke out on a bus in Paris's Gare de Lyon between Thomas Perez, a former legionnaire, and two Indochinese students just back from the Communist-sponsored World Youth Congress in Budapest. The origins of the dispute are obscure, in part because Perez disappeared into the legion, which refused to identify him. But the fracas appears to have been manufactured by the colonial intelligence service, to call attention to a serious security leak: When the two students were arrested, a copy of the Revers report was found in their possession. Subsequent police raids on the Vietnamese community in France turned up literally hundreds of copies of the Revers report held by both pro-French and pro–Viet Minh factions.

What became known as "the Generals' Plot" had important results, both in France and in Indochina. In France, the discredit heaped upon Revers and his report further obfuscated, if that was possible, an already hopelessly confused French policy in Indochina. It revealed an indecision and confusion that stretched from the highest echelons of the French Fourth Republic, a regime badly riven by ideological, party, and personal quarrels. This made it vulnerable to pressure by colonial and military interests hostile to Revers's recommendation that a greater degree of autonomy be accorded the French-sponsored Vietnamese government under Emperor Bao Dai. For these reasons, the Fourth Republic was not a government capable of setting a firm policy for the war, but one in which prevarication and unsatisfactory compromise were the order of the day. In Indochina, Giap was alerted that sooner or later, the French would pull out of their posts along the R.C. 4. And he would be waiting for them.

The second event that postponed the planned withdrawal occurred in Hanoi. Just at the moment when General Blaizot was preparing to evacuate the R.C. 4, he was replaced as commander in chief by General Marcel Carpentier.

On the surface, at least, Carpentier's appointment appeared to offer the French army in Indochina the quality leadership they had often been lacking. He was one of the French military's "stars" and had already made a name for himself by 1915, when, as the youngest captain in the French army, he had won both the Legion d'Honneur and the Croix de Guerre with five citations. He rose from major in 1940 to major general by 1944 as a result of brilliant service as chief of staff to both of the French army's leading commanders in the later stages of World War II: General Alphonse Juin and General Jean de Lattre de Tassigny. Carpentier had himself commanded the elite 2nd Moroccan Infantry Division during the hard fighting in Alsace in the winter of 1944–45. Outwardly confident, cordial, and full of common sense, he appeared the embodiment of the perfect commander.

Yet Carpentier's veneer of self-assurance thinly disguised a deep apprehension about his new command. Like so many officers who had spent most of their careers in the European or North African theaters, he found Indochina complex and disorienting. His unease at being thrust into a situation for which he felt unprepared accentuated a lack of imagination and a lack of instinct for command, which Juin had detected earlier. With no firm convictions of his own and no definite orders from Paris, Carpentier found it difficult to dominate the old Indochina hands led by General Marcel Alessandri, who commanded the Tonkin region.

Alessandri had been a candidate for supreme command in Indochina, but his absence from the corridors of power in Paris and his associations with the pro-Vichy factions that had ruled Indochina during World War II combined to remove his name from the list. In Indochina his opinions carried extra weight because he was a good general: He had earned fame by leading a fighting retreat of five thousand French troops through the jungles of northern Tonkin to China after the Japanese treacherously attacked French garrisons in 1945. His campaign in 1949 to shut the Viet Minh out of the Tonkin Delta, thus depriving them of rice and recruits, was one of the most successful carried out by the French and added to his prestige. And Alessandri firmly believed that the R.C. 4 garrison of Cao Bang must not be abandoned.

As often in history, there are many good reasons for doing the wrong thing. Alessandri and Carpentier, each in his way, would bear that out. The argument was advanced that the victory of the Chinese Communists made maintenance of the line of frontier posts more important than ever as a way to constrict the arrival of supplies to the Viet Minh from the north. The R.C. 4 was the first line of defense for the vital Tonkin Delta, the barrier upon which any Viet Minh offensive must invariably shatter. Alessandri even drew up plans for an ambitious offensive against Viet Minh bases in the Tonkin highlands, plans Carpentier rejected out of hand as pure adventure.

Revealing a prejudice that was to afflict the French throughout the Indochina war despite ample evidence to the contrary, Alessandri argued that operationally and tactically, the Viet Minh lacked the ability to overrun these garrisons, especially Cao Bang, which he believed could be held against an attack of fifteen Viet Minh battalions backed by artillery. To bolster their case, those who advocated holding fast on the R.C. 4 pointed to Giap's failure to take the company-size satellite posts around Lao Cai on the Red River, which he attacked in 1949. These arguments would find a tragic echo four years later, when it was alleged that Giap's inability to take Na San the previous year proved that *bases aero-terrestre* like Dien Bien Phu were invulnerable. (These represented a new military concept in 1952—posts linked to French bases only by air.)

Departure from Cao Bang would also require abandoning much equipment, which could never be evacuated via the ambush-lined route. In the end, the French were victims of their own prejudices and myths: They believed in the historical inferiority of Vietnamese soldiers, labeled anyone who argued for withdrawal a defeatist, and asserted that abandoning the cemeteries that lined the R.C. 4 would insult the memory of dead comrades.

While the French high command was ruled by discord and division, Giap forged a clear, if flawed, strategic picture based on Mao Tse-tung's theories. Giap believed that the Communist victory in China permitted him to pass to a stage in which the two armies could meet on the battlefield as military equals. Guided by these theories and aided by his Chinese allies, he trained and equipped five combat divisions—the 304th, 308th, 312th, 316th, and 320th—of twelve thousand men each. These divisions were primitive by Western standards, but their rusticity was actually advantageous in the battle conditions of the remote Tonkin highlands against the road-bound French. Giap's next task was to make them proficient in the art of attacking French fortified posts.

In February 1950, Giap hurled his 308th Division, which would come to be celebrated as the "Iron Division," at the company-size post of Pho Lu on the R.C. 4 and overran it in a matter of hours. Nghia Do, another outpost in the Lao Cai area near the Chinese border, was attacked by the 308th the following month and was saved only by the timely arrival of an entire French paratroop battalion. Rather than expend casualties on such an isolated and strategically insignificant place—and perhaps also because his supply lines, assured by an army of coolies, were overextended—Giap backed down. Instead, he decided that his army was ready to take advantage of the French overextension on the R.C. 4.

At 6:45 on the morning of May 25, 1950, a violent artillery barrage suddenly rained down upon the two companies of Moroccans at Dong Khe, on the R.C. 4 some two hundred miles to the east of Lao Cai. Unobserved by the garrison, the Viet Minh had succeeded in hoisting five well-camouflaged 75mm cannon onto the heights above the town. There, for two days, they "fired down the tubes" into the French post, using the same techniques they were to employ at Dien Bien Phu, seconded by a number of heavy mortars and machine guns. A heavy monsoon cloud cover, together with well-positioned antiaircraft guns, kept French air support to a minimum.

On the evening of May 26, the bombardment increased in intensity as pre-

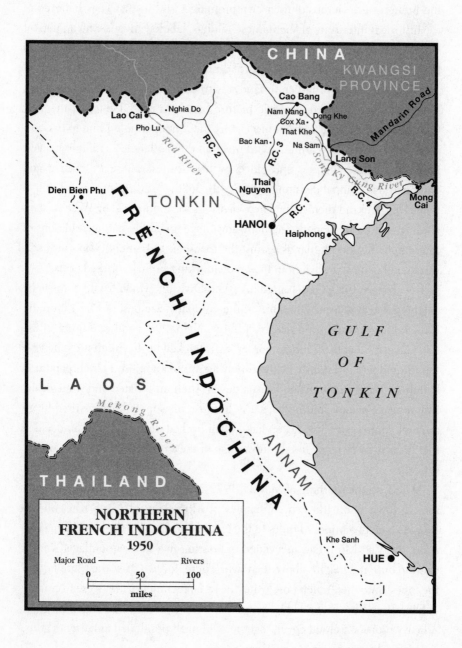

CHINA

KWANGSI
PROVINCE

Cao Bang

Nam Nang
Cox Xa   Dong Khe
That Khe
Bac Kan   Na Sam
Nghia Do
Lao Cai
Pho Lu

R.C. 2

Mandarin Road

Lang Son

Red River

R.C. 3

Song Ky Cung River

R.C. 4

Mong
Cai

Thai
Nguyen

TONKIN

Dien Bien Phu

R.C. 1

HANOI

Haiphong

GULF

OF

TONKIN

LAOS

FRENCH INDOCHINA

Mekong River

ANNAM

THAILAND

Khe Sanh

HUE

**NORTHERN
FRENCH
INDOCHINA**
1950

Major Road ——   —— Rivers

0   50   100

miles

lude to an attack by the 308th, which was unleashed on the citadel of Dong Khe just before midnight. Early on May 27, around fifty survivors of Dong Khe filed down the R.C. 4 toward That Khe. Cao Bang had been cut off.

In Hanoi, Alessandri reacted immediately. Collecting thirty-four aircraft, he dropped a battalion of French colonial paratroopers on Dong Khe at around five o'clock on the evening of May 27. Despite having to run a gauntlet of violent antiaircraft and machine-gun fire, the paratroopers took a brigade of the 308th completely by surprise as they ransacked the town and, after fierce fighting that cost the Viet Minh three hundred dead, ejected them into the jungle. In the following days, operations were carried out to clear the R.C. 4 of Viet Minh.

Despite the impressive amount of heavy equipment lost by the French, and the fact that twenty-five of the thirty-four aircraft that had flown the paratroopers in had been damaged by antiaircraft fire, the French persisted in calling Dong Khe a victory. They attributed the success of the Viet Minh assault to skittishness of the Moroccan garrison, while the counterattack by the French paratroopers proved to French satisfaction that one of their parabattalions was worth an entire brigade of the Iron Division.

To be fair to the French, the struggle along the R.C. 4 was one part of a large war, a war that they could claim with some justification to have stabilized by the summer of 1950. They had enjoyed great success in Cochin China, the southernmost of Vietnam's three provinces, in pushing the Viet Minh away from Saigon. Indeed, a Viet Minh offensive launched in the south in August–September 1950 to cover Giap's preparations in Tonkin resulted in heavy Viet Minh losses. The pacification campaign in the Tonkin Delta appeared to be going well, although, as time would show, it lacked the essential political ingredient to make it stick: The absence of a government political infrastructure on the local level allowed the Viet Minh to filter back as soon as French troops had waded out of sight over the rice paddies. The French government also had authorized reinforcements for the expeditionary corps, and a Vietnamese army was on its way to being established. Furthermore, the outbreak of war in Korea in June 1950 promised to produce active U.S. support for the French in Indochina. The Indochina war was no longer an unfashionable colonial conflict. It now was one front in a global struggle being waged by the free world against international Communism.

Carpentier believed that a Korea-style invasion of Indochina by Chinese and Viet Minh forces was imminent, and that the frontier posts must be maintained at all costs. Nevertheless, he was not blind to the danger he was running on the R.C. 4. Convoys could no longer travel beyond That Khe, and Dong Khe and Cao Bang were supplied entirely by aircraft, a commodity in which the French were not rich. Cao Bang and Dong Khe were islands in a Viet Minh sea, and on September 2, 1950, Carpentier at last decided to abandon them.

The next question was how. There were three options open to him, and Carpentier chose the worst. He rejected the first, an air evacuation of Cao Bang, because while the troops could be withdrawn by Dakotas and old German Ju-52s in two days, it would mean sacrificing Cao Bang's several hundred civilians—a motley of Chinese and Vietnamese merchants and prostitutes. A more prolonged air evacuation would attract Viet Minh attention and make life very difficult for the elements holding the perimeter.

The second option was to pull the garrison out down the R.C. 3. This would mean a 115-mile trek through Viet Minh territory to the Tonkin Delta. The advantage of this route was that it would march the garrison away from the main Viet Minh divisions along the Chinese frontier, through country that was less difficult and less tightly held by the enemy.

However, Carpentier decided to pull out along the R.C. 4, reasoning that the thirty-three miles from Cao Bang to Dong Khe, and the thirteen miles separating Dong Khe from That Khe, could be covered in quick stages. On September 16 he ordered Alessandri to prepare to evacuate Cao Bang and Dong Khe just as soon as French forces launched a successful diversionary capture of Thai Nguyen on the R.C. 3, which he expected to be complete by October 1.

Even before Carpentier's order was issued, it was hopelessly out of date. At seven A.M. on September 16, another hail of artillery and mortar shells pummeled Dong Khe, this time held by two companies of the *Troisieme etranger*. After the two days of softening up, by now familiar, a human wave overran the post at dawn on September 18. A week later, an officer and thirty-one legionnaires appeared out of the jungle at a French post on the R.C. 4 just outside of That Khe—the only survivors of Dong Khe.

The commander of the frontier zone, a Colonel Constans, was directing the battle by radio from Lang Son over fifty miles away. He tried to organize a repeat of the successful May 27 paratroop assault on Dong Khe, but was overruled by the man who had temporarily replaced General Alessandri, now on leave in France. The replacement—a General Marchand—concluded correctly that the Viet Minh would not be surprised by this maneuver a second time. In fact, they were waiting for it, guns pointed skyward. That Colonel Constans was willing to try shows the measure of the fantasy world in which some French commanders lived, and how little they appreciated the Viet Minh's strengths.

At this point Carpentier made a series of decisions that turned what was already an unpromising plan into a catastrophic one. With Dong Khe strongly held by the Viet Minh, it no longer made any sense to evacuate the Cao Bang garrison down the R.C. 4. The only options were an air evacuation or a retreat down the R.C. 3 toward French forces moving upon Thai Nguyen from the delta.

Carpentier did neither. Instead, he reinforced Cao Bang by air with a *tabor* (battalion) of North Africans while he assembled a force of three Moroccan *tabors* and the crack *Premier bataillion etranger parachutiste*, in all about 3,500 men, at That Khe. The Premier BEP, code-named "Task Force Bayard," was placed under the command of Lieutenant Colonel Marcel Le Page. Carpentier's overall plan was for Task Force Bayard to seize Dong Khe and hold it for the Cao Bang garrison coming down the R.C. 4—but he failed to mention this to Le Page.

Moreover, when he announced on September 20 to Alessandri, who had just stepped off the plane from Paris, that he was to organize this retreat, the choleric Corsican exploded with rage and railed against the withdrawal. Carpentier told him to organize it anyway, and boarded a plane for Saigon. Thus, like Cogny (the commander of the Tonkin region during the Battle of Dien Bien Phu), Alessandri was placed in charge of an operation with which he was fundamentally out of sympathy.

Nevertheless, after the disaster, Alessandri insisted that his seven battalions, backed by airpower, should have sufficed for the breakout, even though the Viet Minh outnumbered them by more than eight to one. For this reason, no one bothered to organize an intervention force of paratroopers as insurance against misfortune, nor did they seem in a hurry. Le Page dithered with his force at That Khe from September 19 to 30 before he was ordered to push his battalions up the R.C. 4 to seize Dong Khe.

French general Yves Gras has written that this movement might have succeeded had the departure of Le Page coincided with that of a Lieutenant Colonel Charton from Cao Bang: The French forces would have converged upon Dong Khe from two directions simultaneously.

However, the French plan called for Task Force Bayard to seize Dong Khe on October 2, the date when Charton would blow his magazines and strike out down the R.C. 4 to join them. This assumed, first, that Bayard would be powerful enough to seize Dong Khe single-handedly; and, second, that Charton could move his garrison down the R.C. 4 before prodigious numbers of Viet Minh troops hovering about fifteen miles off the road could move into a blocking position. A third assumption implicit in the plan was that each officer realized the urgency and importance of his part and moved to execute it efficiently. Alas, because of Carpentier's insistence upon secrecy, Giap was better informed about French intentions than were the men who were to carry them out.

On the evening of September 30, Le Page left That Khe to march the thirteen miles to Dong Khe. Everyone—including Le Page, who protested in vain that he had been given no intelligence reports on Dong Khe—realized that surprise was their best ally. However, when advance elements of the Premier BEP hit opposition as they neared Dong Khe, Le Page, cautious to the point of timidity, rejected the furious pleas of the legion paratroopers that they be allowed to punch through what they reckoned were lightly held Viet Minh positions. Instead, he postponed the attack until the following morning, by which time, as the legionnaires had predicted, the Viet Minh had called in reinforcements.

As a consequence, Le Page's two-pronged advance upon Dong Khe sputtered on the limestone ridges that surrounded the town. This hardly improved the disposition of the paratroopers, who had become openly contemptuous of his leadership—and of the fighting abilities of the Moroccan troops. Their attitude, while perhaps justified, helped to undermine cohesion in a heterogeneous force whose morale was already fragile.

This need not have been immediately fatal, as Charton had not yet left Cao Bang. Le Page could have retreated before his forces were cut off from That Khe. However, Colonel Constans, directing the battle from a comfortable distance at Lang Son, failed to realize that the pressing need was to save the forces under his command from catastrophe. Instead, he persisted with the original purpose. A letter was dropped by plane to Le Page on the afternoon of October 2 explaining—for the first time—the purpose of his operation.

The letter directed Le Page to bypass Dong Khe to the west and return to the R.C. 4 at Nam Nang, about eleven miles north of Dong Khe, where he was to meet the garrison from Cao Bang. From the perspective of Lang Son, the maneuver appeared perfectly feasible, even brilliant. But it was based on the fallacy that Le Page was threatened by only three Viet Minh battalions.

At five-thirty on the evening of October 2, the advance elements of Viet Minh caught a company of Moroccans by surprise and inflicted sixty casualties, while elsewhere mortar attacks and assaults announced that the Viet Minh were arriving in force. Nevertheless, the following morning Le Page assigned the Eleventh *tabor* and the Premier BEP the mission of holding Na Keo, an abrupt limestone ridge four hundred meters high; it paralleled the R.C. 4 for about a mile and therefore was supposed to offer a blocking position against the Viet Minh forces approaching from the east while he plunged west into the jungle with his remaining two *tabors*.

Giap realized that he had been handed a golden opportunity to destroy Task Force Bayard. While some of his forces tied down the paras and the Moroccans on Na Keo, others swept to the south and struck at Le Page's column as it struggled through the jungle. It was painfully clear that Constans had underestimated both the number and the abilities of the Viet Minh.

It was also obvious that perhaps for the first time in the war, the legionnaires were outgunned: Their heavy machine guns, Rebvel 31s, had been designed for the Maginot Line and were absolutely unsuited to mobile warfare; the grenades had no fuses and were therefore useless; and they had been issued a ridiculously small amount of ammunition for rifles, mortars, and light machine guns. The only thing that kept them alive as they clung to the top of Na Keo was the fact that the ridgeline was so narrow that the Viet Minh shells usually passed over their heads and fell harmlessly into the valley below. Nevertheless, constant attacks and machine-gunning by Viet Minh occupying peaks overlooking Na Keo caused considerable casualties.

At twelve-thirty on the morning of October 4, the Eleventh *tabor* withdrew from Na Keo, but it was badly cut up by the Viet Minh. Just before first light, the Premier BEP withdrew, following Le Page into the jungle. Their march was a calvary. Exhausted after three nights without sleep, the legionnaires hacked a passage through the dense foliage, hoisting the stretchers of the wounded up the precipitous cliffs only to lower them farther on.

For the next two days, without adequate maps and constantly harassed by the Viet Minh, the Le Page column made slow progress toward the valley of Cox Xa, where they expected to meet Charton. They reached the valley on October 5, and at five o'clock that evening Le Page made radio contact with Charton, grasping at the prospect of a meeting as if it were salvation itself.

When Lieutenant Colonel Charton had left Cao Bang at noon on October 3, this energetic legionnaire looked less like the commander of a military operation than like Moses leading his people into the wilderness. His 1,600 soldiers and 1,000 irregulars advanced warily down the road, watching for ambushes. They were followed by a gaggle of families and townspeople, including the garrison's numerous prostitutes.

Had Charton departed earlier and marched faster, he might have arrived in time to help Le Page seize Dong Khe. As it was, Charton's column straggled unmolested along the R.C. 4 toward Dong Khe. However, at ten o'clock on the morning of October 4, as the head of his column completed the eighteen miles between Cao Bang and Nam Nang, a radio message informed him of Le Page's failure before leaving Dong Khe. Charton was ordered to leave the R.C. 4 and head southeast along the Quang Liet trail, where, he was told, Le Page waited for him on the ridges to the east of Cox Xa. Charton set about blowing up his trucks, cannon, and heavy equipment in preparation for plunging into the jungle.

Unfortunately, if the Quang Liet trail existed on the staff maps in Lang Son, no one at Nam Nang could find it. Charton decided to follow a stream that ran south from Nam Nang, but it was heavy going. His irregulars cut a path through the vegetation while his column followed single file. By nightfall they had covered five miles since morning. The next day, October 5, was much the same, except that the Viet Minh mounted a few small ambushes. On October 6 some of Charton's advance elements pushed forward, trying to make contact with Le Page, and ran into serious Viet Minh resistance. However, with his column strung out over almost four miles, and with the civilians in the middle preventing the third battalion of the *Troisieme etranger* in the rear from moving forward, Charton's ability to maneuver was severely limited.

In fact, he began to have an inkling that he and Le Page had filed into an enormous ambush. Fifteen Viet Minh battalions had blocked Le Page's escape toward That Khe and Charton's back toward Cao Bang. Le Page, exhausted, had settled into the valley of the Cox Xa, trusting in the apparent security provided by the ridges that surrounded him like the crumbling walls of Roman amphitheaters. But Giap's troops drew around him like a noose. In the blackness before dawn, the Premier BEP led a sacrificial attack to break out of the Cox Xa valley and join with Charton.

Despite their fatigue, this action was regarded as one of the legion's finest. Attacking across a succession of dips and stone ledges against murderous fire, the paratroopers managed to break out, though at enormous cost. The corridor, easily traceable in the dawn light by the bodies of dead legion paras, quickly filled with Moroccans at the end of their psychological tether, crying, "Allah Akbar! Allah Akbar!" They fled over the rocks and down the cliff faces. Only 560 men of the Le Page column remained. Of the Premier BEP, only nine officers and 121 legionnaires were still alive, and many of these had been wounded.

The panicked and disheveled aspect of the survivors seriously lowered morale in Charton's group. At four o'clock in the afternoon, the Third *tabor* panicked and broke in the face of a feeble Viet Minh attack. The French force was dissolving into a mob. The only coherent unit that remained was the battalion of the *Troisieme etranger*. Charton moved south with it and with about three hundred Moroccans, avoiding the Viet Minh, until he was wounded and captured.

Le Page gathered the remaining battalion commanders around him, and they decided to break into small groups and flee toward That Khe. Only a handful of officers and a small group of men actually made it. Most went through the same experience as Hungarian legionnaire Janos Kemencei: Following the Song Ky Cung River, which flowed to That Khe, he periodically heard the rattle of automatic fire, followed by shrill Vietnamese voices crying, "*Rendezvous, soldats francais! Rendezvous, vous etes perdus!*" ("Give up, French soldiers! Give up, you're lost!") He threw himself into the undergrowth when one of these fusillades erupted near him. "*Lai-Dai*" ("Come here"), a small Vietnamese said, the barrel of his gun pressed to Kemencei's forehead. Le Page surrendered to a Viet Minh officer who spoke excellent French, and who threw his arms around him in delight at capturing the commander of the French expedition.

The loss of the combined Le Page/Charton columns was bad enough in itself—of over 5,000 soldiers in the two groups, 12 officers and 475 men managed to escape to That Khe; only three officers and 21 legionnaires of the Premier BEP escaped death or capture. But when news of the debacle reached Hanoi, complete panic set in. Carpentier compounded the error he had made at Cao Bang by ordering the evacuation of That Khe in the face of strong Viet Minh forces moving to invest it. At six P.M. on October 10, the demoralized garrison of That Khe set out on the R.C. 4 for Lang Son, harassed by Viet Minh. The rear guard, made up of legion and colonial paratroopers, was cut off and forced into the jungle, where they suffered the fate of the Premier BEP. Only five paras managed to struggle into Lang Son.

But they had no time to linger. Colonel Constans, who, only days before, had held Viet Minh capabilities in utter contempt, now completely revised his opinion. Claiming that fifteen to eighteen Viet Minh battalions were converging on Lang Son, and that French forces available to defend the garrison were utterly inadequate, he ordered Lang Son evacuated. Actually, Giap had been profoundly surprised by the scope of his victory, but his troops were in no state to take on Lang Son, which had adequate forces to defend it.

When he visited on October 14, even Alessandri found the atmosphere of panic reigning in Lang Son contagious. He hopped on a plane to Saigon and, in a dramatic night conference, convinced Carpentier that a disaster greater than that at Cao Bang stalked Lang Son. Orders from Paris to hold Lang Son caused Carpentier to countermand the withdrawal the following morning, but it was too late: Running scared, Constans and Alessandri began the evacuation anyway, and persuaded Carpentier in Saigon that it was the only viable option. By October 20 the Lang Son garrison had reached the delta without a shot being fired.

What the Viet Minh discovered when they strolled into the town varies according to the account one reads, but the booty was substantial. It included gasoline, uniforms, food, tons of rifle and artillery ammunition, machine guns and rifles by the thousands, and some say thirteen howitzers and an airplane— all told, enough to equip a Viet Minh brigade.

On November 3 the French garrison at Lao Cai on the Red River began a fighting retreat to the delta, leaving the Vietnamese frontier region completely in the hands of the Viet Minh. Between five and six thousand men had been thrown away in a matter of days in what French journalist Bernard Fall called the greatest French colonial defeat since Quebec in 1759.

The French disaster on the R.C. 4 was to have many consequences. In Washington it was decided that America should assume a more active role in the war. In Paris the government of Rene Pleven was tumbled by the news, the twelfth French Cabinet to fall since the beginning of the war and another indication of political confusion over France's goals in Indochina. The accelerated arrival of American arms, together with the appointment of Jean de Lattre de Tassigny as commander in chief and high commissioner in Indochina, gained some important breathing space for the French. Giap obliged his new foe by launching a series of offensives against the Tonkin Delta, offensives brilliantly parried by de Lattre.

However, most tragic for the French was that the R.C. 4 disaster could not be ascribed simply to bad luck or to the bad judgment and poor leadership of just a few local commanders. Although both Le Page and later Colonel Christian de Castries at Dien Bien Phu proved to be mediocre commanders, the sad fact is that many of the errors and weaknesses revealed at the R.C. 4 were systemic ones that returned to haunt the French at Dien Bien Phu.

Perhaps the most significant French failure was their gross underestimation of the Viet Minh. In many respects, it was this contempt for the Vietnamese as soldiers—a contempt as old as the French Indochinese empire—that gave rise to many of the most spectacular French disasters; it caused them to undertake operations beyond their capacities. And when they did this, the weaknesses of their army were glaringly exposed: disagreements over strategic priorities in Paris, Saigon, and Hanoi; mediocre generalship; the paucity of their air force; often poor staff work and inadequate logistical capabilities; and the low morale of the heterogeneous imperial force, especially among their North African troops. In the final analysis, the only troops the French could count on in all circumstances were their paratroopers and legionnaires. And while these men were courageous, the courage of small numbers was not enough to swing the strategic balance.

The Battle of the R.C. 4 was a major turning point in the Indochina war. Both the psychological and the strategic balance of the war had shifted in favor of the insurgents, and the stage was set for the final confrontation four years later in another remote highland valley in upper Tonkin, Dien Bien Phu. That battle would end the French war in Vietnam and signal the beginning of the American war.

Dien Bien Phu

WILLIAMSON MURRAY

Once Vo Nguyen Giap swallowed up the garrisons along the R.C. 4, the French had all but lost the struggle for Indochina. In retrospect, that seems clear now. But they did not see it that way at the time, and the war would go on, bloodily, for the next forty-five months. Through that time they would try to bring about the kind of set-piece battle in which Western armies excelled, the conventional stand-up slugfest in the open— one, they hoped, that would prove decisive (which battles rarely are). It became the obsession of each successive commander in chief. In the spring of 1954, they would achieve their wish in a mountain-ringed valley whose Vietnamese name, Dien Bien Phu, might be translated as "Seat of the Border County Administration." But by that time, Giap was pursuing the same aim.

As Douglas Porch has written, "perhaps the greatest strength possessed by the Viet Minh was patience." Giap, ever the model Communist military leader, followed Mao Tse-tung's three-step prescription for victory in revolutionary warfare, and in the process added some elaborations of his own. What had worked for the Chinese Communists, he believed, would work even better for their brethren in the jungles of Indochina. He was right. The first phase was the strictly guerrilla combat that Giap practiced through 1950. Its main purpose was to wear down the French and eventually to establish a balance of strength. (The secondary object, of course, was to avoid being destroyed himself.) Phase two saw guerrilla and conventional ground warfare combined, with attacks in the open based on concentrations of mortars and, as time went on, artillery. (Here, the help of the Chinese Communists was imperative.) Giap's R.C. 4 attacks were the model for the transition from the first phase to the second. Then, in this "war of long duration" (Giap's phrase), came the point when his forces would take the offensive. "We shall attack without cease," he wrote, "until final victory, until we have swept the enemy forces from Indochina. During the first and second stage, we have gnawed away at the enemy forces; now we must destroy them."

Only once did Giap deviate from the Maoist formula. In January 1951, flush from his R.C. 4 triumphs, he tried to leap from the first stage to the last, without the crucial intervention of the second. "Ho Chi Minh in Hanoi for the Tet," Communist leaflets proclaimed—in other words, by the middle of February, when the Chinese lunar new year generally falls. For five days in January, Giap sent human-wave attacks against the French outpost at Vinh Yen, some thirty miles northeast of Hanoi. Again and again, French fighter-bombers would lay down a curtain of napalm, roasting the attackers. In this biggest of French victories, Giap lost six thousand dead. He returned to patience and stage two.

Henceforth, Bernard Fall has written, the Viet Minh would "refuse combat on any terms but their own." They inevitably chose to strike in places where the French could not use tanks or other heavy equipment; where they could not detect the presence of camouflaged troops hidden under the canopy of the jungle; where the hit-and-run nature of Viet Minh tactics kept them forever off balance. Fall speaks of their "uncanny tactical sense." They made ambush a fine art. Attacks on fixed positions seemed to come out of nowhere, sudden mortar barrages "smashing barbed wire, ploughing passages through the minefields, and knocking out French gun crews." Within minutes Viet Minh infantry appeared on top of battered dugouts. French air support often arrived "just in time . . . to witness the departure of the prisoners, with their hands raised, between a double column of Viet-Minh guards."

But the French were in for ruder and more psychologically debilitating shocks. In his extraordinary history/memoir, *Street Without Joy*, Fall quotes a paratroop commando on a perilous flight through the jungle in October 1952: "You should have seen us. Along the route of retreat of the paratroops, the Viets had planted on bamboo pikes the heads of the soldiers they had killed, like so many milestones. Some of the men went berserk from it, other cried hysterically when they recognized the head of somebody they had known. . . ."

It was that kind of war.

Even when they did win engagements, the French lacked the air- or the man power to exploit their tenuous victories. Thrusts at Viet Minh bases that seemed initially promising accomplished little except the siphoning off of mobile reserves from other theaters of war: The enemy would simply regroup and strike elsewhere. All the while the U.S. poured money (but never men) into Indochina, $2.6 billion in 1954 alone. But the U.S. sent mostly World War II surplus, already obsolete. Giap's forces also relied on American equipment, much of it captured in Korea or left behind by the fleeing Nationalists; the Communists sent it south, along with fire-control personnel and artillerymen. The Soviet bloc weighed in with regular shipments of mortars, artillery, automatic weapons, and Molotova trucks. By the end of the war, Viet Minh firepower was actually superior to that of the French—who were, in Porch's words, "outgunned, outmanned, and outmaneuvered."

Indochina was a war of little dramas, ending with one big one, Dien Bien Phu. There was a piecemeal quality to French losses, but over the years they added up—as Fall puts it, "one convoy annihilated here, one battalion mauled there, a truck convoy lost in an ambush elsewhere." The war took an especially high toll on young officers. Lieutenants died by the hundreds, 1,300 in all. (In 1953 alone, more junior French officers were killed in Indochina than were graduated that year from the national military academy at Saint-Cyr.) This was one of those rare wars in which the number of KIAs exceeded the wounded. The French and their Indochinese allies lost 94,000 dead or missing and 78,000 wounded. "To maintain major communications lines," Fall has written, "cost on the average three to four men *per day* for every hundred kilometers of road." The Viet Minh losses were even more appalling. No casualty figures were kept, but estimates go as high as four hundred thousand, with another quarter of a million civilian deaths. Victory would not come cheaply.

Nevertheless, at the end of 1953, a virtual draw existed. Giap had originally intended to mount a series of attacks in the Tonkin Delta: He hoped to capture Hanoi or Haiphong, preferably both. The Chinese

Communists, whose role in the war was becoming increasingly dominant, feared that the French, fighting from interior lines, would hold off the Viet Minh in a series of set-piece battles, just what they had been hoping for all along. The Chinese suggested that Giap strike instead at the Montagnard hill tribes along the Laotian border; they had long presented a significant guerrilla threat to the Viet Minh rear.

The bait in what they hoped would prove a trap for the French was opium, a largely unspoken reason for one of the major battles of the twentieth century. The Viet Minh wanted the Montagnard opium, much of which grew in the Dien Bien Phu area, because it was one of the principal sources of finance for their war effort. The French wanted the same opium because it paid for their special operations in the back country (and made some members of their secret service wealthy). The French commander in chief, General Henri Navarre, Porch has written, "calculated that he simply could not stand by and allow the Viet Minh to replenish their war chests with Montagnard opium. Therefore, the French occupation of Dien Bien Phu was neither a foolish nor short-sighted decision, as it has often been portrayed."

However, when Navarre set up a fortified air-land "hedgehog," or *base aéroterrestre*, far from his center of operations in the Tonkin Delta, he was taking a gamble. In addition to protecting his opium supplies and blocking the Viet Minh invasion route to Laos—the more customary explanation for Dien Bien Phu—Navarre was not averse to luring Giap into a set-piece battle. But did he reckon that Giap would respond with a gamble of his own, dispatching a hundred thousand men, or approximately half the force available to him, to the mountains that surrounded Dien Bien Phu? Could he have foreseen that Giap, with the aid of the Chinese, would build up a four-to-one superiority in artillery? Even so, the gamble was one that Giap came close to losing, had it not been for the stiffening the Chinese provided. They not only continued to supply him, especially with artillery, but, more important, they persuaded him to abandon human-wave assault tactics in favor of a tightening web of trenches, reminiscent of the French marshal Vauban's seventeenth-century siege tactics. The result, as Williamson Murray tells it here, was a first, a victory not just of Asians over Westerners—since World War II, that was no longer novel—but of colonial subjects over their former masters. Dien

Bien Phu would be the greatest single Communist military triumph of the Cold War.

WILLIAMSON MURRAY, a senior fellow at the Institute for Defense Analyses, is a professor of history emeritus at Ohio State University and, with Allen R. Millett, the author of *A War to Be Won: Fighting the Second World War.*

THE BATTLE OF DIEN BIEN PHU in the spring of 1954 ended a century of French rule in Indochina. It represented the triumph of an indigenous Nationalist movement, one completely dominated by fanatical Communists. It also confronted the United States with the question: Should it attempt to rescue a French garrison that was clearly going down to defeat? The American decision was a cold, rational statement that Indochina was not worth the price of success—that the conditions under which American land forces would have to fight in Southeast Asia were far worse than they had been in the just concluded Korean War.

How had the French found themselves in a major battle in a gloomy valley in one of the most isolated parts of Indochina? What were the strategic, political, and operational factors that drew French military leaders in Hanoi to stake all, far from their centers of power, with tenuous lines of communications, and in an area of no great strategic significance?

The French had colonized Indochina (Vietnam, Laos, and Cambodia) in the nineteenth century. Utilizing the weapons of the industrial revolution, they easily dominated the locals and established a colonial regime that represented both the strengths and weaknesses of the French empire. They brought a modern, relatively honest administration, technological and medical benefits, and French education. Not surprisingly, they also administered Indochina for their own economic benefit and ruthlessly suppressed any signs of dissent. But Vietnamese Nationalism smoldered under the surface.

Ironically, the schools the French established were to play a crucial role in their eventual defeat. In the early 1990s, an American-Vietnamese filmmaker interviewed Vo Nguyen Giap, who had played such a major role as the military leader in the wars against the French and Americans. Giap chose to speak in

French, not Vietnamese, and in the film *From Hollywood to Hanoi*, he conveyed the fanaticism of the French Revolution. He was the very embodiment of Robespierre: ice-cold, passionate, doctrinaire, prepared to make any sacrifice for the cause. In fact, he had received an admirable education at Quoc Hoc, one of the best lycées in Vietnam, where he had drunk deeply the lessons of the French Revolution. Giap had been second only to the man who would take the nom de plume of Ho Chi Minh and who would lead Communist forces in two wars.

In March 1945 the Japanese destroyed the pro-Axis French colonial administration in Indochina that had cooperated with them since 1940. Within six months, the Japanese themselves would surrender. Thus they provided Ho and his nascent Communist-Nationalist movement with a political vacuum, which Ho's movement eagerly sought to fill. In the immediate postwar period, Ho and his followers seized and then consolidated a tenuous hold over most of Vietnam, particularly over the northern sections. The French deployed major forces to Vietnam to suppress what they regarded as a local insurrection. These forces were led by a military embittered by the catastrophe of 1940 and never really controlled by the constitutional authorities in Paris. The war for Vietnam began in 1947—a war that lasted until 1975, at a terrible cost to all involved, with the greatest price paid by the Vietnamese themselves. Initially, French forces in Indochina received almost no aid from the United States, which regarded the struggle with considerable distaste because of its colonialist nature. The French government exhibited similar ambivalence and refused to allow conscripts to participate in the war. The result was a stalemate: The French dominated the countryside where their troops happened to be, while the Viet Minh tightened their hold when the French moved on.

The nature of the war changed in 1949, when the Chinese Communists arrived on Indochina's frontier after having chased the Chinese Nationalists to Taiwan. Supplied with substantial amounts of weaponry—much of it American, captured from the Nationalists—Ho's Viet Minh launched a series of attacks against French bases along the frontier in the fall of 1950. The garrison towns of Dong Khe, Cao Bang, and Lang Son fell in rapid succession. The French seemed on the brink of collapse. But the international situation again shifted. Far to the north, Kim Il Sung had unleashed the Korean War, and the rapid escalation of that conflict had a profound effect on the war in Indochina. Suddenly, the Americans loosened the purse strings to support the French struggle against international Communism; American suspicion of colonialism disappeared in reaction to the desperate struggle in Korea. Now, at last, the French received massive amounts (at least in their terms) of weapons and ammunition to fight the Viet Minh. At the same time, Chinese aid to the Viet Minh substantially decreased as Mao concentrated on the war in Korea.

But their victories in the fall of 1950 led Ho and Giap to believe that success was around the corner. Early in 1951 they threw their forces against French positions in the Red River Valley in an all-out bid for victory. Giap even predicted that Ho would arrive in Hanoi in time to celebrate the lunar new year, Tet. But the French had received more than an infusion of American weaponry. They had a new commander, General Jean de Lattre de Tassigny, one of the outstanding soldiers in the French army. Lattre infused his troops with a new enthusiasm; in one case he flew into a beleaguered garrison and then radioed out to his forces to "come and get me." The first Viet Minh offensive came in January 1951; the French held, while the Viet Minh suffered more than 6,000 killed and 8,000 wounded out of 20,000 attacking troops before Giap broke off the attack. By early summer the Viet Minh had withdrawn from the delta and were licking their wounds in the jungles that surrounded the Red River Valley.

But the French were not in a position to follow up their victories. They, too, had suffered heavily in the fighting; their forces were stretched to the breaking point, and de Lattre was already dying of cancer. Once again the war in Indochina settled into a stalemate. The French possessed the firepower and training to defeat whatever Viet Minh forces chose to stand and fight. Thus, they dominated the great Mekong and Red River deltas during the day. But the Viet Minh fought a war of subversion—one that aimed to control the countryside politically—and the French could not be everywhere. For the next two years, they pursued the illusion that they could force the Viet Minh into a stand-up battle. Major French offensives, launched from the Red River Delta, drove deep into Viet Minh territory, but they rarely struck anything except empty terrain. The problem lay in extracting such forces, for Giap would rapidly concentrate his reserves and then strike the French as they retreated. He accepted battle only on his own terms. More often than not, the French paid a heavy price to escape. It was like punching a feather pillow and then having a bear trap snap shut. Besides ill-fated strikes against Giap's main forces, the French launched search-and-destroy missions throughout the countryside against guerrillas who were disrupting political administration even in the Red River Delta. These operations were no more successful in reestablishing control over the countryside than similar American efforts a decade later.

By summer 1953, the French high command in Indochina confronted a number of problems, none of which provided much hope for the future. Admittedly, the United States appeared willing to bankroll the war for an indeterminable period (although, of course, American support brought with it advice from people who had not a clue about the nature of the conflict). But the Korean War was about to end, and that would bring increased logistic support from the Chinese back to the Viet Minh. Moreover, the endless war in Southeast Asia was finally wearing on French patience at home. The French people and their representatives were sick of a war that had obviously deadlocked, even if no conscripts were dying. These factors came together to push French military leaders to make a series of strategic and operational decisions that led directly to the battle of Dien Bien Phu.

Significantly, a fundamental misassumption underlay all French planning. The French high command still did not take the Viet Minh seriously as a military force, or Giap, the former history professor, as a general. At the end of 1953, French planners in Hanoi sought to create a trap for the Viet Minh by launching a significant portion of their reserves at a target they believed to be of considerable strategic significance: a sprawling village in a mountain valley, Dien Bien Phu. There, they hoped the Viet Minh would at last fight in the open, where superior French firepower, training, and discipline would destroy the revolution.

Planning for Dien Bien Phu reflected a number of misassumptions by General Henri Navarre, the new French commander in Vietnam, beyond a mere underestimation of the Viet Minh and the seriousness of the situation. *Time* magazine quoted the general: "A year ago none of us could see victory. There wasn't a prayer. Now we can see it clearly—like light at the end of the tunnel" (a phrase that echoed again and again through this war and the next). Yet the French government had made clear that it would not supply substantial reinforcements. Even more important was the inability of the French high command in Indochina to enunciate a clear rationale for the operation. On the one hand, they argued that possession of Dien Bien Phu would prevent the Viet Minh from moving into Laos, as they had the previous year. On the other hand, they argued that their forces in Dien Bien Phu could serve as a center for strikes into northern Vietnam's highlands to disrupt supplies and foodstuffs from reaching the Viet Minh. But underneath everything was the hope that the Viet Minh would take the bait.

Thus, Dien Bien Phu was supposed to be a fortress capable of standing up to a full-fledged conventional assault. Given the fact that the French had barely enough troops to protect an airstrip at the center of the valley into which reinforcements and supplies would have to flow, much less the great ring of hills surrounding the valley, it was hard to see how Dien Bien Phu could serve as both a fortress and a base for mobile operations against Viet Minh supply lines. But the real problem was that Dien Bien Phu was indefensible under almost any conditions except absolute superiority. Everything was observable from the heights overlooking the valley, and if the Viet Minh concentrated heavy artillery on those heights, they would dominate the battlefield. The commander of ground forces in northern Vietnam, General René Cogny, was ambivalent about the operation; in the summer of 1953, he had proposed seizing the valley, but by the fall, he was strongly objecting to the plan. Nonetheless, as was to occur with many other commanders in this war, he executed an operation with which he disagreed. Some French officers were suspicious that Cogny's doubts reflected a political ploy in case the plan turned out badly.

The operation almost did not occur. Bad weather closed in but then cleared at the last moment. The men who jumped in and fought at Dien Bien Phu were to rue the change in the weather. So on November 20, 1953, a force of 1,827 French paratroopers dropped on the valley. They met light resistance, the Viet Minh being content to withdraw and await further developments. The following day, another major drop reinforced the first wave, this one led by the paratrooper commander Brigadier General Jean Gilles, who carefully stashed his glass eye in his combat smock before jumping. The last drop occurred on November 23 and included Brigitte Friang, a woman reporter who had gone through jump school and who already had five combat jumps to her credit. The paratroopers were the French army's elite reserve in Indochina, and having seized the ground, they set about establishing an airstrip and defensive positions so that reinforcements and heavy equipment could be flown in.

The paratroopers, along with legionnaires, would form the heart of the defenses. They were to be reinforced by a mixture of troops drawn from other French units in Indochina, some very good, some of doubtful utility. The North African units of the French army had a long history of exceptional bravery—it was they, after all, who made the crucial breakthrough of German lines in Italy in May 1944 that led to the capture of Rome. But already among the Algerians, the deep frustrations of their countrymen, which soon would result in the Algerian War, were impacting on their military effectiveness. Some Algerians fought well, others not so well. But the real weak link turned out to be the T'ai mountain tribesmen, who made up nearly a third of the garrison. The tribesmen were excellent guerrilla fighters on their own terrain, much of which was now under Viet Minh control. But away from their homeland, they proved unreliable. Besides the infantry committed to the garrison, the French provided substantial artillery and a small force of tanks. The gunners, despite the greater numbers of Viet Minh artillery and their accurate counterbattery fire, stood by their guns to the bitter end. The tankers fought with brand-new M-24 "General Chaffee" light tanks, straight from America. The tanks had been disassembled in Hanoi, flown into Dien Bien Phu, and then reassembled on the spot by their crews.

While the paratroopers had seized the valley, command of Dien Bien Phu fell to a highly decorated fifty-one-year-old cavalryman, Christian Marie Ferdinand de la Croix de Castries—a man who had a reputation for both his dashing bravery and his sexual appetites. The rumor was that he christened Dien Bien Phu's strongpoints with the names of his mistresses. Sadly, under the strain of command and combat, de Castries was to snap, and a hard-boiled, laconic paratrooper officer, Pierre Langlais, would assume de facto control of the battle. He was to be aided by what soon became known as the paratrooper mafia; in the terror and confusion of the collapse of French assumptions, command devolved on the toughest and most competent, while rank counted for little.

Giap was delighted to take up the French challenge. But he refused to play by French expectations. Instead of striking quickly before he was ready, he carried out a careful and meticulous redeployment across the highlands. As Giap recorded: "We came to the conclusion that we could not secure success if we struck swiftly. In consequence . . . we strictly followed this fundamental principle of revolutionary war: strike to win, strike only when success is certain; if not, then don't strike."

With the French making the opening move, the Viet Minh shifted their forces to the far western reaches of northern Vietnam. The weather and jungle conditions represented a nightmare, especially when one considers that virtually everything—men, weapons, ammunition—had to move on foot. But Giap and his officers were more than fanatical revolutionaries; by now they were thorough professionals, entirely capable of handling the operational and logistical challenges posed by such a complex redeployment.

Once the Viet Minh had cleared the neighboring highlands, they methodically closed in around Dien Bien Phu until they had it surrounded. Raiding actions by the French brought few results except heavy casualties and, as the Viet Minh arrived in strength on the heights overlooking Dien Bien Phu, the French lost control of everything but the valley. In the valley itself, the garrison continued its desultory work on defensive strongpoints, but the lack of command interest—a reflection of the underestimation of Giap's capabilities—and the macho attitude of elite troops that fortifications were for others hardly made Dien Bien Phu a solid defensive position. Not until March 23 would de Castries ask Hanoi for the basic French engineering manual on the construction of fortified positions. By then the French had already been under attack for ten days. Virtually none of the French strongpoints possessed enough barbed wire to divide their positions into defensible segments. Consequently, when the Viet Minh succeeded in making a breach, the entire position became vulnerable. And the Viet Minh proved very good at exploiting breaches. Further compounding the vulnerability of the defenses was the fact that the French stripped the landscape bare to build field fortifications. Viet Minh observers in the hills now had a clear view of everything that happened in the valley.

By early February the outline of the French defensive system had emerged. In the center, the vital airstrip was surrounded by a series of fortified strongpoints: in the east, Dominique and Eliane; to the north and northwest, Anne-Marie and Huguette; and on the southwest, Claudine. To the north, separated by a considerable distance, lay Gabrielle, while Béatrice, also separated from the center, lay close to the jungle and mountains to the northeast. Finally, six kilometers to the south was strongpoint Isabelle, placed in a swamp that made the living conditions of its garrison miserable. Isabelle provided crucial artillery support for the main French defensive positions, particularly in the killing battles of April, but it lay too far south to support the outer strongpoints in the north, where the first Viet Minh attacks would come. The position in the central garrison consisted of a number of strongpoints that gave 360-degree coverage from trenches connected to a number of bunkers and mortar positions. Each of these defensive bastions—called, for example, Dominique 1 and 2 or Huguette 7—was provided with some barbed wire and mines, but not nearly enough. Moreover, most of the bunkers gave relatively little protection against artillery bombardment.

The basic assumption under which the French fought was that superior firepower—air as well as artillery—would keep the enemy at bay. Counterbattery fire and air strikes would thus dominate and then eliminate whatever artillery the Viet Minh might drag across the jungle highlands. Aerial resupply efforts would then proceed through the small landing strip. In fact, with more than a three-to-one superiority in artillery, the Viet Minh were able to disrupt the landing strip early in the battle, and only a desperate effort by the Americans, who gathered up virtually all the equipment-drop parachutes in the Pacific and sent them posthaste to Hanoi, allowed the French to turn to resupplying their garrison by parachute. But beyond the Viet Minh's artillery superiority lay the fact that their engineers and artillerymen meticulously sited and dug in each artillery piece. What made even the parachute resupply effort a trial was the fact that, through the help of the Chinese, Giap brought substantial antiaircraft capability to the siege. So dense was the flak over Dien Bien Phu that some French pilots who had flown over Germany in World War II thought the Viet Minh were putting up more effective barrages.

Nevertheless, the French felt confident enough about their "artillery superiority" that throughout January and February, they brought in a series of visiting firemen, including their own minister of defense and Lieutenant General Iron Mike O'Daniel, commander of U.S. Army forces in the Pacific. Most visitors, including apparently O'Daniel, left impressed with what they had seen and with the garrison's confidence. By mid-March, Giap and his Viet Minh forces were ready. By now he enjoyed more than a three-to-one advantage over the defenders (approximately 13,000 French and empire troops—many of doubtful utility—against 50,000 Viet Minh). His artillery, which had been harassing the French with increasing severity over the past month, was in place.

At five P.M. on March 13, the Viet Minh artillery opened up with a thunderous roar that not only smashed into Béatrice but blanketed French positions throughout the central sector. Béatrice was of crucial importance, because its possession by the French would keep the Viet Minh artillery and observers back from the airfield. It was defended by the 3rd Battalion of the 13th Foreign Legion Demi-Brigade. Within an hour and a half, the Viet Minh were pressing in on all sides, and the defenders were calling for final protective fire from the main batteries of French artillery (the batteries on Isabelle were too far away to support Béatrice). To add to French woes, Viet Minh artillery destroyed Béatrice's command bunker and, shortly afterward, the command bunker in the central sector. Of course, one couldn't miss where the main French command posts were, since they had large aerials poking up from the barren earth. By eight in the evening, Giap's soldiers were inside the position and mopping up the legionnaires. By midnight the fight was over; a few survivors made it back to the main positions at daybreak, but the battle had opened with a disaster for the French.

Not only had the defenses on Béatrice collapsed, but the artillery had neither suppressed the enemy's guns nor held off the attacking enemy infantry. It was not for want of trying; the French fired off no fewer than six thousand 105 shells, one quarter of their stock. But the Viet Minh had too many artillery pieces and were too well dug in for anything other than massive artillery superiority to destroy their positions.

Still worse followed on the heels of Béatrice. Over the night of March 14, Gabrielle's garrison thwarted a Viet Minh attack. In the early-morning hours of March 15, a massive barrage further reduced Gabrielle's garrison; as had happened at Béatrice, one of the Viet Minh shells then hit the command post and wiped out most of the staff. Another infantry assault followed up on the bombardment; the main garrison failed to launch an effective relief effort. By mid-morning another position had fallen; a few escaped, but most of Gabrielle's garrison of five hundred men were either dead or in Viet Minh hands.

Béatrice and Gabrielle shattered French illusions. French artillery, for all the bravery of its crews, had failed. Counterbattery work had not silenced Viet Minh guns emplaced in deep revetments (admittedly limiting their targets to a narrow band); nor had it placed sufficient shells on Viet Minh infantry to prevent them from swamping French positions. The shocking failure of French artillery led Dien Bien Phu's artillery commander, Colonel Charles Piroth, to commit suicide on March 15 to atone for the failure of his guns—a suicide that the paratroop commander Langlais may have encouraged by remarking to him that expiation was in order.

Meanwhile, Viet Minh artillery had blanketed all the French defensive positions. It had destroyed French fighter-bombers on Dien Bien Phu's landing strip or driven them off, while the landing of resupply aircraft was rapidly coming to a halt. Ambulance aircraft and helicopters would continue to land until the end of the month, but from that point on, the garrison was totally cut off except for aerial drops. The fall of Béatrice, which was on high ground, brought Viet Minh artillery to positions looking directly down into the central position, while Gabrielle's loss allowed Giap to set antiaircraft positions on the flight path into the airstrip, making aerial resupply a nightmare throughout the remainder of the battle. To compound the problem of using air effectively, the

French remained so dismissive of Viet Minh capabilities that they continued to direct most of the close air support and resupply missions on the radio en clair; the Viet Minh knew what was going on as quickly as did French pilots.

To compound these difficulties in the days after the fall of Béatrice and Gabrielle, most of the T'ai troops on the Anne Marie positions deserted. Nevertheless, there was a slight improvement in the garrison's morale as the legendary Major Marcel Bigeard and his 6th Parachute Battalion dropped into Dien Bien Phu. Bigeard, wrote one American reporter who spent time there, "had the physical presence of a medieval warlord, a tall, lean, hawk-nosed man with a fine disregard for danger and an innate gift for leadership." But there was little help from Hanoi, where Cogny seems to have spent his time feuding with Navarre and preparing the historical record to show himself in a favorable light. On March 24 he found time to send de Castries the reassuring message that "[T]he rainy season, now close at hand, will compromise [the enemy's] communication lines and will oppose a major obstacle of mud to the development of his field fortifications." Cogny was wrong on both counts: The bad weather interfered more with French resupply efforts, while Viet Minh defensive positions were on the high ground and thus far less vulnerable to the effects of the monsoon.

But the Viet Minh had suffered heavy losses in the attacks on Béatrice and Gabrielle. With possession of the high ground, Giap turned to strangling the central position. Viet Minh troops began digging approach trenches that would allow them to launch their infantry over shorter distances at the French defenses and therefore suffer fewer casualties. If the Viet Minh were learning, so were the French. Moving out of Huguette and Claudine with support from Isabelle, paratroopers and armor drove to the west of Dien Bien Phu and caught the enemy completely by surprise. Bigeard was at his best; his meticulous planning resulted in a sharp setback to the Viet Minh. But in the end, the French could not take the casualties involved in such ripostes: Aerial resupply was becoming increasingly expensive and less effective, and many of the drops completely missed areas controlled by the French. Their opponents could better bear heavy casualties, and the movement of supplies and reinforcements to Viet Minh forces around Dien Bien Phu continued unabated despite the heavy attacks launched by the French air force.

On the evening of March 30, Giap launched his next series of attacks against the central sector. As had happened on Gabrielle and Béatrice, the Viet Minh began with a heavy artillery bombardment that targeted Dominique and

Eliane, as well as French command centers. Following a rolling barrage, Viet Minh assault waves left their approach trenches, so assiduously dug during previous weeks, and destroyed the defenders on Dominique 1 and 2. But they failed to take the third strongpoint on Dominique. Artillerymen on that position remained with their guns and, firing over open sights, blasted the attacking Viet Minh infantry to pieces. Their stand prevented Giap's troops from breaking into the center of the fortress. At the same time, the Eliane position came under heavy attack from the Viet Minh 316th Division; Eliane 1 fell. But a mixed force of Frenchmen, Foreign Legion paratroopers, and Moroccans counterattacked and regained most of the lost territory.

Late on the afternoon of March 31, Bigeard launched one of his patented counterattacks. His troops regained Eliane 1 and Dominique 1, but at a heavy price in casualties and artillery shells. That day, eighteen French 105s fired off thirteen thousand rounds at the attackers. By this point both the garrison and its tormentors were exhausted. Despite desperate calls by de Castries to Hanoi, Cogny was too busy with social engagements to meet with Navarre. In spite of the availability of a battalion of paratroopers, Hanoi dithered away the chance to reinforce Dien Bien Phu at the moment when the Viet Minh were in serious trouble.

Giap now shifted to the west. While attacking Dominique and Eliane, the Viet Minh were also pressuring Huguette. By early morning of April 2, they had pushed the defenders on Huguette 7 into a small bunker on the corner of the strongpoint; but a French counterattack, supported by tanks, drove the Viet Minh off the position to the northwest of the airstrip. Over the night of April 4–5, it was the turn of Huguette 6, and again Viet Minh regulars gained control of most of the strongpoint despite a steady dribble of reinforcing small units. But in the early-morning hours a French counterattack, supported by all of the remaining French artillery, hit the Viet Minh 165th Regiment before it had consolidated its position. The French had learned that if they were going to regain a position, they had to strike immediately with what was at hand, rather than wait to get everything ready. In this case, what was ready were two companies of Bigeard's paratroops, each with barely eighty men. Nonetheless, their counterattack hit the Viet Minh when they were most vulnerable, and with the support of deadly artillery fire, the French drove the Viet Minh out.

The French had weathered Giap's second offensive. They had lost some of the outer strongpoints of the central position, but they maintained its integrity.

The cost had been heavy, in both reserves of ammunition and the steady attrition of the garrison. The driblets of reinforcements hardly made up for the casualties, especially since the parachute bureaucracy in Hanoi insisted that the resupply efforts adhere to peacetime procedures. On the night of April 3–4, Langlais threw away the rule book and ordered transport aircraft circling above to drop their reinforcements directly on the central fortress rather than on a regulation drop zone. When the drop commander objected, saying that such an action was not in accordance with regulations, Langlais exploded: "*Merde!* You can tell Colonel Sauvagnac that I'll take the responsibility for the drop-zone violations. Drop those men!" The arrival of 305 paratroopers, with only two dead and ten wounded, justified Langlais's gamble. In addition, the garrison was feeling the loss of specialists, such as artillerymen and tankers. Langlais forced the authorities in Hanoi to drop these men in (provided they were willing) without jump training. Again, the losses were small.

If Giap was facing his own problems, most of which arose from the heavy casualty bill, he was not willing to take the pressure off the garrison. He aimed to finish Dien Bien Phu before the Geneva Conference on the future of Vietnam convened in mid-May. That conference, attended by the foreign ministers of China, France, Britain, the Soviet Union, and the United States, was supposed to solve the problems raised by the Korean and Indochinese conflicts. In the end, it did nothing about Korea, divided Vietnam, split off Cambodia and Laos, and created the potential for another conflict.

On the other side of the world, a major policy debate was raging in Washington. The debate was between those who believed that the United States should intervene with airpower to prevent a French defeat at Dien Bien Phu—in particular the secretary of state, John Foster Dulles, and the chairman of the Joint Chiefs of Staff, Admiral Arthur B. Radford—and those who believed that such involvement would lead to the commitment of ground forces in a war that was not in America's strategic interest. Radford argued that a major raid out of the Philippines by a large force of B-29s would turn the tide at Dien Bien Phu and gain the French the breathing room needed to survive until the peace conference at Geneva convened. The journalist and historian Bernard Fall suggests that at Clark Field the U.S. insignia on some B-29s may have been painted out and replaced with the French tricolor circles.

But to the anguish of the French, Radford's position ran into substantial opposition elsewhere in the American military. In particular, General Matthew Ridgway and Lieutenant General James Gavin (both former commanders of the 82nd Airborne and among the most outstanding combat leaders of World War II) did not believe that any number of air raids would suffice to bail the French out at Dien Bien Phu, and that the inevitable result of such attacks would be the commitment of U.S. ground forces to Indochina. They argued that the United States should not involve itself in a colonial war, where the costs in lives and treasure would bring no commensurate gain in strategic, economic, or political terms. They felt—to paraphrase Omar Bradley about war with China in 1951—that Vietnam was the wrong war, in the wrong place, and at the wrong time. In retrospect, their strategic calculus was on target, and they did not find it difficult to win over President Dwight Eisenhower. The United States would stand aside as the French garrison went down to defeat. There would be no American strikes in the Dien Bien Phu area until the summer of 1965, when Operation Rolling Thunder began.

Despite the gallantry of their stand, French forces at Dien Bien Phu were on their last legs by mid-April. Major Viet Minh attacks went in on the Eliane positions on April 10; only a desperate last-ditch attack by Vietnamese paratroopers drove the Viet Minh off Eliane 1. In *Hell in a Very Small Place*, Bernard Fall describes the scene:

> As the Vietnamese paratroopers in turn emerged on the fire-beaten saddle between the hills, there arose, for the first and last time in the Indochina war, the Marseillaise. It was sung the way it had been written to be sung in the days of the French Revolution, as the battle hymn of the French Republic. It was sung that night on the blood-stained slopes of Hill Eliane 1 by Vietnamese fighting other Vietnamese in the last battle that France fought as an Asian power.

Now, as the two opposing sides struggled to regain their balance—the French almost out of men and supplies and with a failing airlift, and the Viet Minh forced to use boys in place of the troops devastated by French firepower—Giap's forces turned to siege tactics as well as direct attacks. They dug their trenches ever closer to French positions, harassed their enemy with constant artillery fire and probing attacks, and did everything in their power to hinder the airlift. Between April 12 and 21, Giap's soldiers drove the French off the Huguette positions to the north and west of the airstrip, thus making airlift operations ever more difficult. The French hung on, but they no longer had the reserves or the ammunition to regain what they lost. Cogny's headquarters in

Hanoi added to the air of unreality by asking de Castries what engineering supplies he needed to protect the garrison from the monsoon rains that were turning its positions into waterlogged swamps—the one advantage being that the mud made the Viet Minh artillery slightly less effective. His request came on April 23, when only thirty-five men arrived to replace the sixty-seven casualties suffered that day.

The final turn on the road to defeat came on April 23. A counterattack by paratroopers to regain Huguette 1 got caught in the open and pinned on the airstrip; the commander of the operation had his radio tuned on the wrong frequency and never picked up that things were going wrong. Bigeard, awakened from a deep sleep, rushed across the central position in a jeep, but too late. A major counterattack had failed with heavy losses (150 men killed or wounded), and Dien Bien Phu's last operational reserve had gone down the drain. The morale of even the best units began to crack. The cost to the Viet Minh in the Huguette fighting had been heavy; they would not launch their final series of attacks until May 1, after a full week of replenishing supplies and bringing up cadres and soldiers to replace their losses.

The end would come with relative suddenness. Astonishingly, as the garrison slowly collapsed under the weight of Viet Minh attacks, legionnaires were still engaged in vigorous patrolling and attacking enemy bunkers, perhaps to pay their eventual captors back ahead of time. On May 5, Cogny, ever the cad, sent a final message to the garrison, undoubtedly for the historical record: "I need not underline inestimable value in every field, and perspectives offered, by prolonging resistance on the spot, which at present remains your glorious mission."

Despite the hopelessness of the fight, Frenchmen, incredibly, continued to parachute into the fortress. Over the last four nights of airdrops, 383 troopers of the 1st Battalion Colonial Paratroopers jumped into Dien Bien Phu; even more incredibly, 155 of these were Vietnamese, who had to know their fate if they fell into Viet Minh hands. Over the night and early-morning hours of May 6–7, the Viet Minh finally pried the French off the Eliane positions, and the collapse became general. At five-thirty in the afternoon of May 7, with the Viet Minh all over the central position and his own bunker about to fall, de Castries radioed to Hanoi that he was blowing up the ammunition and supply dumps. Cogny replied, "Well then, au revoir, old boy." To the south, the troops in the isolated Isabelle position soon followed de Castries' surrender. They had rendered crucial artillery support to the end of the battle; moreover, they had beaten off every attack the Viet Minh had launched on their position and had survived despite being inundated by the monsoon rains. They had held out past the point of any reasonable expectations. The total dead for the siege was well over ten thousand, of which the French and their allies had suffered close to a quarter.

The most direct result of Dien Bien Phu was the end of French rule in Indochina. The Geneva Conference would turn over all of North Vietnam to Ho Chi Minh and the Viet Minh; within a year the French had, for all intents and purposes, withdrawn from Southeast Asia. The Viet Minh returned about three thousand French prisoners in July and August. But of the rest, close to ten thousand had died on what became a death march to the prison camps, or in the camps themselves. Many who survived would soon be fighting a new guerrilla war in Algeria, one that would put paid to the French empire.

But longer-term results of Dien Bien Phu proved even more far-reaching. For the United States, the French defeat represented a distinct blow to the policy of containment. The failure of the United States to help the dying garrison at Dien Bien Phu would scar Franco-American relations and lead the French to withdraw from the military portion of the NATO alliance. Under Charles de Gaulle's unforgiving leadership, they would chart their own defense course. The strategic significance of the loss of part or all of Indochina hardly should have mattered on the harsh scale of economic and political power that would determine the course of the Cold War over the next thirty-five years. In the larger sense, the United States could have been the winner. Tragically, the strategic wisdom that had characterized the Eisenhowers, the Ridgways, and the Gavins disappeared with the next generation of political and military leaders. In 1964 the French government, recognizing the path on which the United States was so eagerly embarking, made available to American leaders their massive after-action report on the Indochinese war. It was placed by polite American officers in the library of the National Defense University, where it remains to this day, unread and unused.

The French military, however, assiduously studied the "revolutionary war." In a sense they learned from it, and when the Algerian revolt broke out in November 1954, they applied the lessons to the new conflict. But they had learned only the military lessons. They won the Algerian war in military terms but lost the political war—and Algeria. And the terrible level to which they sank in winning that war came close to breaking their army and their nation.

In the end, it was the Vietnamese who lost the most from the Viet Minh's victory at Dien Bien Phu. When Bernard Fall visited Hanoi in the early 1960s, he warned his hosts that the Americans were coming; the North Vietnamese reply was that the Americans were just like the French, with a little more fire-power. A single incident at the battle of Khe Sanh in March 1968 suggests the extent of Hanoi's miscalculation. In a simple raid on a North Vietnamese bunker 850 yards outside of the perimeter, the attacking marine company re-ceived the support of no less than 3,600 rounds of artillery fire—approximately one fifth of all the artillery ammunition expended during the entire siege of Dien Bien Phu. Through 1972 the North Vietnamese were to persist in the pursuit of a decisive victory that would do to the Americans what Dien Bien Phu had done to the French. One can argue that in 1968 they sought not one but two decisive victories over the American military, one at Khe Sanh and the other with the Tet Offensive against South Vietnam's cities. In military terms, the result was a catastrophe for the North Vietnamese and the Vietcong. They may have achieved their goal of a united Vietnam, but the cost staggers the imagination: They destroyed virtually every year group of young males from 1962 through 1975. Vietnam's current position as one of the poorest countries in a sea of Southeast Asian prosperity is very much the result of the hubris that the Viet Minh leadership gained from the victory at Dien Bien Phu.

The General at Ease:
An Interview with William C. Westmoreland

LAURA PALMER

No American commander of the past century, except Douglas MacArthur, has been the center of more controversy—indeed, has received more opprobrium—than William Childs Westmoreland. He headed the U.S. Military Assistance Command in Vietnam (MACV) for nearly four years, from June 1964 (ten years after Dien Bien Phu) until March 1968, and became the chief enforcer of the strategy of containment in Southeast Asia. It was a period that saw the Americanization of a struggle that had begun as a civil war, as our troop commitment rose from 16,000 to 500,000. In Korea, Mark W. Clark may have presided over the first war in our history that did not end in an obvious victory; Westmoreland will be forever associated with our first outright loss, even if he did not exit a loser.

For Westmoreland, Vietnam should have been the pinnacle of a distinguished military career. He had fought with distinction at the debacle of Kasserine Pass and later, in the invasion of Sicily. He had gone ashore at Normandy, had fought his way across France, and had crossed the Remagen Bridge under fire. He had led troops in Korea; had commanded one of the most prestigious of American divisions, the 101st Airborne; and had been superintendent of his alma mater, the U.S. Military Academy at West Point. A brave man who was a methodical planner and a gifted administrator, Westmoreland placed the characteristic American reliance on crushing force—the wielding of overwhelming military power that, he would argue, Washington continually denied him. He was probably right, to an extent. His critics would fault him for a lack of imagination, for an inability to see that he could win all the battles (which he did) and still lose the war. They argued that he placed too much emphasis on military solutions and not enough on political ones. They were probably right, too.

Instead of adapting to the unconventional methods of Communist revolutionary warfare, Westmoreland chose to emphasize increasingly massive search-and-destroy missions. Unlike the French, who sought to take on and defeat the Viet Minh (now, with their own country, the North Vietnamese) in set-piece battles, Westmoreland had a simpler objective: to kill as many of the enemy as possible. The more casualties he could inflict, the more he could undermine the enemy's will to fight. The insurgency would end once its manpower pool dried up. It was as if, in initiating the Era of the Body Count, Westmoreland had ripped a page out of the 1916 German playbook at Verdun, when the principal object had not been to gain territory but to bleed the French white.

The strategy of attrition was at the heart of a 1982 CBS documentary charging that Westmoreland had ordered that statistics of Vietcong and North Vietnamese strength levels be "cooked," to show that their force size was diminishing and that the expensive search-and-destroy efforts were achieving potentially war-winning results. The documentary, hosted by the tenacious Mike Wallace, was titled *The Uncounted Enemy: A Vietnam Deception*. Westmoreland sued for libel. It was a court action that backfired against the plaintiff nearly as much as Alger Hiss's 1948 suit for slander against Whittaker Chambers, which led the defendant to produce the famous "Pumpkin Papers," documents that Hiss had passed to the Communists through Chambers. Now, in the 1985 trial, the defense called a witness, a retired colonel in army intelligence who testified that Westmoreland had indeed ordered him to reduce estimates of Communist strength. The suit was settled out of court.

The trial was still in the public mind when Laura Palmer, a former journalist in Vietnam, interviewed the general in the summer of 1988 for the first issue of *MHQ: The Quarterly Journal of Military History*. Westmoreland, who had retired as chief of staff of the army in 1972, was unbending in his own defense. He may well have had a point in arguing that after the shattering defeat of the Vietcong in their Tet Offensive in the winter of 1968, the U.S. should have provided the men and matériel to launch an overpowering counteroffensive. It didn't. Quite to the contrary, the American public viewed Tet as a defeat, and President Lyndon

B. Johnson, like any good politician, counted heads. Westmoreland was called home soon after.

We may come to regard William C. Westmoreland as a good man trapped in an impossible role, trying to win an increasingly unpopular war, the most unpopular in our history. It was a war that could not be won, no matter what strategy the U.S. pursued.

LAURA PALMER worked as a journalist in Saigon during the Vietnam War. She is the author of *Shrapnel in the Heart: Letters and Remembrances from the Vietnam Memorial*. She writes and produces for television news.

T HE BUMPER STICKER *on the back of his blue Buick says simply,* I AM A VIETNAM VETERAN. *He is General William C. Westmoreland, and with pride resonating behind every word, he'll tell you that he is the nation's number one Vietnam vet.*

Westmoreland is perhaps the only American general to fight first for his country and then for the reputation of his soldiers. His message is blunt and succinct. In a speech delivered this summer before the Vietnam Veterans POW Association in Washington, D.C., he said, "Our children must know that we answered our country's call, to fight a war the military was not allowed to win, that we fought on even after our Congress, and indeed our people, lost their will to continue the battle, and we came home to a greeting of hostility or silence."

During his forty years as a soldier, Westmoreland fought in three wars, including Vietnam, where he served as commander of all U.S. forces from 1964 until early 1968. He then returned to Washington, D.C., and became army chief of staff, a post he held until his retirement in 1972. During his career, he also served for several years as superintendent at West Point, his alma mater. With the exception of World War I, William Childs Westmoreland has lived the military history of this century, and he has the awards and decorations to prove it.

Westmoreland, now seventy-four, is a man at peace with his present and his past. He and his wife, Katherine, known to all as Kitsy, spend part of each summer in Linville, North Carolina, in the gentle grasp of the Blue Ridge Mountains. They have reared three children, and their forty-one-year marriage has both strengthened and nurtured them, and is still an obvious source of joy. Last July we sat down for a chat, and my image of a man with the warmth of Mount Rushmore slowly dissolved. The public Westmoreland is the first man you meet: tough, proud, tenacious, and smart. He is the four-star general who will always be asso-ciated with two three-letter words: Tet and CBS.

But there is another Westy, a private man who is tender, witty, and kind. Watching and listening to the play between the public and private personas is both fascinating and revealing. Imagine the commander in chief of American forces in Vietnam, sitting alone, late into the night, signing all of the next-of-kin letters by hand, and you'll begin to see what I mean.

How strongly do you identify with these veterans?

Very strongly. They were my boys. And they were boys. The average age, less than nineteen. The first thing that happened in the morning in Saigon was that I received the casualty lists. The whole time I was in Vietnam, and then when I was the army chief of staff, I personally signed the letters to the next of kin. I wouldn't allow the auto-pen to be used.

You signed every one?

I signed every one of them.

You'd do that in the morning?

Sometimes I'd be doing it at midnight. I worked it in. I gave it very top priority. Because of the importance of that letter and the sacrifice that had been made, I felt it was wrong for me to have a mechanical pen. There was a certain phoniness about those pens that I just couldn't accept.

Some of these casualties must have been people you knew.

Let me give you a good example. One day I was sitting in my office with the casualty lists in front of me. It was probably seven o'clock in the morning. On that list was a Pershing—General John J. Pershing's grandson, Second Lieutenant Richard Warren Pershing. I'd known him as a little boy that high.

Did you ever get used to situations such as that?

One of the first events that happened when I became army chief of staff was that Kitsy's brother, Lieutenant Colonel Frederick Van Deusen, was killed, at almost the exact time I was sworn in. I heard the news before the ceremony, but I didn't tell her until afterwards. The date was July 3, 1968.

What went through your mind?

A military man has to be able to accept these tragedies. I mean, you've got so much on your plate. You look and you grieve for about five minutes, and then you think about it the rest of the day; but in the meanwhile, you have people coming in the office, you have decisions to make, and so you set your feelings aside until you have a chance to reflect.

And when did that happen?

That evening with my wife. She loved that kid. He was the baby of the family. Outgoing, happy-go-lucky; everybody liked him. He and I used to play golf together, and we used to jog. He was so enthusiastic about commanding a battalion. I was devoted to him. He left a wife and three children.

Did the death of your brother-in-law change you?

No, I think a professional soldier realizes there are going to be casualties—unforeseen, unhappy developments. You can't let them totally upset your life and interfere with your duty.

But clearly, anyone who signed those next-of-kin letters was ready to face the human side of the war?

After my brother-in-law was killed, it took about a week for his body to come back. We went to Fayetteville, North Carolina, for his funeral. I contracted pneumonia. When a person is under tremendous stress, and this happens to me, I develop temporary health problems. This was a good case—the stress of a new office, of going back to the Pentagon, the stress of having to deal at that level with an unpopular war with an ambiguous strategy—and then having a brother-in-law killed. Those things accumulated, and I found myself in the hospital for a week.

Why have you become so involved in the process of healing and reconciliation? When did you start getting involved in this?

I retired on the first of July, 1972. At that time, the war was an unpopular war, which rubbed off unfavorably on the warriors. I was very sensitive about this. I felt it was so terribly unfair. I felt that when I retired, I had an obligation to take the darts, and to try to explain this very complex war to the American people. I decided nobody knew more about the Vietnam War than I did, and I was going to make myself available to talk to anybody. You can't believe the abuse I got, but I didn't let it get to me.

I'm sure some people said that what Westmoreland was fighting for was his own reputation as well.

I don't think you can separate the two. I'm a veteran. I'm the number one veteran. I'm symbolic of the others.

They came back from the war and were tagged as losers.

But they never lost a battle.

I am aware of that, but we are talking about what people perceive, and as the number one veteran, you were perceived as the number one loser.

No question about that, no question about that. Many of them had hid the fact that they were Vietnam veterans, and they will admit that to you. The turning point in the public attitude was when the Vietnam veterans converged on Washington and had a "Welcome Home" parade for themselves; nobody else would do it. I led the parade, and they loved it.

That parade took place in November 1982. You came down to Washington from the CBS trial in New York.

I've been to many parades, and I've found it's great for morale if the old man can mingle with the troops while they are forming up. When you have a parade like that, the troops start forming about two hours ahead of time, so I went around to every state group, and any number of them said, "General, please march with us." I said, "Naw, naw, I'm not going to march with you guys." I like to kid troops, and have fun bantering back and forth.

"Who are you going to march with?" some of the soldiers asked me.

"I'm going to march with Alabama."

"General, why the hell are you going to march with Alabama?"

I said, "Alabama starts with A, it is leading the parade, and I'm going to lead them!"

It was an exhilarating thing for me. As I talk about it, I get tears in my eyes, and I admit it.

What do you think about the Vietnam Veterans Memorial in Washington—the Wall?

I've been there twice. I was there for the dedication. I found Fred's name and made a rubbing of it to bring to Kitsy. She has never been to the Wall.

What went through your mind when you found his name?

There was a big crowd around me, so I didn't physically weep.

Were there tears inside?

Well, certainly, certainly. That kid was the closest thing I ever had to a brother. Of course, when I approached his name, there were hundreds and thousands of names just like his. Many of them had been cadets under me at West Point. The names of some of my finest cadets are on that Wall.

When you look at the Wall, it must be like looking at your family.

Yes, in a sense, a family of Americans, young men that I relate to. With all those names, you get an impression and understanding of the price we paid during that war.

To change the subject—what was the hardest decision you had to make in Vietnam? The one that caused you the most anguish or turmoil?

The initial commitment of American troops in 1964.

Did you have doubts about sending combat troops?

Oh, boy, I tell you this was a very, very tough decision. Nobody wanted to do it. I didn't want to do it. I was hoping the American military adviser effort could work for the Vietnamese and make them fight their own battles.

Why did you think committing our troops was a bad idea?

I didn't think it was a bad idea. I thought it was essential after I evaluated it, but it was a very tough decision to come to—to commit American troops in a foreign land where a unique type of war was being fought. But I saw that it would be impossible for the Vietnamese to cut it. Does that slang expression mean something to you?

Yes, it does.

The decision to commit American troops was one that none of us wanted to take, but it was a question of whether or not we abandoned Vietnam, which was going down the drain. They had lost confidence, they were in the dumps, they were losing a battalion a week. My judgment was that if we had not committed American troops, it was just a matter of time till they disintegrated. I think the same thought process took place in Washington with the Joint Chiefs of Staff and the president.

What did you think of LBJ? How would you characterize your relationship to him?

LBJ always did what he said he would do. He didn't always do what I asked, but he always listened. I was very candid. But I put a premium on loyalty. I wouldn't undercut the chain of command. In no way did I try to undercut the Joint Chiefs of Staff or the secretary of defense. But I was forthcoming when LBJ asked me questions. I said we couldn't expect immediate results, that this was primarily a war of attrition. During his first year in office—1964—we went from 500 advisers to 15,000 military personnel. We assumed the responsibility of shoring up the South Vietnamese.

Another key player in 1964 was Robert McNamara. What did you think of the secretary of defense?

I don't dislike Bob McNamara. He was fair to me. He came over in March or April of 1964. I remember I talked to him in 1964, one-on-one, in the old embassy in the middle of Saigon. He was really quite surprised by the complexity of the situation he found in Vietnam and the ambiguity of the solutions. I knew it was a complex situation and would take a long time to solve. Maxwell Taylor was the ambassador at the time, and his deputy was U. Alexis Johnson. We discussed at great length what to do, and came to a consensus that we would ask for combat troops. But we did not visualize that it would take as many as it finally did.

I wondered if the American people would stick with our effort. I felt the American people had to get emotionally involved. I suggested to McNamara something like a people-to-people program between South Vietnam and the United States to facilitate this. Later, I talked to one of his aides about following up on this idea. But McNamara apparently didn't want to get the American people emotionally involved in the war—he wanted to play it low-key. He wanted to fight on the cheap—to program and manage it so that we wouldn't end up with huge stockpiles like we did after World War II. McNamara was managerially oriented.

I want to go back for a moment to what you originally said. I find it a striking statement that out of your four and a half years in Vietnam, the initial decision to send combat troops was the most difficult to make.

We were actually operating in the unknown. Young American boys would have to perform on the battlefield with hardened Vietcong forces and the tough North Vietnamese troops that had defeated the French at Dien Bien Phu, in an alien land with all the problems of terrain, disease, etc. These presented formidable problems.

Now, in 1954 I had been on the Army General Staff as a brigadier general when consideration was made to put troops into Dien Bien Phu. The administration was totally disenchanted about going into another war. We had finished World War II and had just negotiated the armistice with the North Koreans, and politically, another military involvement wasn't feasible. I was in on those deliberations, where all the negatives were exposed. Had I not been in on them, my doubts about the wisdom of committing American troops in 1964 may not have occurred to me.

Of the decisions you made as commander in Vietnam, which are you most proud of?

The decision to hold Khe Sanh.

Why?

I interpreted the intelligence and the performance of the enemy during the Tet Offensive to mean that they were trying to dominate and take over Thua Thien and Quang Tri provinces and to establish a provisional government and political headquarters at Hue, the ancient capital. The holding of Khe Sanh thwarted the enemy plans. Let me go a little further. If they had overrun Khe Sanh, they could have moved into the lowlands with two divisions and mingled among the people. It would have been hard to ferret them out. The armchair strategists back in the U.S. said it was crazy to hold Khe Sanh. Arthur Schlesinger, Jr., the historian, said that I ought to be relieved of my command, that I was the worst general since Custer. [Laughs.]

Then why, if Khe Sanh was so important, was it later abandoned?

Once it became evident that the enemy had abandoned the area, I could not afford to tie down troops there. We were in a position to reoccupy Khe Sanh at any time, and the enemy was not about to move in, having lost so many men. The terrain in Vietnam was so extensive that we could not afford to tie down troops unless they were essential to the prosecution of the war. We had an eight-hundred-mile front. That was unprecedented, unless you go back to the Civil War. There are many similarities between Vietnam and the Civil War.

Give me an example or two.

The common denominator between the two was that they were wars of mobility, in which you only tied down troops when necessary. You had to keep troops mobile. In the Civil War, you had foot soldiers, horses, and boats on the Mississippi, Cumberland, and Tennessee rivers. In Vietnam we also had boats, and we exploited the river-ways. The thing that replaced the horse was the helicopter, and without the helicopter, we could not have accomplished what we did. In neither war was the holding of terrain the primary emphasis. And in both wars, it was a question of bringing the enemy to the battlefield in order to attrite his ranks.

That Laos-Cambodia frontier really bothered you, didn't it?

Oh, it plagued us. The enemy would cross it and fight us. He chased us, but we couldn't chase him. I tell you, I think the finger points at Averell Harriman. Are you familiar with the book *Key to Failure*, by Norman Hannah? The essence of the book is that because of the prestige of an earlier ambassador to the Soviet Union—who must have been Harriman—tacit agreement was made with the Russians that if we would not cross the border, they would not be part of the capture of Laos. Harriman had a lot of prestige, and he carried the day on that.

Do you think there has been a good Vietnam movie?

I haven't seen one.

What went through your mind when you watched Platoon?

I was aghast when they had soldiers killing other soldiers, smoking pot at night in their bunker. It didn't happen.

Are you saying it didn't ever happen?

No, I was about to qualify that. If it happened, it was very exceptional. The marijuana that was used was in the main used in the rear areas by the stevedore types who were kind of bored with what they were doing and had more access to drugs. A well-trained, well-disciplined combat unit would not tolerate marijuana because it would jeopardize their own safety.

Let me throw another factor into this equation that you may be aware of, but my feeling is probably you aren't. One of the real liabilities that influenced Vietnam was the decision made to call up—I think this was in 1965 or '66—a hundred thousand category fours. Now, does category four mean anything to you?

I think I've heard it mentioned.

Category four is a dummy. You can probably make a soldier out of ten percent of him. Give him menial jobs, and he is not a troublemaker. But it is awfully difficult to utilize that many category fours.

Now, whose decision was that?

It was alleged that it was McNamara's, but I'm not sure. It was a political decision. To understand that is important when you start reflecting on the drug syndrome, the fragging, or on the type of person who had been dismissed by a judge from a criminal charge if he would join the army and go to Vietnam. And that did happen. So that introduced a weak-minded, criminal, untrained element into the army. When those people came to Vietnam—and they started arriving in late '68, '69, '70—that's when disciplinary problems began on the battlefield.

What would have happened if you had taken thousands of men from Harvard, Yale, or Princeton?

There would have been an uproar. The army, over the years, had always drawn its officer corps from the college campuses, where you presumably have men of character and leadership. That avenue was mostly cut off by educational deferments, but the army still had to have officers. So they had to lower their requirements for the officer candidate schools. That brought about the commissioning of people like Lieutenant Calley.

What were the differences between the World War II soldier, the Korean War soldier, and the GI in Vietnam?

The World War II soldier was fighting a war that the American people perceived as a war concerned with the survival of America and the American way of life. He was older—his average age was twenty-six. Everybody was expected to serve, and most did. Men who were drafted would have volunteered anyway. The whole country was mobilized; the war was viewed as a crusade.

And in Korea?

Korea—let me just make some parenthetical remarks. The Korean War has not been studied and analyzed, and there is more to be learned from that war than from any of the three. There are so many lessons to be learned.

Give me one or two of the most important lessons.

We didn't have a national objective. When the North Koreans came down in 1950, the policy makers in Washington did not face up to what the objective was. Was it to restore South Korea, along the 38th Parallel? Or was it to defeat North Korea? Or was it to go to the Yalu, which they did, and it was a terrible mistake. They could have given MacArthur firm instructions: You will destroy the enemy south of the 38th Parallel. If that had been done, I am not sure that the Chinese ever would have come in. This was our first experience with limited war, and our policy makers blew it. The Korean War only lasted three years; if it had lasted five, you would have had the same public reaction as you did with Vietnam.

How old was the average soldier in Korea? He couldn't have been as young as the one in Vietnam.

Oh, no, I think I can make a fairly reasonable guess, it was probably twenty-three, twenty-four years of age. In Vietnam we threw a terrible burden, under very difficult circumstances, on soldiers who were even younger—as I've said, less than nineteen.

What was our objective in Vietnam?

It was not to conquer Vietnam. It was to get the Communists off the backs of the people who wanted to live in a non-Communist state. The objective was made clear by the National Security Council. Now, you hear time and again that there was no strategy. That is an erroneous statement. One can say that it was not the optimal strategy, and I would agree with that. But there was a strategy. That was to bring the North Vietnamese to the conference table, as we had done in Korea. It was not to unify the two Vietnams, it was not to defeat the enemy as we had done in World War II. Now, one can criticize the tactics involved, and that airpower was not used by Johnson in 1968, as it might have been. If he had done what Nixon did four years later, they would have come to the conference table and we would have been in a position of strength.

Are you referring to the Christmas bombing in 1972?

Yes. Have you ever heard of a man named John Colvin? Several years ago, John Colvin wrote a piece for *The Washington Quarterly*. Colvin was the British consul in Hanoi in 1966 and 1967. He was in constant contact with many of the senior leaders in Hanoi. And in this article, he stated that at the end of '67, Hanoi's morale was so low that the leadership was on the verge of capitulation—by virtue of the damage done by our air strikes. Our planes would bomb a bridge, and they would work every night for a week to repair it. We would take a photograph of it, and then the next day we'd drop it again. This was beginning to wear on them, and Colvin thought they were on the verge of capitulation. But the interesting thing is that you saw no visibility in our media about efforts being made to bring the North Vietnamese to the conference table. After their defeat in the Tet Offensive, I thought there was really a good chance of that.

What about the Tet Offensive? In these past twenty years, have you had any new thoughts about Tet?

No new ones, but some earlier ideas have been reinforced. When Tet hit, we knew they were going to attack. We didn't know how massive that attack would be, but we knew it would be in multiple places. At that time, I put a cable in to Admiral U. S. Grant Sharp, Jr., the U.S. Pacific commander, and the Joint Chiefs of Staff, saying, in effect, that the enemy has changed his strategy and we should reevaluate our own. I felt that if we had done that, if the bombing campaign had been stepped up then, that the outcome of the war could have been different.

The Tet Offensive was a terrible gamble by the enemy, and they were crushed. After that defeat, I think there was a really good chance of bringing them to the conference table. But public opinion was disgusted with a war that was dragging on and on. The president later told me that he didn't have the votes. Johnson counted the votes; most politicians do. But I object to saying that was the point when the war was lost. That was the point when it became evident that America was not going to make good its commitment to the Vietnamese.

Tet was our last chance. We had thrown away all our trump cards when we finally got them to the negotiating table in Paris. Their big trump card was the POWs. We didn't have any trump cards because we were already withdrawing our troops. We'd even sanctioned letting their troops remain on South Vietnamese soil.

Hypothetically, if you could sit down with any of your opposing NVA commanders, who would it be and what would you ask?

At that time, General Giap was the commander of the NVA forces, and I think I would ask him why they launched the Tet Offensive. They proceeded to fight our type of war—and where did they get the impression that there would be a public uprising? That the South Vietnamese would flow to their ranks? That Tet would be a success, militarily? I would also be very curious to know how they knew that we were not going to cross the Laotian and Cambodian borders. Did they get that from the Russians?

Was consideration ever given to using nuclear weapons in Vietnam?

We had no tactical weapons in South Vietnam, but if we needed them, they could have been flown in. This was my thought process: It was conceivable that a situation would arise when the president, through the chain of command, would ask me if it would be feasible to use a tactical nuclear weapon. After I had that thought, I talked to Admiral Sharp. We agreed it was conceivable, not probable, that we could be asked about the use of a tactical nuclear weapon. Both of us knew what was available. We decided that we would study the options. For example: Under what circumstances could a tactical nuclear weapon be used? What type of weapon would be appropriate? How would it be delivered? What would be the influence of factors like weather patterns, etc.? When LBJ heard about the study group, he said, "Knock it off." It was rather ironical. We were doing the study so we could have answers in case he asked. I wasn't disposed to recommend it. But you can't make a decision unless you do a study.

In your autobiography, you write, "I later learned that President Johnson and his advisors did not want to get the American people stirred up, because there was a

fear that the hawks would get the upper hand, and possibly provoke a confronta-
tion with China or Russia." Do you still believe that?

I did at the time I wrote the book. In view of Red China's conduct since that
time, I'd be inclined to back off. What they didn't appreciate was the historical
animosity between the Chinese and the Vietnamese. Whether the Vietnamese
would have invited the Chinese to come in, I don't know. The last time the
Chinese came down, they stayed for a thousand years.

Does Vietnam ever get to you?

I had three cases of amebic dysentery. [Laughs.] I never let Vietnam get to
me. The psychological pressures on a commander are there; you can't escape
them. But frankly, I don't have any strong sense of pressures as I look back, even
though I was putting in sixteen hours a day, seven days a week.

Has your country ever let you down?

Well, I don't think so, except— Let me put it this way. I was a little surprised
that the government didn't in some way come to my rescue after that hatchet
job by CBS. [The CBS documentary *The Uncounted Enemy* alleged that Westmoreland manipulated enemy troop strength figures.] That was a disillusioning
experience for me.

Philosophically and psychologically, they were in staunch support, but from
the practical standpoint, there wasn't anything they could do.

What do you mean?

The government picking up the legal tab of a private individual.

There is one solution that has come to me that did not occur to me at the
time. This is interesting, and you're the first person I've ever mentioned this to.
In retrospect, there was another course of action I could have taken. As a retired
officer, I could have demanded that the Department of the Army try me for
doing what CBS said that I had done. That would have put the burden of proof
on CBS in a court-martial atmosphere, where there would be a jury of officers.
It would be a military tribunal with officers who knew what the war was all
about. You can't get a civilian jury that understands something as technical as
intelligence on the battlefield, the chain of command, the responsibility of a
commander.

Can someone ask for that and get it?

Well, theoretically, I think so, but practically, I don't know. But it is something that rather intrigues me. CBS would have looked like fools after it was over. It would have cost me a lot less money, too.

How was the money raised?

By a not-for-profit foundation.

Did it actually cost you anything?

Oh, yes, about sixty thousand dollars.

That's a lot of money.

It was tax-exempt. But not peanuts.

Doesn't it take courage to do what you've done during the last ten or fifteen years?

I don't think of it as courage. Facts are facts.

I always ask veterans if they dream about the war after it's over. Do you have Vietnam dreams?

Not that I can recall. In most of my dreams, I'm dreaming that I lost my baggage, or the keys to my car.

The Mystery of Khe Sanh

JAMES WARREN

Nineteen sixty-eight was one of those years marked by its tumult, a historic year probably, a turning point possibly. Did the New Order of youth take over, with long-lasting results? Did an older, more conservative one reassert itself in the end? Vietnam, the war that seemed eternal, underlay everything that year: the American cities that went up in flames, the assassinations of Robert Kennedy and Martin Luther King, Jr., the student riots in Paris, the "occupation" of Columbia University that began almost festively and ended in a riot, more riots at the Democratic Convention in Chicago, the Prague Spring put down by Soviet tanks in August—and, finally, almost as an afterthought, the election of Richard M. Nixon, as the buds of tomorrow were abruptly pinched off. For the nations of the non-Communist world, 1968 had been a terrible interval, one that must have given the prolegarchs of Moscow and Beijing immense satisfaction.

Fittingly enough, the year began with an event that became a national obsession for Americans that winter: the North Vietnamese siege of the combat base at Khe Sanh. It was, as James Warren points out, "the longest and most dramatic battle in America's longest war." Sensing what seemed to be the importance of Khe Sanh, print and TV journalists, photographers, and film crews descended on the menaced outpost. There were so many that they were allowed to stay only a day or so at most. Roughly one quarter of all TV reports that winter dealt with the plight of the marines at the beleaguered outpost. Then the media swarms returned to Saigon to write speculations on whether or not Khe Sanh would turn into an American Dien Bien Phu. President Johnson was haunted by the same fear. He commissioned a three-dimensional terrain model for the windowless White House basement chamber known as the

Situation Room. In the words of *Washington Post* reporter Don Oberdorfer, LBJ "insisted on a formal paper from the Joint Chiefs, 'signed in blood,' as he put it, that Khe Sanh could be held." The president didn't want a major military catastrophe on his watch. The Khe Sanh malady was contagious, from the top down. The American public caught it. The siege—and the Communist Tet Offensive that began on January 30 at the beginning of the South Vietnamese lunar new year—put paid once and for all any optimistic visions of the war.

Warren's account deals with the many questions of Khe Sanh, some of which are still unanswered and may not be until the archives of the former North Vietnam are fully opened. Was the Dien Bien Phu comparison truly apt? Had General Westmoreland concentrated too many men—over 50 percent of all U.S. maneuver battalions—in the northernmost provinces of South Vietnam, close to the 17th Parallel boundary? Was Khe Sanh merely a Communist ruse designed to distract Westmoreland from the countrywide Tet Offensive? Was he correct in calling Khe Sanh his proudest moment, as he did in the interview with Laura Palmer? Why did holding the base seem so important that he even considered dropping tactical nuclear bombs on the area held by two North Vietnamese divisions? ("Although I established a small secret group to study the subject," Westmoreland wrote in 1976, "Washington so feared that some word of it might reach the press that I was told to desist.") Tactical nukes or no, did he manage to turn Khe Sanh into a death trap for the North Vietnamese—partly because they, too, gave in to the same obsession that gripped the Americans? And why was the base eventually, and so unceremoniously, abandoned? Some may ask why this backwater was even contested. Who really won? And, in the end, did it matter?

JAMES WARREN, a New York editor, is the author of *Portrait of a Tragedy: America and the Vietnam War* (with Harry G. Summers) and *Cold War: The American Crusade Against World Communism, 1945–1991.*

IT WAS A SERIOUS PROBLEM, and it required a quick response: A team from the 3rd Reconnaissance Battalion had been patrolling north of Khe Sanh Combat Base (KSCB), the westernmost U.S. Marine outpost along the demilitarized zone separating North and South Vietnam. On January 17, 1968, the recon team was moving slowly and quietly along one of the many gnarled ridges that made up Hill 881 North when they were ambushed by soldiers of the Vietnam People's Army—regular troops of what is popularly known in the United States as the North Vietnamese Army (NVA).

Within just a few seconds, the team commander and his radio operator were dead. The six other Americans, all wounded, pulled back from the NVA firing positions as fast as they could and called the commanding officer of India Company, 3rd Battalion, 26th Marine Regiment, Captain Bill Dabney, whose command post was on Hill 881 South. The team was in big trouble. As luck would have it, Captain Dabney had a platoon from his company based on the very same hill. It was quickly dispatched to attempt a rescue. With the help of helicopters from the combat base, Lieutenant Thomas Brindley's 3rd Platoon managed to pull off the rescue with great aplomb. But in the excitement of the action, the rescuers left behind a radio and the sheets of radio codes called shackle cards.

The cards were considered vital; Dabney didn't want them in NVA hands. Two days later, he sent out another platoon to collect the gear. This platoon, too, came under attack from an estimated twenty-five North Vietnamese soldiers. Lieutenant Harry Fromme's marines withdrew under the steady cover of mortar fire. It was the second time the NVA had engaged his marines on the same terrain: That was unusual. Something big was in the wind, or so Dabney believed. And the captain was not the only marine officer to think so.

Since November, signs of increased enemy activity—fighting holes, bunker complexes, widened trails, even newly created, paved roads—were uncovered on a regular basis uncomfortably close to the KSCB and the surrounding hills that protected the approaches to the main marine outpost. Recon teams were spotting NVA soldiers brazenly marching out in the open. Often the enemy soldiers were wearing new uniforms and carrying new AK-47 assault rifles. Meanwhile, the U.S. Army Green Berets at Lang Vei, which lay seven miles to the west of KSCB, were discovering ominous signs of an enemy escalation on their deep patrols into Laos. What the foot patrols observed, the vast array of electronically gathered intelligence—from both the air and the ground—confirmed. There were more than ten thousand enemy soldiers in the area, and more were en route.

Perhaps the most dramatic evidence of the big build-up came in the form of a group of NVA officers who had been shot on January 2 while attempting to gather intelligence just a few hundred meters from the eastern perimeter of the Khe Sanh base. This incident, more than any other, ratcheted up concern over whether KSCB could be held—concern that reached to the highest levels. Walt Rostow, the president's national security adviser, told Lyndon Johnson that in the estimation of the field commander in Vietnam, General William Westmoreland, "The NVA were massing for another major offensive in this area, perhaps targeted this time around Khe Sanh."

On January 11 a gravely concerned General Earle Wheeler, chairman of the Joint Chiefs of Staff, cabled the field commander in Saigon from Washington, asking for contingency plans in the event of an attack, and asking if such an attack might be forestalled by a marine withdrawal to the east. The next night, after conferring with the III Marine Amphibious Force commander, Lieutenant General Robert R. Cushman, Jr.—commander of the marines in all of I Corps, the northernmost military region of South Vietnam—Westmoreland cabled back his answer: Two marine battalions could be on the scene in twelve hours if needed. He had already alerted an army brigade about going north to fill the marines' shoes if they had to. And Westmoreland vigorously rejected the withdrawal option:

This area is critical to us from a tactical standpoint as a launch base for SOG [Special Operations Group, a Saigon-based joint CIA-military command] teams and as flank security for the strong point obstacle system [a series of manned outposts and unmanned barriers stretching across much of the demilitarized zone (DMZ)] it is even more critical from a psychological viewpoint. To relinquish this area would be a major propaganda victory for the enemy. Its loss would seriously affect Vietnamese and U.S. morale. In short, withdrawal would be a tremendous step backwards.

Recalling the situation on the eve of the battle, artillery aerial observer Major Jim Stanton "saw literally hundreds of North Vietnamese soldiers in their bright green, easy-to-see uniforms. They were in large numbers, they were bivouacking in the open, they were doing things that made it very difficult to patrol. I could go out and recon areas by fire and *always* get North Vietnamese to scatter."

It was against this backdrop that Dabney asked his battalion commander for clearance to conduct a reconnaissance in force on the morning of January 20. He would use most of India Company's infantry to determine just what the enemy was up to in the area of Hill 881 North.

The first several hours of the patrol were slow going. Progress was hampered by fog—it was the tail end of the monsoon season—and by waist-high elephant grass and the hilly terrain. As the marines advanced toward Hill 881N along two ridgelines, approaching a series of four small hills, NVA infantry opened fire from their fortified positions on those small hills.

Within thirty seconds, twenty marines were dead or wounded. Brindley's platoon, leading the right column, was stopped cold and went to ground in the folds of the hillside. Firing and maneuvering continued for several hours. In the course of the engagement, the NVA shot down a CH-46 chopper sent in to retrieve the wounded. Brindley called in artillery fire on the NVA positions, momentarily silencing their guns. Once the artillery barrage lifted, the lieutenant rose to lead his men in an attack on the NVA positions. It was described by one observer as a classic U.S. Marine frontal assault, like "a page out of Chesty Puller. . . ."

It worked. The NVA broke and fled their positions as the Americans continued to pour small arms, mortar, and artillery fire in the direction of the enemy withdrawal. But Thomas Brindley was killed at the moment he reached the summit of the NVA stronghold, and the recon team that had joined in the assault was overrun and shot up by the fleeing NVA troops. The next objective for the marines was to retrieve that recon team, all of whom were wounded or dead. This, too, was accomplished, but several more marines fell in the process.

It was now late in the afternoon. Dabney could see the NVA were preparing to counterassault the ground that had cost him the lives of seven men, and he acted fast. He called in jet strikes on the enemy positions and then pulled his weary marines off Hill 881 North. By the order of Colonel David Lownds, who commanded the entire 26th Regiment, they were to return to their own real estate on Hill 881S.

Although they couldn't have known it at the time, Dabney's marines had just concluded the first fight in the longest and most dramatic battle of America's longest war. Within weeks, an apprehensive American public was transfixed by the developments around Khe Sanh, and they remained so even as the war's great turning point, the Tet Offensive, came and went. From late January through March, stark and striking images of an isolated garrison of some 6,000 American troops (and one battalion of South Vietnamese Rangers) locked in combat against an estimated 20,000 NVA soldiers were transmitted via nightly newscasts, newspapers, and magazines.

It seemed to many Americans, including a number of military strategists, a deadly gambit; the marine outpost was in effect totally surrounded. Route 9, the only road connecting the base to the string of other U.S. strongpoints along the DMZ, had been under enemy control since August 1967, when the marines determined that too many men were required to protect the "Rough Rider" truck convoys that brought food, ammunition, and desperately needed construction supplies to KSCB. This meant that the 150 tons of supplies a day it would take to keep the marines in fighting shape had to be transported by air alone.

Lyndon Johnson, the man who had first committed combat troops to Vietnam in March 1965, became obsessed with the fate of the marines and the dynamics of the battle, with its dangers, and with its potential to alter the whole calculus of a mystifying and frustrating war against a third-rate power. On many nights during the siege that followed the fierce combat, Johnson could be found in the basement of the White House in his bathrobe, poring over the latest strategic assessments. Indeed, Johnson was delighted when the National Photographic Center provided him with an exact model of the combat base and surrounding environs so he could better acquaint himself with each day's developments. "No single battle of the Vietnam War has held Washington and the nation in such complete thrall as has the impending struggle for Khe Sanh," observed *Time* magazine in mid-February.

No one was more focused on the impending battle than its chief architect,

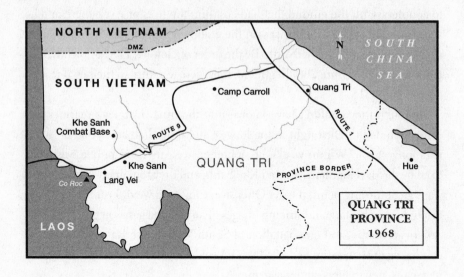

QUANG TRI PROVINCE 1968

NORTH VIETNAM

DMZ

SOUTH VIETNAM

SOUTH CHINA SEA

N

• Camp Carroll

• Quang Tri

ROUTE 1

Khe Sanh Combat Base

ROUTE 9

QUANG TRI

• Khe Sanh

PROVINCE BORDER

• Hue

Co Roc ▲

• Lang Vei

LAOS

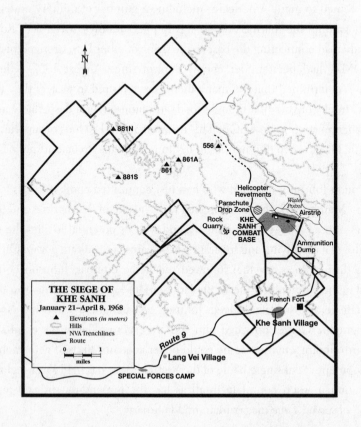

N

▲ 881N

556 ▲

▲ 861A

▲ 861

▲ 881S

Helicopter Revetments

Parachute Drop Zone

Water Point

Airstrip

Rock Quarry

KHE SANH COMBAT BASE

Ammunition Dump

THE SIEGE OF KHE SANH
January 21–April 8, 1968

▲ Elevations *(in meters)*
⌒ Hills
▬ NVA Trenchlines
⌒ Route

0   1
miles

Old French Fort

Khe Sanh Village

Route 9

• Lang Vei Village

SPECIAL FORCES CAMP

William Childs Westmoreland, who had for over a year pressured and cajoled marine command in Da Nang first to keep Khe Sanh operational, then to expand the size of its garrison. Westmoreland had moved a number of army battalions up north to I Corps in preparation for what he plainly conceived of as the war's Big Battle.

For their part, General Lew Walt, who commanded all the marine units in Vietnam from June 1965 through May 1967, and his successor, General Robert Cushman, couldn't see the wisdom of holding the line so far to the west of South Vietnam's highly populous coastal plains. It was, at least in marine command's estimation, a war for the villages. The area around the village of Khe Sanh, under twenty miles from Laos, was thickly jungled, mountainous terrain, populated largely by isolated pockets of Bru Montagnard tribesmen. To the marines, Khe Sanh seemed a distraction from the main theater of the war. They saw their large infantry units' primary use as providing a shield for the Combined Action Companies, which worked to win hearts and minds in the village hamlets by providing security, training, medical care; improving the lot of the Vietnamese people; and, of course, denying the Vietcong access. As Marine Corps Brigadier General Lowell English put it, "When you're at Khe Sanh, you're not really anywhere. . . . You could lose it and you haven't lost a damn thing."

So why did Westmoreland persist with such ardor in having it out with the NVA at Khe Sanh when the people ostensibly in charge of the war in I Corps thought it futile? Both during and after the battle, the army general was never at a loss for reasons. He described the base as the "crucial anchor of our defense along the demilitarized zone." It was, in his view, necessary to cut off infiltration into South Vietnam from the Ho Chi Minh Trail, and KSCB was an optimal place to conduct operations against the trail. Westmoreland also told his senior officers in Saigon that the base would be necessary for his ambitious plan to launch a devastating thrust into Laos, designed to destroy the enemy's base camps as well as the network of trails and roads by which he moved his supplies into the heart of South Vietnam. (The invasion into Laos in 1967 and 1968 was not a live option, as Washington had ruled out any combat actions in either Cambodia or Laos. Hence, Westmoreland's plan rested on the assumption that he could convince Washington to jettison that restriction.)

Over twenty-five years after the battle, it seems to this observer that the overriding reason for Westmoreland's ardent desire to fight it out with the NVA at Khe Sanh was not rooted in any particular tactical equation. Rather, he saw the impending battle in the context of a larger canvas: If he did not react to Hanoi's movement of two elite divisions into the area, he would be letting the Communists gain a key psychological edge in a war where psychology and perceptions played a truly defining role.

What was more, if the enemy could be lured into the area of the KSCB in large concentrations, the general reckoned, he could inflict shatteringly high casualties on their units by using U.S. air assets, which included hundreds of fighters, fighter-bombers, helicopters, prop planes, and even strategic B-52 bombers. It was a force capable of unleashing ordnance with a destructive power the likes of which had never been deployed against ground troops in the history of warfare. It might very well cause the Communists to recognize that their effort to conquer South Vietnam was destined to fail. "In a war that frustrated traditional analysis or easy measurement," comments historian Robert Pisor in *The End of the Line*, "Khe Sanh would be the single, dramatic blow that would cripple the North Vietnamese beyond any question or doubt. It would be the definitive victory, the perfect finishing stroke for [Westmoreland's] generalship in Vietnam, and he had prepared for it painstakingly."

Adding to the drama, and very much on Westmoreland's mind on January 20 as Dabney's marines made their way back to the comparative safety of Hill 881S, was a bit of history in the form of another battle of some note. In April 1954 a French garrison in a remote fortress at Dien Bien Phu in northern Vietnam, considerably larger than that of the marines at KSCB, found itself under a choking siege by the Viet Minh. Displaying great patience, sacrifice, and resilience, the Vietnamese troops under General Vo Nguyen Giap hauled large artillery pieces through the jungle, often pulled by hundreds of porters, not trucks or animals, and pummeled the French positions out of existence one at a time. More than 10,000 of France's finest troops surrendered; only 73 members of the 15,000-man garrison at Dien Bien Phu escaped the grasp of the Viet Minh. With the humiliation of the fall of Dien Bien Phu, the war in Indochina ended for France.

The Big Question in January 1968 was whether the NVA could turn in a performance similar to that of their predecessors, or whether the Americans—with far greater firepower and air support than the French could even have imagined, and with their unrivaled intelligence-gathering technology—could accomplish a "Dien Bien Phu in reverse." Throughout the siege at Khe Sanh, Bernard Fall's book about the French disaster, *Hell in a Very Small Place*, was much read by marine officers and by the increasingly large army of reporters inevitably drawn to what was shaping up as Vietnam's long-awaited Big Battle.

Surely Dien Bien Phu was also on the mind of Colonel David Lownds on January 20, when he learned that a low-ranking NVA officer had defected, turning himself in to marines at the KSCB and revealing that his former brothers-in-arms were poised to strike Lownd's marines within twenty-four hours. The officer, Lieutenant La Thanh Tonc, told marine intelligence interrogators that Hill 861, which lay about five kilometers to the northwest of the base, was to be attacked and overrun that very night. Once that key hill outpost was in North Vietnamese hands, said the NVA officer, a regimental-size attack on the KSCB would commence. Colonel Lownds and his boss, General Ravthon Tompkins, commander of the 3rd Marine Division, decided there was nothing to lose by assuming the information was accurate. That night all units were put on 50 percent nighttime alert. Sure enough, at precisely twelve-thirty A.M. on January 21, more than two hundred NVA soldiers, led by elite sappers called Dac Cong, assaulted the Hill 861 mini-fortress from their positions on nearby Hill 861A, blowing holes in the marines' perimeter wire with bangalore torpedoes and satchel charges. The company commander was wounded three times, and his gunnery sergeant was killed. Within a few minutes, the helicopter landing pad was in enemy hands, and NVA soldiers were running all around the firing positions of the marines, who were forced to withdraw to a smaller, higher position.

With the help of expert mortar support from Dabney's India Company marines on nearby Hill 881S (which wasn't attacked at all that night), the K Company marines regrouped and counterattacked, inflicting heavy punishment on the NVA with knives and rifle butts as well as small arms fire. By five-fifteen A.M. the only North Vietnamese on Hill 861 were dead.

But Lownds and his marines had little time to celebrate the success of the K Company victory. Just a few minutes after the fighting had stopped, the KSCB itself came under rocket attack from the NVA positions on Hill 881N. One of the first hits occurred in the eastern sector of the base perimeter, landing directly in the main ammunition dump and setting off, in Robert Pisor's words, "a colossal explosion that bathed the Khe Sanh plateau in a glaring white light of apocalypse." To some of the marines near the explosion, it must indeed have seemed like the world was about to end, as helicopters tumbled over and clouds of tear gas enveloped the landscape. All sorts of artillery ammunition, some white-hot, were scattered about the base, and fires burned within the marine positions for two full days.

At six-thirty A.M. the North Vietnamese mounted their assault, but not on the main base, as the NVA defector had predicted. Instead, their target was the village of Khe Sanh, which happened to be the seat of the regional South Vietnamese government. There, a small contingent of civic action marines were stationed. They led poorly armed local security forces in the defense of the village. To the surprise of many, the small contingent repulsed two attacks with minimal casualties. After the second attack, and a thousand rounds of support artillery fire, Lownds decided that he couldn't defend a position so far from his main outpost, so he ordered helicopters to retrieve the marines in the village. The local forces would have to walk back to KSBC.

The effect of the first (of many) NVA bombardments of the base was devastating. Over 90 percent of the marines' ammunition had gone up in smoke. The airstrip had been damaged: Just 2,000 feet of the 3,000-foot aluminum runway were usable. Most of the aboveground bunkers had been severely damaged or destroyed. That meant smaller transport planes had to be used to replenish desperately needed ammunition. The situation, Lownds remarked, "was critical, to say the least."

The hill fights and the artillery barrage on January 21 set the tone and pattern for the battle of Khe Sanh, a struggle that lasted two and a half months. Almost every day the base would take fire from rockets, mortars, and large-caliber artillery, most of which originated in three brilliantly camouflaged locations: Hill 881N; Co Roc Mountain in Laos (which lay maddeningly out of range of even the largest American artillery, the 175mm U.S. Army guns to the east of Khe Sanh at Camp Carroll); and "position 305," about ten thousand meters northwest of Hill 881S. Meanwhile, navy, air force, and marine airpower continued to punish the NVA by dropping tons of high-explosive ordnance and napalm on suspected troop and headquarters positions of the two crack enemy forces in the area: the 304th and the 325C divisions. As the marines busied themselves each day digging deeper into their cloud-shrouded plateau, reinforcing their bunkers, revetments, and minefields along suspected routes of approach, they were sporadically probed by NVA sappers and snipers. And they steeled themselves for the assault that every day seemed more and more likely. "Thus," writes Marine Corps historian Captain Moyers Shore II, "the two adversaries faced each other like boxers in a championship bout; one danced around nimbly throwing jabs while the second stood fast waiting to score the counter punch that would end the fight."

What happened on the last day of January—or rather, what did not happen—added another element of mystery to the cat-and-mouse game around the Khe Sanh plateau. Hanoi on this day launched its biggest offensive of its war against the United States and South Vietnam. Combined Vietcong–North Vietnamese forces struck ferociously at five district capitals, military installations, and all of South Vietnam's major cities, including Saigon, where a VC sapper team made its way into the U.S. embassy compound. But on this day KSCB received not even a single probe. Most of the Tet attacks resulted in disastrous casualties for the Communists, and they were quickly repulsed. Hanoi did succeed, however, in greatly discrediting the American military's rosy predictions that the end of the war was coming into view in early 1968.

The Tet Offensive attacks also ratcheted up concern over the enemy's true intentions regarding Khe Sanh: Would the flurry of attacks on January 31 be the trigger for the big assault on the isolated marine garrison? It was in this context that General Westmoreland considered the possibility of using "a few small nuclear weapons" at Khe Sanh—the first time that option had seriously been weighed by an American general since the Korean War.

If the NVA were going to overrun KSCB, they would have to neutralize the company of marines dug in on Hill 861A, northeast of Hill 861 and about four kilometers northwest of KSCB. Pfc. Mike Delaney of Echo Company, 2nd Battalion, 26th Marines, remembered that "there was nothing but double- and triple-canopy jungle on the hill [861A] when we got there. It was heavy growth, and we saw a lot of wildlife. . . . It was super hot. It was like a smothering heat. Very little wind. The vegetation held the heat close to the ground. It was . . . constantly humid. The fog would roll up from the valley . . . that was scary because we couldn't see anything below us."

What lay below the marines on the night of February 4–5 was a battalion of NVA assault troops. At 3:05 A.M. that night, the Americans on the hill were on the bad end of a mortar barrage that led to one of the most ferocious engagements of the entire siege. The NVA, an estimated battalion from the 325C Division, overran Echo Company's first platoon. Captain Earle Breeding's troops quickly mounted a counterassault, attacking the enemy with bayonets, handguns, and bare hands. The company commander remembered that one marine knocked an enemy soldier unconscious with a roundhouse punch, then finished him off with a knife. "It was uncontrolled pandemonium," Breeding recalled. The engagement lasted over three hours, during which time the NVA mounted their own counterassault. Bill Dabney's India Company on Hill 881S was kept quite busy, firing some 1,100 mortar rounds in support of their brother company on Hill 861A. Air strikes were called in and may well have broken up the enemy's reserve battalion, as it was on the verge of attacking (it never did). The North Vietnamese left 109 bodies on the battlefield that night. Seven marines died, and thirty-five had to be evacuated from the hill with serious wounds.

On Hill 861A, the marines prevailed. An extraordinary five Navy Crosses were awarded for heroism in action that night. On February 7 it was the NVA's turn: The Special Forces camp seven miles west of KSCB was overrun; and for the first time in the Vietnam War, the enemy used tanks on the battlefield. Ten of the twenty-five Green Berets at Lang Vei that night were killed in the fighting, and as many as several hundred of the Civilian Irregular Defense Group (CIDG) strikers who were stationed in the Special Forces compound were lost to enemy fire as well.

The fall of Lang Vei greatly increased the rancor between the Special Forces and the marines, largely because Colonel Lownds had refused to mount an infantry relief force, fearing that it would face almost certain ambush. It also brought more than six thousand Bru and Laotian refugees to the front gate of the KSCB, seeking refuge from the increasingly intense artillery and aerial barrages that were turning the once lush landscape around Khe Sanh into a wasteland of charred earth and shrapnel-laden trees. The arrival of the civilians unnerved the marines, who feared the NVA might try to use them as a human screen behind which to mount an attack. Lownds was sympathetic to the locals, most of whom had family members fighting with the Americans, and he managed to evacuate the Laotians and some Vietnamese, but the Bru Montagnards, who had fought bravely and with great loyalty, were denied the right to evacuate to the lowlands by the Vietnamese government and had to fend for themselves in a hazardous combat zone.

Lang Vei emboldened the NVA—or so it seemed, for at 4:45 A.M. on the morning of February 8, they attacked painfully close to the KSCB perimeter, this time against the reinforced marine platoon on Hill 64, very near the rock quarry just to the west of the combat base. The NVA assault was murderously intense: Within fifteen minutes the force of sixty-five marines was reduced to just more than twenty fighters—everyone else was dead or too seriously wounded to carry on. The fight raged for hours, with the marines barely hanging on to a small portion of their original perimeter until reinforcements arrived with airpower at around eight-thirty A.M., driving off the attacking force.

On one of the 150 NVA corpses was found a map of KSCB showing that, as one veteran recalled, "almost to a bunker, they knew where almost everything we had was, including the positions of our underground ammo bunkers. If they had hit [in an assault on the main combat base], I'm sure an initial wave of RPG [rocket-propelled grenade] men . . . would have decimated many of these positions." That night on Hill 64, the official tally has it that twenty-four Americans were killed in action, and twenty-nine were wounded. (In fact, the total was probably somewhat higher: Many veterans hold firm to the belief that all U.S. casualty figures at Khe Sanh were deliberately set far below the real totals.)

By the second week in February, Khe Sanh and the fate of the marines had become an abiding concern of President Johnson and the Joint Chiefs of Staff. They were attempting to gauge not only the enemy's intentions but the soundness of their own field commander's strategy. In the National Security Council and in the highest reaches of the Pentagon, voices of skepticism were more and more in evidence. The marines were taking a daily pounding from gun positions that apparently could not be knocked out by artillery or airpower. The U.S. troops were unable to patrol more than a few hundred meters from their base, and even then invited ambush. Thoughtful men, even Westmoreland's protégé, the scholar-soldier General Maxwell Taylor, were beginning to have grave reservations about the rationale for holding on to so remote an outpost. And there was vigorous debate over whether the United States could effectively use marines as bait to lure the NVA infantry units into the open, to be crushed in a well-orchestrated bombing campaign. It was a new kind of tactic. Who knew if it would work?

In a reasoned and provocative memo to the president dated February 14, Taylor, then serving as the chief executive's personal military adviser, argued for a careful consideration of alternatives to keeping Khe Sanh. He felt that Westmoreland's own cables and statements revealed that the rationale for holding the base was faulty:

> [Westmoreland] concedes that Khe Sanh has not had much effect on infiltration from Laos, and it is not clear whether he regards the role of blocking the Quang Tri approach as of current or past importance [Taylor's emphasis]. Thus, General Westmoreland does not appear to argue strongly for the defense of Khe Sanh because of its present value. . . . Whatever the past value of the position, it is a positive liability now. We are allowing the enemy

to arrange at his leisure a set-piece attack on ground and in weather favorable to him and under conditions which will allow us little opportunity to punish him except by our air power.

The tremors of doubt running through official Washington led a determined Westmoreland to redouble his efforts to ensure that the United States stuck it out. He worked furiously at Military Assistance Command Vietnam to preserve a unified front among the senior staff, insisting that there was no room for negativism and defeatism, and in March that "there are no advantages of military significance accuring [sic] from abandoning Khe Sanh if it is indeed our purpose to eject or destroy the invading NVA forces."

While the president and the JCS doubted and debated, the NVA infantry entered a quiet phase. For two weeks, no major attack was attempted on either the hill strongpoints or the base. But the steady shelling went on and on. Often more than five hundred rounds a day struck inside the base, and the marines grew ever more weary of waiting for the big assault, eating K rations, and getting by (very often) on less than a canteen of drinking water a day.

Meanwhile, keeping the base in food and ammunition proved a daily struggle. A big KC-130 transport was hit by incoming fire and exploded on the runway on February 10, killing six people. Khe Sanh's airstrip, dreaded by fliers all over Vietnam, was a favorite target of NVA artillery men, and one of the most dangerous places in a country chock-full of them. So hazardous was the airstrip that the air force stopped landing its star transport, the big, vulnerable C-130, and began to drop supplies out of the back hatch of the C-130s and the smaller C-123s. The so-called low-altitude parachute extraction system required steady nerves and a strong heart, as pilots had to bring their planes to within five feet of the tarmac and then pull up hard, while parachutes dragged the cargo pallets out of the rear. In March and February alone, eight transports were lost to NVA antiaircraft fire. Hundreds more were tagged by small arms and machine-gun fire on the way in or out.

While the marine infantry and artillery struggled against their NVA counterparts, an astonishing array of combat, transport, and intelligence-gathering aircraft crisscrossed the skies over the plateau. Marine and navy A-6 Intruders, A-4 Skyhawks, and air force F-4 Phantoms and F-105s—indeed, planes from all over South Vietnam, Thailand, and even aircraft stationed on carriers in the South China Sea—were ready for action should they be called on by either the Tactical Air Direction Center of the First Marine Air Wing or the 7th Air

Forces Airborne Command and Control Center, both of which orchestrated the air war (not without friction) during the siege.

And then there were the B-52 bombers. During the course of the battle, these behemoths dropped 60,000 tons of ordnance on NVA positions. Add that to the 40,000 tons dropped by the tactical aircraft, and you have five tons of bombs dropped for each of the 20,000 NVA soldiers suspected of being in the general area of operations. NVA veterans still speak today with a mixture of terror and awe at the thunder that rained down on them. Some have said the B-52 strikes, coming as they did without any warning, were far and away the worst aspect of an extremely rough campaign.

And what of the marines' morale? It remained, by most accounts, surprisingly high, especially considering the rapidly deteriorating conditions the men were forced to endure. Sleep was a hard commodity to come by amid the sporadic shelling, and it was not at all unusual to see marines who'd fallen asleep standing up in their fighting holes. The condition of the base, and the marines' rough-edged up-the-middle approach to war, horrified U.S. Army officers who visited during the weeks of the siege. Major General John J. Tolson, commander of the 1st Cavalry Division, the outfit that ultimately relieved the marines at Khe Sanh in April, recalled that the base was "the most depressing and demoralizing place I ever visited. It was a very distressing sight, completely unpoliced, strewn with rubble, duds, and damaged equipment, and with the troops living a life more similar to rats than human beings."

The marines would have found humor in this statement, as they did about so much of their grim experience at Khe Sanh, for rats, big rats, were an integral part of life at KSCB. A favorite trick of the men was to lace peanut butter with C4 explosive and then watch their rodent companions drink themselves to death trying to quench their burning insides.

And there were always the digging and the preparing. Their lives depended on these, and nowhere so much as on the isolated hill positions that were favorite targets of the NVA guns. Lance Corporal Phil Torres of India Company, 3rd Battalion, 26th Marine Regiment, remembered:

We lived like moles, never leaving the trenches or bunkers. We were constantly digging—it never stopped—day and night, filling sandbags, digging trenches, carrying food. We were always laying German tape concertina wire, which was very dangerous to work with because it was covered with razor blades. . . . There was about a hundred meters of clearance between the concertina and the trenches. We built homemade bombs from 106mm recoilless-rifle shell canisters filled with C4 plastic explosive, machine-gun links, expended M-16 cartridges, anything we could find.

Rats, sporadic artillery rounds whistling toward their positions, cold food, bad weather, snipers, mortar fire—the catalog of irritants was indeed a long one, and those reporters who made the dangerous trip to KSCB were often struck by the peculiar horrors of the place. Michael Herr, whose reflections on Khe Sanh take up a good part of his masterpiece, *Dispatches*, recalled that "nothing like youth ever lasted in their faces for very long. It was the eyes: because they were either strained or blazed-out or simply blank, they never had anything to do with what the rest of the face was doing, and gave everyone the look of extreme fatigue or even a glancing madness."

The last week in February brought with it an unnerving revelation: On February 23 the shelling of the base reached an all-time high: 1,307 rounds landed within the perimeter. Two days later, NVA trenches approaching the base were detected for the first time. Hanoi's daily newspaper, *Nhan Dan*, turned up the volume on the propaganda, claiming that the actions in Quang Tri province had "shown the aggressors that they cannot avoid not only one but many Dien Bien Phus."

One of the newly discovered trenches ran due north, just twenty-five meters from the base perimeter. The Americans countered NVA efforts by saturating the trench areas with fire from C-47 "Spooky" gunships and jet strikes.

For the marines, February 25 was the darkest day of the siege. Increasing enemy pressure called for a response, and a large reconnaissance patrol (forty-seven men) was mounted to locate a mortar that had been particularly troublesome. About an hour into the patrol, the reinforced squads stumbled into an NVA ambush and were cut to ribbons; when another group of marines tried to come to the rescue, they, too, were caught in ferocious fire, and most of the men were killed outright. The toll for venturing beyond the confines of the base was great: twenty-eight dead and more than twenty wounded.

The appearance of trenches, the high level of shelling, the "lost patrol" of February 25—all of these deepened the apprehension and foreboding of Colonel Lownds and his troops. Meanwhile, the acoustic and seismic sensors that had been dropped along all the approaches to the base indicated ever increasing levels of activity just hundreds of meters from the marine positions.

On February 29, Lownds, thinking "this might well be the main attack," called in B-52 strikes on suspected NVA positions just a thousand-plus meters from the base. The results, recalled the marine colonel, "were devastating . . . those strikes caught at least two battalions." Later that night, the enemy assaulted the perimeter where the sole South Vietnamese army (ARVN) battalion of the battle was in place, and they were repulsed handily.

Was that attack meant to be the main one? Records of NVA radio traffic that night indicate that a big assault may have been brewing, but like so much about the battle, the truth remains a mystery, in large part because we don't yet know when and why the NVA decided to scale down the number of combat units in the area of Khe Sanh. We do know, however, that the attack on the ARVN Rangers' positions following the B-52 attacks that night was the last serious probe by a large force of infantry of the KSCB.

On March 8 a front-page story in *The New York Times* offered a sobering comparison of Khe Sanh and Dien Bien Phu, at once reflecting the level of concern over the fate of the outpost and heightening it. Ironically, it was around that day that CIA and marine intelligence sources began to report a sharp diminution of enemy activity in the immediate area of KSCB. The heavy shelling, however, continued. On March 30, B Company of the 1st Battalion, 26th Regiment, fought a three-hour battle in close proximity to where their comrades had fallen during the lost patrol on February 25. Once the guns were silent, 115 NVA bodies were counted on the battlefield, against nine marines killed in action. It was the last big firefight of the battle of Khe Sanh.

The great ground assault that the marines had long awaited simply never came. By the end of the month, marines were running patrols farther and farther from the confines of the base perimeter. By the end of March, the siege of Khe Sanh had slipped into history. The North Vietnamese Army remained in the area and proved more than up to a good fight on occasion, but the clashes of the next months had none of the strategic overtones of those in January, February, and March.

Operation Pegasus, the relief of Khe Sanh, began on April 1, as the U.S. Army's 1st Cavalry Division pushed westward at breathtaking speed along the DMZ, meeting little resistance. The four battalions of the 26th Regiment under David Lownds, the men who'd done most of the fighting—and the waiting—at Khe Sanh, began being airlifted out of the area on April 18. They would never return as a unit.

Even before Lownds's troops left the base, the controversy over what role Khe Sanh played in the entire complex conflict had begun. It continues unabated today. In reflecting on the battle, William Westmoreland, the man who had insisted—against strong protest from the Marine Corps—that the base be held, felt that the siege would be remembered as "a classic example of how to defeat a numerically superior besieging force by coordinated application of firepower." Indeed, "Khe Sanh [was] one of the most damaging one-sided defeats among many that the North Vietnamese incurred, and the myth of General Giap's military genius was discredited."

Giap and his fellow Vietnamese soldiers have always held that they prevailed by manipulating Westmoreland, by causing him to focus his attention and his precious combat troops in the remote northwestern corner of Quang Tri province, far from where the real battle was in the cities and towns to the east. A number of respected American historians have accepted this view, including Stanley Karnow and Neil Sheehan, who writes in *A Bright Shining Lie*, "Khe Sanh was the biggest lure of the war. The Vietnamese Communists had no intention of attempting to stage a second Dien Bien Phu there. The objective of the siege was William Westmoreland, not the Marine garrison. The siege was a ruse to distract Westmoreland while the real blow (the Tet Offensive) was prepared."

The ruse theory has many merits, but it rests on no small measure of conjecture and takes a perhaps overgenerous view of the famous Vietnamese general's strategic acumen. If Giap did have a plan to assault the base—and he could have thought seriously about attacking, if the opportunity had arisen—it is naive to believe he would ever reveal it. And even if one grants that Giap had never contemplated overrunning the garrison, one has to ask whether the diversion of American forces to Quang Tri significantly altered the outcome of the "real battle": Tet.

Surely, considering the outcome of Tet, with so many fine Viet Cong units utterly destroyed by U.S. and South Vietnamese counterattacks, that is a hard case to make. If six or seven battalions of U.S. infantry had remained among the population centers instead of up north near the DMZ, if all the air assets focused on Khe Sanh had been evenly dispersed throughout the rest of the country, the Tet Offensive might have ended more quickly, but the strategic impact would not have changed an iota. Tet was a strategic victory for the

North Vietnamese, as it crushed the American public's will to continue the fight in Vietnam.

Giap, it would seem, paid for his "ruse" at Khe Sanh with the lives of at least ten thousand men, and he got precious little for it. Khe Sanh, it must be said, was a tactical victory for the United States. Yes, the NVA often got the best of the marines in brief firefights and ambushes at the squad level. But the Americans prevailed in all the major hill attacks, and U.S. artillery and airpower undoubtedly broke up many assaults before they managed to come off. Airpower, more than any other combat arm, crushed the American adversary around Khe Sanh. The diaries of North Vietnamese soldiers confirm the grim hardships of the campaign and the atrocious casualties caused by incessant aerial bombardment. The Americans suffered greatly, but their casualties were almost certainly under one tenth of the enemy's. (The official marine tally is 205 killed in action, which most veterans believe is a significant underestimation. In any case, it doesn't include more than fifty servicemen who were killed in the dangerous airspace above the base, nor the Green Berets who were killed at Lang Vei.)

The irony of Khe Sanh is that the tactical victory was sadly irrelevant. General Westmoreland, the Joint Chiefs of Staff, and the president had envisioned the confrontation as a great turning point. American military power was meant to crush two divisions of NVA infantry and, in the process, break Hanoi's will to carry on the fight against so powerful a foe. But that did not happen. The Vietnamese will to carry on the fight was just as strong after Khe Sanh as before—a tribute to the tenacity of the enemy.

Khe Sanh, the battle without a proper last act, helped to seal the fate of the war by highlighting the conflict's incomprehensibility to a weary public. To many observers, the battle demonstrated the futility of the American mind-set and way of war in Vietnam. Westmoreland, like many of the nation's military and political leaders, seemed utterly obsessed by his country's raw military strength and battlefield technological wizardry. In reading his statements and proclamations about Khe Sanh both during and after the battle, one senses that his faith in the vast array of killing tools at his disposal blinded him to the war's complexities and subtleties.

In June 1968, a few days after General Westmoreland surrendered command of MACV to General Creighton Abrams, marines began to dismantle the runway and raze Khe Sanh Combat Base with bulldozers and explosives.

Nothing was to be left for propaganda photos by the enemy. When the story reached the press, it set off a furor in the United States. MACV, aware of the public relations problem that came with abandoning a base described several months earlier as "the anchor of our defense" along the DMZ, issued a communiqué, explaining that with greater numbers of army troops in Quang Tri province facing fewer NVA units, it no longer made sense to hold so remote an outpost. Holding "specific terrain" was no longer necessary. Vietnam, the communiqué made clear, was a mobile war.

EPILOGUE

On the night of Sunday, March 31, 1968, President Johnson addressed the American people. He announced that naval vessels and aircraft would cease attacks on North Vietnam. The U.S., moreover, was ready to enter into negotiations. He ended his speech with a single surprise sentence: "I shall not seek, and will not accept, the nomination of my party for another term as your president."

In living rooms all over the country, people cheered. Car horns honked. The "twenty words that shook the world," *Newsweek* said, "gave the nation an almost cathartic sense of relief at the prospect of a move toward peace." Three days later came another surprise. Radio Hanoi announced that the Communists would come to the table. For a brief moment, it really did seem that the end of the war in Vietnam was just around the corner.

The Evacuation of Kham Duc

RONALD H. SPECTOR

Peace talks, after much argument about where they should take place, began in Paris on May 13, 1968. It was already a given that their fate would depend on the military situation half a world away. Indeed, the Communists went back on the offensive. They kept it up through much of May. They attacked across the thirty-nine-mile-long buffer at the 17th Parallel that formed the boundary between the two Vietnams: the famous demilitarized zone (though it wasn't)—or DMZ, as it was known more familiarly—that had been set up in the mid-1950s after the French vacated Indochina. They attacked Saigon and struck elsewhere along the seven-hundred-mile crescent of South Vietnam. The Americans called the new offensive "Little Tet." This time, without the distraction of Khe Sanh, they were better prepared.

The coastal wetlands south of the DMZ first saw a series of interconnected actions that, taken as one, may have constituted the largest single battle of the war. It was called Dai Do, after a contested river village, but the names of a number of hamlets might have done just as well. In a month of continuous fighting, the Communist push was stopped, but the North Vietnamese then went on the defensive, which they were better at anyway. American troops, Ronald H. Spector writes, were "sent against superbly concealed and protected Communist bunker complexes without benefit of adequate reconnaissance and sometimes without appropriate supporting arms. Units were often fed into battles piecemeal without any clear idea of enemy strength and dispositions." In terms of weaponry alone, the American M-16 rifle, which had a tendency to jam at the worst moments, was clearly inferior to the Communist AK-47. Was Dai Do a diversion for the more important attacks to the south? The

Americans did end in charge, but at a price. As Spector writes, they "suffered more than 1,500 casualties, including 327 dead, a figure equal to the number of marines killed at Khe Sanh over the entire seventy-seven days of the so-called siege."

On May 5, Saigon exploded, as rocket and mortar fire swept the city of 3 million. VC troops concealed by the Communist underground took over entire sections and held them for several days. Some 30,000 homes were destroyed; 500 civilians died, and another 4,500 were wounded, most of them in house-to-house fighting. "The Vietcong has no air force," the Saigon police chief remarked, "so it uses ours." Another Vietnamese official told a *Newsweek* reporter that "We cannot go on destroying entire blocks every time a Viet Cong steps into a house." As far as increasing numbers of Americans at home were concerned, our military in Vietnam could do nothing right.

The numbers of Communist attacks that May were impressive (as were their casualties), but the results were less so. There was one exception: the envelopment of Kham Duc. Ten miles from the Laotian border, Kham Duc was a base for the so-called Studies and Operations Group (SDG), reconnaissance teams that performed special operations inside Laos and along the Ho Chi Minh Trail. The Communists were especially eager to rid themselves of its annoying presence. The fighting at this Khe Sanh in reverse, which Spector describes here, may have been the most unequivocal debacle for American arms in Vietnam, though its final hours were also heroic ones. The end came on May 11–12 and may have provided the Communists with the victory they sought as the peace conference opened.

RONALD H. SPECTOR is a professor of history and international affairs at George Washington University in Washington, D.C. He is the author of *After Tet: The Bloodiest Year in Vietnam*, from which the story of Kham Duc is excerpted; *Eagle Against the Sun: The American War with Japan*; and *At War at Sea*. Spector served in Vietnam as a Marine Corps historian.

A T THE BEGINNING of April 1968, U.S. Marines and Air Cavalry troops in Vietnam lifted the siege of Khe Sanh in one of the largest operations of the war. As the North Vietnamese withdrew from the area of the beleaguered marine base, leaving behind evidence of their heavy losses, a communiqué from the headquarters of the U.S. commander, General William Westmoreland, declared that for the Communists, the battle of Khe Sanh had been "a Dien Bien Phu in reverse." Under two months later, however, U.S. forces were to suffer a sharp defeat at another remote outpost near the Laotian border—a defeat that was, in a sense, a Khe Sanh in reverse.

The months following the Tet attacks at the end of January had been a time of stress and of calamity not always averted. Early in February, Communist troops, supported for the first time by tanks, overran the Lang Vei Special Forces camp near Khe Sanh, killing 200 of its 500 defenders, including ten of its more than two dozen American advisers. After the much publicized fall of Lang Vei, Kham Duc was the last remaining Special Forces camp of I Corps along the Laotian border. Far from the urban centers and coastal farmlands, Kham Duc sat in the center of a mile-wide green bowl in the rugged country of northwestern Quang Tin province. Route 14, the principle north-south road through the border region, ran through the base. Just across that border, ten miles away, the roads and tracks of the Ho Chi Minh Trail extended their fingers south and east, some already reaching Route 14 itself.

Like Khe Sanh and Lang Vei, Kham Duc and Ngoc Tavak—its satellite camp three miles closer to Laos—did not truly block the enemy's infiltration into South Vietnam. The border country was too rugged, the Communists' lateral roads were too numerous, and the camps' garrisons were too small to do that; yet the units holding them kept the Communists under observation and frequently interdicted their movements. Their presence meant that there would always be some sand and gravel thrown into the smoothly meshed gears of the Laotian infiltration system.

Since early April, U.S. Army engineer units had been at work upgrading Kham Duc's runway and constructing a concrete base to support the radio navigation facility. As the improvements to the base progressed, so did Communist preparations for attack. By late April, U.S. intelligence was reporting large enemy units in the area, including elements of the 2nd Division of the North Vietnamese Army. A prisoner taken on May 3 reported that his unit was planning to attack Kham Duc. Four months before, when Khe Sanh had been similarly threatened, the Americans had poured in reinforcements and air support. Now the Americans again began reinforcing. A battalion task force of the Americal Division, consisting of the 2nd Battalion, 1st Infantry, an additional infantry company, and some supporting artillery, began arriving by air at Kham Duc late in the morning of May 10. Lieutenant Colonel Robert B. Nelson, commander of the 2nd Battalion, took charge of the camp.

Nelson's men joined about 60 army engineers, approximately 400 Civilian Irregular Defense Group (CIDG) soldiers, and the latter's South Vietnamese and U.S. Special Forces leaders and advisers. Neither as well armed nor as well trained as the North Vietnamese and the Vietcong, the CIDG were mercenaries that the Special Forces had recruited and organized from among the various highland, non-Vietnamese tribal, ethnic, and religious minorities. The CIDG's key missions were surveillance, scouting, patrol, and local security. Although their leaders were sometimes bound to the Special Forces and the government by personal ties or political deals, they were primarily freelance soldiers, hired as a group on a contractual basis. Their behavior in a crisis varied from cowardice and treachery to stalwart heroism, depending on the specific situation and the tribal group involved.

Even as reinforcements were arriving at Kham Duc, Ngoc Tavak was already under attack. Located on the site of an old French fort, Ngoc Tavak was defended by a 113-man CIDG Mobile Strike Force company, with eight U.S. Army Special Forces troops and three Australian training-team advisers. Thirty-three U.S. Marines manned two 105mm howitzers, which had recently been moved to Ngoc Tavak to interdict nearby North Vietnamese routes and trails. However, the howitzers were short of ammunition and could be resupplied only by air from Kham Duc.

At about three in the morning on May 10, the Communists opened their final heavy-artillery and mortar barrage against the base, followed by a ground attack some thirty minutes later. During the height of the action, some of the CIDG troops abandoned their positions and fled toward the compound, yelling, "Don't shoot, don't shoot, friendly, friendly." But once inside the compound, these "friendly" troops tossed grenades and satchel charges at the marine positions, causing heavy casualties. Some of the surviving Americans believed they could also hear the distinctive sound of carbines being fired at them by the CIDGs. (Only the CIDGs had carbines; NVA troops carried AK-47s, whose high-velocity rounds sound quite different.)

The Special Forces commander, Captain Christopher J. Silva, and the commander of the marine battery, Lieutenant Adams, were both badly wounded during the night. As the North Vietnamese attackers penetrated the perimeter and advanced into the eastern end of the camp, the remaining defenders pulled back and called for support from air force gunships and fighter-bombers. The defenders believed that some of the wounded were still on the western side of the camp, though as the North Vietnamese closed in, the Americans had no choice but to call for the gunships to blast the western side with their deadly fléchettes (artillery rounds with dartlike metal projections) and cannon fire.

At dawn two Australian warrant officers managed to organize a counterattack by the CIDG troops who were still loyal: They cleared the perimeter and recaptured the howitzer positions abandoned during the nighttime attack. Yet the marines were almost out of shells for their 105s.

Four CH-46 helicopters carrying reinforcements from Kham Duc arrived later that morning, greeted by a hail of fire from the North Vietnamese forces surrounding Ngoc Tavak. The first chopper managed to land safely and unload its cargo of about twenty-five CIDG troops, but as the second approached the landing zone, its fuel line was severed by automatic-weapons fire. The damaged chopper, fuel streaming from its fuselage, settled safely on the ground and unloaded its troops. The third helicopter landed alongside and discharged its reinforcements as the crew of the crippled CH-46 jumped aboard. But as the third chopper was about to lift off, it was hit by a rocket-propelled grenade round and burst into flames. The landing zone was now unusable, and only small UH-l medevac helicopters could land at the camp to take off the severely wounded. As one medevac chopper came in to hover off a nearby hill, a large number of panicky CIDG soldiers rushed aboard; others held on to the skids as the helicopter lifted off, then fell to their deaths several hundred feet below.

The senior surviving officer, Captain White of the Australian training team, was now in command. Requesting permission to evacuate the camp, he was told to hang on. But with the helicopter pad unserviceable, water and ammunition nearly exhausted, most of the Americans killed or wounded, and the steadiness of the CIDG a doubtful proposition, White believed he had no choice but to abandon the camp before darkness brought renewed attacks. The men destroyed the damaged helicopter and any weapons that they could not take with them.

Avoiding the obvious routes to Kham Duc, where the enemy was almost certain to be waiting in ambush, White led his men southeast through heavy jungle to a hill about a mile from Ngoc Tavak, where they hacked out a landing zone. CH-46s quickly swooped in to take the survivors back to Kham Duc.

The loss of Ngoc Tavak had been a costly one. Of the forty-four Americans and Australians at Ngoc Tavak, fifteen had been killed and twenty-three wounded, and two were missing. Of the hundred-odd CIDG troops, sixty-four were missing or had deserted, and thirty were dead or wounded. By the time the dazed and exhausted survivors reached Kham Duc, that camp, too, was under attack.

Scattered mortar fire rained down on the camp on May 11, as the last of the Americal reinforcements and additional supplies were flown into the besieged base. By the end of that day, there was a total of some 1,500 U.S. and CIDG soldiers at Kham Duc, as well as almost 300 dependents of the CIDG troops who had been evacuated from their village near the base. Many of the Americal troops had been sent to reinforce the outposts in the hills surrounding the bowl-shaped valley where the camp was located.

Late in the night of the eleventh, troops of the 1st Vietcong Regiment, 2nd NVA Division, began their final preparations for an assault on Kham Duc. Around four A.M. the Communists overran the first of the outposts, Number 7, on a hill northeast of the base. By that time, General Westmoreland had already decided to abandon the camp.

Since the arrival of U.S. forces in Vietnam, some of the largest and most stubborn battles had begun as contests for the control of Special Forces camps such as Khe Sanh. Kham Duc had appeared likely to be the next such battleground, with powerful enemy forces converging on the base, U.S. reinforcements arriving, and support and strike aircraft being summoned to aid the defenders.

Yet as U.S. commanders studied the impending battle, they began to have second thoughts. When Colonel Jonathan Ladd, commander of Special Forces in Vietnam, met with Lieutenant General Robert E. Cushman, Jr., the commander of the III Marine Amphibious Force (MAF), he found Cushman unwilling to commit more troops to Kham Duc. Ladd pointed out that strong reinforcements would be needed to hold the camp against an attack by a reinforced North Vietnamese regiment. But Cushman had few uncommitted troops to spare and was concerned about a new threat posed by the build-up of Communist forces in the An Hoa basin area southeast of Da Nang. A reserve CIDG Mobile Strike Force company had already been dispatched to another threatened Special Forces camp, Thuong Duc, located on the main western approaches to Da Nang. Cushman also pointed out that Kham Duc would be difficult to resupply and was beyond the artillery range of friendly supporting bases.

On the afternoon of May 11, Ladd accompanied the deputy commander of Military Assistance Command, Vietnam (MACV), Creighton Abrams, to a meeting with Cushman and Major General Samuel Koster, the Americal Division commander. Koster had assumed operational control of the Kham Duc battle. At the meeting, the III MAF staff briefed the generals on the situation at Kham Duc. They recommended that the camp be abandoned—or, as they phrased it, "relocated." Colonel Ladd strongly disagreed, pointing out that Kham Duc was the last South Vietnamese outpost of southern I Corps in the western mountains. He also emphasized that it was an important launching site for the super-secret teams innocuously called the Studies and Observation Group, which conducted reconnaissance missions and raids into Laos and other parts of Southeast Asia to observe and interdict lines of communication, capture prisoners, assess bomb damage, and collect intelligence. By 1968 the number of such missions had risen to more than three hundred a year. Further, Ladd suggested that the Communists might put a Kham Duc victory to propaganda use, especially in view of the peace talks opening in Paris.

Unmentioned but ever present during the deliberations were memories of the recent siege at Khe Sanh. Although American generals had always spoken of the battle with confidence and enthusiasm when addressing Washington or the media, they had found it an anxious and wearing experience, superimposed as it was on the widespread and bloody fights of Tet. Now, with this new mini-Tet looming, neither Abrams nor Cushman was inclined to begin another protracted battle. "The decision to evacuate was brought on considerably by the

Khe Sanh experience," wrote Westmoreland's operations officer. At the conclusion of the discussions, Abrams instructed Cushman to prepare plans for a withdrawal. Westmoreland approved the decision a few hours later.

By the time word of the decision to evacuate reached Colonel Nelson at Kham Duc, all seven of the hill outposts were under heavy attack. Squads and platoons of American soldiers reinforcing the CIDG troops on the hills fought desperately, supported by C-47 gunships dropping flares to illuminate the area and peppering the attackers with their mini cannon. As the outposts were overwhelmed, the defenders directed gunships and artillery fire onto their own positions. A few managed to escape into the Kham Duc perimeter, but many died in the hill outposts.

The fate of the outposts added to the sense of terror and foreboding within Kham Duc. The morning began with a fresh disaster when one of the first evacuation helicopters, an army CH-47, was hit by heavy ground fire as it landed on the runway. The chopper exploded, and its flaming hulk blocked the runway for over an hour. An A-1E fighter also was shot down.

As the sun rose over Kham Duc, burning away some of the morning fog, aerial observers beheld a grim sight: The camp was under almost continuous mortar fire, and heavy ground attacks were taking place against the northwestern perimeter. The burning CH-47 sent clouds of black smoke into the sky. On the nearby hills, radio antennae sprouted above the newly established NVA command posts.

Inside the perimeter, men tensely awaited the ground attack. The enemy mortar barrage increased in intensity, and a near-miss showered one squad with shrapnel. An 82mm mortar round scored a direct hit on a nearby mortar manned by CIDG personnel, killing or wounding all three of the crew. Specialist 4 Todd Regon, leader of a mortar team, quickly rounded up some Americal infantrymen, led them to the pit, and gave them a crash course in mortar firing. Scrambling back to his own mortar position, Regon was astounded to see illumination rounds bursting harmlessly over the daytime battlefield. An instant later, the mortarman realized that he had failed to show his infantry trainees the difference between high-explosive and illumination rounds for the CIDG mortar. Despite his grim situation, Regon managed a smile. "This ought to confuse the hell out of the enemy."

As enemy pressure on the base increased, MACV directed all available air support to Kham Duc. Fighters and attack planes from Pleiku, Da Nang, Cam Ranh Bay, and Phu Cat—as well as bases in Thailand—converged on the beleaguered base in answer to the call from the Seventh Air Force commander, General W. W. Momyer, for a "Grand Slam" maximum air effort. An airborne command post in a converted C-130 coordinated the air attacks as dozens of aircraft responded to Momyer's call. At times there were as many as twenty fighters over Kham Duc. Two forward air controllers (FACs) in light planes flew parallel to each other at opposite sides of the Kham Duc runway, each controlling fighter strikes on his side of the field. Traffic was so thick that by late morning the FACs could specifically select fighters based on their load: napalm, cluster-bomb units, 500- or 750-pound bombs, or high-drag bombs.

"We've got a small Khe Sanh going on here," an air force officer at Kham Duc recorded. "I hope we finish it before night comes." The evacuation, when it came, was marked by confusion, panic, and tragedy. Many of the defenders at Kham Duc were not informed of the decision to abandon the camp until many hours after it had been made. The CIDG forces, panicky and on the verge of mutiny or surrender, feared that the Americans would abandon them. Suspicion was mutual, since American troops had heard the stories of CIDG forces firing on other Americans at Ngoc Tavak.

The air force's 834th Air Division, whose giant C-123s and C-130s would have to make the actual evacuation, was also dogged by confusion and last-minute changes. At 8:20 A.M. on May 12, the 834th was alerted for an all-out effort to evacuate the base. Two hours later, fighting at Kham Duc had grown so intense that the Seventh Air Force canceled the evacuation and directed the transports to fly in additional ammunition to Kham Duc. By the time the MACV operations center directed the 834th to resume evacuation operations, around one-fifteen P.M., transports loaded with ammunition were already on their way to Kham Duc. Other planes on the ground had to unload their cargo before proceeding empty to Kham Duc to bring out the defenders. To complicate matters further, Colonel Nelson's command post could not communicate with many of the supporting aircraft because the America's radios were incompatible with those used by most of the planes. Messages had to be relayed from the Special Forces command post, whose radios could talk to the planes. At times the heavy volume of incoming message traffic almost jammed the two available networks. The communications mess made it nearly impossible for ground commanders to coordinate transport and helicopter landings with supporting air strikes.

That complete disaster was averted was due largely to the deadly skills of the fighter pilots and their controllers and to the iron nerve and brilliant improvisation of the tactical airlift crews. The first C-130 into Kham Duc landed on the debris-strewn runway at about ten A.M., in a hail of mortar and automatic-weapons fire that punctured a tire and fuel tanks. Lieutenant Colonel Daryl D. Cole's plane, dispatched before the evacuation order had been reinstituted, had a full load of cargo for Kham Duc, but panic-stricken civilians and CIDG troops rushed the plane as soon as it taxied to a stop, preventing either orderly unloading or evacuation. With mortar shells landing ever closer to the aircraft, Cole decided to attempt a takeoff with his overloaded plane, crowded with CIDG personnel and much of the remaining cargo. His first attempt was unsuccessful, and the increased attention that the plane was attracting from NVA gunners convinced the passengers to make a hasty exit. In the meantime, the crew had succeeded in cutting away part of the ruined tire. Dodging the runway debris, with fuel streaming from the wing tanks and under heavy fire, Cole managed to get his stricken C-130 airborne and safely back to Cam Ranh Bay. Cole was followed by a C-123 piloted by Major Ray Shelton, which loaded about sixty army engineers and Vietnamese civilians in under three minutes before taking off under heavy enemy fire.

Throughout the day, army and marine helicopters continued to dodge heavy fire to bring in ammunition and evacuate the wounded from Kham Duc. Yet the helicopters could not carry the large numbers of people now desperate to escape from the doomed camp. Only the large transports of the 834th could do that, and since eleven o'clock there had been no planes. Then, around three in the afternoon, a C-130 piloted by Major Bernard L. Bucher landed at Kham Duc. CIDG troops, women, and children swarmed aboard the plane. The CIDG soldiers and their families were convinced that the Americans intended to leave them behind. Two hours earlier, Special Forces sergeant Richard Campbell had watched in horror and disbelief as a woman and her small child who had fallen while climbing the rear ramp of a CH-46 helicopter were trampled by fear-maddened CIDG soldiers in a rush to board the chopper. Now nearly two hundred women and children were crowded onto Bucher's bullet-riddled C-130.

Because he had received heavy fire from the southwest corner of the field on landing, Bucher elected to take off to the northeast. A few minutes before Bucher's takeoff, fighters raked the NVA machine guns on the low ridges north of the runway with loads of cluster-bomb units. The deadly CBUs killed the gun crews, but replacements from nearby enemy positions soon had the guns back in action. Bucher's plane, struck by heavy machine-gun fire, crashed and exploded in an orange ball of flame less than a mile from the runway. There were no survivors of what has to be counted as one of the worst air disasters of this century, and the costliest one in the Vietnam War.

After watching Bucher's crash, Lieutenant Colonel William Boyd, Jr., pilot of the next C-130 into the camp, decided on a steep, sideslipping descent. Just as Boyd's plane was about to touch down, a shell exploded a hundred feet ahead on the runway. Pushing his throttle forward, Boyd climbed steeply into the air. Landing successfully on his next try, he loaded about a hundred CIDG and Americal soldiers and took off under heavy fire for Cam Ranh Bay.

The fourth C-130 of the day, commanded by Lieutenant Colonel John Delmore, had been forced to make a second pass to avoid Boyd's takeoff. This time the Communist gunners were ready, and .50-caliber bullets ripped six-inch holes in the sides of the fuselage as the giant C-130, its hydraulic system shot away, bounced along the runway, glanced off the wreckage of the CH-47 destroyed that morning, and plowed into a dirt mound on the side of the runway. Miraculously, the entire crew escaped. A few minutes later, the crippled plane burst into flames.

The remaining C-130 pilots circling above Kham Duc, awaiting their turns to land, had seen Bucher's plane crash and burn, Delmore's wrecked on landing, and two helicopters destroyed by ground fire. The runway was littered with debris and burning wreckage. Undeterred, Lieutenant Colonel Franklin Montgomery brought his C-130 into Kham Duc, followed by two more C-130s; together, the three planes brought out more than four hundred people just as the Seventh Air Force was issuing orders to cancel further landings. As the order was given, Major James L. Wallace's C-130 was able to make a pickup, bringing out the remaining soldiers and civilians.

But in the confusion, according to some reports, another C-130 landed briefly just as Wallace's was taking off. In the mistaken belief that personnel were still on the ground, the three men in the combat control team (CCT), who had been pulled out of the camp that morning after spending two days helping to bring in the Americal Division reinforcements, were now dropped off again—to find themselves alone, surrounded by exploding ammunition dumps and the advancing enemy.

Heavy fire forced the C-130 that had brought them to fly out before the three men could return to the plane. The airwaves fell silent as the pilot, Major Jay Van Cleff, radioed that the camp now was not fully evacuated and ready to be destroyed by air strikes.

On the ground, Major Gallagher and Technical Sergeants Freedman and Lundie took cover in a ditch, began shooting at the enemy—silencing one of the two machine guns firing at them from the sides of the runway—and hoped for a miracle. Lieutenant Colonel Alfred J. Jeanotte, Jr., given cover by fighter aircraft, touched down on the north side of the runway, but the crew couldn't see the three men and had to take off right away because of enemy fire. Once airborne, however, the crew spotted the men running back to their ditch after seeing the rescue plane leave without them. Their position was radioed to the next plane in line to attempt a rescue.

Lieutenant Colonel Joe M. Jackson brought in his C-123 with a sideslipping descent, to make the smallest possible target. Despite sharp objects and holes on the runway, the plane landed safely, rolled as close as possible to the ditch, and swung back around for a departure as the three men raced from their cover and were pulled on board. In under a minute, with bullets, shells, and even a 122mm rocket striking all around them, the C-123 took off and got away without a single hole in the plane. Jackson's daring rescue of the last three defenders of Kham Duc earned him the Medal of Honor.

It was over before five P.M. Communist troops advanced cautiously into Kham Duc and along the runway perimeter as explosions from the burning aircraft and ammunition dumps lit up the twilight sky. The following morning, sixty B-52 bombers, the entire force available in Vietnam, rained twelve thousand tons of bombs on the camp, and MACV proclaimed that the enemy had suffered severely. Yet nothing could disguise the fact that Kham Duc had been an American defeat—a Khe Sanh in reverse. Twenty-five Americans had been killed and nearly a hundred wounded, and there were several hundred Vietnamese casualties; seven U.S. aircraft and all the camp's heavy military and engineering equipment were also lost. American commanders had vacillated between reinforcing the camp and evacuating it, finally opting for evacuation under the worst possible circumstances. Command, control, and communications had been confused and often ineffective. General Abrams termed the operation "a minor disaster." "This was an ugly one and I expect some repercussions," wrote the chief of Westmoreland's operations center.

Yet the repercussions were few. Abrams angrily ordered I Corps commanders to review their command, control, communications, and planning, so "that when your command is confronted with a similar imminent problem, appropriate action would be taken so that we would not lose another camp." But the general's expression of unhappiness was confined to top-secret messages. No heads rolled; no investigations were launched. Saigon and Washington remained unruffled, barely concerned. The news media, preoccupied with the Communist attacks in Saigon and the peace negotiations in Paris, paid little attention. In a war in which the distinctions between success and failure, victory and defeat, had long been blurred, even an unequivocal debacle like Kham Duc could be obfuscated, obscured, and ignored.

MIA

MARILYN ELKINS

The fate of MIAs—the missing—was the bleakest of issues in the Vietnam War, and one that refuses to go away. The war may be decades behind us, but even today many Americans believe that somehow, somewhere, in the Socialist jungles of Vietnam, unredeemed captives remain. In towns all over the nation (including my own), you can spot those black MIA-POW flags, with a bowed silhouetted head in a stark white circle and behind it, a guard tower: The words YOU ARE NOT FORGOTTEN complete that doleful scene. The MIA issue is one that long ago became politicized. At a time when the nation was splitting apart over American involvement in the war, the Nixon administration flaunted it in an attempt to rally the faithful who still supported our presence in Vietnam and the bombing of the North. The message on that black flag has taken a tenacious hold on the American imagination, acquiring a life of its own. No doubt it helped to delay U.S. recognition of the united nation of Vietnam by a good twenty years. That did not happen until 1995, twenty-two years after the North Vietnamese released 591 POWs and President Richard M. Nixon announced that "All our American POWs are on their way home."

The government at present identifies 1,859 men as still missing in Southeast Asia (down from a maximum of around 2,600), not an especially high figure compared to other major wars the U.S. has fought. That is not to dismiss the number or the compounded suffering of survivors. Doubt disables. But it is worth comparing the figure to that of the Vietnamese missing, which includes not just Communist Vietcong and North Vietnamese but the Army of the Republic of South Vietnam (ARVN). No one will ever come up with the exact number, which is estimated to be at least three hundred thousand. Communist dead were typically buried in unmarked graves, if their bodies had not been pulverized or vaporized in B-52 raids. The Pentagon's treatment of MIA families, as Marilyn Elkins writes here, was frequently, and inexcusably, callous. But it was positively humane contrasted with the ordeal of silence that families in the North had to endure. Years often passed before the government notified them of a death in battle—if it did so at all—and it provided no information about where the bodies were buried. The North Vietnamese authorities probably didn't know. Families had to content themselves with a red-bordered certificate bearing the name of the deceased and the words "Vietnamese martyr in the struggle against America."

Marilyn Elkins, the wife of an MIA, did eventually get more than just a comfortless certificate, but she had to wait twenty-three years for the proof she sought and dreaded. She had been married to navy lieutenant Frank C. Elkins just nine months when he flew his A-4 Skyhawk from the U.S.S. *Oriskany* on October 13, 1966, on a mission over North Vietnam. He never returned, joining the growing official numbers of the missing. He did leave a diary, which a friend forwarded to his wife—who, for years, was not prepared to think of herself as his widow. That diary, which she edited and had published, is one of the remarkable documents to come out of the war. Elkins, like his wife, had a talent for writing: He eventually hoped to become a college professor of English, as she is now.

Lieutenant Elkins had been flying in action just three months when he disappeared. The record he left of that time is memorable for its honesty and refusal to hide his own misgivings—and his fear. "Today was our first day of actual combat flying," he wrote on June 30, 1966. "I almost gagged in my mask when the forward air controller (FAC) said they were shooting at us." Later, he added, "It never occurs to you while you're flying that there are people down there. . . . The area we hit yesterday was walked through afterward by the cavalry units, and the body count of VC was up around six hundred. . . . The real shame that I feel is my lack of emotional reaction. I keep reacting as though I were simply watching a movie of the whole thing. . . . I only hope and pray that I don't change my mind about what I am doing here. I will lose my mind if I do." To him, the conclusion was inescapable: "War is legalized murder."

What did happen to Frank Elkins that day in October? Did a surface-to-air missile destroy his plane, and him with it? Or was he, as the Pentagon kept hinting to his wife, possibly still alive, a prisoner of war? For years her quest would continue. Politicians, both right and left, would try to use her. Spokespeople for supposedly friendly causes would try to silence her when she asked uncomfortable questions. In an attempt to get a direct answer, she would go to Paris, making daily visits to the North Vietnamese consulate. Even when she thought she had found that answer, years would pass before she could be absolutely sure. She would never remarry.

The story of Marilyn and Frank Elkins is a Cold War story, too.

MARILYN ELKINS is a professor of English at California State University, Los Angeles, where she teaches twentieth century American literature. She edited her husband's war diary, *Heart of a Man,* which was originally published in 1973 and republished in 1990 after his remains were recovered in Vietnam. She has also published a number of critical studies, and has been a visiting professor at the University of Cape Town in South Africa and the U.S. Military Academy at West Point. She lives in Los Angeles.

E VERY WAR HAS PRODUCED some number of men whose remains could not be recovered. In previous centuries, accurate counts of those missing in action (MIAs) were often unobtainable. When Napoleon Bonaparte embroiled Europe in war, for example, soldiers were recruited as armies advanced. The result was huge numbers of men about whom relatives heard nothing and about whose whereabouts the military cared little.

In the past hundred years, the numbers of American MIAs have been reasonably well documented: In World War I, there were 2,912; in World War II, almost 79,000; in Korea, 8,200; and in Southeast Asia, as a result of the Vietnam War, 1,859 remain unaccounted for. The Department of Defense (DOD) still lists three unaccounted for from the Persian Gulf War and one from the War with Iraq. (The DOD also lists 126 who disappeared during the Cold War. The DOD continues to make efforts to account for them.) Since World War II, reported sightings of prisoners of war (POWs)—with attendant claims that Americans are still being held in captivity—have also been common.

Compared to the numbers of American MIAs from earlier wars, the 1,859 listed from Vietnam seem almost insignificant. The number in relation to the total killed—4 percent—also pales compared to some earlier wars: 5.5 percent in World War I; 27 percent in World War II; and 15.1 percent in Korea. It is insignificant, that is, unless you happen to be related to one of them.

Few of their wives or other family members were prepared for the length of time these servicemen would be listed as either POWs or MIAs. No American soldiers had ever officially been held for over three and a half years. While the law provides that a person who has been missing for seven years can be presumed dead, this does not apply to MIAs during a time of war. Americans had never fought in such a long war, and no military policy on MIAs had been established. A majority of the MIAs in Vietnam were pilots—America's best and brightest. Exceptional athletes, intellects, and aviators, they had seemed invulnerable. They had not been expected to fall prey to a small Asian enemy.

Certainly I thought my husband, U.S. Navy lieutenant Frank Callihan Elkins, was immune to MiGs and SAMs. We'd been married for only nine months; he was twenty-seven and I was twenty-two when his A-4 Skyhawk disappeared during a flight from its vessel, the U.S.S. *Oriskany*. I still believed that death was for other people. When I received the notification on October 13, 1966, I had just returned from spending two weeks with Frank in the Philippines and Hong Kong. He had December orders to a test squadron in China Lake, California; I was residing with my parents in Tennessee while I waited out his Vietnam tour. When the casualty assistance officer arrived, I answered the doorbell in a blue floral housecoat, half awake and half smiling: I knew that this man would be embarrassed when he learned he had delivered his message to the wrong wife.

The officer told me that Frank had been killed. After making a telephone call to report that he had delivered his message, he returned to say that he had misunderstood the original communication: Frank was only missing. Eager to see this as portentous, I interpreted the whole episode as additional proof that Frank was invulnerable.

Because Frank's father had a serious heart condition, I immediately contacted my brother-in-law and asked him to break the news to his parents. I didn't want them to receive the same misinformation I had. I could not cry but was shiveringly cold, despite the numerous quilts my parents wrapped around me. I seemed to be watching myself participate in conversations, observing these events as though they were happening to someone else.

While official policy demanded that such news be delivered in person by an officer of equal or higher rank, practice—as in my case—sometimes fell short of the ideal. No matter how it bungled the delivery of such news, the Pentagon assumed that families of MIAs in the Vietnam War would maintain the official expected silence—the traditional stiff upper lip that guaranteed a husband's continued military success—as they had done in past wars.

The Korean War was the first one in which the behavior of POWs under stress had been blamed on the prisoners rather than on their captors. Suspected of conspiring with the enemy and succumbing to Communist brainwashing (this was during the McCarthy era), the Korean POW became a symbol of national dishonor, although the number of Americans who chose not to return—twenty-one—was small compared to the eighty-eight thousand Chinese and North Korean prisoners who refused repatriation (over half of those who fell into American hands).

Consequently, the U.S. military code of conduct used in the 1960s insisted that a captive conduct himself as a fighting man rather than as a powerless prisoner. The code was designed to produce soldiers who could resist torture, remain silent, and attempt escape against overwhelming odds and under brutal conditions. As part of this doctrine, pilots who were being prepared to fly over Vietnam were sent to a weeklong survival school in which they were beaten, forced to curl up in a tiny black box for hours, and verbally assaulted if they failed to escape from their "captors." When he returned from this week in March 1966, Frank had bruises on most of his body and slept for a full twenty-four hours from exhaustion. While many of the simulations were classified and therefore not subjects he could discuss, he confided that he had found the solitary confinement most difficult. To occupy his mind during these seemingly endless episodes, Frank had imagined happy scenes from his childhood and of his return home.

I soon found that equal stoicism was expected of military wives. The official policy was to give us as little information as possible so that we could not harm our husbands with any indiscretion. The government ensured our silence through effective manipulation of our concern for our husbands' safety. The navy's telegrams and other communications insisted that because my husband might be "held by hostile force against his will," "for his safety" I should reply to inquiries from outside sources by revealing "only his name, rank, file number, and date of birth." These were exactly the orders given to Frank during his survival training.

Determined not to compromise him in any way, I began a period of intense, silent waiting. My own needs for comforting were subordinated to government policy that, for most of the period of 1966–68, insisted secrecy was in the MIAs' best interest. Designed to protect national policy without considering their effect on family members, the government's instructions did not include tips on how to survive this vigil. No one suggested that I might find psychological counseling helpful. No one offered to explain what Frank's chances for survival might be. No one offered suggestions as to what I should do—except wait in silence. Treatment of MIA wives during the Persian Gulf War seemed to indicate that this atavistic attitude toward the exigencies of military wives remains relatively unchanged, even though American soldiers now are instructed to give transparently false "confessions" if they are captured. (During the war with Iraq, the rules for appropriate behavior for families of POWs and MIAs have become more relaxed. The DOD no longer forbids families to speak to the media and has a website that offers family support.)

I, however, was left in the hands of whatever emotional support I could find—primarily a group of navy wives who generously called me from their homes in California to extend what comfort they could spare from their concern about their own husbands. I now realize how emotionally costly this solace must have been; I must have reminded these women that their husbands could suffer Frank's fate at any moment. No wonder they sometimes presented me with unfounded rumors and speculations.

Except for my cousin Shirley, whose husband was also a pilot on the U.S.S. *Oriskany*, no one in my immediate family or community knew what to say or do. My parents lived on a farm in rural Tennessee; the nearest town, Pikeville, has a population of about a thousand people. I soon found that even though I had remained silent, most of these people knew about my husband's status and wanted to help. However, no one had provided any of us with a script for appropriate behavior. I couldn't understand why people kept arriving with casseroles, pies, and cakes—rural custom following a death. On the other hand, a friend of my father's who had been a POW in World War II returned home after everyone but his immediate family had given up hope; Clint's experiences, known by everyone in our community, became the repeated evidence they could offer that Frank would survive.

But I needed no assurance of that. Within a few weeks I insisted that my father install another telephone line so I could be reached immediately when Frank came tap-dancing out of the jungle. I was certain my teenage brothers' constant conversations were responsible for the delay in news about Frank.

On October 26, 1966, fire broke out on the U.S.S. *Oriskany*, and many of Frank's friends were killed. One friend, Bill Johnson, had already sent me Frank's diary, which I carefully stored away for Frank; he had kept it with the intention of writing a novel about his Vietnam experience. Bill was killed in the fire, before he could ship the rest of Frank's gear. When the navy finally forwarded Frank's belongings, many items—including the typewriter I had given him and a surprise Christmas gift that I knew he had purchased for me in Hong Kong—were missing. The navy was unhelpful in retrieving these items, which I had embroidered with sentimental significance.

By December, I had become accustomed to the fact that my presence often made other people uncomfortable; I had lost twenty pounds and had nearly perfected the role of zombie. I remained intent on fooling myself: I was convinced that I was helping Frank by staring at my special phone, willing it to ring. Finally, my first bout with Crohn's disease, a chronic ailment that is exacerbated by stress, forced me to spend Christmas week in the hospital. My doctor convinced me that I might die if I continued to do nothing but wait. Even I knew my death wouldn't help Frank.

So I decided to get on with plans we had made prior to his disappearance. We both had wanted to become English professors, and I took my first step toward that goal by enrolling in graduate school. A large number of other MIA wives also earned degrees while they waited for their husbands' return. Initially, we were not entitled to benefits mandated by the GI Bill because we weren't widows, and we were not allowed to collect our husbands' full salaries; the Defense Department required that a percentage be held in savings. When the length of time men were listed as MIA continued beyond that of earlier wars, wives who persisted were given full benefits. I did not apply because neither my casualty assistance officer nor my monthly updates from the navy informed me that I was eligible. Instead, I held part-time jobs to finance my studies.

I was still under government orders not to reveal my husband's status, so when I was asked about the wedding ring I wore, I'd reply, "My husband's in Vietnam." I often didn't like the immediate response that statement received: an almost instantaneous look of pity or, rarely, a diatribe about how reprehensible U.S. activities in Vietnam were.

Within a year of Frank's disappearance, the government negotiated with the North Vietnamese to allow wives to send letters and, eventually, packages to their missing husbands. Soon, navy communiqués detailed what could be included in the monthly letters (good news and cheer) and what could not (the war or any other bad news). Last year the navy returned one of my letters; it had been "found" in materials that they received from the North Vietnamese. Speaking encouragingly about Frank's family and my continuing education, the letter closes with this:

> What else can I say? I love you and am here waiting. And will be. I do live
> chiefly by longing, cherishing our past, trusting in our future, but I endure.
> I keep a thousand experiences to share with you; buy records I know you'll
> want to hear, books you'll want to read, and clothes I think you'll like. You

are the controlling force in my life. I hope you are able to have me with you as much as I have you here. Oh, Frank, I love you so much! I pray I can be worthy of such love.

Rereading these words today, I am embarrassed by how closely they follow navy guidelines. Had he received this letter, I suspect Frank might have found it disconcerting. To anyone who knows my independent nature, it sounds as artificial as the deliberately staged confessions of captured American fliers during the Persian Gulf War. Coming from someone who, prior to her marriage, had negotiated an agreement that she didn't have to be the kind of military wife who held squadron teas and luncheons and would be free to pursue a career, this letter sounds suspect. But it illustrates just how fully I had adopted the official government role.

Whenever the government's rules changed, I followed the new orders. Every two months I could send Frank a six-and-a-half-pound package. Suggested contents included toothpaste, playing cards, vitamins, socks, underwear, soap, canned meat, bouillon cubes, raisins, candy, cheeses, and photographs. I remember how apprehensive I was the first time I also included cigars, an item not mentioned on the list.

About once a month I received a letter that detailed any changes of policy. With each letter, the government's insistence on silence about MIAs grew increasingly irritating. Why couldn't I talk about my husband? Why was I being treated as though Frank and I had done something shameful? And though I had been asked to remain silent, information about me was being used by politicians. Many of them were not interested in Frank's fate or mine so much as in furthering their careers. My local congressman, Bill Brock, told a story in his local campaign speeches about my asking him for help (which, following navy guidelines, I had stressed should remain confidential); he colored both my request and the possibility of what he could do to appeal to local voters.

In 1969, I joined the National League of Families of American Prisoners and Missing in Southeast Asia, an organization founded by the families but fundamentally upholding government policy and receiving government support and encouragement. The league's primary spokeswoman was Sybil Stockdale, the wife of Commander James Stockdale, who was a frequently photographed prisoner and had been the commander of the first air wing of the U.S.S. *Oriskany*. She supported the government's argument that we must win the war to free the prisoners. Angered by my congressman's actions, I had written to Allard Lowenstein, the congressman who started the dump-Johnson campaign and had been a mentor of Frank's at the University of North Carolina, asking for his help and suggestions. I tried to arrange a meeting between Lowenstein and Stockdale, but she refused to cooperate because of his antiwar stance. I have always suspected that her actions were being dictated by government policy, but I have no way of knowing how much official advice she received or followed.

I often resented the rhetoric of war protesters as well. *The Saturday Review* published a letter from a writer who called the first prisoners released by the North Vietnamese in 1969 "obscene biological charades" who wore their uniforms like "the skin of a predator." I responded with a letter of my own, which the magazine also printed. Yet I continued to talk to people like Cora Weiss, cochair of the left-wing Committee of Liaison, whom I asked for help in establishing communications with the North Vietnamese.

From these disparate sources I tried to piece together a realistic picture, one that would allow me to act in Frank's interest. It became clear to me that the MIA/POW issue was being presented as an excuse to continue an otherwise unpopular war; the missing were being used to justify our increased bombing. Repeatedly calling attention to Hanoi's refusal to abide by the Geneva Convention, President Nixon's speeches included his promise to continue the U.S. presence in Southeast Asia "until the prisoners of war are freed."

Al Lowenstein suggested that my going public might actually help Frank, rather than harm him. He put me in touch with John Siegenthaler, the editor of the Nashville *Tennessean*. (By this time I had moved to Nashville and enrolled at Vanderbilt University in another master's program.) Siegenthaler sent Kathy Sawyer to interview me, and she wrote a story that the paper timed to appear on the third anniversary of Frank's disappearance.

The government did not object. For reasons never clearly stated, its policy had changed. After the release of the first three prisoners in 1969, the word went out through our monthly newsletters from the military, through our casualty assistance officers, and through the National League of Families that we could take our suffering to the public. At league meetings we were asked to conduct letter-writing campaigns to show the Vietnamese what the people in the villages of America thought of their treatment of prisoners. Businessman H. Ross Perot spoke at these meetings, garnering support for his attempts to take food and supplies to the prisoners. (Perot would run for president as an independent in 1992, with Stockdale as his vice presidential candidate.) The Pentagon encouraged us to woo the media to mobilize world opinion against the

North Vietnamese. In an international contest for moral approval and good-will, our government started calling attention to North Vietnam's refusal to follow the rules of the Geneva Convention.

Kathy Sawyer's well-written, sensitive article received a lot of attention, and many of my fellow graduate students seemed shocked to learn that my husband was an MIA. Generally, they were kind and supportive. But I received a number of phone calls from heavy breathers who offered to help me out with my sex life, and others who offered to find Frank for me using a variety of methods that ranged from witchcraft to prayer. When I was interviewed on local television and radio shows, I was surprised by the questions some interviewers and callers asked. They seemed more interested in knowing intimate details about my life than in learning about the MIA situation. Many people just wanted me to look pretty, vulnerable, and sad; they certainly didn't want me to have a political opinion. Privately, I had felt for some time that the war was wrong—both morally and practically—but I hesitated to express these sentiments because I feared such remarks might have serious repercussions for Frank, or might be used as propaganda tactics against other POWs. So I remained officially silent about my doubts.

In the spring of 1970, encouraged by both our government and the trips other wives had made, I went to Paris. Calling on the North Vietnamese consulate at 2 rue le Verrier, the two translators I had found through the American embassy and I were greeted civilly and allowed to enter. But a Vietnamese gentleman, who never told me his name, insisted that we should "ask President Nixon" about my husband's whereabouts, and he asked us to leave.

I was struck by the contrast between the elegance of the American embassy and the shabbiness of the North Vietnamese consulate. This was my first encounter with Vietnamese people, and I was also humbled by their small physical stature. By comparison, I felt Brobdingnagian, insensitive, and clumsy. The difference in our size seemed somehow a metaphor for the war in which America's superior numbers and strength were becoming liabilities.

When I returned to the States, I continued to criticize Hanoi's policy concerning prisoners. But often my speeches, and those of other wives of MIAs, were used for different political purposes. At a Veterans of Foreign Wars meeting, when the local commander suggested that he and members of the audience should "go over to Arkansas and whip Fulbright's ass for this little lady and her husband," I announced that I was not present to support the continuance of the war in Vietnam or to attack those people who opposed it; I had come only to express my concern about the prisoners. My audience became quiet and unresponsive. No one spoke to me afterward.

The National League of Families meeting held in Washington in July 1970 crystallized my decision to pursue my own course and ignore the one our government was dictating. When Vice President Spiro Agnew made an appearance to address the members, I didn't stand; the rather stout woman beside me started tapping me on the shoulder with her handbag, increasing the force with each tap. At last I stood up, then left—both the meeting and the organization. I had had it with everyone's political agenda. I wanted no part of a group whose allegiance precluded questioning such leaders as Nixon and Agnew.

By this time President Nixon, Defense Secretary Melvin Laird, and other administration officials had escalated the frequency of their claims that we must remain in Southeast Asia to ensure the release of American POWs. The navy was not happy with my public statements that the "identification, treatment, and release of prisoners should be handled as a separate issue."

In March 1971, I decided to move to Paris and make daily visits to the North Vietnamese consulate, vowing to stay until they told me something about Frank's status. Before my departure, the navy sent an official to caution me about my action and about any statements that I might make: "The foreign press may misinterpret your remarks if you say anything critical about the war, and you don't want your husband to be hurt by your carelessness." He also advised me to watch out for suspicious people who might want to kidnap me.

So commenced a series of days in Paris that always began with a trip to the North Vietnamese consulate. The French police guarding the consulate would often nudge one another and say, "C'est la femme. Encore, eh?" Usually, a Frenchwoman of about forty-five with blue-black hair and bright red lips, dressed in a white blouse and black skirt, would come to the door demanding in French, "Who's there? What do you want?" I would respond, "It's Madame Elkins. I would like to ask you about my husband." Her "We can't give you any information; go away!" would follow.

More than two hundred relatives of MIA/POWs had already come knocking on this door, but I was the first to make it a daily activity. If I knew foreign visitors were likely to be present at the consulate, I would try to time my visit to coincide, making an effort to embarrass the North Vietnamese. Occasionally, I would be given admittance and admonished to "go home and tell President Nixon to stop bombing our country. Then you'll get your answer." Sometimes members of the North Vietnamese delegation would yell at me and criticize the American bombing; at other times they would apologize and look genuinely moved by my request.

Once I asked the secretary directly if Frank was dead. Lowering her eyes, she replied, "*Oui.*" But she would provide me with no additional information. I explained that it would be to her advantage to give me all the information she had on all the men so that President Nixon would have fewer names to use as an excuse for keeping our troops in Vietnam, but she refused. Eventually, she began greeting me with "*Bonjour,* Madame Elkins," but I never obtained the audience I requested with Delegate General Vo Van Sung.

Sometimes I tried to get the secretary to pass Vo Van Sung copies of articles that Kathy Sawyer had written about me for *The Tennessean,* notes explaining my position and my plans to return every day, and cards with my address and phone number. Occasionally, the secretary would give me pamphlets that restated her instructions to me in English. The details changed, but these conversations always ended with my standing in the shadows before a closed door and saying, "À *demain.*"

Because I had great sympathy and respect for these people, the adversarial role was especially stressful for me. I couldn't blame the North Vietnamese for shooting down Frank's plane when he had been bombing their country. Sometimes I would run into members of the delegation in shops. If I spoke, they usually refused to acknowledge me. I suspect they feared I was a little crazy. Perhaps I was.

Other wives of MIAs or POWs would arrive for short stays in Paris, and I would accompany them to make their requests. After almost three months, the North Vietnamese delegation must have realized that I was there to stay. They finally admitted me and told me that Frank was dead. But when I asked them to put the information in writing, they refused, saying that all the other wives would then come to Paris and harass them.

By March 1971 the North Vietnamese had begun returning letters addressed to men whose names were not included on the official POW list released to Senator Edward M. Kennedy in December 1970. Stamped KUONG NGUOI NAHAN TRÁLAI ("this person unknown"), my returned letters seemed more official than any information I had received from American sources about Frank. The Defense Department suggested that North Vietnam was reinforcing its contention that the list was complete and final, but insisted that our government would not accept letter or package returns as evidence of the fate of MIAs. Frank Sieverts, an assistant to the secretary of state, maintained that the men's status would not be changed without concrete proof.

My wait for news about Frank continued, and remaining in Paris was more comfortable than returning home. I was relieved to be anonymous, free from people who asked about my husband's status:

"Have you heard anything yet?"

"No."

"Guess you never will, huh? Bless your heart. It's such a pity."

Though well intentioned, such remarks—sometimes coming from the mouths of complete strangers—always left me fighting back tears. I was also tired of the either/or stance that everyone seemed to insist upon when discussing the war. Simultaneously caring about my husband's return and wanting our troops to withdraw did not seem incongruous to me. I was amazed by how angry hawks could become when I refused to denounce the North Vietnamese, and by how upset doves became when I wouldn't criticize the men who were fighting.

But I had begun to realize that Frank might not return, and I began editing his diary for publication—an act I had not attempted earlier because I believed he would use it himself, as the basis for the novel. Publishing his diary now seemed my responsibility. Editing his writings in 1972, I thought I had achieved some catharsis at last. I hoped that writing its prologue had also provided me with closure. When the book was published in the fall of 1973, I returned to the United States to push its sales—and discovered that the public who had once seemed so eager to know about the war had become largely apathetic. They did not want to be reminded of our national defeat.

Almost a year after the return of the 591 POWs in early 1973, I left Paris for San Francisco. Feeling that I had done all I could to ascertain Frank's fate, I hoped the government would assume responsibility for finding him. After all, it had promised to bring him home when the war was over.

Once the war ended, however, public interest in the MIA issue also ended. After the prisoners returned, leadership of the National League of Families shifted from wives to other family members of MIAs. E. H. Mills, the father of Lieutenant Commander James Mills (shot down on September 21, 1966), became the director in 1973, and he was succeeded by his daughter Ann Mills Griffiths. Her long reign has produced various critics and at least one splinter group, directed by Dolores Alfond, who insists that Griffiths has responded less to the needs of the families than to those of the government. Many MIA family members now echo my earlier suspicions that the league is basically a government organization. (During the Nixon administration, its long-distance telephone bill was paid out of White House funds.) In February 1991, Colonel Millard Peck, a highly decorated veteran, quit his post as chief of the POW/MIA unit of the Defense Intelligence Agency, contending that the official government "mind-set to debunk" evidence of live MIAs was encouraged by Griffiths, whom he described as "adamantly opposed to any initiative to actually get to the heart of the problem." He accused Griffiths of sabotaging POW/MIA investigations. (It is worth noting that the League of Families helped sponsor an MIA/POW website that blamed the 2004 Democratic presidential candidate John Kerry for what the League saw as the abandonment of American soldiers when Kerry helped to reestablish trade with Vietnam. The League also had connections with the Swift Boat Veterans Against Kerry.)

During the mid-1970s the league did little to slow down the speed with which the government began perfunctorily changing MIA status to "presumed finding of death" (PFOD). In December 1976 a House panel determined, later with President Carter's agreement, that no live MIAs remained in Southeast Asia. In March 1977 a presidential commission traveled to Hanoi and subsequently agreed with a House select committee that the Vietnamese were acting in good faith to "repatriate" the remains of all American MIAs. The government provided wives and family members with no explanation for these decisions. Because they were made by our government, we were expected to assume they were trustworthy.

These announcements only confirmed my suspicions that Frank had been used as a pawn. I became convinced that our government would make no more real efforts to recover him—alive or dead. And I realized how powerless I remained.

The navy changed Frank's status to PFOD on October 31, 1977. The telegram arrived at my door in Oakland along with a group of young trick-or-treaters. The following year Frank's family and I held a memorial service for him at the National Cemetery in Wilmington, North Carolina. By 1978 the Pentagon had declared all MIAs to be PFODs, except for Colonel Charles E. Shelton of the air force, who remains listed as a POW for symbolic reasons. His wife took her own life in October 1990. She left no explanation, but friends suggest that her suicide is a result of battling about POW/MIA issues for over twenty years. To me, her action seems as symbolic as her husband's status.

In 1983, President Reagan announced that the MIAs were a high priority for his administration. He sent delegations to Vietnam, and 150 sets of remains were identified and returned. The military's Joint Casualty Resolution Center at Barbers Point in Hawaii, established in the 1970s, increased its efforts to recover remains and make identifications. In 1985, Vietnam turned over the remains of another five persons believed to be MIAs; in 1988 the first joint American-Vietnamese team uncovered two more sets of MIA remains.

But no one had asked me for additional information about Frank, and by the time another twelve silent years had gone by, I felt sure that I would never know his exact whereabouts. Consequently, I was unprepared for the telephone call I received from the navy in December 1989 asking me if I "happened to have" a copy of my husband's dental X rays.

"No . . . Why?"

"Well . . . uh . . . we have a piece of a jawbone and some teeth that we think may have belonged to him."

My anger at the unfeeling language obscured my initial shock. How could this stranger choose his words so carelessly, ignoring their possible effect upon me? But his tone of voice indicated that he was not so unfeeling as his choice of words implied. He explained that Frank was only one of several men who were being considered as the possible source for a box of remains that the North Vietnamese had turned over to American authorities in June. I suggested that he contact my husband's family. Then, as I had during the previous twenty-three years, I tried to remain calm as I confronted this latest unexpected reminder of Frank and of my own irretrievable loss.

On January 22, 1990, exactly twenty-four years from the day I married Frank, the navy notified me that the remains had been positively identified as his. (The bones included those of the torso, legs, and a part of the lower jawbone that seemed to be broken. No bones were available from the rest of the face and head or the feet and hands.) If I regarded the pathologists' reports as "inconclusive," I would have the "option" to arrange for someone else to review the paperwork and remains to provide "quality assurance" of this decision.

A few days later, members of Frank's family and I met with military officials to review their evidence. They explained that the government research group had reached their decision based on a combination of evidence. First they looked for the names of all of the men who were listed as having disappeared in the area of Dien Chau district, Nghe Tinh province, the area from which the bones had been recovered. Using a section of the pelvic bone to determine the age of the person at death, they were able to narrow the possibilities even more. By measuring the torso and leg bones, they could estimate the person's height. Because of the prominent muscle insertion in the bones, the pathologists were certain that the person had had an unusually muscular build. Frank's medical records show that he had a forty-two-inch chest, a thirty-one-inch waist, and a twenty-two-inch thigh and could military-press two hundred pounds; he had begun lifting weights when he was in high school, an activity that he had continued. Using information from the computer database of missing persons' dental records, the researchers narrowed the possibilities to three men. And while they were able to obtain dental X rays on all of the men except Frank, none of the X rays fitted the dental work remaining on the lower jawbone. Although no X rays of Frank's teeth were available, the dental charts showing his fillings and earlier extractions matched those of the jawbone. So he filled the description in every possible way, as did no one else who had disappeared within a fifty-mile radius of the site.

With the recounting of each explanation, I was asked if I wanted to see photographs of the bones or medical records substantiating each claim. At first I could only respond, "I don't know yet. Wait a minute, and I'll let you know." Then I would tell myself that I had to look or continue to doubt their judgment. Each decision to look at the evidence became a little easier, and I managed to get through the afternoon without embarrassing any of us by becoming hysterical. Frank's family told me later that if I had not agreed to look at the photographs, they would have done so; they also felt we needed to look to be able to know.

At first I did wonder if the remains were really Frank's. But because I had put no pressure on our government since the early 1970s, its decision to assign them to him, rather than to the husband of a more insistent wife, seems to serve no ulterior purpose. The government had nothing to gain by returning Frank's remains, which made its analysis more convincing to me. I can imagine no other motivation. Frank and I were just lucky.

Frank appears to have died in the crash of his plane. The fragmentation of the bones and the broken jaw make this explanation the likeliest. The bones were encrusted with dirt, since Vietnamese bury the dead directly in the ground without a coffin and then, approximately three years later, after the flesh has rotted away, dig up the bones and place them in a smaller grave. This process also partly accounts for the missing smaller bones. When this ritual was explained to me, it was described as something the Vietnamese do because of

their "superstitions" about the dead. I couldn't help thinking that we characterize our own practices in such matters, really no more civilized, as "respect for
the dead."

I was touched that the Vietnamese had gone to such trouble to bury someone who had been bombing their country. Their humane customs are partly responsible for my having Frank's remains for reburial. And I was beginning to
discover how grateful I was.

Frank's was one of ten sets of MIA remains identified and returned to the
U.S. mainland for interment in 1990. (As of 2004, the DOD has recovered the
remains of more than 400 MIAs.) They were shipped to Travis Air Force Base
and in late February brought home to North Carolina, where our families held
a private, quiet interment in the National Cemetery in Wilmington. Knowing
the whereabouts of Frank's remains has helped me begin a healing process I
was helpless to effect earlier. Unconsciously, I had been unable to forgive myself for "deserting" him, for failing to negotiate the labyrinth of government
policies and foreign terrains. My earlier insistence that his final whereabouts
did not matter had been dishonest. I had been diminishing the importance of
what I could not change. Now I can draw comfort from envisioning his grave
site, from having a specific physical location that automatically comes to mind
when I think of him. His flesh had already become part of Vietnam, but his
bones no longer lie—like those of Thomas Hardy's Drummer Hodge—un-
coffined and unmarked beneath "foreign constellations."

"That's Ocay XX Time Is on Our Side"

GEOFFREY NORMAN

Actual American participation in the Vietnamese War lasted close to a decade, and as long as that national trauma continued, no aspect of it earned more dispiriting attention than the plight of the POWs in North Vietnamese prisons. Most of what the public knew came through propaganda photographs of downed airmen, who often used their moment of worldwide notoriety to send covert messages. They would paste "Merry Christmas" posters to a wall, holding them with their middle fingers; make a series of exaggerated bows to their captors, as if brainwashed; or blink the word "torture" in Morse code for Communist movie cameramen. They were, in fact, tortured and, in some cases, murdered. The majority were downed pilots, whom the North Vietnamese described as criminals, treating them as such. Later, when the Communists recognized how much value U.S. negotiators attached to the POWs, they began to consider them as hostages, pawns in an excruciating diplomatic chess game that went on for four and a half years. To give them up would have meant giving up North Vietnam's most potent bargaining chip.

The number of POWs was long open to debate. In 1969 the North Vietnamese admitted to holding only fifty-nine. That fall, in a gesture to one of the American peace delegations that regularly visited Hanoi, the North Vietnamese released a seaman named Douglas Hegdahl, an ammunition handler who had been blown overboard by a gun concussion two years earlier. What his captors didn't know was that Hegdahl had memorized the names and ranks of all the POWs he had encountered in a prison nicknamed the Plantation: His mnemonic device was to set them to the tune of "Old MacDonald Had a Farm." His superiors ordered him to seek amnesty. Now the Defense Department knew there were at least 250 men still alive.

Late in the 1980s, fifteen-odd years after the last POW had returned home, the writer Geoffrey Norman interviewed many of them. Some had been imprisoned for five or six years; one, eight and a half. It was the longest time Americans had ever been held during a war. What Norman learned, and what he later described in a remarkable little book, *Bouncing Back*, was anything but dispiriting. If, as Ernest Hemingway is supposed to have said, guts can be defined as grace under pressure, then theirs is a story of heroism beyond measure. To be sure, these men belonged to a combat elite. Their average age was thirty-two, and most were career officers, air force captains or navy lieutenants, and college graduates, some of whom were working toward advanced degrees that they had been forced to interrupt for war service. They had taken special training in survival and captivity. The highest-ranking officers established and maintained a strict code of discipline and solidarity among the POWs that their captors tried, with little success, to break down with torture, long periods of isolation, and psychological abuse. Mostly, though, the POWs survived by learning to fill years of empty hours with improvised mental and physical activity, trying as best they could to salvage a youth that seemed to be slipping away.

In the excerpt that follows, Norman details the life POWs led in the Plantation. The year was 1968, though chronology existed for these men mainly as a string of small incidents of determination and passive resistance pursued in semidarkness. The title, "That's Ocay XX Time Is on Our Side," was the ironic epigram tapped out from cell wall to cell wall, using a twenty-five-letter grid (the letter C could be substituted for K). The POWs had adapted the basic matrix that generations of convicts had employed. Communication was the key to staying sane. But there were other constants of prison life to be dealt with, which Norman details. How to make a plaster substitute to seal a rat hole—and, when that failed, what common Vietnamese vegetable would keep the rodents at bay. How to make a toilet pail comfortable. How to exercise without being caught—which might lead, best case, to being locked in irons or, worst, a beating or a session of rope torture. How to play bridge when a potential foursome was in different and not always adjacent cells.

The POWs were held in eleven prisons in the North (which were at least an improvement over the prisoner cages used by the Vietcong in the South). Four were in Hanoi—the most notorious was Hoa Lo, the "Hanoi Hilton." Six were within fifty miles of the North Vietnamese capital, and one was on the Chinese border. The POWs gave them names, hardly out of affection, such as the Zoo, Skidrow, Rockpile, Briarpatch, Alcatraz, and Dogpatch. From 1965 until 1969, conditions were the dismal standard that Norman describes here. Then, in the latter year, Ho Chi Minh died; for some reason, still unexplained, the new leadership of North Vietnam eased up on the severity of treatment. Perhaps it was the delayed recognition, which the peace negotiations brought home, that the Americans were more useful alive than half dead.

GEOFFREY NORMAN has written thirteen books, including *Bouncing Back*, from which this excerpt is taken; *Alabama Showdown*, an examination of the football culture in that state; *The Institute*, a history of the Virginia Military Institute; and *Two for the Summit*, a narrative of climbing mountains with his daughter, including Aconcagua in Argentina, the highest mountain in the world outside of Asia. Norman is a former contributing editor to *MHQ: The Quarterly Journal of Military History* and a frequent contributor to a number of periodicals, notably *The Wall Street Journal*. He lives in Vermont.

O N MARCH 31, 1968, President Lyndon Johnson told the American people that he was suspending bombing of North Vietnam above the 21st Parallel. At the end of his speech, he also announced that he would not be running for reelection. Johnson had been defeated by the North Vietnamese; he was quitting and going home. It remained to be seen if the U.S. prisoners of war, mainly airmen who had been shot down, would be so lucky.

The news was broadcast over speakers in every prison camp. And when there was nothing said about their release, many of the POWs drew the darkest conclusion. In a camp called the Plantation, on the outskirts of Hanoi, Lieutenant Commander Richard Stratton, the senior ranking officer, said to the three other men in his cell, "If we weren't part of some deal—no more bombing in exchange for our release—then we are going to be here for a long time. Probably until they start bombing again." Stratton's prediction was accurate. He and the others would spend five more years in North Vietnam.

While Hanoi was no longer being bombed, the air war continued in the Panhandle of North Vietnam, and new shootdowns arrived with the unwelcome news that the war was still going on. There were no negotiations yet and no reason to believe that peace and repatriation were at hand.

A single rail line ran outside the Plantation, just beyond the back wall of the old building that the men called the Warehouse, which had been divided into cells. In his cell, designated Warehouse One, Stratton and his cellmates could lean a pallet bed against the wall, climb the ladderlike studs that held the boards together, and look through the gunports at the passing trains. Even after Johnson's decision to halt the bombing of Hanoi, the passing cattle cars were full of young men in uniform on their way to the fight. More than any information from recent shootdowns or the small seeds of truth amid the propaganda of the camp news, this was the most vivid proof that the war was not winding down.

Guards still came to take prisoners out for interrogations, but these increasingly became what the POWs called "temperature quizzes." Instead of being pumped for military information or pressed for propaganda, they were asked how they were getting along and how they felt about their captors and the war. Most of the POWs maneuvered to avoid head buttings. They answered vaguely and were eventually returned to their cells. They began to suspect that in many cases the quizzes were merely a pretext for interrogators to practice their English. Still, to see the door open and the guard point his finger at you was a frightening experience.

There was no way of knowing, when you left the cell for the walk up to headquarters, if you were in for a temperature quiz or something a lot more serious. Delegations were still coming into Vietnam for tours; prisoners in all the camps were still being pressured to make statements, sometimes with the promise of early release; punishments were still being inflicted on men caught violating camp rules. In short, the weeks and months that followed the Tet Offensive of early 1968 were not better by any objective measure.

The POWs began psychologically digging in, adjusting to the long haul. Most were in their twenties or early thirties. A few were barely old enough to have voted in one election before they were shot down. Some were fathers of children they'd never seen; husbands of women they had lived with for only a few weeks. It seemed increasingly possible—even probable—that they would be middle-aged or old men before they left Vietnam. Their survival now included facing this hard reality. Somehow, they had to find ways to fill those years, to salvage something from their youth.

At all of the POW camps in North Vietnam, communication between prisoners was strictly forbidden. Roommates managed to communicate without being overheard, but a man could not shout through walls or windows, or leave messages, or try in any other way to make contact with fellow prisoners in the camp. Men were thrown into solitary, locked in irons, hung by ropes, and beaten when they were caught trying to communicate.

Still, it was worth the risk, since communication was the foundation of any kind of resistance. The senior man had to get his orders out to everyone in the camp, and everyone had to be tied in; four men alone in a room were not part of a unified resistance. With something called the "tap code," prisoners were able to communicate and establish an organization. Working together helped them overcome feelings of isolation and boredom, and ultimately enabled them to resist.

The principle of the tap code is ancient, at least as old as Greek civilization. In modern dress, it appears in Arthur Koestler's descriptions of life in the Soviet prison in his novel *Darkness at Noon*. POWs believed that it had been invented by an air force captain named Smitty Harris, who came up with it while he was in survival school and remembered it in Hoa Lo after he had been shot down. Although the POWs may have been wrong about the origins of the tap code, no group in history ever employed it more successfully or more enthusiastically. Learning the tap code was like getting a telephone: It opened a world.

The basis of the code is a grid that looks like this:

```
A  B  C  D  E
F  G  H  I  J
L  M  N  O  P
Q  R  S  T  U
V  W  X  Y  Z
```

The letter C could be substituted for K, and the code was read like the coordinates on a map—down and right. For example, the letter M would be three down and two across. To transmit an M through the wall, a prisoner would tap three times, pause, then tap twice.

Most men learned the code from a roommate, but it was possible to teach it through a wall to a man who was all alone and needed it worse than anyone. A man who knew the code would simply tap on the wall until he got a response. He might tap out the familiar rhythm of "Shave and a Haircut" until the man on the other side came back with "Two Bits." Once that happened, they were in communication. Then the tedious business of teaching a language began, first using a more primitive system. The first man would tap once, pause, tap twice, pause, tap three times, pause . . . and so on, until he reached twenty-six. Then he would do it again. Eventually, the other man would understand that the twenty-six taps represented the alphabet. A was one, B was two, and so on.

When this had been established, a few messages would be transmitted. The men would exchange names, perhaps, and shootdown dates. It was exceedingly slow and tedious, but it established the link and the rudiments of the method. The next step was to tap out the message "Make a matrix." That done, the newcomer was instructed to fill in the alphabet. In this way the first code was used to explain the much shorter, more efficient one.

At the Plantation, as well as the other camps, the walls were alive with the sounds of men urgently tapping out messages.

When it became clear to the men at the Plantation that they were not going home in return for an end to the bombing of Hanoi, they began trying to improve the physical conditions of their captivity. They would never be comfortable—the cells were crowded and unventilated, and the men slept on boards and wore the same clothes day after day—but they could try to keep clean, and they could improvise several other ways to reduce their misery.

In Warehouse Four there was a lieutenant (j.g.) named Tom Hall who gained a reputation among his fellows as an especially gifted improviser. A farmboy from outside of Suffolk, Virginia, who had grown up learning how to doctor animals, fix cars, and make all of the endless repairs necessary to keep a farm running, he knew how to "make do." After graduating from Virginia Tech, he had gone into the navy and learned to fly fighters. He had been stationed on the *Bonhomme Richard*, on Yankee Station, when his F-8 was hit by a SAM. He had gone to afterburner and pointed the plane toward the beach. Over the Gulf of Tonkin, safely out of reach of the patrol boats and fishing junks, he ejected. The rescue helicopter picked him up and flew him back to the carrier, whose captain was waiting to greet him. A photographer caught the moment, and the picture made the papers back in the States.

Like any pilot who has ejected, Hall was ordered to stand down for a day. The following morning, the weather was so bad over North Vietnam that no missions were flown from the ship. The next day Hall was flying again, and he caught another SAM. This time he bailed out near Hanoi—and the North Vietnamese got him. That was June 1966.

To the men who shared space with him in North Vietnam, Tom Hall was the perfect roommate. He knew how to be quiet, but when he talked, he always had something interesting to say. He told them stories about life back home on the farm, including one about how his family kept a hummingbird flying free in the house to keep the bugs down. The other pilots loved this story; the idea of a hummingbird in the house was somehow otherworldly.

Hall never got too high or too low. He maintained an even strain, as pilots say, and he looked after his comrades first and himself second. He didn't bitch and he didn't quit and he knew, by God, how to cope. It was Hall who figured out how to ease the problem of the drafty cells in the winter of 1968, when the men would wake up in the morning close to hypothermic and spend the first hour or two of the day trying to warm up. HATS, he tapped through the wall. Use extra cloth or, better, a sock to make a hat. Stretch it until it fits over your head like a watch cap. You lose most of your body heat through your head, he explained, and this would help. The men tried it, and it did help. Nevertheless, it was cold, especially during the night.

MOSQUITO NETS, Hall tapped. When it is below forty outside, he explained, you do not need to guard against mosquitoes, but the net can be turned into a kind of insulation, like the fishnet material that Scandinavians use for underwear. Before you lie down to sleep, wrap your upper body in your mosquito net. Like the hats, the improvised underwear was a help. The men were not exactly warm, but they weren't chilled to the bone any longer.

Tom Hall improvised sewing needles from fish bones, or from pieces of wire picked up in the yard. The POWs could now mend their clothes, and they even amused themselves by learning to do a kind of needlepoint. The favorite pattern was, far and away, the American flag.

Hall was also given credit for discovering that a man could use his sandals, which were cut from old rubber tires, as a toilet seat by laying them across the cold, sharp, dirt-encrusted edges of the bucket before he squatted. This, in the minds of many POWs, was the most inspired bit of improvisation in the entire war.

Another persistent, seemingly unsolvable problem at the Plantation was the rats. They were abundant and they were bold. You could chase them out of your cell during the day, but they returned at night. Men were frequently awakened by the pressure of small feet moving across their chests.

Using items that he scrounged—pieces of metal, string, and an empty tin can—Hall built a working mousetrap that kept his cell rat-free. He could not use the tap code to teach the other men how to build such a trap from odds and ends, but he could tell them how to improvise a substitute for plaster out of brick dust and water and use that to seal the rat holes. The other prisoners went to work plastering the holes, and for a while this worked as well as all of Hall's other ideas. But the rats were not pushovers. They began to gnaw their way through the weak plaster barricades, and soon the men had to struggle to replaster the holes faster than the rats could gnaw them open again.

Once more, Hall came through. The Vietnamese grew a kind of bell-shaped pepper, which the men ate with their rations. The pepper was fiercely hot, hotter than any jalapeño the Americans had ever eaten. It was possible to sneak one or two of these peppers out of the mess hall when you were on food detail, and Hall advised the other prisoners to plug the rat holes with them. Checking the holes a day or two later, the men noticed that the rats had tried gnawing through the new plugs but had given up before breaking through. The peppers were too hot even for them.

The rats remained a problem—there were no complete, unequivocal victories for the POWs—but Tom Hall had made it into a fight, and the POWs got their innings.

Housekeeping was humdrum stuff for men who flew supersonic fighters and were accustomed to turning their dirty uniforms over to a laundry run by enlisted men. But it became vastly important at the Plantation and the other camps. The camp was dirty, and sanitation was nonexistent. Spiders, roaches, and flies were everywhere. One man tapped out a message designating the housefly as the national bird of North Vietnam. Keeping clean was important not only for its own sake but because it represented a challenge, however small. It wasn't the stuff of a fighter pilot's dreams, like shooting down a MiG, but under the circumstances it would do.

In their weakened condition, the POWs were prey to all sorts of infections and parasites. They worked hard at keeping their cells, their clothes, and themselves clean. Each man was issued a small bar of lye soap every week, and since it seemed to be almost as abundant as pumpkins, they washed their uniforms vigorously with it when they were taken out to bathe. But they still got sick. Medical lore was dredged up from memory and passed through the wall. When you had diarrhea, you should drink only the broth from your soup and leave any greens or meat it might contain. If you were constipated, you should eat whatever solids were in the soup and leave the liquid. It was not much, but it was a regimen and they followed it.

Boils were a constant, painful problem, as were abscessed teeth. One man remembered a doctor telling him an old piece of medical shorthand—"piss and pus must come out"—so he sneaked razor blades from the shower and used them to lance the boils and open the abscesses. It was painful and messy, but it seemed to work.

Many of the prisoners had been seriously injured when they ejected, and there was a lot of discussion through the wall about how to treat those injuries. What could you do about a broken bone that had not been set properly and was healing crooked?

Al Stafford—one of Stratton's roommates—had suffered a broken upper arm when he was blown out of his plane. The arm seemed to be mending, after a fashion, but he could not raise it to the level of his chest or move it laterally beyond an arc of about 30 degrees. He improvised slings and used his good arm for support, but this only increased the stiffness. He imagined himself returning home—whenever that day came—as a cripple.

Down the line of cells somewhere, another POW learned about Stafford's problem and tapped back that he should begin exercising the arm as much as possible to prevent muscle atrophy and to break up the deposits of calcium that were forming around the break. It was something he'd learned after a football injury.

This led to a debate within Stafford's cell about exercise in general. Should prisoners exert themselves? Dick Stratton, never a man for fitness regimes even before he was shot down, was against strenuous exercise programs. In Stafford's case, he thought it would merely aggravate the injury. As for the other men, he said exercise would burn calories, and they could not afford to waste a single BTU. They were on starvation rations; sit-ups and push-ups would only exhaust whatever small reserves they had. But Stratton was careful not to overexert his authority in this matter. He did not order the men not to exercise strenuously; he merely recommended against it. (Later, he began exercising himself.)

Stafford tried some simple flexing movements. How much worse, he asked himself, could it make his arm? So he would raise it, tentatively, until he reached the point where pain told him to stop. Then he would raise the arm another inch or two, stopping when he could hear something inside begin to tear. It sounded almost like a piece of paper gently ripping. Tears would fill his eyes and he would feel himself growing faint. He would lower his arm until the pain had passed and he had his breath. Then he would slowly raise the arm again, until he reached the same point, and then he would bite down on his back teeth and go another inch, and one more. . . .

After a couple of weeks, he noticed that the arc of mobility had grown by a couple of degrees. So he massaged the arm and kept on. He set goals: Get the arm loose enough that he could use it to drink a cup of water; then enough that he could touch the top of his head. Every day he worked the arm until he could hear that sound of tearing paper and he was on the edge of passing out. The other men in the cell would look away while he was exercising. Now and then, one would say, "How's the arm, Al?"

"Better. Lots better. I can touch my nose."

"That's great, man. Really great. Hang in there."

Other prisoners, desperate for some kind of physical activity, began doing calisthenics. This was tricky, since the sounds of a man running in place or counting off push-ups would alert guards. They would open the cell's little Judas window, wave a finger at the man, and tell him to stop. If he was caught repeatedly, he might be taken up to the headquarters building, which the POWs called the Big House, for interrogation and punishment. Prisoners were to sit quietly in their cells, eat their two bowls of soup a day, come out for a bath and a shave once a week, and otherwise do nothing.

So prisoners who wanted to do calisthenics had to depend on the "clearing system." Along the line of cells, men would watch—and if a guard approached, they would bang on the walls hard enough to alert everyone along the line. When a heavy thud sounded along the wall, men would scramble up from the floor to sit on their bunks with their hands folded in their laps, like subdued children waiting silently in church for services to begin. Between the warning thuds, they did their push-ups and their sit-ups and kept meticulous records of their repetitions. Scores were tapped through the wall, and competitions inevitably followed.

The sit-up count reached into the thousands. A man would fold his blanket into the shape of an exercise mat, get down on his back on the floor, and begin knocking them out with the easy rhythm of a metronome—up and back, up and back, up and back . . . breathe in, breathe out, breathe in, breathe out. . . . Soon the steady, repetitious flexing of his own body would shut out everything else, and he would be alert to nothing except movement and the possible thump from a man in another cell, clearing. Up and down . . . six hundred, six hundred one . . . two . . . Time seemed to slide by when a man was doing his sit-ups. And when he finished, or had to quit, he would feel an overall exhaustion that seemed so much better than the angry tension that grew tighter and tighter inside, like a rope being slowly twisted, when he simply sat on his bunk, hands folded in his lap, waiting for time to pass, feeling his life go by, leaving behind it a trail of . . . nothing.

For some men, calisthenics were insufficient. After thousands of push-ups, tens of thousands of sit-ups, miles of running in place, they wanted something more challenging. For some reason, it seemed essential to start lifting weights.

There were, of course, no weights available, and nothing in the cells even came close. The sawhorses and pallet beds were too big and cumbersome. The only other things in the cells were the buckets. So the physical-fitness fanatics began curling buckets full of human waste to develop their arms. Some days the buckets were heavy and some days they were light. They always stank, but that seemed less and less important to men who had learned to share space with rats and sit on those buckets with absolutely no privacy. They did their curls, concentrating to make the lifting motion smooth and fluid so the contents of the buckets would not slop around too much inside or spill over the edges.

Years later, when he was home, one of the men went to a movie about weight lifting and bodybuilding. The movie was *Pumping Iron*, and it occurred to him that hour after hour, day after day, for almost six years of his life, what he had been doing was pumping shit. It seemed the perfect description.

It was not enough to work on housekeeping, health, and fitness. Even after you had done all you could to keep the cell and yourself clean, exercised until you were exhausted, and taken your turn tapping or clearing, there were still long empty stretches of time that had to be filled. Somehow, you had to keep your mind occupied; otherwise you would dwell on your situation and sink into a swamp of self-pity. The POWs found they had more resources than they could have imagined for keeping themselves diverted. It came down to discovering what they already knew.

Stafford was on the wall one day when someone from the next cell tapped out a riddle. "You are on a path," the message read, "and you come to a place where the path goes off in two directions. There is a guard at the head of each new path. If you take one path, you will meet certain death. If you take the other path, you will live. One guard always lies and the other always tells the truth. You do not know which is which, and you may ask only one question of one of them. What is the question that will allow you to proceed safely?"

It took a long time for the man in the next cell to tap out that message. It took much longer—months, in fact—for Stafford, who had never been good at math and logic and the other empirical disciplines, to mull over the answer. But this was the point. When one of his roommates, who knew the answer, tried to coach him, Stafford said, "No, goddammit. Don't ruin it. I'll get it."

Like virtually all of the prisoners, Stafford finally gave up and asked someone to tell him the answer—which was simplicity itself. You ask either guard, "If I ask the other guard which is the road to safety, what will he tell me?" And then you take the opposite path. This was the best of many brainteasers that went through the wall.

Killing time was not an altogether new experience for the aviators. They had always had time on their hands while waiting to fly, especially in the days before the war. One way of killing time had been with card games that could be put down before takeoff and resumed when the planes were back down. Ready-room and alert-room bridge games could last for weeks. It took some resource-fulness, however, to get a rubber going in prison when all four players were in different and not always adjacent cells.

First you needed cards. The Vietnamese were not handing any out. Al-though they were included in Red Cross and other packages sent to the POWs, these were not distributed until very late in the war. So the POWs had to make the cards. Toilet paper was available. A quill could be made from broom straw, ink from ashes and water. The cards were made small so they could be easily concealed.

Next came the fundamental problem of how to play the game. The men who decided to make up a bridge foursome would each arrange their cards the same way. Then the instructions for how to shuffle would be tapped through each wall. Sometimes these instructions would be relayed by a man who did not play bridge but was willing to help keep the game going and do a little tap-ping to pass the time.

> CUT . . . DECK . . . TEN . . . CARDS . . . DEEP
> CUT . . . LARGE . . . PILE . . . FIFTEEN . . . CARDS . . . DEEP
> PLACE . . . THIRD . . . ON . . . FIRST . . . PILE . . .

And so on until the deck was shuffled.

Then every man would deal four hands, pick up the one that was his, and begin the bidding. Once the bidding was complete, the dummy hand would be turned over. The other hands would remain facedown, and as a card was played, the man making the play would identify the card and its place in the original pile by tapping, so the other players could find it without looking at the rest of the cards in the hand. It would have been easy to cheat, but also, under the circumstances, utterly pointless.

A hand of bridge that might have taken ten minutes to play under normal conditions could last for two or three weeks when every play had to be tapped through several walls. Now and then a new man would decline an invitation to play, saying that it couldn't be done, that tapping all the bidding and the rounds and the scorekeeping through several walls would just take too much time. The other men had an answer, which went back to a time when Dick Stratton had been thrown into a totally darkened cell for punishment.

Long periods of light deprivation are known to cause disorientation and severe emotional distress. Stratton had been kept in that cell for nearly six weeks. His only lifeline was the wall and the man on the other side, Jack Van Loan. At first, simply to give Stratton some kind of reference point, Van Loan would estimate the passage of time and give Stratton a hack every fifteen minutes. It was something. Then, as time went on, Van Loan began asking Stratton to explain things to him: books that Stratton had read, courses he had taken in college, anything that he could remember and describe in detail. Eventually, they came to the subject of philosophy, and Stratton was trying to tell Van Loan, through the wall, about a course he had taken in existentialism. That word alone was tough, and Van Loan missed it several times. Each time Stratton would patiently tap it out again. When they had finally gotten that single word straight, Stratton began tapping out the name Kierkegaard. It seemed to take hours. At one point, Stratton tapped out an apology: SORRY THIS TACING SO LONG.

Van Loan tapped back: DONT WORRY ABT IT XX I THINC TIME IS ON OUR SIDE XX CEEP TALCING.

From then on, whenever a man protested that a bridge game would take too long to tap through several walls of the Warehouse, the man on the other side would tap back: THATS OCAY XX TIME IS ON OUR SIDE.

Card games and chess were good for filling time, but they were not enough to fully engage the minds of college-educated men accustomed to learning as a routine discipline. So they began memorizing lines from poems or plays that they might have been taught to recite as children and had never forgotten, even if they had to work hard at the job of recall. When a man had the lines, he would tap them out to a prisoner in the next cell, who recited them over and over until he had memorized them himself. The music of the lines, the hard cadences—especially of Kipling—provided a kind of solace.

> Then it's Tommy this, an' Tommy that, an' "Tommy, 'ow's yer soul?"
> But it's "Thin red line of 'eroes" when the drums begin to roll—

Men who had never cared much for poetry began to crave the verses, waiting eagerly for them to come through the wall. The POWs in one cell were in the midst of learning "The Highwayman," line by painstaking line, when they were ordered to move. The order came just as they were reaching the climax of the poem and Bess was prepared to "shatter her breast in the moonlight" to warn the highwayman. It was like losing a mystery novel when you are three or four chapters from the end. From their new cell, which had no common wall and could not receive messages by tap code, the men smuggled a message asking what had happened. A message was smuggled back to them—at some risk—and it read: HIGHWAYMAN AND BESS—KIA.

As in some old, preliterate society, storytelling became an important art. The stories and myths of their generation were often films, so after the evening meal and the order to put up nets and lie down on the hard wooden pallets, it would be time for movies. A cellmate who could remember a film would lie on his bunk and begin patiently narrating the action, scene by scene, going into character for dialogue and adding as much detail to the physical descriptions as he could remember or invent. Many of the men had favorite movies they had seen more than once, so they were able to relate a passable summary. Some had a real talent for the work and, with the help of other men who had seen the movie, could assemble a fairly complete account. Certain movies became very popular. *Doctor Zhivago* was easily the best-loved movie at the Plantation.

Still, there were long stretches of dead, empty time when nothing happened and a man was reduced to mute awareness of his situation. He was hungry. In the summer, he was hot and eaten up with skin infections; in the winter, cold and shivering. He was desperately uncertain about the future. He did not know if he would be hauled out for a quiz in ten minutes, still be a captive in ten years.

Almost all of the POWs learned to fantasize. There was a distinction, however, between idle daydreaming and disciplined fantasizing. No one needed to be told that simply crawling under a blanket and dreaming childhood dreams of mother and dog and painless innocence was unhealthy. That kind of random, formless escape would lead a man further and further into passivity, self-pity, and isolation. Instead, when you fantasized, you tried to create real situations and solve real problems. Properly done, a good session of fantasizing would tire you out, leave you with a sense of having accomplished something.

Al Stafford had always loved to sail, so he would sit up straight with his eyes closed and imagine himself out in Chesapeake Bay. He would decide on the season and then try to remember just what the prevailing weather would be. In the summer, when the cell was stifling and full of bugs, he would picture himself out for a winter sail on the bay, with the water the color of lead, the wind blowing whitecaps off the tops of the swells. He saw himself wearing oilskins, and except for a lone freighter moving up the channel, he had the bay to himself. In the winter, while he huddled under his blanket, he would imagine himself stripped down to a bathing suit, skimming past crab boats and other crafts scattered across the mild green expanse of the bay.

At the end of an hour or two of sailing, Stafford could taste the salt on his lips and feel the sun on his skin. He sailed for hours and hours. He used real checkpoints and kept a real logbook. "Five knots equals a mile every twelve minutes. . . . I'll be at the Oxford lighthouse by 1610. . . ."

In another cell, farther down the Warehouse, another man played golf. He would spend two hours a day playing a course he remembered hole by hole. He concentrated so hard on his shots that he could feel the tick of the ball when he made contact with the sweet spot. When his mind wandered for a few moments, he would feel the ugly, metallic sensation all the way up his arms and into his shoulders. A goddamned duck hook, he would tell himself, and trudge off into the rough, hoping that he would be able to find his ball and learn not to use too much right hand.

During his golf games, his cellmates left him alone. It was easy to tell when he was playing, because he would be sitting on his pallet in something like a lotus position, with his eyes closed and his lips moving just slightly as he talked himself through the round. Then, after a couple of hours, he would open his eyes and begin to stretch, as though to relieve the tension. One of the other men in the room would say, "How'd you hit 'em today, Jerry?"

"Not bad, I was two under when I made the turn, but I pushed my drive on fifteen, a long par five. Had to play safe out of the rough and double-bogeyed the hole. Then I three-putted seventeen from twelve feet out. Really blew it. So I was one over for the round."

"That's not bad."

"No, it was a good round. Great weather, too."

"So what about the handicap?"

"I'm still sitting on a two."

"Little more time on the driving range and you'll be a scratch golfer."

"Putting green is more like it. That three-putt killed me."

There was only one limit to this kind of fantasizing: You had to know enough about the situation or the task to make it realistic. You could not simply decide you were going to be a professional golfer and imagine yourself in a playoff against Jack Nicklaus if you had never played a round in your life. But if you put yourself into a world that you did know and understand, and you took your time and forced your mind to follow the consequences of every single choice, you could create a world of almost tangible reality.

It was an escape, but it was also a discipline. If you were a golfer and you played every day, you might feel yourself actually getting better. Though he had not seen blue water for two years, since the morning he last crossed the coast of Vietnam at twenty thousand feet, Al Stafford felt sure he was a better sailor than he had been when he was shot down. He knew so much more now. He had been through certain situations so many times in his mind that he now did the right thing automatically. It was like the time you spent in a flight simulator on the ground, which prepared you for situations you later encountered in the air.

But even if it was a productive way to use long, empty stretches of time, it was still no substitute for the real thing. When it was too hot and he was too dispirited even to fantasize, Stafford wondered when he would see blue water and feel the wind again—or, in his worst moments, if he ever would.

Along the row of cells in the Warehouse, men strained to keep busy, finding the solution in everything from a serious form of make-believe to the most elaborate improvisation. A man named Charles Plumb "played" music on the keyboard of a piano diagrammed in brick dust on the floor. He would patiently play the pieces he could remember, practicing until he got them right. Like Tom Hall, Plumb was an innovator. He had grown up in rural Kansas, where he had been an active Boy Scout and 4-H member. Like many boys his age, he had also fooled around with ham radios and had once sent away for a kit to build his own receiver. He remembered enough about it to try building one at the Plantation so he could listen to news from some source other than Radio Hanoi.

The yard at the Plantation was littered with scrap and debris. On his way to a rare and welcome work detail, Plumb would walk in the typical prisoner fashion, head lowered and shuffling his feet dejectedly. Actually, he was looking for wire. He easily found enough for an aerial and a ground.

During interrogations, prisoners used pencils to write out confessions or letters of apology to the camp commander. They routinely pressed too hard and broke the lead. While a guard was sharpening the pencil, the prisoner would sneak the small piece of broken lead into his clothing to smuggle back into his cell. An eighth of an inch of pencil lead set into a sliver of bamboo made a wonderful, highly prized writing instrument. The POWs would carefully hide their pencils against the possibility of a search. Being caught with a pencil brought punishment for breaking the rule against contraband. Worse, the pencil would be confiscated.

For his radio, Plumb used one of these small pencil points as a detector, balancing it on the edges of two razor blades. For the antenna coil, he wrapped wire around a spool that he made from scrap wood, which he shaped by rubbing it against the rough wall of the cell. He built a capacitor from alternating sheets of waxed paper and aluminum foil smuggled from the kitchen or saved from cigarette packages.

This left the earpiece, which required an electromagnet, diaphragm, and housing. A nail served for the electromagnet. The housing was an unused insulator stuck in the wall, probably dating back to the time the French built the camp. He had worked the insulator loose from the wall and was preparing to wrap the nail with fine wire when the guards conducted a search and confiscated all the parts to his radio. He was taken to the Big House, put in the ropes, and forced to write a letter of apology to the camp commander. He never heard the "Voice of America" on his little radio.

While Plumb was busy with one of his projects, his roommate, Danny Glenn, concentrated on designing and building his dream house. Glenn had studied architecture at Oklahoma State before going into the navy and was shot down four days before Christmas 1966. At the Plantation he filled the hours working on the plans and blueprints for the house he promised himself he would build—exactly to his specifications, with exactly the materials he wanted—when he finally got out of North Vietnam and went home. In his cell, he would rough out the plans on the floor, carefully working out the dimensions and noting the placement of headers, joists, and studs. Then he would draw up his materials list, room by room. His lists were exhaustive and specific, down to the precise gauge of the electric wire. The blueprint of a room would stay on the floor for days, then weeks, while he made his corrections and pondered his decisions.

Lying under his mosquito net at night, Plumb frequently was awakened by his cell mate's voice.

"Hey, Charlie?"

"Yeah."

"You asleep?"

"No."

"Listen, if I'm bothering you . . ."

"That's okay. What is it?"

"Well, you know that upstairs bathroom, the little one at the head of the stairs?"

"Uh-huh."

"Well, I've been thinking about it, and I've decided to go with Mexican tile. What do you think?"

"I think it would look real good."

"You sure?"

"Absolutely."

"It's not too fancy?"

"No. I'd say Mexican tile would be just right."

"Well, what about the color?"

"Hell, I don't know."

"I was thinking green. That dark green like you see on sports cars. British racing green, they call it."

"I think that would look real good."

"Okay, Charlie. Thanks a lot."

"Sure."

"Good night."

In the morning Glenn would go to his blueprints and materials list and write in green Mexican tile for the upstairs bathroom. Then he would check the dimensions and do the arithmetic to calculate just how many three-inch squares he would need and where he would need to cut to fit. He would memorize as much as he could and make notes in tiny script on a piece of paper from a cigarette package, using one of the contraband pencil points or an improvised pen. Then he would fold the sheet into the smallest possible square and hide it in a crack in the wall, erase the schematic of the room he'd been working on, and start another.

That night, after the mosquito nets were down, he would say softly, "Charlie, I'm thinking about paneling that family room downstairs. What do you think . . . ?"

Nearly ten years later, after he had come home and started a new life, Plumb got a call at his home in Kansas.

"Charlie, this is Danny Glenn."

"Yeah, Danny, how you doing?"

"Good. How about you?"

"Real good. What's up?"

"Charlie, I want you to come see me. There's something I want to show you."

"Well . . . all right. Where are you?"

"Oklahoma. Let me tell you how to get here."

Plumb wrote down the directions, and said he would drive down that weekend.

"Great, Charlie. Can't wait to see you."

Plumb followed the directions, and when he made the last of several turns, the one that would take him up to the driveway where he was to turn in, he saw the house. It was the very same house that he had heard described a thousand times and had helped design while his roommate scratched out the plans and prints on the floor of their cell. He stopped the car and studied the house for a long time. It was unbelievable, like something from a dream.

"Hey, Charlie, come on in. Let me show you around."

Everything was there in exact detail. Plumb could walk around the house as if he had lived there all his life. When he came to the end of a hall and opened a door, he knew exactly what would be on the other side, knew where every bathroom was and what kind of tile would be on the floor. Nothing was out of place, and nothing had been changed from the way this house was planned, all those years ago.

"It's beautiful," he said. "I can't believe you got everything just right."

"Oh, it was a bitch, let me tell you. They'd stopped making a lot of the materials I had in mind when I designed this baby. I had to go to salvage yards and warehouses all across the Southwest to find some of this stuff. But, by God, I wasn't going to compromise. I had too much invested—you know what I mean."

Plumb understood.

EPILOGUE

Events continued to move at their Asian snail's pace. In November 1970, Special Forces rescuers, hoping to pluck out a large number of POWs, landed by helicopter at the Son Tay prison camp, the place known as Hope. There were enough Vietnamese (and perhaps some Soviet advisers) for a brisk firefight, but no American POWs: They had been removed after monsoons flooded some of the buildings and fouled the wells. "The raid," Norman writes, "plainly rattled the North Vietnamese. . . . The country immediately went on alert, as though a full-scale invasion might be next. Certainly a resumption of the air war was likely, or perhaps another, more determined attack aimed at freeing the POWs. In a way, these few hundred men had suddenly become the focus of the entire war, on both sides."

POWs were moved by truck from various camps to the Hanoi Hilton, deemed to be safer. Between thirty and fifty men were confined in eleven concrete rooms, each the size of a basketball court. Two more years passed. It was, in its way, an unusual interval. Men, summoning nearly forgotten skills and specialties, began to teach classes without books, beginning in the morning after cleanup and lasting all day. They taught higher math, Spanish, German, international relations, history, psychology, American and British literature, thermodynamics, and automobile mechanics. There were electives in meat cutting from a former butcher's assistant, beekeeping from a man who had grown up on a farm, wine appreciation from an officer who had been stationed in Europe. Someone even taught a course in classical music, humming or whistling the opening bars of symphonies. In one of the rooms, a POW directed a glee club. If a teacher was at a loss for, say, the date of the Battle of Waterloo, he would resort to tapping on the wall: Someone among the hundreds in the Hanoi Hilton would know the answer.

A peace treaty was signed at last on January 27, 1973. The North Vietnamese and the Provisional Revolutionary Government in the South released 591 men in what was called Operation Homecoming. Bands played when the planes carrying them landed. Genuine heroes of a thankless war, they deserved every adulatory note. Time may have been on their side. But how ocay had it been?

The Christmas Bombing

STEPHEN E. AMBROSE

The last significant American military action of the Vietnam War may be, even now, the most controversial. Most people thought of it as the Christmas bombing of 1972, though the man who set it in motion, President Richard M. Nixon, preferred not to emphasize the aspect of holiday uncheer: He called it the December bombing. Nixon was splitting crosshairs, as it were. He did suspend the attacks on Hanoi and Haiphong for the thirty-six hours surrounding December 25. The official designation of the aerial offensive, which (with the intermission) lasted from December 18 to 30, was Linebacker II, a reflection of the nation's —and its president's—fascination with that sporting approximation of war, professional football.

For the United States, the war was winding down, even if Henry A. Kissinger's negotiations with the North Vietnamese remained stalled. All through 1971, the timetable of troop withdrawals had been speeded up: By the spring of the new year (and the beginning of an election campaign), America's military representation was down from its 1968 peak of 550,000 to 95,000, of whom only 6,000 were combat troops. The war had been increasingly Vietnamesed, though it was the Americans who pursued the search for "peace with honor"—to use one of Nixon's favorite phrases. In February 1972 he became the first president to land in Beijing; a Moscow summit was scheduled for late spring. The North Vietnamese saw that time was running out. In March they launched a powerful offensive out of Cambodia. Equipped with Soviet tanks and rockets, they mounted an uncharacteristically conventional attack, one that nearly worked. This was no mere guerrilla strike but a massed strike by 120,000 troops. Clearly, they wanted to achieve a decision before the presidential election in the fall. They menaced Saigon and took large chunks of the two northernmost provinces of South Vietnam.

Although Nixon knew that he could not return ground troops to South Vietnam—that would have been political suicide—he could depend on one immediate resource: airpower. On May 8 he announced that U.S. fighter-bombers would seal off the entrance to the harbor of Haiphong with two thousand–pound mines and institute a naval blockade of North Vietnam. Nixon gambled that the Soviets would not retaliate by calling off the late-May summit. They did make pro forma protests, but the summit went forward as planned. At this point, they did not want the Vietnam War to interfere with détente. "The Soviet Union," writes the historian George C. Herring, "continued to send economic assistance to North Vietnam, but it also sent a top-level diplomat to urge Hanoi to make peace. The Chinese issued perfunctory protests against Nixon's escalation of the war, but behind the scenes they also exerted pressure on Hanoi to settle with the United States." The two Communist giants "had apparently come to regard Vietnam as a sideshow which must not be allowed to jeopardize the major realignment of power then taking place in the world."

Meanwhile, the air campaign known as Linebacker I had begun. It was, true to its name, a defensive action (as its misnamed successor would not be). In the words of one military writer, Linebacker I was "arguably the most effective use of airpower in the Vietnam War." Few air campaigns in the twentieth century equaled its success. Linebacker I interdicted the flow of supplies to the south; carpet bombing by the lumbering B-52 giants out of Guam or Thailand broke the advance of the fourteen divisions of the People's Army of North Vietnam. Fighter-bombers destroyed railroad bridges and tunnels leading from Hanoi to the Chinese border; they were not easily repaired. The historian of airpower Mark Clodfelter registers some of the results of Linebacker I: Mining "decreased seaborne imports from more than 250,000 tons a month to near zero." Perhaps because they wanted to let the North Vietnamese know who was boss in the Communist world, the Chinese refused to ship any goods south for a number of weeks. "They denied the transport of Soviet goods across their territory for *three* months." By destroying stores of fuel and ammunition, Linebacker I robbed the North Vietnamese of the capacity to wage conventional warfare. As one British military authority has observed, "You cannot refuel T-54 tanks with gasoline out of water bottles carried on bicycles."

The North's Easter offensive continued through the summer and into the fall; it suffered a costly defeat. Early in October the North Vietnamese returned to the bargaining table. In just over two weeks, the two sides reached a draft agreement. Days before the election (Nixon triumphed in one of the great landslides of American history), Kissinger could declare with virtual certainty, "We believe that peace is at hand." It was not to be. The South Vietnamese president, Nguyen Van Thieu, balked at the terms. In December talks broke off. The stage was set for the Christmas bombing—Linebacker II.

Peace did come at the end of January 1973. Though both sides made concessions, the eventual agreement was very much like the one Thieu had blocked in the fall. Still, as Stephen Ambrose notes, many questions surrounding the Christmas bombing remain unresolved. Did Linebacker II reinforce the success of Linebacker I? Did the bombings force the North Vietnamese back to the negotiating table, where they finally accepted an armistice and set the POWs free? Did Linebacker II truly bring "peace with honor"? Or did we, as one of Kissinger's aides wrote, bomb North Vietnam "into accepting our concession"? Were the Christmas bombings directed more at Saigon than at Hanoi? Were they, to use the phrase of the *New York Times* columnist James Reston, "war by tantrum"? Were the losses of fifteen B-52s and the sixty-two crewmen who died a price too high to pay? Did Linebacker II vindicate the supremacy of airpower? Or did it merely show its limits? Was the peace treaty a blunder that would doom South Vietnam three years later? Or, if there had been no Watergate—then just a mote in the public eye—would Nixon have felt emboldened to save South Vietnam in 1975, as his successor Gerald Ford did not?

If history is enjoying a resurgence of popularity, one of those chiefly responsible is the late **STEPHEN E. AMBROSE**. By the time of his death in 2002, Professor Ambrose had written more than thirty books, including multivolume biographies of Dwight D. Eisenhower and Richard M. Nixon (from which this article was excerpted), as well as such bestsellers as *Undaunted Courage,* the story of the Lewis and Clark expedition; *Nothing Like It in the World: The Men Who Built the Transcontinental Railroad, 1863–1869;* and his accounts of the end of World War II in Europe, *D-Day, Citizen Soldiers, The Victors, Wild Blue,* and *Band of Brothers* (which was made into a hit television miniseries). Ambrose was founder of the National D-Day Museum in New Orleans.

O F THE MANY CONTROVERSIES that swirl around the American role in the Vietnam War, one of the most contentious centers on the Christmas bombing of Hanoi in December 1972. This event followed Henry A. Kissinger's October news conference in which he said, "Peace is at hand," and President Richard Nixon's triumphant reelection in November. It preceded the signing of the armistice in January 1973 and the release of the American POWs.

According to Nixon and his supporters, the Christmas bombing forced the North Vietnamese to make concessions, accept an armistice, and release American POWs. It was a great U.S. victory that brought peace with honor.

According to Nixon's critics, the armistice agreement signed in January 1973 was identical to the one reached in October 1972. The bombing brought no concessions from the enemy, nor was it intended to; its purpose was to persuade the South Vietnamese to go along with an armistice to which they were violently opposed. The bombing ended not because the enemy cried "enough" but because American losses of B-52s were becoming intolerable. In addition, conservative critics called the bombing an American defeat that brought a temporary cease-fire at the cost of a free and independent South Vietnam.

Like so much else in the Vietnam War, the issue of the Christmas bombing was divisive and remains so. To the prowar hawks, it was done with surgical precision, sparing civilian lives; to the antiwar doves, it was terror bombing, pure and simple. These differences in view cannot be reconciled or settled, but they can be examined.

For three years, Kissinger, as national security adviser, had been engaged in secret talks with Le Duc Tho in Paris, seeking a negotiated peace. In the spring of 1972 the Communists had launched their largest offensive ever and had almost overrun South Vietnam. Nixon had responded by bombing Hanoi and mining Haiphong Harbor. The offensive was stopped. In October, Kissinger and Le Duc Tho finally reached an agreement. Its basic terms were a cease-fire in place; the return of POWs; total American withdrawal from South Vietnam; and a National Council of Concord and Reconciliation in South Vietnam to arrange elections, its membership to be one third neutral, one third from the current government in Saigon, one third Communist. Nixon was satisfied that this agreement met his conditions for peace with honor.

President Nguyen Van Thieu of South Vietnam, however, felt betrayed. He perceived the agreement as a surrender: It gave the Communists a legitimate role in the political life of his nation; it allowed the Vietcong to hold on to the territory it controlled in South Vietnam; worst of all, it permitted the North Vietnamese Army (NVA) to continue to occupy the two northern provinces and retain more than 150,000 troops in his country. Thieu absolutely refused to agree to the cease-fire. In early December, Kissinger went to Paris to persuade Le Duc Tho to remove the NVA from South Vietnam; Le Duc Tho adamantly insisted on going through with the October agreement.

On December 13, 1972, Kissinger flew back to Washington to meet with Nixon and an aide, General Alexander Haig, to discuss the options. The doves urged them to make a separate deal with Hanoi for the release of the POWs in return for a total American withdrawal, leaving Thieu to sink or swim on his own. This proposal had no appeal to Nixon and his aides. To abandon South Vietnam now, after all the blood that had been shed, all the money that had been spent, all the uproar that had overwhelmed the American political scene, would be wrong, cowardly, a betrayal. To abandon Thieu would amount to surrendering the fundamental American goal in the war: the maintenance in power of an anti-Communist government in Saigon.

To get Thieu to sign the agreement, and to force Le Duc Tho to give just a bit more, some dramatic action by the United States was necessary. With fewer than 25,000 U.S. troops remaining in South Vietnam, down from a high of 550,000 when Nixon took office, there was no possibility of escalating on the ground. The only real option discussed was to expand the bombing campaign against North Vietnam.

There were, however, powerful arguments against that course. Sending B-52s over Hanoi meant risking those expensive weapons and their highly trained crews, because the Soviets had been rushing SA-2 SAMs (surface-to-air missiles) to North Vietnam. The SAMs fired a ten-meter-long missile that U.S. airmen ruefully called "the flying telephone pole." Each missile carried a 286-pound warhead with fuses that could be set to detonate close to a target, on impact, or on command. Guided by a radar tracking beam that honed in on its target, they traveled at a speed of Mach 1.5. The range was thirty horizontal miles and about eleven miles up. Fighter-bombers could evade the missiles by diving toward them and then veering off sharply, but that technique was not possible for B-52 pilots.

There were other technological problems for the big bombers. Built in the 1950s, they had been designed to drop nuclear weapons over the Soviet Union. They had only four 4.5mm tail guns—and, in any case, the SAMs came on too fast to be shot down. The B-52s' best defense was altitude: They usually dropped their bombs from 30,000 feet. But the SAMs were able to reach almost 60,000 feet.

And there were political as well as technological problems. Because of the strength of the antiwar movement in the United States, the government—under both Lyndon Johnson and Nixon—had imposed many restrictions on targets in the air war, which, naturally, infuriated the airmen. This policy had little effect on public opinion—the doves and foreign critics still charged that the U.S. Air Force was carrying out a barbaric, terrorist campaign—but it was a great help to the North Vietnamese. They knew what was off-limits and could concentrate their SAMs around such predictable targets as railroad yards and radar sites.

The technological advantage was with the enemy; for this reason, Secretary of Defense Melvin Laird, his deputy, Kenneth Rush, and the chairman of the Joint Chiefs of Staff, Admiral Thomas Moorer, were opposed to using B-52s over Hanoi, and they so advised the president. Many of Nixon's political advisers were also opposed, because to escalate the bombing after Kissinger's "peace is at hand" statement would drive the Nixon-haters in Congress, in the media, on the campuses, and among the general public into a frenzy.

But something had to be done to convince Thieu that, whatever the formal wording of the cease-fire agreement, he could count on Nixon to come to the defense of South Vietnam if the NVA broke the cease-fire. And Le Duc Tho had to be convinced that, despite the doves in Congress, Nixon could still punish North Vietnam.

That made the bombing option tempting. Although the B-52s were relatively slow and cumbersome, they packed a terrific punch. They carried eighty-four 500-pound bombs in their bomb bays and twelve 500-pound bombs on their wings. They could drop those bombs with relative accuracy, much better than World War II bombers. (The Seventh Air Force commander, General John Vogt, complained that the internal radar systems of the B-52s were "notoriously bad" and that "misses of a thousand feet or more were common." However, in World War II, misses of a thousand meters—three times as much—had been common.) They flew from secure bases in Guam and Thailand. They had been used with devastating effect in the Battle of Khe Sanh in 1968 and again to stop the NVA spring offensive of 1972. The temptation to use them against Hanoi was great, and growing.

Kissinger tried to resist it. He recommended more bombing south of the 20th Parallel, against NVA units that were not as well protected by SAMs as Hanoi was, and reseeding the mines in Haiphong Harbor. On the other hand, Haig, always a hard-liner, argued forcefully for an all-out bombing campaign by the B-52s against Hanoi itself.

Nixon later said that ordering the bombing was "the most difficult decision" he had to make in the entire war. But, he added, "it was also one of the most clear-cut and necessary ones." He issued an order on December 14 to reseed the mines, from the air—and also to send the B-52s against Hanoi. He told Kissinger he was prepared "for new losses and casualties and POWs," and explained, "We'll take the same heat for big blows as for little blows."

To Kissinger, the president seemed "sullen" and "withdrawn." Nixon "resented" having to do what he did, because "deep down he was ready to give up by going back to the October draft" of the armistice agreement. His bombing order, according to Kissinger, was "his last roll of the dice . . . helpful if it worked; a demonstration to the right wing if it failed that he had done all he could."

Once Nixon set the policy, public relations became his obsession. John Scali, White House adviser on foreign affairs information policy, put the problem succinctly to Nixon's chief of staff, H. R. Haldeman, in a telephone conversation: "We look incompetent—bombing for no good reason and because we don't know what else to do." On May 8, 1972, Nixon had gone on television to explain his reason for bombing Hanoi and mining Haiphong: It was in response to the Communists' spring offensive. Scali had thought the television appearance unnecessary in May, as the justification for Nixon's strong action was obvious then. But in December, when his critics and even some of his supporters could not figure out his reasons, Nixon refused to go on television to explain his actions.

Kissinger badly wanted Nixon to make a broadcast; he had been urging it for days. But Nixon, according to Kissinger, "was determined to take himself out of the line of fire." Nixon feared that any attempt to rally the people to support more bombing after "peace is at hand" would fall flat.

On the evening of December 14, four days before the bombing was set to begin, Nixon told Kissinger to hold a news conference to explain the status of the negotiations. The president followed up with a five-page, single-spaced memo on December 15 and another of two pages on December 16, instructing Kissinger on what to say. He told the national security adviser to "hit hard on the point that, while we want peace just as soon as we can get it, that we want a peace that is honorable and a peace that will last." Kissinger should admit the U.S. goals had been reached "in principle" in the October agreement, but add that some "strengthening of the language" was needed "so that there will be no doubt on either side in the event that [the agreement] is broken." He should accuse Le Duc Tho of having "backed off" on some of the October understandings.

Kissinger should emphasize that with the Christmas season coming on, the president had a "very strong personal desire to get the war settled." But he should also point out that the president "insists that the United States is not going to be pushed around, black-mailed or stampeded into making the wrong kind of a peace agreement." Finally, he should say that "the president will continue to order whatever actions he considers necessary by air and sea"—the only reference to the bombing order, which had already gone out.

In his memos, Nixon was repetitious to a degree unusual even for him, an indication of the strain he was under, due perhaps to the difficulty of his position. As an example of his dilemma, it was the Americans—in response to demands from Thieu—who had backed off the October agreements, not the North Vietnamese. But Nixon could not have Kissinger straightforwardly tell the American people his administration was bombing Hanoi to convince Thieu to sign. Thieu was seen increasingly in the United States as the sole obstacle to peace and thus was increasingly unpopular. On December 15, Senator Barry Goldwater, an Arizona Republican and one of the toughest hawks, said that if Thieu "bucks much more," the United States should proceed with its withdrawal and "to hell with him."

Kissinger held his briefing on December 16 and said what he had been told to say. He stressed the president's consistency, unflappability, firmness, patience, and farsightedness. He mentioned Nixon fourteen times (he had been criticized by Haldeman for referring to the president only three times in his October news conference).

By this time the tension in the Nixon-Kissinger relationship was threatening to lead to an open break. Kissinger was unhappy with his boss because of his interference, and his back-and-forthing, on the negotiations. Nixon was furious with Kissinger for his "peace is at hand" statement, which had raised public expectations to a high level, expectations that were going to be dashed when the bombing began. Nixon also resented the way Kissinger had thrust himself onto center stage, his constant leaks to reporters, and the way the reporters responded by giving Kissinger credit for the huge margin of the election victory. Further, earlier in December, *Time* magazine had named Nixon and Kissinger "Men of the Year," with their pictures on the cover; Kissinger correctly feared that Nixon resented having to share the honor.

On December 17, Nixon wrote a letter to Thieu. Usually, the president signed drafts of letters to foreign heads of government prepared by Kissinger; in this case, he wrote the letter personally. Nixon had Haig fly to Saigon to hand-deliver it. In the letter Nixon made a threat: Unless Thieu accepted the agreement, the United States would go it alone. "You must decide now whether you want me to seek a settlement with the enemy which serves U.S. interests alone."

Although Nixon himself would do anything possible to avoid a break, the threat was not meaningless, because, as Goldwater's statement indicated, Congress might carry it out regardless of the president's wishes. Thieu knew that, and he also knew how to read between the lines of Nixon's letter. After reading it, he told Haig it was obvious he was being asked to sign not a peace agreement but rather an agreement for continued American support.

On December 18 the air force launched its B-52s and fighter-bombers against Hanoi. The orders were to avoid civilian casualties at all costs; for example, a missile-assembly plant manned by Russian technicians in the heart of Hanoi was off-limits, partly because of fear of Soviet casualties, partly to avoid near-misses that would devastate residential areas. Still, Linebacker II, as the operation was code-named, greatly damaged railroads, power plants, radio transmitters, and radar installations around Hanoi, as well as docks and ship-yards in Haiphong.

It was not Nixon but Johnson who had imposed the restrictions on targets; in fact, they frustrated Nixon. The day after the bombing began, he read a report about targets that had been avoided for fear of civilian casualties, and he called Admiral Moorer. "I don't want any more of this crap about the fact that we couldn't hit this target or that one," Nixon said. "This is your chance to use military power effectively to win this war, and if you don't, I'll consider you responsible." But the armed forces, concerned about their reputation and perhaps doubtful of the effectiveness of area bombing, continued the restrictions.

Nevertheless, a French reporter in Hanoi referred to "carpet bombing," a line repeated by Radio Hanoi. As a result, there was an immediate worldwide uproar and many expressions of moral revulsion. There had been no presidential explanation or announcement of any kind. People everywhere had taken Kissinger at his word, that only a few t's needed to be crossed and a few i's dotted and the negotiations would be wrapped up. The shock when the bombing was announced was even greater than that following the Cambodian incursion of 1970.

The adverse congressional and editorial reaction was unprecedented. Senator William Saxbe, an Ohio Republican, said Nixon "appears to have left his senses." Democratic Senate leader Mike Mansfield of Montana called it a "Stone Age tactic." Democratic Senator Edward Kennedy of Massachusetts said it was an "outrage." In an editorial, *The Washington Post* charged that the bombing caused millions of Americans "to cringe in shame and to wonder at their President's very sanity." James Reston, in *The New York Times*, called it "war by tantrum."

Nixon did have supporters, including Governors Nelson Rockefeller of New York and Ronald Reagan of California and Republican senators James Buckley of New York, Howard Baker of Tennessee, and Charles Percy of Illinois. John Connally, former governor of Texas and treasury secretary, called Nixon daily to encourage him and assure him that, regardless of what politicians and the media said, the people were behind him.

That was probably an exaggeration, but not as gross as the exaggerations of Nixon's critics. They charged that he had ordered the most intensive bombing campaign in the history of warfare. That was nonsense. In comparison to the human costs at Dresden, Hamburg, Berlin, and Tokyo—not to mention Hiroshima and Nagasaki—in World War II, the bombing of Hanoi during the Christmas season of 1972 was a minor operation. Under the severe targeting restrictions followed by the air force, civilian casualties were only around 1,500, and at least some of those were caused by SAM missiles falling back on the city after missing their targets. In World War II a bombing raid that killed fewer than two thousand German or Japanese civilians was not worth even a minor story in the newspapers, not to mention expressions of moral outrage from opinion leaders and prominent politicians.The Christmas bombing of Hanoi was not terror bombing, as the world had come to know terror bombing in the twentieth century.

Nixon's private response was to personalize it and assign to his critics the lowest possible motives. In his diary he wrote that they "simply cannot bear the thought of this administration under my leadership bringing off the peace on an honorable basis which they have so long predicted would be impossible. The election was a terrible blow to them and this is their first opportunity to recover from the election and to strike back."

That was by no means the whole truth. The most basic cause for the moral revulsion was the nature of the war itself. Few in the United States had protested the firebomb raids of World War II, which set out deliberately to kill civilians. Why the difference three decades later, especially when the air force was doing its utmost to avoid killing civilians? Because from 1942 to 1945, the United States was fighting for its life against a foe who was not only pure evil but also powerful enough to threaten the entire world. In World War II there had been no ongoing negotiations with the Germans and Japanese, only a demand for their unconditional surrender. In 1942–45 the Americans were bombing in order to hasten that surrender.

But in 1972 no one believed that the United States was fighting for its life, or that the NVA could conquer the world, or that there could be no end to the war until Hanoi surrendered; and few believed that more bombing would bring a quicker end to the war.

Despite the protest, Nixon continued to send the B-52s and fighter-bombers, and the battle raged in the sky above Hanoi. If Hanoi was far from being the most heavily bombed city in history, it certainly was one of the best defended. The SAMs shot down six of the ninety B-52s that flew missions on December

20; the following day, two of thirty were destroyed. The air force could not long sustain such losses; on the other hand, the Soviets could not long continue to supply SAMs in such quantity to the North Vietnamese (they were shooting a hundred or more per day at the attackers).

Nixon felt his resolve was being tested; he was determined to prevail. Kissinger, however, broke under the pressure of the protest and began leaking to reporters, especially Reston, word that he had opposed the bombing. This infuriated Nixon. He instructed his aide Charles Colson to monitor all Kissinger's telephone calls and contacts with the press. The president, according to Colson, "was raving and ranting about Henry double-talking." Colson did as instructed and discovered that Kissinger was calling Reston and others, "planting self-serving stories at the same time he was recommending Nixon be tough on Vietnam."

When Haldeman confronted Kissinger, the national security adviser simply denied the facts. "I have never given a personal opinion different from the president's," he claimed, and said he had not given an interview to Reston. Haldeman got him to admit that he had called Reston on the telephone, just before Reston wrote a column stating that Kissinger had opposed the bombing and implying that Kissinger was the one moderate, sensible man among Nixon's advisers. Kissinger concluded his conversation with Haldeman by suggesting that it was time for the president to give him a vote of confidence: a letter from Nixon giving Kissinger backing and credit for the progress in the negotiations.

Nixon went to his home in Key Biscayne, Florida, for Christmas. He ordered a thirty-six-hour halt in the bombing for the holiday. In his diary he complained he was "more and more" a lonely individual. "It is a question not of too many friends but really too few—one of the inevitable consequences of this position." He received very few Christmas salutations, even from Republicans on Capitol Hill and members of his Cabinet. As a result, he told interviewer David Frost four years later, "it was the loneliest and saddest Christmas I can ever remember, much sadder and much more lonely than the one in the Pacific during the war." He did make some telephone calls, including one to Ronald Reagan, who complained about CBS News coverage of the bombing and said that under World War II circumstances, the network would have been charged with treason.

The day after Christmas, despite urgings from some of his aides and much of the media that he extend the Christmas Day truce, Nixon ordered the biggest bombing raid yet, 120 B-52s over Hanoi. Five were shot down, but that afternoon Nixon received a message from Hanoi. The Communists, who had evidently exhausted their supply of SAMs, proposed that the talks resume in Paris on January 9. Nixon replied that he wanted technical talks resumed on January 2, and he offered to stop the bombing of Hanoi if the Communists agreed. Hanoi did so.

General Haig was furious. He did not want to stop the bombing when Hanoi was all but on its knees. He was incensed when he discovered that "every single adviser of the president . . . [was] calling the president daily, hourly, and telling him to terminate the bombing." But even Haig realized that Nixon had little choice, because if he continued the bombing after the congressional session began on January 3, "there would have been legislative restrictions which would have been national suicide from the standpoint of ever negotiating a settlement."

Nixon decided to call off the bombing. On December 29 he announced that he had suspended offensive operations north of the 20th Parallel and that the Paris talks would resume.

So who won the eleven-day battle? The North Vietnamese had shot down fifteen B-52s, and eleven fighter-bombers had gone down. Ninety-three American airmen were missing—thirty-one became known POWs. The enemy had fired 1,200 missiles and lost three MiG jets to achieve these results. Some 40,000 tons of bombs had fallen on Hanoi—40 kilotons, or the equivalent of two Hiroshima-size bombs. However, visitors to Hanoi soon after the battle ended, including Americans, all testify that although great destruction was done to military and industrial targets—such as the airfields, railroad network, and factories—residential areas were mostly untouched.

There was no clear-cut winner. Thus the last American action in the Vietnam War was characteristic of all those that had come earlier: cursed by half measures. From 1964 to 1969, Johnson's actions, as described by Nixon, were always "too little, too late." That had been true as well as Nixon's ultimatum in November 1969; of his Cambodian incursion of 1970; of his Laotian operation in 1971; of his May 8, 1972, air offensive; and now of his Christmas bombing. He had taken the heat for an all-out offensive without delivering one. It was not that he did not want to, but rather that it was overwhelmingly obvious the American political system would not allow him to do so.

Nixon called Hanoi's willingness to resume the talks a "stunning capitulation," one presumably brought about by the bombing. But it had been Saigon, not Hanoi, that had created the stalemate in the talks. In his message to Hanoi, Nixon had referred to the October agreements; going back to them represented an American, not a North Vietnamese, concession. Kissinger's reference to "normalization" of relations continued the hints he had been secretly making to Le Duc Tho that when peace came, the United States would aid in the reconstruction of North Vietnam, just as it had helped Germany and Japan after World War II.

On December 30, Senator Henry Jackson, a Democrat from Washington, called Nixon to ask the president to go on television and explain that "we bombed to get them back to the table." Nixon passed the message along to Kissinger with a note: "He is right—but my saying it publicly would seriously jeopardize our negotiations."

Nixon had another reason to hesitate over making the claim that Jackson wanted him to make. It would have been extremely difficult to get informed observers to believe that Nixon had bombed Hanoi in order to force North Vietnamese acceptance of terms they had already agreed to. It was much easier to believe that Nixon's real target was not Hanoi but Saigon. And as 1972 came to an end, there was no indication that Thieu was prepared to sign.

On January 2, 1973, the House Democratic Caucus voted 154 to 75 to cut off all funds for Vietnam as soon as arrangements were complete for the withdrawal of American armed forces and the return of the POWs. On January 4 the Senate Democratic Caucus passed a similar resolution, 36 to 12.

Nixon passed the pressure on to Thieu. Initially, he tried to do so through Anna Chennault, the widow of General Claire Chennault, whose influence on the right wing of the Republican Party was considerable. He had her friend John Mitchell, his former attorney general, ask her to use her influence with Thieu, but the "Dragon Lady," as she was commonly called, refused. There was irony here. In 1968, Mitchell had persuaded Mrs. Chennault to intervene with Thieu to get him to refuse to help Johnson in his election-eve bid for peace, which, if successful, might have given Hubert Humphrey the presidency. Now Nixon wanted her to persuade Thieu to cooperate with the president and accept an unsatisfactory peace. She would not.

Nixon again wrote directly to Thieu. The letter, dated January 5, was less threatening than previous ones and contained a more explicit promise:

"Should you decide, as I trust you will, to go with us, you have my assurance of continued assistance in the post-settlement period and that we will respond with full force should the settlement be violated by North Vietnam."

Nixon was not in a position to give such a promise. Without congressional appropriations, he could not come to Saigon's aid.

That same day he had a meeting with the leaders of both parties. The atmosphere was cold. He spoke briefly about Vietnam. He said he knew many of the men in the room disagreed with his policies but added that he was determined to persist.

Nixon concluded, "In any event, you have indicated your own positions—some of you—which is in direct opposition. I understand that. I have the responsibility. Gentlemen, I will take responsibility if those negotiations fail. If they succeed, we all succeed."

On January 6, Nixon went to his retreat at Camp David, where he met with Kissinger, who was flying to Paris the next day. The president said that if Kissinger could get Le Duc Tho to go back to the October 8 agreement, "we should take it." Kissinger demurred, but Nixon insisted. He did want Kissinger to get some wording changes so that "we can claim some improvement," but the point was that the war had to end, on whatever terms, in this round of negotiations; otherwise the Ninety-third Congress would force the administration to end it on even worse terms.

The president did agree that Kissinger could threaten the North Vietnamese with a resumption of the bombing of Hanoi if they did not cooperate, but Nixon then warned him that "as far as our internal planning is concerned, we cannot consider this to be a viable option." As for Thieu, Nixon referred to Haig's report of his December visit to Saigon: Thieu was saying that "it is not a peace agreement that he is going to get but a commitment from the United States to continue to protect South Vietnam in the event such an agreement is broken." Nixon said that was exactly right.

January 9 was Nixon's sixtieth birthday. In an interview, he gave his formula for living: "Never slow down." He admitted that he had many problems, "but boredom is the least of them."

He also wrote by hand a piece of self-analysis: "RN approaches his second inauguration with true peace of mind—because he knows that by his actions, often in the face of the most intense sort of criticism, what he is bringing to the world is a 'peace of mind'—that is, a peace formed by the exercise of hard reason and calm deliberation, and durable because its foundation has been carefully laid." Nixon instructed Haldeman to pass the piece along to the staff and called it "an excellent line for them to take" when talking to the press about the president.

That afternoon Nixon got what he called "the best birthday present I have had in sixty years." Kissinger cabled from Paris that there had been "a major breakthrough in the negotiations. In sum, we settled all the outstanding questions in the text of the agreement."

Le Duc Tho had accepted Kissinger's revised wording on the demilitarized zone. But it made no practical difference; the accord that had been reached was basically the same as in October. Kissinger aide John Negroponte was disappointed. He told friends, "We bombed the North Vietnamese into accepting our concession."

Getting the Communists to accept the accord had never been the problem; the problem was Thieu, and that remained. Nixon was eager to have the situation resolved before Inauguration Day, January 20, but he worried that Thieu would refuse to cooperate.

On January 13, Kissinger returned from Paris. He flew down to Key Biscayne to brief the president. They talked until two A.M. Nixon walked out to the car with Kissinger to say good night and to tell him that the country was indebted to him for what he had done. Nixon later wrote that "it is not really a comfortable feeling for me to praise people so openly," but "Henry expects it, and it was good that I did so." Kissinger replied it was only Nixon's courage that had made a settlement possible. In his memoirs Kissinger wrote that he felt "an odd tenderness" that night toward Nixon.

The next morning they turned their attention to Thieu. Nixon wrote him another letter and told Haig to fly to Saigon to deliver it. The letter was full of threats: "I have therefore irrevocably decided to proceed to initial the Agreement on January 23, 1973, and to sign it on January 27, 1973, in Paris. I will do so, if necessary alone." There were also promises. If Thieu would sign, Nixon would make it "emphatically clear that the United States recognizes your government as the only legal government of South Vietnam; that we do not recognize the right of any foreign troops to be present on South Vietnamese territory; that we will react strongly in the event the agreement is violated." Of course, there was a big difference between not recognizing the right of the NVA to stay in South Vietnam and requiring the NVA to leave the country when the American armed forces left. Nixon concluded, "It is my firm intention to continue full economic and military aid."

Nixon feared that his words would not be enough, but he was determined to prevail. "Brutality is nothing," he told Kissinger. "You have never seen it if this son-of-a-bitch doesn't go along, believe me." To add to the pressure on Thieu, Nixon had Senators John Stennis, a Mississippi Democrat, and Goldwater warn publicly that if Thieu blocked the agreement, he would imperil his government's chances of receiving any further aid from Congress.

Still Thieu would not yield. He sent a letter to Nixon raising the same complaints he had made in October—naturally enough, since it was the same agreement. Nixon replied on January 20 with an ultimatum.

On the public relations front, meanwhile, Nixon was also busy. On January 19 he told Haldeman, "We need to get across the point that the reason for the success of the negotiations was the bombing and the converse point that we did not halt the bombing until we had the negotiations back on track." He instructed Kissinger to brief the staff on the settlement: "The key to this briefing will be to get a lot of people out selling our line." Nixon wanted "an all-out effort with inspired leaks, etc."

On January 20, Nixon was inaugurated for his second term. He had hoped to be able to announce that peace had been achieved, but Thieu's intransigence made that impossible. Under the circumstances, the hoopla that ordinarily occurs at inaugurations was distinctly absent, and Nixon's inaugural address was short and somber.

The parade following the ceremonies was marred by small groups of demonstrators chanting obscenities and throwing eggs and debris, but it was nowhere near as bad as four years earlier. If Nixon had not brought peace quite yet, he had gone a long way toward achieving that objective. The madness and hatred that had been so prominent in 1969 had abated by 1973. Sadly, in part it had been replaced by a bitterness because of the Christmas bombing and a suspicion because of the growing furor over the Watergate break-in. If Nixon deserved credit for the gains, he also deserved blame for the bitterness and suspicion.

On January 22 word arrived that Thieu had finally bowed to the inevitable and consented to the agreement. The following evening Nixon went on television to announce that on January 27 the formal signing ceremonies would be held in Paris. A cease-fire would begin at midnight that day.

After this announcement Nixon met with Kissinger. Nixon said he did not want to have any hatred or anything of that sort toward "our enemies"—by which he meant the American doves, not the Vietnamese Communists. "On the other hand," he continued, Nixon's foes had to recognize that they "are disturbed, distressed, and really discouraged because we succeeded."

Nixon later wondered whether commentators would appreciate what he and Kissinger had accomplished; he decided "probably not." He told Kissinger that every success was followed by a "terrific letdown," and he urged Kissinger not to let it get to him. There were many battles left to fight; he should not be discouraged.

For his part, Nixon wrote later that he had expected to feel relief and satisfaction when the war ended, but instead was surprised to find himself with feelings of "sadness, apprehension, and impatience." Kissinger was struck by Nixon's being "so lonely in his hour of triumph."

Beyond the letdown he always felt after a crisis, Nixon had reasons for his negative feelings. In the weeks that followed, he often and vehemently maintained he had achieved peace with honor, but that claim was difficult to sustain. Seven years earlier, when pressed by reporters to explain what kind of settlement he would accept in Vietnam, he had held up the Korean armistice of 1953 as his model. What he finally accepted was far short of that goal.

The Korean settlement had left 60,000 American troops in South Korea; the Vietnam settlement left no American troops in South Vietnam. The Korean settlement left no Communist troops in South Korea; the Vietnam settlement left 150,000 Communist troops in South Vietnam. The Korean settlement had established the 38th Parallel as a dividing line, and it was so heavily fortified on both sides that twenty years later, almost no living thing had crossed it; the Vietnam settlement called the 17th Parallel a border, but the NVA controlled both sides of it and moved back and forth without interference. The Korean settlement had left President Syngman Rhee firmly in control of his country, to the point that the Communist Party was banned; the Vietnam settlement forced President Thieu to accept Communist membership on the National Council of Concord and Reconciliation.

Small wonder that Thieu regarded the settlement as little short of a surrender, and feared that the cease-fire would last only until the Americans got their POWs back and brought their armed forces home. Small wonder, too, that he worried about his future, as his army was woefully inferior to Rhee's army (not to mention the NVA).

Thieu did have one asset to match Rhee's: a promise from the American president that if the Communists broke the agreement, the United States would come to his aid. But in South Vietnam, in the spring of 1975, that promise proved to be worthless, because by then Nixon had resigned to avoid impeachment. In some part the resignation was brought on by the Christmas bombing. Kissinger's "peace is at hand" promise, followed by Nixon's triumphant reelection, and then by the bombing, created feelings of bitterness and betrayal and led many Democrats to want to punish Nixon. Nixon gave them their excuse with Watergate.

Nixon's defenders assert that had it not been for Watergate, the North Vietnamese would not have dared to launch their offensive in 1975. Or, if they had, that Nixon would have responded with the fury he showed in the spring of 1972, and the American bombing support would have made it possible for the South Vietnamese to turn back the invaders once again.

Nixon's detractors call this scenario nonsense. They assert that all he ever wanted or expected from the cease-fire was a "decent interval" before the NVA overran Saigon. That decent interval was until Nixon had successfully completed his second term. They argue further that Congress was never going to give Nixon the funds to resume bombing in Vietnam and that he knew it, even as he made his promises to Thieu.

No one can know what might have been. Everyone knows what happened.

V

THE END

The ICBM and the Cold War:
Technology in the Driver's Seat

JOHN F. GUILMARTIN, JR.

From the beginning of the Cold War to its end, technology held the whip hand. Of all the unprecedented, indeed dramatic, advances in weaponry, John F. Guilmartin, Jr., writes here, "None had a more profound strategic impact than the intercontinental ballistic missile, icon of the Cold War and central pillar of mutual deterrence." The very nature of the East–West confrontation came to be shaped by the ICBM and its potential visit of apocalypse on both sides. Never in history has a weapon influenced statecraft and strategy so thoroughly. It was like a real-life replay of *The Sorcerer's Apprentice*. Inventions had not only taken over; they threatened to get out of hand. Men may have prevailed in the end, but the margin was terrifyingly small.

As if in recognition of technology's dominance, the Cold War became the era of the acronym: the ICBM; its little sisters, the IRBM (intermediate-range) and the SLBM (submarine-launched); the missile tip with several warheads, MIRV (multiple independently targeted reentry vehicles); ABMs (antiballistic missiles); PALs (permissive action links), the remote-controlled digital codes that could unlock and activate a nuclear weapon; TELs (mobile transporter-erector-launchers); SIOP (single integrated operation plan), which identified *all* Soviet and Chinese targets to be attacked, enabling the simultaneous use of every available nuclear weapon; SDI (strategic defense initiative), the "star wars" chimera that is still with us; and, of course, that most tellingly sinister acronym of all, MAD (mutual assured destruction).

"Like the early fathers of the church" (the writer John Newhouse's phrase), the brethren of the nuclear priesthood squabbled over positions that might have seemed the stuff of theology had not their impli-

cations been so real. The disputants did not just conjure hell; they held
the keys to it. Should there be more emphasis on first-strike or second-
strike capability? Should the defense of cities be put on a par with the
protection of missile sites and airbases? How much accumulation of
nuclear weaponry was too much? Presumably, the same sort of arguments went on in the Soviet Union. Igor Kurchatov, the father of the
Soviet atomic bomb, stopped further work after viewing the effects of
the first air-dropped hydrogen bomb in 1955. "That was such a terrible,
monstrous sight! That weapon must not be allowed ever to be used." Not
long before, however, that Bolshevik warhorse Viacheslav Molotov, had
taken a different tack: "A Communist should not speak about the 'destruction of the human race' but about the need to prepare and mobilize
all forces for the destruction of the bourgeoisie." He went on to say that
if one believed that "in the event of war all must perish . . . then why
should we build socialism, why worry about tomorrow? It would be better to supply everyone with coffins now." The Molotovs were clearly
winning out.

Meanwhile, the clock of terror had begun to accelerate. It took under
fifteen years to go from the first atomic bomb in 1945 to ICBMs that
could carry a nuclear charge from one continent to another. Some
chronology will provide useful background to Professor Guilmartin's article. By August 1949, soon after the Berlin crisis ended, the Soviets exploded their first atomic bomb. November 1952 saw the first successful
American hydrogen bomb, tested on the Pacific atoll of Eniwetok. Nine
months later, the Soviets responded with a thermonuclear device of
their own. Stalin had died in the interval, and now the Soviets, who had
a substantial lead in rocketry, were rushing to launch an ICBM. (If the
U.S. was behind, it was partly through choice. The Americans emphasized SAC—another of those ominous acronyms—and the delivery of
nuclear bombs by aircraft; the U.S. had 1,309 long-range bombers by
1955.) Shortly after Stalin's demise, Nikita Khrushchev, the lapsed shep-
herd, recorded his first incredulous sight of one of the rockets designed
by Sergei Korolyov, a former gulag inmate, at a private viewing for the
Soviet leadership:

I don't want to exaggerate, but I'd say we gawked at what he showed us
as if we were a bunch of sheep seeing a new gate for the first time.

When he showed us one of his rockets, we thought it looked like nothing but a huge cigar-shaped tube and we didn't believe it could fly. Korolev took us on a tour of a launching pad and tried to explain to us how the rocket worked. We were like peasants in a marketplace. We walked around and around the rocket, touching it, tapping it to see if it was sturdy enough—we did everything but lick it to see how it tasted.

The fact that he had as yet no long-range nuclear weapons did not prevent Khrushchev from a noisy rattling of destructive potential. During the Suez crisis of late October 1956—at the same time Soviet tanks were overrunning Hungary—he threatened Great Britain and France with rocket-borne nuclear destruction if they didn't pull out of Egypt. (Eisenhower quietly ordered his two allies to do the same thing, but it was Khrushchev's bluff that, by frightening the world, earned the most publicity and emboldened him to push his gambler's luck.) It wasn't until the next summer that one of Korolyov's rockets, history's first ICBM, flew four thousand miles to a target in the Pacific. In October, using the same type of rocket that had powered their ICBM, the Soviets lofted Sputnik ("fellow traveler"), the first satellite to orbit the earth. This had to be counted as Khrushchev's masterstroke, perhaps the greatest publicity stunt of the entire Cold War.

A month later, on November 7, 1957, the fortieth anniversary of the Bolshevik Revolution, the Soviets added to their Sputnik triumph by sending a dog into orbit, the first living creature from our world in space. (Unfortunately for Laika, the little terrier of distinction, her rocketmasters had been too rushed to provide for reentry.) These Soviet space enterprises were not just astounding feats of technology; they also carried the fear of nuclear holocaust to American skies. Quite suddenly, there were no places on earth that seemed safe any longer. As Khrushchev proclaimed in November 1959, "We now have stockpiled so many rockets, so many atomic and hydrogen warheads, that if we were attacked, we could wipe from the face of the earth all our probable opponents."

But neither the Soviet nuclear present nor its future was quite that rosy.

To be sure, more triumphs would follow: the first man in space—Yuri Gagarin lifted off just three days before the Bay of Pigs Cuban disaster in April 1961—and the first woman, Valentina Tereshkova, both again ferried by the same rocket that could transport a nuclear warhead to North America. But the United States, shaken by *Sputnik*, had already caught up to the Soviet Union in ICBM production, and even edged ahead. As the Americans knew from their own new satellite spy cameras, the Soviet's total arsenal of functional ICBMs was, by the summer of 1960, just four, all based at a single swampy and unprotected site south of Archangel.

In the fall of 1962, Khrushchev would make one final gamble: the importation of missiles to Cuba. By bringing IRBMs and MRBMs (medium-range) into the island off the U.S. coast, he was, in effect, converting them to ICBMs: The IRBMs could reach in an arc from Newfoundland to San Francisco. One can argue how much Kennedy gave him in return, but the humiliating fact remains: The missiles were removed. "You Americans will never be able to do this to us again," the Soviet deputy foreign minister Vasily Kuznetsov remarked to a U.S. diplomat. His grim promise would come true before very long. By the end of the 1960s, the Soviets could boast 1,487 ICBMs, over 400 more than the Americans.

The most frightening phase of the Cold War may actually have been over. But few at the time saw it that way.

JOHN F. GUILMARTIN, JR., is a professor of history at Ohio State University, where he teaches military history and naval history; he is a leading authority on the development of military technology. He did two combat tours flying long-range air force rescue helicopters during the Vietnam War.

S CHOLARS, SOLDIERS, AND STATESMEN have long debated the nature of the relationship between technology and war, particularly the interaction between strategy and developments in weaponry and transportation. Does technology drive tactics, and thus strategy? Or, rather, do strategic imperatives dictate the pace at which key technologies are developed and fielded? Were railroads, high-explosive artillery shells, and the machine gun to blame for the slaughter in the trenches of 1914–18? Or did the fault lie with flawed strategic and operational concepts? Was the airplane to blame for the rain of destruction unleashed on European and Japanese cities in 1939–45, or were flawed or skewed strategies responsible? The history of the intercontinental ballistic missile (ICBM) and its relationship to the Cold War provides a rare opportunity to test the technology-versus-strategy hypothesis, for technology was clearly a major driving factor in the way the Cold War played out, and the ICBM was clearly the driving technology in the strategic, operational, tactical, and technological matrix that set the strategic rhythms of the conflict. The political and military trajectory of the Cold War might be likened to that of a speeding car, racing toward an uncertain destination. The geopolitical realities of national location and natural resources formed the car's body; the inescapable tension between Marxist-Leninist command economics and supply and demand provided the engine; Soviet hegemonic ambitions (and suspicions) and fear of them in the West, particularly America, were the fuel; diplomacy—hopefully—provided the brakes. Technology was in the driver's seat.

Dramatic advances in weaponry, many of them frightening in their strategic and moral implications, were a central feature of the Cold War, beginning with the awful reality of the atomic bomb: intercontinental jet bombers, radar-guided surface-to-air missiles, infrared and radar air-to-air homing missiles, supersonic fighters, nuclear submarines, over-the-horizon radar, massive arrays of sensitive sonar detectors on the ocean bottom, spy satellites, cruise missiles, and sophisticated encryption and code-breaking computers. The list could be extended indefinitely. But of all these unprecedented technologies, none had a more profound strategic impact than the intercontinental ballistic missile, icon of the Cold War and central pillar of mutual deterrence. The very thought of an offensive capability, securely based in the inner recesses of the homeland, that could reach out across oceans and continents to vaporize enemy cities and bases less than an hour after launch was so mind-boggling as to utterly change the way statesmen, military leaders, and, above all, ordinary citizens and politicians thought of war. When Carl von Clausewitz, the nineteenth-century Prussian philosopher of war, entertained as his limiting case the possibility of war as a single, unrestrained act of total violence, he rejected the notion as incredible. The intercontinental ballistic missile, armed with a nuclear or thermonuclear warhead, threatened to make him a prophet.

The Cold War began before the advent of ICBMs and surely would have been waged without them, but in a manner difficult to imagine. The crux of the matter was that an ICBM attack could be delivered in a remarkably brief span of time and, in practical terms, was unstoppable. But the incoming warheads had no place to hide in the empty vastness of space and could be detected by radar as they rose above the curvature of the earth, leaving ample time to deliver a counterblow. Later, geosynchronous reconnaissance satellites armed with infrared detectors tuned to the heat emission spectra of rocket exhaust plumes extended warning time to the moment of liftoff. In round figures, an ICBM could traverse the distance between America and the Soviet Union in about thirty minutes, but from 1961–62, American ICBMs, and presumably Soviet ones, could be out of their silos within a minute of receiving an authenticated launch order.

The essential elements of the equation were in place by the early 1960s and, the Soviet deployment of antimissile missile batteries around Moscow notwithstanding, remained in place through the end of the Cold War. Without the residual threat posed by ICBMs standing ready in their silos in the missile fields of Central Asia and North America, a disabling surprise attack by manned bombers or submarine-launched ballistic missiles would, in principle, have been possible. Ironically, the transparently self-evident nature of ICBM deterrence left both the Soviet Union and the United States free to wage conventional war, both by proxy and in person, by relaxing the fear that tensions rising from, say, war in Korea, Vietnam, or Afghanistan might unleash an unanswerable thermonuclear attack out of the blue.

Conversely, the balance of terror in Europe was complicated by intermediate-range ballistic missiles (IRBMs), vastly increasing the dangers posed by conventional warfare and—with benefit of hindsight—effectively ruling it out. With much shorter flight times than their intercontinental cousins, IRBMs complicated the warning-and-notification deterrent calculus, all the more so since they were based close to, and ostensibly targeted against, vital industrial and population centers. The problem was particularly acute for the Soviets, inasmuch as the western Soviet Union was within IRBM reach of European NATO. The United States was not, of course, within reach of Soviet IRBMs, and by the mid-1970s the specter of a "limited" nuclear exchange in Europe seemed plausible, at least to some; analysts grimly joked about America's willingness to fight to the last European. The story is an involved one, as much a part of diplomatic as military history, and is too complicated to recount here. Suffice it to say that concern for a surprise attack by European-based IRBMs, including Soviet missiles west of the Urals, was a major driving force in nuclear arms control negotiations almost from the beginning—the quid pro quo for the removal of Soviet missiles from Cuba in 1962 was the removal of U.S. IRBMs from Turkey and Italy—and that here, as with the Soviet and American response to the strategic dilemmas posed first by the possibility and then by the reality of the ICBM, technology ruled. The presence of mobile Soviet SS-20 IRBMs in Europe from 1977, and the threat of a subsequent tit-for-tat Pershing II deployment by the U.S., loomed large in the logic behind the negotiations between President Ronald Reagan and Premier Mikhail Gorbachev that, as we now know, marked the beginning of the end of the Cold War.

The logic of the scenarios posited above is debatable. What is not is that ICBM-based mutual deterrence was central to the Cold War, a reality reflected in the strategic vocabulary. Such expressions as circular error probable (CEP), preemptive first strike, survivable second-strike capability, and launch on warning, while not exclusively related to ICBMs, arose within a context shaped by the intercontinental ballistic missile. IRBMs were important mainly as a theater-level deterrent or, as we shall see, a first-strike threat. Manned bombers, the first nuclear delivery system and the only one with intercontinental reach until the late 1950s, influenced Cold War strategic calculations not so much because of the awesome power of their bombs but because, unlike ICBMs, they could be launched and then recalled to "send a message." It is worth not-

ing, too, that while ICBMs had a major impact on strategic bomber operations, driving the U.S. Strategic Air Command to a fifteen-minute runway alert
posture and to continuous airborne alert during times of heightened tension,
the converse was not true: So long as a launch order could get through, the
ICBM in its hardened silo of reinforced concrete or, in its final Soviet incar-
nations, on a mobile transporter-erector-launcher (TEL), was operationally
self-sufficient and thus strategically credible. The ballistic missile submarine
assumed strategic importance not because of the power or accuracy of its
weapons—submarine-launched ballistic missiles (SLBMs) were generally inferior to gravity bombs and ICBMs on both counts—but because the submarine, hidden in the ocean deeps, was effectively immune to preemptive attack
by ICBM.

The ICBM had its origins in the aftermath of World War I, in the space-
flight societies of Weimar Germany. Advocating manned exploration of space,
the societies combined utopian futurism with hardheaded technological real-
ism. Their first and most basic contribution was to recognize that black powder,
hitherto the only rocket propellant, would never suffice to lift a payload beyond
the atmosphere. Although powerful, black powder fell short when it came to
imparting acceleration to a rocket. The relevant measure of merit was specific
impulse; that is, the number of pounds of thrust produced by each pound of
propellant burned per second. Expressed in seconds, specific impulse is in fact
a measure of efficiency: The higher the value, the more efficient the propellant. As the formula indicates, the key integer was the molecular weight of the
decomposition products, the lighter the better, and the products of a black-
powder explosion were heavy indeed. Oxidizing alcohol, gasoline, or kerosene
with liquid oxygen offered substantially better performance, and it was on these
combinations that the rocket pioneers based their calculations. To highlight
the difference, black powder's specific impulse is about 150 seconds, while that
of liquid oxygen and kerosene is on the order of 300. Other combinations
that offered better performance—for example, liquid oxygen or liquid fluorine
and liquid hydrogen—were clearly impractical: Hydrogen is liquid only at extremely low temperatures (the stuff boils at −423 degrees), posing formidable
containment problems, and fluorine is horribly corrosive. The German space
enthusiasts were remarkably good prophets; all first-generation ICBMs used
the propellants they identified. Liquid hydrogen, the most efficient fuel of all,
was not tamed until the mid-1960s and even today is used only for the most demanding applications, in the upper stages of rockets for deep-space exploration

and in the space shuttle's main engines, where extreme performance requirements justify the immense time, effort, and cost that liquid hydrogen entails and where quick launch response is not important.

The story of the German army's co-option of the rocket societies, of the establishment of the Peenemünde test facility, of the development of the A-4/V-2 bombardment rocket, and of Wernher von Braun's pivotal role in the process is well known. In essence, von Braun and his engineers solved the two most basic problems of high-performance rocketry: propulsion and guidance-and-control, the former with a liquid oxygen/alcohol engine weighing 2,484 pounds and producing 28 tons of thrust; the latter by graphite vanes thrust into the rocket exhaust, assisted by aerodynamic control surfaces on the tail fins and controlled by an electronic analog computer that could be reprogrammed to accommodate changes in range and direction, the first reprogrammable electronic analog computer ever.

The V-2 had a maximum range of only 180 miles, indifferent accuracy—miss distances of a mile in range and two and a half miles laterally were typical—and a warhead containing only 1,650 pounds of high explosive. In terms of its contribution to the Third Reich's war effort, the V-2 was a gross waste of resources, not least of all because, as historian Gerhard Weinberg has noted, it was useless on the Eastern Front by the time it became operational, since the urban complexes it could hit were out of range. It was, however, effective in bombarding the cities of an industrialized nation, as the British learned to their dismay, and von Braun and his group had toyed with the idea of extending its range to intercontinental dimensions by adding wings or a second stage. In the aftermath of Hiroshima and Nagasaki, the possibility that such a vehicle could be used to loft a nuclear warhead was starkly evident, and, at least theoretically, there was no limit to range. Engineers in the Soviet Union and the United States had initiated design studies for such a combination before the Cold War started.

There is a general mistaken notion that the V-2 was the direct ancestor of all American and Soviet ICBMs and high-performance space boosters. Without diminishing the technical achievements of the Peenemünde design group, that is at best a half-truth. The Soviet Union was well advanced in rocketry before World War II and successfully tested a rocket-powered fighter plane in 1941, well ahead of the Germans. But the Soviet lead was compromised by Stalin's paranoia, for the Great Purge decimated not only the ranks of his officer corps but those of his engineers as well. Sergei Korolyov, designer of the first Soviet ICBMs, was condemned to the gulag in 1938 and released only in 1944, when rocketry's strategic importance became evident. The United States came late to high-performance rockets, as it had to jet engines, but, with its seemingly bottomless reservoir of competent engineers, quickly made up lost ground. North American Aviation had begun design studies on high-performance liquid-fueled rocket engines before war's end, and other companies, notably Douglas and Martin, were not far behind.

To be sure, both the Soviets and the Americans milked the V-2 for what they could. The U.S. Army absorbed the von Braun group, giving it responsibility for army ballistic missile development at the Redstone Arsenal near Huntsville, Alabama. The group was later absorbed by NASA to become a major component of America's space program. By contrast, the Soviets exploited German rocket engineers individually before releasing the survivors to go home. The Soviets put the V-2 into production in 1950 and fielded enhanced versions later in the decade, in large part to train the launch crews of what was to become the Strategic Rocket Forces, independent of the Red Army and Air Force. That said, the only direct V-2 descendants of consequence were the huge first-stage booster rockets, designed at Huntsville under von Braun's guidance, that powered Apollo astronauts into earth orbit en route to the moon. While inspired by the V-2 and exploiting German engineering breakthroughs, the American and Soviet ICBMs fielded during the Cold War were distinctive products of their respective national industries. Nor could it have been otherwise, for as World War II drew to a close, the means by which intercontinental range might be achieved with a nuclear-tipped ballistic missile were anything but clear—if, indeed, it could be done at all.

Three basic problems confronted would-be ICBM designers: propulsion, guidance-and-control, and warhead design. Measured against existing systems, propulsion required the greatest advances but, ironically, would be easiest to master. The Germans had solved the basic problems of combustion-chamber design and had developed turbopumps to deliver fuel and oxidizer under pressure. The challenge was to increase scale and efficiency, which, while hardly simple, required no major breakthroughs. In guidance-and-control, too, the Germans had shown the way, using gyroscopically stabilized platforms to provide precise vertical and horizontal orientation, linear accelerometers and integrating circuits that compared acceleration with elapsed time to calculate velocity, and an electronic computer to translate the inputs into discrete commands in thrust, roll, pitch, and yaw. Mechanically deflecting exhaust gases was a crude stopgap, but the idea of controlling thrust by gimballing—that is, mounting the entire rocket engine on a ball joint and swiveling it to control the direction of thrust—had an intellectual pedigree that went back to the prewar rocket societies. Development of the hydraulic pistons, servomotors, and electronic control boxes capable of aligning a rocket motor firing at full thrust within tenths of a degree in pitch and yaw would be difficult, but the basic technologies were reasonably well understood.

Warhead development was another matter. First, the warheads had to be sufficiently light and compact for the rocket to loft, and the shrinking of warheads entailed forbidding problems of nuclear physics, of precision manufacture, and of controlling the focused implosion of the high-explosive charges that squeezed the bomb's plutonium or uranium core to critical density. Second, intercontinental trajectories involved reentry into the atmosphere at unprecedented velocities, and that, for reasons of basic physics, entailed unprecedented temperatures. The short-ranged V-2's modest reentry velocities produced a fraction of the heat generated by the collision with the atmosphere that intercontinental trajectories entailed, and the engineers started with blank paper. They quickly learned that the V-2's sharply pointed nose was *not* the way to go. The intense concentration of heat caused by the formation of a hypersonic shock wave around a single point created temperatures nearly twice the melting point of steel. The obvious solution was a massive metal shield that would absorb the heat until the warhead reached the lower atmosphere, where convective cooling could take over.

We are unsure about developments in the Soviet Union, but American engineers favored copper heat shields, both because of copper's great heat-absorptive capacity and because it was easy to calculate the thickness needed for a given reentry velocity. But copper is extremely heavy. The Germans came to the rescue, recalling that a plywood-encased instrument package installed in an experimental V-2 had survived reentry intact, though with the plywood charred. In charring, the plywood had clearly been an efficient heat absorber; moreover, plywood was light and provided good thermal insulation. From this insight came the development of heat shields made of materials designed to dissipate reentry heat by ablation, literally by wearing away. American engineers initially balked, for calculating the thickness of an ablative shield was dauntingly complex, depending not only on thermal conductivity but also on heat loss due to burning, melting, sublimation, and physical loss of material. Indeed, the required thickness could be determined only by repeated testing. But the weight advantages of ablatives were compelling, and their use became standard.

Ablative heat shields were only half of the solution. The other half was discovered in 1952 by the National Advisory Committee on Aviation (NACA, later NASA) engineer H. Julian Allen in wind tunnel tests that showed blunt shapes pushed the heat-laden shock wave well out in front, dissipating some 60 percent of the reentry heat in a parabola-shaped wave. In combination with ablative heat shields and warhead miniaturization, their discovery made the ICBM a practical reality. It also put America's Mercury astronauts into orbit: John Glenn and his successors returned to earth aboard Atlas ICBM reentry bodies fitted with a cockpit instead of a warhead. The early Soviet cosmonauts returned to earth aboard larger, and conceptually cruder, spherical spacecraft exploiting the same basic phenomenon.

Meanwhile, beginning with manned bombers, the Soviets and Americans developed other delivery systems as insurance—with great success in the U.S. and indifferently so in the Soviet Union. The relevant comparison is between the Boeing B-52, still a mainstay of America's aerial might half a century after entering service, and the marginally successful Myasishchev M-4, which offered only an incremental performance increase over the turboprop-powered Tupolev Tu-95. (The British fielded a highly capable nuclear bomber force during the mid-1950s but lacked the wherewithal to develop strategic missiles and became increasingly dependent on the American nuclear deterrent as the Cold War progressed.) Next, while pressing the development of ICBMs, both the U.S. and the Soviets turned to intercontinental cruise missiles. The initial American contracts were let in 1945–48, and by the early 1950s two prime contenders had emerged: the subsonic Northrop Snark and the supersonic North American Navaho. Both Snark and Navaho were large, a reality dictated by warhead size and weight, but there the similarities ended. Apart from its lack of horizontal tail surfaces, the Snark was a relatively conventional vehicle. Turbojet-powered, it was boosted from its launcher by two strap-on solid-fuel rockets and was guided by an inertial system that incorporated stellar navigation. Development was anything but smooth, and repeated unsuccessful launches from Patrick AFB, Florida, led to quips about Snark-infested waters. Worse, one Snark failed to self-destruct as programmed and proceeded southward, turning up in the Brazilian rain forest and inspiring the couplet "Hark, hark, the Snark. Where she goes, nobody knows!" For all this, the Snark briefly achieved operational status at Presque Isle, Maine, in 1960–61.

The Navaho was considerably more complex, consisting of a ramjet-powered Mach 3 cruise vehicle of advanced design that was launched vertically and accelerated to flight speed by a liquid-fueled rocket booster. The booster was powered by a North American Rocketdyne liquid oxygen/kerosene rocket with exceptional promise but a short track record, and the staging sequence—the Navaho was the first to use "piggyback" staging, with the cruise vehicle mounted atop the booster—embodied major technical unknowns. The ramjet engines were of novel design and unprove; the flight control and navigation systems were complex and (the fatal flaw), like those of the Snark, used vacuum tubes. As the Navaho demonstrated graphically, vacuum tube reliability, while sufficient for relatively straightforward systems with built-in backups, including first- and second-generation ICBMs, was inadequate for a vehicle in which hundreds of interdependent events had to occur in precise sequence for extended periods. In sum, the Navaho was an extraordinary mix of promise and disappointment. A turbojet-powered version of the cruise vehicle, the X-10, was highly successful as an unmanned research craft, and the booster's rocket engine was the progenitor of a host of high-performance American designs, but the total vehicle was an utter flop, earning the sobriquet "Never go Navaho" with a series of spectacular pad explosions and post-launch failures. Still, its promise was so great, and the hurdles to be surmounted to produce a successful ICBM so forbidding, that for a short time in 1955, Navaho enjoyed the highest funding priority, receiving substantially more money than the Atlas ICBM.

The Soviets got off to a more measured start, developing and fielding V-2 derivatives that culminated in the 725-mile-range R-5, the first Soviet missile to carry a nuclear warhead. It was dubbed SS-3 Shyster by NATO. (The actual model designations were unknown to Western intelligence, and NATO identified Soviet systems by an elaborate alphanumeric system: "SS" stood for ballistic missile; "Shyster" was the code name of the third such system identified, and so on. The names were chosen arbitrarily, and many were whimsical or ironic.) Like the Americans, the Soviets hedged their bets by developing rocket-boosted, ramjet-powered, supersonic cruise missiles, one by the Myasishchev design bureau and the other by Semyon Lavochkin. The more advanced Lavochkin design followed a trajectory strikingly parallel to that of the Navaho, pioneering the use of novel materials, notably titanium, and producing much useful test data but no operational vehicle. As with Navaho and Snark, both programs were canceled when ICBMs made them superfluous.

Following the R-5's success, Korolev, by now in effective charge of Soviet rocket design, pressed for the development of a genuinely intercontinental missile, the R-7, nicknamed Semyorka (a diminutive of seven) and named SS-6 Sapwood by NATO. The R-7's boosted fission warhead was considerably heavier than the Atlas's thermonuclear weapon, and the thrust requirement correspondingly greater. Moreover, Korolev's team was handicapped by a lack of alloys suitable for the hundred-ton-thrust engine their calculations called for. They responded by clustering rockets in groups of four, using common oxidizer and fuel turbopumps, and surrounding a core cluster with four booster clusters. Each rocket produced only about twenty-three tons of thrust, somewhat less than that of the V-2, but they were lighter and far more efficient, and the total thrust was more than sufficient (by comparison, the Atlas's booster rockets, direct descendants of the Navaho engine, produced sixty tons of thrust each). The first successful R-7 launch was in August 1957, two months later than that of the Atlas.

A comparison of the two missiles is instructive. Both used liquid oxygen and kerosene for propellant. Both had short careers as operational ICBMs, a consequence of the extended launch sequence that liquid oxygen demanded. Both would enjoy spectacular careers as space boosters, but there the similarities end. Paraphrasing Sovietologist Steven Zaloga, if Atlas's engineering was Gothic in lightness, Semyorka's exhibited Romanesque raw strength. Atlas had just three engines; the central rocket elegantly gimballed for control. Semyorka had twenty and was controlled by comparatively primitive vernier rockets: The thruster nozzles were fixed, and adjustments in pitch, roll, and yaw were provided by small auxiliary rockets, a simple but inherently inefficient solution, since the vernier rockets required independent fuel and control systems. The Russian missile's skin would support a man's weight; that of Atlas was so thin that the internal pressure of the propellants was all that kept it from collapsing.

More telling is a common design feature that underlines the incredible urgency with which both missiles were developed, an urgency rendered more terrifying by each power's ignorance of its rival's capabilities and intentions. Both missiles were stage-and-a-half vehicles; that is, they rose from the pad with all engines firing, Semyorka discarding the four outer rocket clusters and their fuel tankage, and Atlas jettisoning two of its three engines after the initial boost phase. This was less than optimal for reasons basic to rocket engineering. Maximum thrust is required at liftoff when weight is greatest; then, as fuel is expended and as atmospheric drag falls off with increasing altitude, the thrust requirement diminishes. It therefore makes sense to lift off with a separate lower stage that drops off when its fuel is expended, leaving its weight behind. The upper stage or stages then proceed to apogee powered by smaller, more efficient engines. The advantages of staging are enhanced by the fact that optimum rocket-nozzle length varies inversely with air density. Maximum thrust at liftoff calls for a long bell-shaped nozzle to permit the propellant gases to fully expand in the dense air of the lower atmosphere, but such a nozzle becomes increasingly inefficient at higher altitudes. It is for this reason that high-performance satellite and space boosters, designed to loft the maximum payload by minimizing airframe and fuel weight, use multiple stages, typically three, with each successive stage's engines having progressively shorter nozzles. Solid-fueled ICBMs also use multiple stages, but for somewhat different reasons, as we shall see.

Both Semyorka and Atlas were magnificent designs, sufficiently reliable for manned space flight: Yuri Gagarin rode Semyorka into orbit, and Atlas orbited John Glenn (and Ham the chimpanzee before him). But both rockets were first and foremost ICBMs, and their designs were finalized so early that the engineers were not certain liquid oxygen and kerosene would ignite spontaneously in the hard vacuum of space. They therefore accepted substantial penalties of weight and nozzle inefficiency to place hardware on the launch pad capable of lofting a nuclear warhead to intercontinental ranges at the earliest possible date: Atlas in September 1959 and Semyorka that December. Further underlining the haste with which the early ICBMs were developed, the American Titan I—a two-stage missile, still using liquid oxygen and kerosene but stored belowground in a reinforced concrete silo and fueled by high-speed pumps that reduced launch time to fifteen minutes—became operational at about the same time as Semyorka. That all of these competing and highly expensive systems, any one of which could have filled the strategic bill, were rushed to deployment at the same time speaks for itself. Both the Soviet Union and the United States had to be absolutely certain that they had at least one system that actually worked, reliably and on short notice. It is worth noting that the strategic backdrop to this period of frenzied technological development included, to hit the high points, the 1948 Berlin Blockade, the Korean War, and the Hungarian uprising and Suez crisis of 1956. The last of these provided the stage for Nikita Khrushchev's famous and, as we now know, empty "missile rattling" threats.

———

Atlas and Semyorka, in any case, were recognized as interim solutions long before they achieved operational status. Their extended launch sequences rendered them vulnerable to preemptive attack, and they could be held ready to fire only briefly. Their silo-based successors depended on propellants that did not require refrigeration and could be stored in the missile's tanks for extended periods. The American Titan II, which entered service in 1964, burned a mixture of unsymmetrical dimethyl hydrazine (a volatile and environmentally nasty fuel) and nitrogen tetroxide (an even more volatile oxidizer that was worse); the Soviet R-16 (NATO designation SS-7 Saddler), which entered service the same year, was powered by hydrazine and red fuming nitric acid, both dangerous and difficult to work with. Both fuel-oxidizer combinations are highly volatile and hellishly toxic; their sole virtue was that they could be stored in the missile's tanks without refrigeration. That they were used at all speaks volumes for the strategic imperative.

The ideal, of course, was a missile that could be stored indefinitely in a silo, ready to fire, a requirement that no liquid fuel combination could satisfy. The answer lay in solid propellants, rocket fuels that could be poured into a mold to solidify and remain inert until ignited, requiring no pumps, no corrosive liquids, and no refrigeration. The solution was found in asphalt-stabilized, perchlorate-based solid propellants, discovered by engineers at the Guggenheim Aeronautical Laboratory of the California Institute of Technology in 1942 and subjected to accelerated development as the Cold War got under way. By the late 1950s, these propellants were sufficiently stable and had sufficiently long shelf lives for operational use. Their main drawback, like that of black powder, was low specific impulse: They produced impressive initial acceleration but yielded significantly less thrust per pound of fuel per second than liquid propellants. The solution was to use multiple stages. The deployment in 1962 of the first operational solid-fueled ICBM, the three-stage Minuteman I, was a major Cold War benchmark, in part because it heralded the creation of an ICBM force that could be kept indefinitely on a high state of alert, and in part because it underlined a qualitative lead for the U.S. in strategic weaponry: The Soviets would not field their first solid-fueled ICBM, the SS-13 Savage, until 1969. It is worth noting that the Minuteman I and the Minuteman III, which replaced it beginning in 1970, had relatively modest throw weights; that is, the warhead, reentry vehicle, and guidance system were relatively light, positively diminutive when compared with their Soviet equivalents. The compensatory mechanism was the superior accuracy produced by miniaturized guidance systems.

Rapid advances in missile capabilities forced equally swift changes in basing modes and in the way crews lived and worked. The first ICBMs were erected on open pads, then filled with liquid oxygen and kerosene, a process that consumed hours and left the missile and crew horribly vulnerable to a counterstrike. Next came pits in which the missile could be stored horizontally below ground level, with underground fuel storage, launch control centers, and living facilities for the crew. Called coffin shelters, these provided limited protection against a preemptive strike; constructed in haste, they were only partially hardened (that is, made of steel-reinforced concrete thick enough to withstand the force of a nuclear blast). Next came underground reinforced concrete silos in which the missile could be stored and fueled vertically, then raised above ground for launch. The definitive basing mode was a hardened underground silo fitted with vents and cooling systems so that the missile could be launched from underground. The silos were sealed with massive blast doors mounted on tracks and opened and closed by electric motors. The underground launch complex, itself hardened, was typically reached by elevators and isolated from the surface and the silo by multiple blast doors. Equipped with electric generators, air filtering and conditioning systems, and living quarters, the underground complexes were home for missile crews during their periodic alert tours. In them, the crews faced a combination of claustrophobic confinement and boredom on the one hand, and the awful possibility of nuclear war on the other, something that can only be imagined by those who have not experienced it.

So far, I have said little about accuracy, but it was a key element in the strategic equation. ICBM accuracy was commonly (and mistakenly) expressed as circular error probable—by definition the diameter of the smallest circle that can be drawn around half the impact points of a series of firings at the same target. The other component of accuracy was bias, the distance of the center of the circle from the target. The mistake lies in the common assumption that the center of the circle defining CEP was, in fact, the target. From the beginning of the missile race, there was a direct relationship between perceived accuracy and warhead size: The larger the CEP, the larger the warhead. Also from the beginning, American ICBMs had significantly smaller CEPs than their Soviet opposites. The Soviets compensated by installing larger warheads, and—frighteningly—the disparity in warhead size and yield increased as the Cold War dragged on.

Another pivotal factor was intelligence or, perhaps more to the point, the lack thereof, particularly early on. Both the Soviets and Americans focused on engineering development of the ICBM, but the interplay between missile range and accuracy, warhead size, and intelligence had an impact on strategic decisions that was at least as great as the outcome of the race to be first on the pad. These factors came together in crisis or near-crisis proportions on at least two occasions. The first was the Cuban Missile Crisis of 1962; the ensuing confrontation was rendered more dangerous by the characteristics of the missiles in question: kerosene and red fuming nitric acid-fueled R-4 IRBMs (NATO designation SS-4 Sandal) with a range of only 1,200 miles, indifferent accuracy, and an extended and vulnerable launch sequence. Lacking the range and accuracy to pose a credible threat to the American ICBM or bomber force, the missiles made sense only as vehicles for a preemptive strike on American cities. Fortunately, heads cooler than Khrushchev's prevailed.

The second came in the 1980s, most specifically in the war scare of 1983, as U.S. intelligence, tracking Soviet missile tests by electronic monitoring and satellite imagery, noted a steady shrinkage of CEPs from miles to hundreds of meters. Soviet launch trajectories, tracked by American radar and radio-monitored telemetry, became steadier, and the dispersion of impact points of dummy warheads in the Soviet Pacific test range, tracked through satellite photographs, became smaller. In American eyes, the stability of mutual nuclear deterrence at that point depended in large measure on the ability of the silo-based ICBM force to ride out, and therefore deter, a Soviet first strike. As CEPs shrank, the number of warheads needed to target a Minuteman or Titan silo with a high expectation of destroying it steadily diminished, placing a preemptive Soviet first strike within the realm of possibility, or so it seemed. The appearance of mobile, solid-fueled Soviet ICBMs, deployed operationally in 1985–87 but detected earlier, heightened concern, accelerated development of the MX—the last American ICBM—and led to serious discussion of elaborate and expensive basing modes. One option actually endorsed by the Carter administration involved a network of mobile launchers and multiple shelters covering most of Utah and Nevada. Another option seriously considered, at least by newspaper columnists, political analysts, and their sources in the Pentagon, was to concentrate the bulk of the silo-based ICBM force in a single, tightly packed missile field to exploit the fact that multiple nuclear warheads cannot be used simultaneously against targets close to one another, since the first warhead to detonate will trigger subcritical reactions in the others, causing them to fizzle. The doomsday finality of this scheme, termed "dense pack" with unintended appropriateness, speaks for itself and is all the more intimidating for having been based on a false premise: that CEP and accuracy were one and the same.

But the impact of ICBM technology went far beyond dry strategic considerations to embrace the human dimension of war at its most elemental level. The interaction took place at the critical intersection between nuclear warhead and command and control. For the ICBM deterrent to be credible, the missiles had to be launched on extremely short notice. They also had to be launched by human decision, for no machine could be trusted to unleash Armageddon. But neither could a single human, and from that awareness arose an elaborate series of safeguards and procedures. In American practice, a missile crew could initiate the launch sequence only after receiving a coded launch order from the commander in chief or his designated representative. After the crew authenticated the message with headquarters and a computerized database, the code would be loaded into the launch console. Then, and only then, could the launch crew commander and his (or, later, her) deputy insert two launch keys into firing locks, physically separated so that a single individual could not turn both keys. Launch was accomplished by turning the two keys at the same time, typically within two seconds, a short enough interval so that one person could not reach the second key after turning the first, and long enough to accommodate normal reflexes. If any step in the procedure was missed or botched, the missile would not fire. Soviet practice was probably similar—we can still only speculate—with the second key belonging to a member of the KGB assigned to ensure political control. In American practice, and surely Soviet practice as well, crews were carefully screened for psychological stability and repeatedly drilled to ensure that they would execute a launch order if one ever came. Mercifully, none did.

A final point emphasizes the awesome threat posed by ICBMs, as well as their central place in the deterrent balance of terror at the strategic heart of the Cold War: Both the Soviet Union and the United States were so terrified of the threat of an ICBM attack and, paradoxically, so determined to preserve the stabilizing deterrent power of the threat that—at least so far as the public record shows—no missile was ever launched from an operational ICBM silo, nor was an ICBM ever fired with a live nuclear or thermonuclear warhead aboard.

The War Scare of 1983

JOHN PRADOS

For four decades and more, we lived in perpetual fear of war. The nuclear doomsday clock appeared to be forever stuck at one minute to midnight, the witching hour for the world. Several times the long hand moved forward by several alarming seconds. To put the feeling another way, it was like walking around with collective aneurysms in our brains that could burst all at once and kill without warning. We might forget about the danger as we went about our daily routines; we knew with certainty that it would never go away. The confrontation between East and West had taken on the aura of permanence.

Those of us who lived through the Cold War—in this age of terrorism, it already feels like ancient history—can number the moments when the clock inched visibly ahead toward the sinister joining of its hands. Most (but not all) of those moments happened during the 1950s and the 1960s, the period of maximum peril. Did we come closest to nuclear catastrophe with the Cuban Missile Crisis of 1962—three or four seconds short of it, let us say? There were other dicey confrontations, too many of them and too close for comfort: the Berlin Blockade, when a new land war in Europe seemed imminent just when another had been concluded; the GDR's Soviet-approved erection of the Berlin Wall in 1961, when, for a few tense hours, American and Soviet tanks faced off muzzle-to-muzzle at Checkpoint Charlie; the Suez Crisis of 1956, when Nikita Khrushchev threatened to nuke Paris and London if the British and French troops occupying the Suez Canal didn't withdraw; the simultaneous Soviet invasion of Hungary, when Russian tanks rolled over the democracy of a week; the Soviet-backed Chinese intervention in Korea during the fall of 1950 that David Holloway in his preeminent study,

Stalin and the Bomb, calls "the most dangerous point in postwar international relations."

Most historians will argue now, however, that the Cuban Missile Crisis was the turning point of the Cold War, even if two thirds of the East-West standoff still stretched ahead of us. That seems a bit like putting the dramatic climax of a three-act play at the end of the first. In the lengthening view of history, it may be accurate; but it is not the way so many on both sides felt at the time. And as John Prados tells us in the essay that follows, one of the most dangerous near-misses took place in 1983, a mere six or seven years before the Soviet Union and its empire abruptly began to crumble. If we think of a Cold War thermometer that goes from room temperature (the breach of the Wall in 1989) all the way up to boiling, the war scare that fall was only slightly less fraught with explosive potential than the Cuban crisis. That human frailty was involved, the frailty of the sclerotic paranoids who ruled the Kremlin, made the 1983 episode, if anything, more full of risk. *Dr. Strangelove* had come to life. But the scariest part was that even as the Soviet leadership elevated their alerts, their American counterparts seemed not to have a clue what was happening.

JOHN PRADOS is a Washington-based author and a senior fellow at the National Security Archive. He is the author of fourteen books and a contributor to many others. His most recent works include *Hoodwinked: The Documents That Reveal How Bush Sold Us a War; Lost Crusader: The Secret Wars of CIA Director William Colby;* and *Inside the Pentagon Papers* (edited with Margaret Pratt-Porter). Prados lectures widely on intelligence, national security, military history, and combat simulation design.

"**P**ERHAPS NEVER BEFORE**," intoned the Russian official, "has the atmosphere in the world been as tense as it is now." The speaker, Grigory Romanov, a leader of the Communist Party of the Soviet Union (CPSU) apparatus in Leningrad and a member of the Soviet Politburo, knew the inner fears of the Kremlin. "Comrades," Romanov thundered, "the international situation at present is white hot, thoroughly white hot." This speech marked the anniversary of the Bolshevik Revolution. Just seven months earlier, Georgi Arbatov, Russia's leading Americanist, had told a reporter that "the situation is worse now than at any time since the Cuban Missile Crisis."

Nothing that happened in the interval between Arbatov's April 1983 interview and Romanov's November 7 speech had done anything to reassure people on the state of Russian-American relations. Negotiations on controlling nuclear weapons were going nowhere, with American conservatives pressing the Reagan administration to abrogate the arms agreements that already existed. Russians and Americans were both proceeding with new missile deployments, including a fresh generation of nuclear weapons in Europe that terrified local populations. Cold War covert actions initiated by one side or the other were under way in Asia, Africa, and Latin America. To end the summer with a bang, on the last day of August a Korean civilian airliner, flight KAL 007, blundered into Russian airspace, to be pitilessly shot down with 269 passengers on board. President Ronald Reagan himself declared the Soviet Union an "evil empire" and the "focus of evil in the modern world."

These events took place in the open, apparent to everyone. But behind the scenes the Cold War was even hotter; in fact, practically boiling. One or both sides had miscalculated, and in a nuclear age, misunderstanding and misinterpretation could lead to the unthinkable. There was a quiet crisis in the early 1980s, the ramifications of which we do not yet understand. It is possible that the Cold War might have ended sooner but for the prevailing atmosphere of confrontation. It is also possible that the critical international situation steeled subsequent Soviet leaders such as Mikhail Gorbachev in their determination to end the superpower struggle. On the other hand, it is equally possible that the end of history could have come right then, in nuclear annihilation. In the spring of 1948, when the government of Czechoslovakia fell to a Russian-backed factional coup, beginning an escalation of tension that culminated with the Berlin Blockade, people spoke of a "war scare of 1948." Today we can begin to consider the untold story of the war scare of 1983.

Reagan administration officials in 1983 were intensely focused upon an ideological competition with the Soviet Union over arms control and the so-called Euromissiles, intermediate-range missiles that both sides were deploying in Europe then. The Americans downplayed the military threat to the Russians posed by the quick-reacting Pershing II missiles that formed part of their own deployment program, and spoke of Soviet "disinformation" attempts to affect the opinions of Western Europeans living with Euromissiles in their midst. (There are, in fact, documents, including annual KGB reports from this period, revealing Russian claims to have influenced peace movements in Western Europe.) Some former U.S. officials still argue that the Soviets conjured an apocalyptic vision of the American threat, then somehow succumbed to it themselves, believing that "the Americans were coming." This much is beyond dispute: The Soviets were fearful in 1983, and Reaganauts were so wedded to their own propaganda messages that they were oblivious to the signs of discomfiture in Moscow. Moreover, unlike 1948, in 1983 fingers on both sides of the Cold War divide rested upon nuclear hair triggers.

The strategic situation in 1983 was not what appeared on the surface, at least from the Soviet point of view. Americans were used to the rhetoric of the "window of vulnerability," a slogan current in the 1980 election, which denoted a time frame in which the United States was supposedly in special danger of being disarmed by a nuclear missile attack. But readers might be surprised to learn that during the final months of the Carter administration, it was the Russians who came to the Americans with a detailed briefing from their own secret data, showing a substantial and growing U.S. threat to Soviet nuclear forces. Beyond the exaggerations and the real meaning of the data (that both sides were vulnerable, depending on who went first), the point is that in 1981, going into the Reagan administration, Moscow had already demonstrated concern over U.S. military intentions.

American weapons programs lent some weight to these concerns. On its Minuteman III intercontinental ballistic missiles (ICBMs), the United States was installing a new guidance system called the NS-20, as well as higher-yield warheads. The new instrumentation greatly reduced the time necessary to change an ICBM's target; held more targets in constant memory; and substantially improved accuracy. In combination with the increased power of the nuclear weapons it carried, each Minuteman III warhead would have excellent prospects against even the most deeply dug-in Russian missile silos. The Peacekeeper, a bigger ICBM carrying ten warheads (there were three in the Minuteman), stood on the verge of deployment. In submarine-launched ballistic missiles (SLBMs), the Americans were developing an improved Trident missile warhead called the D-5 that made sea-based missiles as deadly as ICBMs against hardened targets. As for Russian SLBMs, American designers were seeking new ways to target missile submarines. Meanwhile, American war planners were "gaming out" flexible response scenarios that allowed for the limited use of nuclear weapons, potentially lowering the nuclear threshold.

The KGB officer Oleg Gordievsky, who rose to be the deputy rezident (chief of station) in London, had become a double agent spying for the British. In *KGB: The Inside Story*, which he coauthored with British historian Christopher Andrew, Gordievsky reports a May 1981 conference among senior KGB officials in that agency's foreign intelligence headquarters at Yasenovo, a Moscow suburb. Soviet leader Leonid Brezhnev addressed the assembly, but his somber speech proved only the warm-up for the astonishing pessimism of KGB director Yuri V. Andropov, who told the Russian spymasters they were to begin a special effort to detect American preparations for nuclear war. The Soviets even gave the operation a name, RYAN, for the Russian phrase raketno-yadernoye napadenie ("nuclear missile attack").

Planning and central coordination for RYAN became the responsibility of the KGB Institute for Intelligence Problems. When Gordievsky saw the initial orders that summer, he noted that data on actual nuclear weapons received a relatively low priority. A higher premium was placed on indications of U.S. or Western alliance decisions for war. Some Soviet embassies, like that at Helsinki, were instructed simply to monitor the number of windows lit up in Western embassies at night. These and additional requirements applied to KGB stations in London, Washington, and elsewhere. In 1982 the chief of the KGB institute went to Washington as the new KGB rezident.

According to George Blake, the KGB double agent with British intelligence who defected to the Soviet Union in the 1960s, another member of the small circle of British defectors in Moscow, Donald Maclean, got wind of the consternation at high levels in Soviet leadership. Maclean wrote a paper criticizing Soviet weakness in becoming mesmerized by U.S. nuclear forces. The result, he argued, was undue influence in the Kremlin by the Soviet high command. According to Gordievsky and Andrew, the KGB's American experts believed that Director Andropov's alarmist views were being fueled by the Soviet military. In fact, Russian defense minister Dimitri F. Ustinov was among the most hard-line voices on the Politburo, a fact known at the CIA and among American foreign policy experts as well as at Yasenovo. To make things worse, Brezhnev's health failed, and before the end of 1982, Yuri Andropov emerged as the new top leader in the Soviet Union.

Meanwhile, the indications coming from Washington were alarming to the Soviets on both diplomatic and military fronts. On the diplomatic side, the Americans seemed to show no interest in a summit. On the military side, about the time Andropov came to power, the U.S. press featured a leak of a secret Pentagon document, the *Fiscal Year 1984–88 Defense Guidance*, which mandated programs designed to enable the United States to "prevail" in a nuclear war. The leaks dovetailed closely with Reagan administration budget requests for new communications networks designed to function in a nuclear environment and for a new airborne command post to serve the president in time of war. American strategists were simultaneously beginning to talk of "decapitation," the idea of wiping out the adversary high command through a series of strikes aimed specifically at centers of government and prearranged evacuation sites.

In February 1983 a KGB document later published by Gordievsky shows Moscow giving its rezidenturas (intelligence stations) an overstated briefing regarding U.S. nuclear capabilities, plus a new list of intelligence reporting requirements. These included identifying specially equipped blast and fallout shelters, evacuation data on government officials, data about blood supplies acquired by the government, and places visited by officials most frequently outside working hours. One suggestive instruction: "Keep under regular observation the most important government institutions, headquarters, and other installations involved in preparation for RYAN."

It is worth noting that these instructions from the KGB's Moscow center, with their hint of immediate alarm, are dated almost three weeks before Ronald Reagan's "evil empire" speech of March 8, 1983. In introductory comments to this text in a collection of his speeches, former president Reagan writes, "At the time [this speech] was portrayed as some kind of know-nothing, arch-conservative statement that could only drive the Soviets to further heights of paranoia and insecurity."

On March 23, two weeks after the "evil empire" speech touched off the KGB's latest jitters over Soviet-American relations, Reagan spoke from the Oval Office and proposed his Strategic Defense Initiative (SDI). As the president's national security adviser, Robert C. McFarlane, makes clear in a memoir, the SDI program, particularly in the highly technological form President Reagan selected—with such frills as space-based laser weapons—represented more of a wish than a weapon. McFarlane admits, "I was a little worried about the scientific community." Some of McFarlane's subordinates on the National Security Council (NSC) staff go further and admit that SDI was a piece of gimmickry, more a tool for intimidation than a real program. The hasty launch of the entire program is epitomized in the fact that Reagan's formal decision for an SDI, contained in a directive called National Security Decision Document 85 (NSDD-85), is dated two days after the president's speech.

In contrast to NSDD-85, there was no quality of afterthought about U.S. policy on the Soviet Union. On January 17, 1983, President Reagan had signed NSDD-75, which laid down his Soviet policy. With respect to military strategy, the memorandum had specified: "Soviet calculations of possible war outcomes under any contingency must always result in outcomes so unfavorable to the U.S.S.R. that there would be no incentive for Soviet leaders to initiate an attack." Reagan's order had much more to say about Cold War competition, technology transfers, economic and geopolitical policy, and the like, but the war scare of 1983 would flow from the military strategic propositions of the policy.

It is a tenet of nuclear strategy that the side in distress, outclassed by the adversary, may maximize its limited chances by shooting first. That is the foundation for such bits of nuclear jargon as "launch on warning" or "preemptive attack." As 1983 opened, the Kremlin feared an American strategic nuclear advantage, and NSDD-75 shows the Reagan administration indeed intended to act from a position of strength. The addition of SDI to the mix suggested the

United States sought means to neutralize such Soviet forces as might remain following an initial nuclear exchange. Computer models show that SDI might have considerable impact blunting a retaliatory attack ("second strike") but relatively little against a first strike. No doubt the secret war games of the Soviet general staff (and American Joint Chiefs of Staff) showed the same thing. The net effect of these developments would be that a weak adversary at some point would be forced to choose between launching a nuclear war by preemption, to preserve its "deterrent," or permitting itself to be disarmed.

This point was appreciated in the Kremlin, and it sparked far more than a debate about esoteric strategies or stochastic nuclear exchange models. In *Pravda*, the Communist Party newspaper, Yuri Andropov commented on Ronald Reagan's SDI just four days after Reagan's presentation. Accurately enough, Andropov summarized Washington's aim as "an intention to secure the potential with ballistic missile defenses to destroy the corresponding strategic systems of the other side, that is, to deny it the capabilities to mount a retaliatory strike, counting on disarming the Soviet Union in the face of the American nuclear threat."

On top of these developments, the NATO allies were making final preparations for deploying America's Euromissiles as the summer of 1983 began. Two U.S. systems were involved, the ground-launched cruise missile and the Pershing II. The latter would be an accurate ballistic missile with the range to reach Moscow—and with a much shorter flight time than ICBMs based in the United States. The Pershing II posed a threat to Russian command centers, making the possibility of "decapitation" concrete. The Soviets, in turn, might be expected to use force against those places where Euromissiles were deployed, which terrified the peoples of Western Europe. For several years, peaking as the Euromissiles were about to be installed, political protests and demonstrations on nuclear issues roiled around this controversial program. In Bonn, West Germany, alone, more than five hundred thousand people took to the streets in just one of the 1983 demonstrations. But the Reagan administration refused to be deflected and moved steadily toward Euromissile deployment scheduled for the fall. This impending development, combined with lack of progress in arms control talks, cast a pall over the Kremlin. Throughout the summer, the Soviets made private and semipublic threats to walk out of arms negotiations.

Then came KAL 007. The Soviet shootdown of the Korean airliner on September 1, egregious error that it was, proved less damaging to U.S.-Soviet relations than Moscow's initial inclination to deny everything. Kremlin confusion increased because Yuri Andropov, sick with failing kidneys, had left Moscow for a Black Sea resort, his vacation becoming a convalescence. His absence from Moscow left various sectors of the Soviet apparat adrift. Washington was willing to fish in these troubled waters. Reagan's NSDD-102 declared that "Soviet brutality in this incident presents an opportunity to reverse the false moral and political 'peacemaker' perception that their regime has been cultivating." There followed a series of acrimonious charges in Washington and Moscow, and the release of American recordings of radio chatter by the Soviet interceptor pilot and his controllers, which showed the fighter plane had fired without much thought for the target. Both sides alleged deception.

Secretary of State George Shultz recalls the KAL 007 incident as the end of a superpower "minithaw" summer during which Soviet concessions on human rights had opened a way to progress. That view is far cheerier than the recollections of Soviet foreign minister Andrei Gromyko, who had yet to get in to see President Reagan and who would be prevented from attending the United Nations General Assembly when U.S. authorities refused to assure landing rights and security for his airplane. Gromyko met Shultz in Madrid on September 8 to discuss European issues, but the secretary of state proved determined to press the Russians on human rights and KAL 007. Following a chilly private talk, Shultz heard Gromyko tell the larger group, "Problem number one for the whole world is to avert nuclear war."

Don Oberdorfer, the distinguished diplomatic correspondent for *The Washington Post*, told an audience in 1993 that "Ronald Reagan was not the man I thought he was. It was a scary time from [my] perspective." President Reagan had the Russians where he wanted them. He held the high ground in terms of propaganda and had determined to exploit the Soviet error in the KAL 007 incident. He had frightened Moscow with the Strategic Defense Initiative, had continued nuclear programs that posed dangers to Soviet nuclear forces, and had stood at the point of deploying Euromissiles that directly threatened Moscow's command-and-control centers and its political leadership. The question is: Had Reagan thought through the consequences?

According to Gromyko's memoir, at the Madrid meeting the Soviet foreign minister did not confine himself to a simple statement of the main problem. Rather, speaking "in the name of the Soviet leadership," Gromyko went on, "The world situation is now slipping toward a very dangerous precipice. It is plain that the great responsibility for not allowing a nuclear catastrophe to occur must be borne by the U.S.S.R. and the U.S.A. together. In our opinion, the U.S.A. should reevaluate its policies, and the president and his administration should look at international affairs in a new way."

No one on the American side took the point. The Russians were evil, had massacred innocent passengers, and so on. A number of senior Soviet officials, from Georgi Arbatov to Ambassador Anatoly Dobrynin, Moscow's man in Washington, would later agree that the KAL shootdown was a blunder. But Dobrynin would also observe that Washington's criticisms were "hasty and dangerous accusations," and there can be no doubt that the Soviet leadership as a whole felt the same way. Though sophisticated Russians figured the checks built into the American political system minimized the risk of an unprovoked first strike against the Soviet Union, that never became a uniform belief. Yuri Andropov himself, according to Dobrynin, stood as a *"probable exception"* (my italics) to the view that "an attack could take place unexpectedly at any moment, like Hitler's attack on the Soviet Union, or the Japanese attack on Pearl Harbor in 1941." Ominously, in the Soviet system, only Andropov's hand rested on the nuclear button.

As it had been when he was director, the KGB remained responsive to Andropov's moods. Operation RYAN was in full swing. In mid-June 1983, just prior to leaving for what became his sickbed, Andropov remarked that there had been an "unprecedented sharpening of the struggle" between East and West.

KGB stations assumed a posture of increased readiness. Yasenovo followed up on August 12 with a supplement to the list of war indicators KGB officers were supposed to track. Stations were to report every two weeks. Moscow center wanted new items of intelligence that must have had KGB officers pulling their hair out. These included warning of increased intelligence efforts against the Warsaw Pact; dropping of agents and/or equipment into the U.S.S.R. or Pact countries; CIA and National Security Agency liaison with other NATO intelligence agencies; infiltration of sabotage teams; appearance of special security detachments; and increases in Western disinformation efforts. What, if anything, KGB stations reported in response to this directive remains unknown. However, the Soviet practice of fulfilling production "norms," or quotas, and Moscow's continued alarm suggest that the KGB received at least some data that Yasenovo interpreted as preparation for war.

Other world developments heightened the sense of emergent crisis. Polish labor leader Lech Walesa, who had defied the Soviet-backed Communist government of his country, received the Nobel Peace Prize in early October. The United States exhibited outrage after a bombing in Beirut that destroyed a barracks and killed almost 250 U.S. Marines. Only days later, the Americans invaded the Caribbean island of Grenada, a friend of Moscow's ally Cuba. Washington appeared to be in an aggressive mood.

In this charged atmosphere occurred a NATO military exercise called Able Archer 83, scheduled to last from November 2 through November 11. A so-called command post exercise in which only headquarters and higher echelons participated, Able Archer tested "nuclear release procedures." While the U.S. government obviously would have the key role in ordering the use of such weapons in wartime, the decision would have to be ratified by a standing committee of NATO national representatives, part of the chain of command. Getting a decision through this network could take half a day or more, and its awkwardness required that the system be regularly exercised. The initial plans had called for President Reagan himself to participate in Able Archer, though the maneuver was scaled back at the last moment. Had Able Archer occurred as first planned, no doubt it would have been of even greater concern to the KGB. More White House and Pentagon windows certainly would have been lit at night.

In any case, Soviet intelligence apparently panicked. According to Oleg Gordievsky, the KGB observed a change in the message formats NATO used, the kind of thing that often happens as a security device when military operations commence. The NATO command posts also transitioned through every level of readiness from peacetime activity through full alert. On November 6, Gordievsky reports, Moscow transmitted a further appeal for KGB officers to search for RYAN indicators. On either November 8 or November 9, he says, there followed a "flash" message to KGB posts ordering an unprecedented "superalert."

There is some doubt that the superalert was actually ordered. American analyst Raymond Garthoff, among our foremost experts on Russia, concludes in a study of the end of the Cold War that any such alert would have been kept very quiet by Soviet intelligence. Garthoff interviewed a number of key Moscow officials, including the first deputies to the foreign minister and chief of the general staff, and the chief of the international department of the Communist Party, and no one had any recollection of an alert. Mikhail Gorbachev, then a Politburo member, also said the matter never came before that body. On the other hand, Gorbachev affirms the general proposition that 1983–84 proved the most delicate moment in the superpower relationship. Ambassador Dobrynin confirms that he heard of the KGB alert from his rezident in Washington. The CIA also apparently learned later from different sources that Soviet military intelligence was put on a state of high alert.

Certain concrete actions of a military nature did take place. All sources agree that a Soviet nuclear-armed tactical bomber regiment based in East Germany went on combat alert. Some others report that Russian commanders were told to take steps to secure their aircraft, ships, and weapons against surprise attack.

Fortunately for all, November 11 came and went with no move by the West, and Able Archer also ended. However, just days later, the first Euromissiles actually arrived in Europe. Moscow walked out of arms control talks, with Andropov complaining it was impossible to do business with partners like the United States.

The Russians had sabers of their own to rattle. During 1983 there were nineteen Soviet nuclear weapons tests, plus nine so-called peaceful nuclear explosions. In 1984 came another eighteen tests and eleven explosions. There were also a multiplicity of missile tests, including the beginning of testing for the large SS-24 ICBM and the mobile SS-25. Though suffering from numerous malfunctions (over half its trials were rated failures in the West), the SS-24 testing program proceeded at a rapid rate. The SS-25 program went smoothly and, if anything, even more rapidly. In submarine-based missiles, the Soviets were flight-testing their SSN-23 and conducting submerged launches from Typhoon-class submarines of the SSN-20 to test ranges in the Kamchatka Peninsula and the Pacific Ocean.

In military maneuvers for the Soviet Strategic Rocket Forces, American experts were told later, the scenarios used in 1982 and 1983 featured practice of the technique known as "launch under attack"—that is, nuclear preemption by means of offensive missile attack (in response to a confirmed attack by the other side, while the enemy's missiles are still in the air). Even more ominous, the 1984 scenario for Soviet nuclear exercises featured a U.S. surprise attack combined with a Soviet preemptive response.

Soviet defense minister Dimitri Ustinov put a public spin on developments in mid-December 1983, when he addressed a convocation of Soviet war veterans. "Imperialism is not all-powerful," Ustinov thundered. "Its threats do not frighten us. The Soviet people have strong nerves." The danger of such posturing lay in its fueling a cycle of misperception that could lead to crisis and war. Luckily, Ustinov chose this moment to soothe as well as warn. "No matter how complicated the political-military situation," Russia's defense minister declared, "there is no point in overdramatizing it."

Americans, too, were beginning to heed the drift in superpower relations. "We got their attention," Robert McFarlane is quoted as saying at about this time. "Maybe we overdid it." McFarlane's NSC director for Soviet and European affairs, seasoned diplomat Jack Matlock, had suggested the need to cool the other side's fears with some conciliatory rhetoric. McFarlane told Matlock to draft a presidential speech, which he did in conjunction with Shultz's State Department and White House political mavens. Later, professional speechwriters redid the first draft. As Able Archer ended, the speech stood ready, though there were as yet no plans for Ronald Reagan to mouth any of its fine phrases.

At the CIA, meanwhile, concern developed about Moscow's pessimism. Director of Central Intelligence William J. Casey was hearing increasingly ominous news. Reports from Oleg Gordievsky, filtered through British intelligence, supplied the basic picture. The CIA also picked up the bomber alert in East Germany as well as certain changes in Russian communication patterns. Intelligence sources say the Soviets, though not all at once and not in an operational sequence, rehearsed every step they would take in starting a nuclear war.

Periodically, the CIA and other U.S. intelligence agencies jointly compiled studies of key issues called national intelligence estimates (NIEs). Among the most important NIEs was the Soviet estimate, and the one current at this time was NIE 11-3/8-82, approved by William Casey and circulated on February 15, 1983. Among other things, it concluded that the Russians would expect a crisis to precede a war, and during that period would "heighten their surveillance of enemy activity" in addition to shifting to a wartime posture and seeking to carry out deception measures. At the outset of any hostilities, the NIE remarked, "The Soviets would try to implement a theaterwide air offensive [in Europe]" to neutralize NATO nuclear assets. Ominously, the CIA estimate contains this: "If [the Soviets] acquired convincing evidence that a U.S. intercontinental strike was imminent, they would try to preempt." This would be most likely if conventional war were already under way in Europe, but war out of the blue — for example, a preemptive attack based on a gross miscalculation of the other side's intentions—was not excluded. In short, the CIA's standing estimate in the fall of 1983 mirrored some of the same things that were on the minds of planners in Moscow.

Jack Matlock attended all the White House meetings where Bill Casey was present, and a more conciliatory American approach to the Soviet Union was discussed—including the presidential speech Matlock helped to draft. Matlock himself had presented a briefing in September at which President Reagan sat for a two-hour exposé of the CIA's data on the Russians. Matlock does not recall Casey pressing the president to quell Soviet fears. The CIA director liked Matlock's proposed speech as a token in the propaganda war but did not see a conciliatory gesture as unusually urgent. Matlock's recollections of Reagan's opinion of the first draft are that it contained little new; again there seemed no special urgency.

Something changed between September and December, and not through standard National Security Council channels. Matlock believes that Nancy Reagan, who favored softer rhetoric on the Russians, had much to do with it— or, rather, the First Lady's Los Angeles astrologer did. Intelligence sources say that Bill Casey, no astrologer, approached Reagan through Nancy. In this version, Casey had been won over by warnings from his Soviet analysts and set up a meeting with the president.

Secretary of State George Shultz returned from a European trip in mid-December to find a new tone at the White House. He saw the president on December 17. Reagan specifically referred to the warmer passages in Russian defense minister Ustinov's talk to Soviet veterans, with its appeal for the abolition of all nuclear weapons. Robert M. Gates, then the CIA's deputy director for intelligence, records in his memoirs that the Casey-Reagan meeting occurred on December 22. Gates quotes a CIA report presented at the meeting that cited the KGB and Soviet military intelligence alerts, remarking that the Russian posture "seems to reflect a Soviet perception of an increased threat of war."

President Reagan decided to go ahead with the speech. He delivered it over a global satellite link from the East Room of the White House on January 16, 1984. He added a few homey touches, which turned out to be the phrases people remembered. Secretary Shultz made a speech along similar lines nearly simultaneously in Stockholm. In his memoirs Ronald Reagan writes, "Three years had taught me something surprising about the Russians: Many people at the top of the Soviet hierarchy were genuinely afraid of America and Americans. Perhaps this shouldn't have surprised me, but it did."

Chairman Yuri Andropov reacted negatively to Washington's sally, but the Russian leader proved to be on his last legs, in rapid decline since before Christmas. Andropov collapsed during the final week of January and died on February 9, to be replaced by Constantin Chernenko, another aged leader. Chernenko also would be wary of the United States, but he lacked Andropov's sense of immediate confrontation. Moscow resumed arms control negotiations in 1984. The following year, when Chernenko passed away, Mikhail Gorbachev assumed leadership and traveled to Geneva for the first Reagan-era summit conference between the superpowers. Soviet sources report that Gorbachev at first tried to compete with the United States but soon realized the futility of the arms race.

Like the leadership, the Russian military remained skeptical of the United States. They continued a vigorous missile testing program. An article in *Military Thought*, the journal of the Soviet general staff, discussed the danger of war beginning under the cover of normal military exercises, then, paragraphs later, mentioned Able Archer by name. Marshal Nikolai Ogarkov commented, in a May 1984 interview with the Russian military newspaper *Krasnaya Zvezda* ("Red Star"), "With the quantity and diversity of nuclear missiles already achieved, it becomes impossible to destroy the enemy's systems with a single strike." Nevertheless, Ogarkov opposed arms control and bore responsibility for the KAL 007 incident. He would be replaced in the fall of 1984, about the time Moscow resumed nuclear arms talks.

The Russian answer to the so-called decapitation threat posed by the Pershing II came in the form of a new technology. On November 13, 1984, a command post at Leningrad sent a missile launch order to a military radio facility near Moscow, which rebroadcast it to an SS-20 intermediate-range missile that had just taken off from the Soviet test center Kapustin Yar (now in the Ukraine). The rocket itself then transmitted a launch order to an SS-18 heavy ICBM, which fired from its silo in Kazakhstan. Here the Russians demonstrated the ability to execute an automated launch of their missile force. Without knowing exactly which rockets were configured as airborne launchers (and destroying them), or blanketing all of Russia with high levels of radio interference (physically very demanding), there would be no way to preclude a Russian missile launch. In effect, the Russians had created a "doomsday machine," an automatic system capable of wreaking destruction even after the immolation of the Soviet Union.

Despite numerous subsequent arms control treaties and the peaceful demise of the Soviet Union, as well as the end of the Cold War, the existence of the doomsday machine is troubling. As recently as 1993 the Russian automatic launch system continued in service; insofar as we know, it remains active today. This kind of automaticity inherently increases the danger of war by accident or miscalculation. It is sad that the security pressures of the early 1980s made such a system seem desirable to Moscow.

Meanwhile, the KGB's Operation RYAN did not simply disappear. Annual reports of the Russian intelligence service discovered in a Moscow archive show the KGB continued to report on RYAN indicators until at least 1987. Documents published by Gordievsky show KGB orders concerning RYAN still flowing as late as 1984. Russian fears apparently continued throughout Gorbachev's rule; RYAN ended in 1991.

In Washington, Ronald Reagan would not be the only American surprised by the depth of Russian anxiety. The CIA, acknowledges Robert Gates, failed to appreciate the dangers in spite of its own people's warnings. Only in March 1984, when Gates read a British compendium of reporting from double agent Gordievsky, did he realize that Soviet leaders must have really been alarmed. Two points stand out. First, since the British share information with the CIA, the Gordievsky data on RYAN must have been of concern to the CIA's Directorate of Operations. Either the CIA spooks discounted the reports, the operations people would not share them with CIA analysts, or the British never passed along some of the Gordievsky data. Significantly, Gates writes that his agency finally went to President Reagan only after it learned that Soviet military intelligence had received the same sort of alert order as Gordievsky claimed for the KGB. Apparently, the KGB's move to a "war footing" was insufficient for the CIA to spring into action.

Second, in its heart, the CIA still did not believe the war scare had been real. People remember details of what they were doing and where they were at critical moments, and the discovery that the world had come close to a nuclear war has to be classed as such a moment. Robert Gates, however, does not recall where he was when he read the British retrospective on Gordievsky. Even more concrete, in 1984 the CIA commissioned a special national intelligence estimate (SNIE) on whether American intelligence had been missing the point. The paper was drafted by National Intelligence Council chairman Fritz W. Ermarth, a Russian specialist who had been brought back to the CIA from the RAND Corporation, and was a veteran of the National Security Council staff. The paper, SNIE 11-10-84/JX, titled "Implications of Recent Soviet Military

Political Activities," held that each of the unusual Russian actions (for example, the bomber alert) could have had an innocent explanation, short of Moscow's succumbing to a war scare. The actual deployment of Euromissiles, not Able Archer or anything else, was taken to be the stimulus for Russian fears. Interestingly, the CIA paper conceded what some American propagandists liked to deny—that the advent of the Pershing IIs had to be worrisome for the Russian leadership.

Intelligence analysts remained divided on the issue for over a year before the press of other matters laid this one to rest. But Bob Gates remained disturbed, however, and followed up in 1990, when he was on the NSC staff as deputy national security adviser. The president's Foreign Intelligence Advisory Board revisited the war scare. Its study, still not made public, reportedly concluded that U.S. intelligence had missed the boat on an actual crisis.

Looking back at the Cold War, Americans have had a temptation to gloat over supposed victory. Those who do for the most part have no idea how close hysteria came to ending it all in the early 1980s. Moscow's fears cannot be dismissed as self-induced—a result of the hype the Soviets had been putting out about America's Euromissiles. "It's not reducible to that," says Raymond Garthoff, "not by a long shot." Able Archer, writes CIA chieftain Robert Gates, marked "one of the potentially most dangerous episodes of the Cold War." Worst of all is the understanding that the United States, dedicated to its own war of words, dismissing the views of the other side as mere propaganda, remained oblivious to a brush with Armageddon. That was one hell of a game of chicken.

There Goes Brussels . . .

WILLIAMSON MURRAY

Let us play a counterfactual game, and suppose for a moment that the one-sided crisis of 1983 had gotten out of control. What if, for example, on the night of September 26, a Soviet officer in a bunker outside Moscow had not had doubts about what he was seeing on a computer screen—first one incoming missile, and then another, five in all. Had Lieutenant Colonel Stanislav Petrov followed regulations, he would have telephoned his superiors to warn them that the Soviet Union was only minutes away from a nuclear attack. Petrov hesitated, convinced that something had gone awry in the computer system. The minutes passed. Nothing did happen. That night one man's hunch may have averted World War III.

"The terrible ifs accumulate," as Winston Churchill said of the opening moves of World War I. Those same terrible ifs might have been the story of 1983. What were the most likely possibilities of an armed confrontation? What form might it have taken? A best-case scenario in the crisis that the Soviet leadership had created for itself might have seen the normally overcautious Yuri Andropov ordering some sort of demonstration, a shot across Western bows, as it were—perhaps rocketing a nuclear bomb to explode harmlessly in the South Pacific or the Indian Ocean. (Such a warning missile would have avoided the polar regions, where it would have set off American radar.) But Andropov was an ill man—he died the following February—who had increasingly ceded decision-making to the ancient hard-liners in the Kremlin. One would have had to expect an immoderate response from them. Chances are that they would have precipitated either a limited or, worst case, a full-scale nuclear war. They didn't, but as we know now, they came close enough.

There is one other scenario that we might consider, and as Williamson Murray writes, it is the most likely one: an attack on Western Europe. Indeed, the Warsaw Pact nations always assumed that they would take the offensive—just as NATO, "an alliance committed to protecting the status quo" (the historian Lawrence Freedman's phrase), would rely on defense. NATO planners had spent years preparing for conventional mass armored attacks. Pact armies, they surmised, would probably head across the North German plain to Hamburg and beyond, or west through the Fulda Gap to Frankfurt. Could NATO fight a holding action until American reinforcements made it across the Atlantic? (That explains why NATO placed such emphasis on antisubmarine warfare, to protect shipping.) But NATO totally miscalculated the form the Warsaw Pact attack would take. The Soviets, we now know, were planning nothing less than a nuclear blitz of Europe. Yet they forgot to take one thing into account: the other side's response.

WILLIAMSON MURRAY, a senior fellow at the Institute for Defense Analyses, is a professor of history emeritus at Ohio State University and, with Allan R. Millett, the author of *A War to Be Won: Fighting the Second World War*.

WITH THE COLLAPSE of the Berlin Wall in 1989 came the overturn of the entire strategic framework within which European politics had run from the end of World War II. For the first time, the West learned what NATO's opponents, the Soviet Union and the nations of the Warsaw Pact, had in mind if war broke out in Europe. This new knowledge came as an extraordinary surprise, since it underlined the level of miscalculation in most Western theorizing about Soviet military plans for the last two decades of the Cold War.

We now know that the Soviet Union's military planners had no intention of beginning a major war in Europe with a conventional attack. There was no debate in the Soviet Union about first use of nuclear weapons. Military operations would begin with a massive barrage of between three and four hundred nuclear weapons against a variety of NATO targets. Not only did the Warsaw Pact possess no defensive plans in this period, a revealing fact in and of itself, but it had no plans for conventional offensive operations.

How the evidence about Soviet military plans fell into Western hands is an interesting story. When the Soviet empire disappeared into the dustbin of history, Russia's military forces returned to their own territory. The commanders and staffs of the former Red Army took along with them virtually everything on Soviet military installations that was not nailed down, and that included sensitive documents. Had the Soviets been the only ones involved in planning for offensive operations, we would know only as much as Russian authorities deigned to tell us—not much, if anything.

But the Soviets could not avoid leaving a paper trail of planning dictates with the military forces of the other Warsaw Pact nations. When the German Democratic Republic collapsed, and when the Communist governments in Poland and Czechoslovakia yielded to democratic regimes, a considerable number of documents on planning fell into the hands of the new rulers. The change happened so quickly that the ousted administrators had no time to destroy the documents. The Germans in particular proved interested in what the evidence suggested—and more than willing to publish the results. Though Western intelligence agencies have probably not yet reconstructed the full Soviet plan, the available evidence has allowed them to sketch, in considerable detail, the framework for what would have happened if a great European war had occurred.

D-Day for a Soviet invasion of Western Europe would have started with nuclear holocaust. Soviet missiles and, in some cases, bombers would have attacked virtually every major air base, nuclear storage area, communications center, and headquarters with tactical nuclear weapons. Such an attack not only would have devastated much of NATO's conventional and nuclear power, it would have caused enormous collateral damage to the towns and cities that lay near the military bases that the Soviets targeted.

The strikes would have ranged across Germany to the United Kingdom and would have fallen impartially on U.S., British, French, and German bases. The aim would have been straightforward: to destroy NATO's command-and-control system and its ability to respond with nuclear weapons *before* the immensely superior (in terms of numbers) conventional forces of the Warsaw Pact rolled over the wreckage. Soviet plans also make it clear why they placed such emphasis on nuclear protection of their combat vehicles and troops, and why they trained their conventional forces to fight in areas contaminated by nuclear weapons—they *knew* that nuclear weapons, *their nuclear weapons*, would be used right from the first in a NATO–Warsaw Pact military confrontation. The rigorous training that the Soviets received to survive on a nuclear battlefield, especially in contaminated areas, was a major feature of Warsaw Pact exercises. Soldiers operated for extensive periods in their nuclear protection gear; tanks and armored personnel carriers remained buttoned up for long periods of time; and air bases practiced operations in which all personnel wore rubberized suits and washed down constantly. All of this was done with utmost seriousness and under the most stringent discipline. There were no shortcuts.

Not all of the targets for Soviet strikes are known, but enough information has surfaced to suggest how extensive the collateral damage would have been. Attacks on command-and-control sites such as Wiesbaden, Frankfurt, and Heidelberg and other West German bases would have practically destroyed many cities. NATO's central headquarters, near Brussels, was targeted, and not much of the Belgian capital would have remained. Major ports would have been attacked: Hamburg, Bremen, and Antwerp would have gone up to prevent U.S. and British reinforcements from reaching the continent. Air bases such as Rhein-Main also would have been hit, adding to the collateral damage in nearby areas. Though London probably would have been spared, American air bases in Britain would have received their share of tactical nuclear weapons: The nuclear capability of aircraft on those bases threatened the massed conventional forces of the Warsaw Pact.

After the first devastating nuclear strikes, Warsaw Pact forces then would have advanced against an opponent whose ability to resist had been thoroughly disrupted, whose command and control no longer functioned, who possessed relatively little airpower, and who had few nuclear weapons left on the continent with which to attack the Warsaw Pact's conventional forces. Increasingly, from the mid-1960s on, Soviet military planners treated the possibility of war in Central Europe as an isolated event. They never seemed to pay attention to the probable strategic response from North America. In many ways, they were as out of touch with the political and strategic realities of the Cold War as the Schlieffen Plan had been with the realities of 1914. Then, no one of influence on the German general staff seemed to have reckoned with the full political consequences of invading Belgium.

This new picture of Soviet intentions explains why the political leadership in the Kremlin chose not to go to war, despite the overwhelming conventional superiority of its armed forces in the 1970s and 1980s. It was not so shortsighted as the military. In the largest sense, of course, students of the Cold War have understood why there was no World War III. Despite the fact that, for much of its duration, the Cold War represented, for both sides, a struggle of hostile ideologies of good versus evil, of truth versus lies, the specter of nuclear war introduced an element of enormous caution into the international arena. The mere existence of nuclear weapons prevented the replication of the war against Nazi Germany that had involved the destruction of most of Europe's major cities and the expenditure of resources and blood on an unimaginable scale. (The forty million deaths suffered by the Soviet Union alone suggests the immensity of the disaster.) Yet one of the many ironies of the Cold War may be that, in the end, deterrence, the talisman that provided tenure for whole generations of political scientists, worked—but only in a way that none of the theorizing academics understood.

The Soviet military plans represented a military solution to a narrowly defined operational problem: how to conquer Western Europe without suffering catastrophic damage themselves. But one must also understand that Soviet military planners analyzed NATO's operational and strategic options and worked entirely within the context of their own perceptions. It was mirror imaging of the worst sort. From their perspective, were they in NATO's position, the sole response to a massive Soviet invasion of Western Europe with conventional forces would be an immediate use of tactical nuclear weapons to break up and wreck the Soviet military juggernaut—in other words, to achieve an operational balance, or what they called the "correlation of forces." The Soviet planners regarded discussions among Western political leaders and academics about conventional defense, forward defense, and no first use as nothing but a massive campaign of disinformation, a smoke screen hiding the true intentions of NATO.

Once Soviet commanders and planners had made the assumption that NATO would use tactical nuclear weapons from the outset—just as they would do in similar circumstances—their response seemed obvious. They determined to eliminate that threat by blasting NATO's nuclear capabilities to smithereens. *Then* their conventional forces could move west to police up the rubble. (In fact, NATO's first-use plan came into play only if it was faced with the collapse of its forces in a conventional war.) The Soviet plans make it clear why they were so worried about the new generation of U.S. weapons introduced in the early 1980s, in particular the Pershing and nuclear-tipped cruise missiles that the Reagan administration deployed to Britain and Germany. Those fears took shape in the deception campaign that resulted in movements such as the nuclear-freeze group.

The operational problem for the Soviets was that the new American weapons systems were mobile, and with even minimal warning, they could be set up in areas not targeted by Soviet nuclear planning. Thus, even after the Soviet tactical nuclear strikes, NATO would have retained substantial means to launch a series of devastating nuclear counterstrikes against Soviet conventional forces and their command-and-control systems.

But it was probably not Western military planning and new nuclear capabilities that exercised the most effective deterrent on the Soviet Union's military and political leaders. Soviet plans by their very nature were self-deterring. They created a host of problems for those in Moscow who had to consider such a contest within the larger context of Soviet-American strategic confrontation. And Soviet leaders, considering that wider context, had to believe that an attack on NATO that opened with a barrage of three to four hundred nuclear weapons would result in an American reply with all the nuclear forces at the U.S. president's disposal. From the Soviet point of view, the Americans would have no choice but to move a tactical nuclear war in Europe to the strategic level. No Soviet leader could fail to believe that the nuclear destruction of NATO would lead immediately and catastrophically to an American response that would destroy the Soviet Union.

Acknowledgments

I wish to express my special thanks to Byron Hollinshead, Sabine Russ, Marleen Adlerblum, and Matthew Ashford at American Historical Publications, and to my old and good friend Robert D. Loomis at Random House, for their assistance and encouragement in all aspects of this book.

Index